AUTHENTIC LEADERSHIP THEORY AND PRACTICE: ORIGINS, EFFECTS AND DEVELOPMENT

MONOGRAPHS IN LEADERSHIP AND MANAGEMENT

Series Editor: James G. (Jerry) Hunt

MONOGRAPHS IN LEADERSHIP AND MANAGEMENT
VOLUME 3

AUTHENTIC LEADERSHIP THEORY AND PRACTICE: ORIGINS, EFFECTS AND DEVELOPMENT

EDITED BY

WILLIAM L. GARDNER
University of Nebraska-Lincoln, USA

BRUCE J. AVOLIO
University of Nebraska-Lincoln, USA

FRED O. WALUMBWA
Arizona State University, USA

Emerald

United Kingdom – North America – Japan – India – Malaysia – China – Australasia

Emerald Group Publishing Limited
Howard House, Wagon Lane, Bingley BD16 1WA, UK

British Library Cataloguing in Publication Data
A catalogue record for this book is available from the British Library

ISBN: 978-0-7623-1237-5

Awarded in recognition of
Emerald's production
department's adherence to
quality systems and processes
when preparing scholarly
journals for print

CONTENTS

PART IV: PERCEPTIONS OF AUTHENTIC LEADERSHIP: EXPLORATORY STUDIES

PART V: MOVING FORWARD

LIST OF CONTRIBUTORS

Neal M. Ashkanasy	UQ Business School, The University of Queensland, Brisbane, Australia
Bruce J. Avolio	Department of Management, University of Nebraska-Lincoln, Lincoln, NE, USA
Donna M. Brazil	United States Military Academy, New York, NY, USA
Adrian Chan	College of Business Administration, University of Nebraska-Lincoln, Lincoln, NE, USA
Marie T. Dasborough	UQ Business School, The University of Queensland, Brisbane, Australia
Ceasar Douglas	Department of Management, College of Business, Florida State University, Tallahassee, FL, USA
Keith M. Eigel	Leadership Development Incorporated, Atlanta, GA, USA
Gerald R. Ferris	Department of Management, College of Business, Florida State University, Tallahassee, FL, USA
Louis W. (Jody) Fry	Tarleton State University – Central Texas, Killen, TX, USA
William L. Gardner	Department of Management, University of Nebraska-Lincoln, Lincoln, NE, USA
Sean T. Hannah	United States Military Academy, New York, NY, USA
Larry W. Hughes	School of Business Administration, Fort Lewis College, Durango, CO, USA

Mansour Javidan — The Garvin Center for Cultures and Languages of International Management, Thunderbird, The Garvin School of International Management, Glendale, AZ, USA

Karin Klenke — School of Leadership Studies, Regent University, Virginia Beach, VA, USA

Thomas A. Kolditz — United States Military Academy, New York, NY, USA

Karl W. Kuhnert — Department of Psychology, University of Georgia, Athens, GA, USA

Paul B. Lester — Department of Management, University of Nebraska-Lincoln, Lincoln, NE, USA

Fred Luthans — Department of Management, University of Nebraska-Lincoln, Lincoln, NE, USA

Pamela L. Perrewé — Department of Management, College of Business, Florida State University, Tallahassee, FL, USA

Todd L. Pittinsky — John F. Kennedy School of Government, Harvard University, Cambridge, MA, USA

Rebecca J. Reichard — Department of Management, University of Nebraska-Lincoln, Lincoln, NE, USA

Christopher J. Tyson — Georgetown University, NE, Washington, USA

Paul Varella — Haskayne School of Business, University of Calgary, Calgary, Alberta, Canada

Gretchen R. Vogelgesang — Department of Management, University of Nebraska-Lincoln, Lincoln, NE, USA

David Waldman — School of Global Management, Arizona State University, Phoenix, AZ, USA

Fred O. Walumbwa   School of Global Management and
                        Leadership, Arizona State University,
                        Phoenix, AZ, USA

J. Lee Whittington   University of Dallas, Irving, TX, USA

Carolyn M. Youssef   College of Business, Bellevue University,
                        Bellevue, NE, USA

ABOUT THE AUTHORS

Neal M. Ashkanasy is Professor of Management in the UQ Business School, and the Faculty Director of Research. He has a Ph.D. (1989) in Social and Organizational Psychology. His research focuses on the role of emotions in organizations. He has published in journals such as the *Academy of Management*, the *Journal of Management Review*, and the *Journal of Organizational Behavior*, and has edited four books. He is a former Chair of the Managerial and Organizational Cognition Division of the Academy of Management and is currently Associate Editor for *Academy of Management Learning and Education* and the *Journal of Organizational Behavior*.

Bruce J. Avolio currently holds the Clifton Chair in Leadership at the University of Nebraska-Lincoln in the College of Business Administration. He is the Director of the Gallup Leadership Institute and is a Gallup Senior Scientist. Professor Avolio has an international reputation as a researcher in leadership having published over 100 articles and 5 books. His latest books are entitled, *Transformational and Charismatic Leadership: The Road Ahead* (Oxford Press: Elsevier Science, 2002) and *Leadership development in balance: Made/Born* (Erlbaum, 2005). His last two published books were entitled: *Full Leadership Development: Building the Vital Forces in Organizations* (Sage, 1999) and *Developing Potential Across a Full Range of Leadership: Cases on Transactional and Transformational Leadership* (Erlbaum, 2000). His latest book proposal is entitled, *High Impact Leader: Every Moment Matters* to *Authentic Leadership Development* and will be published by McGraw-Hill in 2005. His current research grants include a National Science Foundation project with UNISYS to study virtual teams and leadership, and a 4-year project supported by the U.S. Army Research Institute on officer leadership development at Fort Leavenworth. Over the last 10 years, he has successfully won nearly 4 million dollars in research grants to support his research program.

Donna Brazil is an active duty Army Lieutenant Colonel and Assistant Professor in the Department of Behavioral Sciences and Leadership at the

United States Military Academy at West Point, New York. She holds a Bachelor's degree from the United States Military Academy, as well as Masters and Ph.D. degrees in Social Psychology from the University of North Carolina at Chapel Hill. Donna's research and teaching activities include applied social psychology, sociology, and leader development.

Adrian Chan is currently pursuing his MA/Ph.D. in Leadership at the University of Nebraska-Lincoln. Previously, a uniformed organizational psychologist with the Ministry of Defense, Singapore, Adrian's research portfolio includes performance-related skill acquisition, team-level visioning and team-building, organizational change, morale, innovation and stress. Adrian has also worked closely with the Gallup Organization, Hewitt Associates, Boston Consulting Group, Anderson Consulting, and PriceWaterhouseCoopers.

Marie Dasborough is an Assistant Professor at Oklahoma State University, having recently completed her doctorate at the University of Queensland, Australia. Her research interests include leadership, emotions in the workplace, emotional intelligence, and attribution theory. Marie's research has been presented at the annual meetings of the Academy of Management and the Society of Industrial and Organizational Psychology. She has published her research in book chapters and journals such as *The Leadership Quarterly, Journal of Education in Business,* and the *Asia Pacific Journal of Human Resources Management.*

Ceasar Douglas is Associate Professor of Management at Florida State University. He received a Ph.D. in Management from the University of Mississippi. His research interests are in the areas of work team development, leadership, leader political skill, and temporary work force issues. He has published articles in *The Leadership Quarterly, Journal of Organizational Behavior, Journal of Managerial Psychology, Journal of Management, Research in Personnel and Human Resources Management,* and *Supervision.*

Keith M. Eigel is a consulting psychologist with Leadership Development Incorporated. Keith received his Ph.D. from the University of Georgia.

Gerald R. Ferris is the Francis Eppes Professor of Management and Professor of Psychology at Florida State University. He received a Ph.D. in Business Administration from the University of Illinois at Urbana-Champaign. Ferris has research interests in the areas of social influence and effectiveness processes in organizations, and he is the author of articles published in such journals as the *Journal of Applied Psychology, The Leadership Quarterly, Organizational Behavior and Human Decision Processes, Personnel Psychology, Academy of Management Journal,* and *Academy of Management Review.*

Louis W. (Jody) Fry is currently Associate Professor of Management at Tarleton State University – Central Texas. He received his Ph.D. from The Ohio State University. Jody's current research interests include intrinsic motivation and organizational transformation through spiritual leadership. His research has been published in *The Leadership Quarterly, Journal of Applied Psychology, Organization Science, The Academy of Management Journal, Journal of Occupational Behavior, Journal of Management, Journal of Marketing Research, Public Choice, Human Organization,* and *The Academy of Management Review.*

William L. Gardner is the Howard L. Hawks Chair in Business Ethics and Leadership at the University of Nebraska-Lincoln. William received his DBA from Florida State University. His current research interests include authentic leadership development, ethical conduct in organizations, and identity and impression management processes in organizations. His publications have appeared in such journals as the *Academy of Management Journal, Academy of Management Review, Journal of Management, Journal of Organizational Behavior,* and *The Leadership Quarterly,* among others.

Sean T. Hannah is a United States Army officer and faculty member of Behavioral Sciences and Leadership at the United States Military Academy at West Point. Sean is currently a fellow at the Gallup Leadership Institute at the University of Nebraska-Lincoln. His research interests include authentic and moral leadership development, leadership efficacy, and organizational meaning-making and schema diffusion.

Larry W. Hughes is a Assistant Professor of Management at Fort Lewis College in Durango, Colorado, and as a Fellow of the Gallup Leadership Institute at the University of the Nebraska-Lincoln. His chapter was inspired, in part, from his dissertation entitled "Transparency, translucence or opacity?: An experimental study of the effects of a leader's relational transparency and style of humor delivery on followers' performance." His current research interests include humor in leader–follower relations, the use of humor in self-presentation and impression management, the effects of stigma on social identity, and pluralistic ignorance and the study of ethics.

Mansour Javidan received his MBA and Ph.D. degrees from the Carlson School at the University of Minnesota. He is Professor and Director of the Garvin Center for the Cultures and Languages at Thunderbird, The Garvin School of International Management in Arizona. He is on the board of directors of the GLOBE (Global Leadership and Organizational Behavior Effectiveness). His publications have appeared in such journals as *Strategic Management Journal, Academy of Management Executive, The Leadership Quarterly, Management International Review, Human Relations, Journal of World Business,* and *Journal of Organizational Change Management.* Dr. Javidan has designed and taught a variety of MBA and executive development courses, and made presentations in over 20 countries around the world. Dr. Javidan just completed a 3-year term on the editorial board of the Academy of Management Executive. He was named in Lexinton's 2001/2002 Millennium Edition of the North American Who's Who Registry and Empire's Who's Who Registry.

Karin Klenke is Professor of Leadership Studies in the School of Leadership at Regent University. She holds a Ph.D. in Organizational Psychology from Old Dominion University. Her current research interests include leadership and spirituality, authentic leadership development, and women in leadership. Professor Klenke has published four books including *Women and Leadership: A Contextual Perspective.* Her articles have appeared in *The Journal of Leadership and Organizational Studies, Management Decisions, The International Journal of Qualitative Methods, Current Psychology,* and *the Journal of Management Systems,* among others.

Tom Kolditz is an active duty Army Colonel and Professor who chairs the Department of Behavioral Sciences and Leadership at the United States Military Academy at West Point, New York. He holds a Bachelor's degree in Psychology and Sociology from Vanderbilt University, as well as Masters and Ph.D. degrees in Social Psychology from the University of Missouri. He has published across a diverse array of academic and military journals, including *Military Review,* the *Journal of Personality and Social Psychology, Field Artillery Professional Journal,* the *Journal of Personality,* and *Perception and Psychophysics.* Colonel Kolditz's research and teaching activities span applied social psychology and leadership development. In April and

May 2003, he traveled throughout Iraq to study leadership and cohesion in small units during hostilities.

Karl W. Kuhnert is I/O psychologist at the University of Georgia. Karl received his Ph.D. from Kansas State University. He teaches and writes on leadership, ethics, and organizational development. His publications have appeared in the *Academy of Management Review, Journal of Management,* and *Group and Organization Management,* among others.

Paul B. Lester is a doctoral student in the Gallup Leadership Institute at the University of Nebraska-Lincoln. An active-duty U.S. Army officer, Paul graduated from the United States Military Academy in 1996. Paul received his MS from Murray State University. His current research interests include leadership development, strategic leadership, efficacy, and resiliency.

Fred Luthans is George Holmes Distinguished Professor of Management and University Professor at the Gallup Leadership Institute, University of Nebraska. He is also a Senior Scientist with Gallup and co-editor (with John Slocum) of three journals: *Organizational Dynamics, Journal of World Business,* and *Journal of Leadership and Organization Studies.* Fred received his Ph.D. from the University of Iowa and has an honorary doctorate from DePaul University. His current research revolves around positive organizational behavior and psychological capital as part of authentic leadership. He has several books, the latest in press with Bruce Avolio titled *The High Impact Leader: Moments Matter in Accelerating Authentic Leadership Development* (McGraw-Hill) and numerous articles in all the top-tier journals.

Pamela L. Perrewé is Distinguished Research Professor and the Jim Moran Professor of Management at Florida State University. She received a Ph.D. in Management at the University of Nebraska-Lincoln. Perrewé has research interests in the areas of job stress, coping processes, personality, and organizational politics, and she is the author of articles published in such journals as *Academy of Management Journal, Journal of Applied Psychology, Journal of Organizational Behavior, Journal of Management,* and *Journal of Vocational Behavior.*

Todd L. Pittinsky is Assistant Professor of Public Policy at the John F. Kennedy School of Government of Harvard University, and a core faculty member of the Center for Public Leadership. Todd earned his BA from Yale University, his MA in Psychology from Harvard University, and his Ph.D. in

Organizational Behavior jointly from the Harvard Graduate School of Arts and Sciences and the Harvard Business School. The two foci of Todd's research lab are the psychological science of leadership and the nature of allophilia (liking or love of the other) in intergroup relations. Todd has published studies in leading academic journals including the *American Behavioral Scientist, Psychological Science, Self and Identity,* and *The Journal of Social Issues.*

Rebecca J. Reichard is currently pursuing a PhD in Business as part of the University of Nebraska-Lincoln's Gallup Leadership Institute. She is also a Consortium Research Fellow for the Army Reasearch Institute's Leader Developement Research Unit in Fort Leavenworth, Kansas. She earned a BS in Psychology from Missouri Western state University and a MS in Industrial/Organizational Psychology from Southwest Missouri State University. Her research interests include applying positive psychology to leader self-development, the motivation and self-regulation of successful leaders, and self-awareness.

Christopher J. Tyson is a member of the Georgetown University Law Center class of 2006. He earned his BA from Howard University and his M.P.P. from the John F. Kennedy School of Government at Harvard University. His interests include social policy, race, and criminal justice.

Paul Varella is a Ph.D. candidate working on his dissertation at the Haskayne School of Business at the University of Calgary. He received his MBA from the same university and has worked in the fields of social capital and leadership. Some of his early research was presented at annual meetings of the Academy of Management. Recently, some of his research appeared in *The Leadership Quarterly.* He has taught strategic management and management courses and is currently working as a visiting instructor at the Arizona State University-West.

Gretchen R. Vogelgesang is a doctoral student in the Gallup Leadership Institute at the University of Nebraska-Lincoln. Gretchen received her MBA from DePaul University. Her current research interests include authentic leadership development and the development of resiliency as a part of psychological capital.

David Waldman is Professor and Chair of the Department of Management in the School of Global Management and Leadership at Arizona State

University. His research interests focus on the nature of effective leadership practices at strategic levels, and leadership in a virtual context. His publications have appeared in such journals as the *Academy of Management Journal, Academy of Management Review, Journal of Management, Journal of Organizational Behavior, The Leadership Quarterly,* and the *Journal of Applied Psychology.* Professor Waldman is a Fellow of the American Psychological Association and the Society for Industrial and Organizational Psychology. In addition, he is currently on the editorial boards of the *Academy of Management Journal,* the *Academy of Management Learning and Education,* the *Journal of Organizational Behavior,* and *The Leadership Quarterly.*

Fred O. Walumbwa is an Assistant Professor in the School of Global Management and Leadership at Arizona State University. Dr. Walumbwa received his Ph.D. from the University of Illinois at Urbana-Champaign. His current research interests include leadership development, cross-cultural research, how leadership is moderated and mediated through advanced information technology, positive organizational behavior, and team dynamics. His publications have appeared in such journals as the *International Journal of Human Resource Management, Journal of Occupational and Organizational Psychology,* and *The Leadership Quarterly,* among others.

J. Lee Whittington is the Dean of the College of Business and the Graduate School of Management at the University of Dallas. He received his Ph.D. from the University of Texas at Arlington. J. Lee's current research interests include social cognition in leader–follower relationships, spiritual leadership theory, legacy leadership and servant leadership. His research has been published in *The Leadership Quarterly, Academy of Management Review,* and *The Journal of Organizational Behavior.*

Carolyn M. Youssef is Assistant Professor at the College of Business, Bellevue University. She received her Ph.D. from the University of Nebraska. Carolyn's research focuses on the development of measurable human resource strengths and positive psychological capacities that can lead to enhanced performance and leadership effectiveness in the workplace. Her most recent publication is a book on *Positive Organizational Behavior* and *Psychological Capital* to be published by Oxford University Press. Professionally, Carolyn held various human resources, training, and organizational development positions at Thomas Cook, the American University in Cairo (Egypt), USAID, Unilever, Shell, Wadi Holdings, and the Natural Resources Institute (Kent, UK).

PREFACE

Bruce J. Avolio, William L. Gardner and
Fred O. Walumbwa

This edited volume was one of two publication outcomes of the first Gallup Leadership Institute (GLI) Summit held in Omaha, Nebraska, June 2004. The primary goal of that summit was to inaugurate the new GLI at the University of Nebraska-Lincoln and to initiate a research program around what constituted authentic leadership development. The GLI was founded on the basic assumption that many leadership interventions are far from genuine, oftentimes atheoretical, poorly evaluated and have not demonstrated a return on investment. The mission of the new GLI is as follows: "To develop and support basic and applied research that creates the foundation for implementing best practices in leadership assessment, development and performance."[1]

The first set of publications from the GLI 2004 Summit appeared in a special issue of *The Leadership Quarterly* in Summer, 2005 (Volume 16, Issue 3), in which seven papers were chosen focusing on the development of what constitutes authentic leadership and its development. Papers chosen for inclusion in this special issue came from approximately 80 papers submitted to the GLI Summit. Papers were chosen on the basis of their contribution to advancing theory around authentic leadership and were thus more limited in range than the current edited volume.

The specific goals for compiling this second publication outlet from the GLI Summit were threefold. The first goal was to examine the origins of authentic leadership, to further define this construct and to examine the

Authentic Leadership Theory and Practice: Origins, Effects and Development
Monographs in Leadership and Management, Volume 3, xxi–xxix
Copyright © **2005 by Elsevier Ltd.**
All rights of reproduction in any form reserved

influence of individual differences and environmental factors on authentic leader emergence. The second goal was to examine the positive effects of authentic leadership in organizations, including the creation of positive ethical climates and veritable and sustainable performance. The final objective was to examine "authentic" leadership development models/interventions that facilitate the development of authentic leadership. For related topics, the connection to authentic leadership and its development are made clear.

Our highest aspiration for this edited book is that it will open a new dialogue on what constitutes the "root construct" of all positive, effective forms of leadership (Avolio & Gardner, 2005; Avolio, Gardner, Walumbwa, Luthans, & May, 2004; Gardner, Avolio, Luthans, May, & Walumbwa, 2005). We advocate that authentic leadership is such a root construct that transcends other theories and helps to inform them in terms of what is and is not "genuinely" good leadership. Building off this aspirational goal, we also expect to stimulate a conversation around what actually develops genuinely good leaders. For the most part, there are numerous players in the business of leadership development who cannot answer a simple and direct question. *What evidence do you have that you have actually developed even one leader?* That question was posed to one of the top consultants from a very well-known organization that profits from leadership development interventions around the globe and her response was, "someone was examining that issue in another department." We challenge all of those in the business of developing leaders to come up with a better answer – one that at least demonstrates they have actually developed just one leader!

To be clear, we are not advocating creating a new set of terms simply to create some new focus on leadership. Indeed, the concept of authentic leadership is perhaps the oldest, oldest, oldest wine in the traditional leadership bottle! Instead, we are attempting to dig beneath the surface of all leadership theories that have not adequately defined and tested what constitutes authentic leadership and its development, whether leadership is participative, directive, transactional, transformational and so forth.

Before we delve any deeper into what constitutes "authentic leadership development," we need to first define it more precisely as well as our central focus on "authentic leadership." Paraphrasing the definition initially provided by Luthans and Avolio (2003), authentic leadership development is defined as a process that draws from both positive psychological capacities and a highly developed organizational context to foster greater self-awareness and self-regulated positive behaviors on the part of leaders and associates, producing positive self-development in each. Authentic leaders are leaders who: (a) know who they are and what they believe in; (b) display transparency and consistency between their values, ethical reasoning and actions; (c) focus on developing positive psychological states such as confidence, optimism, hope, and resilience within themselves and their associates; (d) are widely known and respected for their integrity.

Greater insight into the authentic leadership construct can be gained from consideration of its theoretical roots. The topic of authenticity has been given varied treatment over the years, in different disciplines ranging from philosophy, sociology, and clinical and social psychology. Authenticity is often associated with the maxim "to thy own self be true" (e.g., Harter, 2002). The contemporary concept of authenticity owes much to modern scholars of identity and the self, although its historical roots can be traced much farther back (Weigert, 1988). In the modern conception of authenticity, the belief that one has a "true self" versus a public or presentational self is a common assumption of the dramaturgical approach to studying the self (e.g., Goffman, 1959; James, 1890). Goffman's ideas spawned a brief spate of research into the construct, particularly in the area of educational leadership (Halpin & Croft, 1963a, b, 1966; Henderson & Hoy, 1983; Hoy & Henderson, 1983; McInnis, 1973). Interestingly, this initial work focused on inauthenticity as opposed to authenticity. However, after this initial spurt of activity, research on the implications of authenticity and inauthenticity for leadership lay dormant for decades.

One effort to rekindle interest and advance knowledge in this area was undertaken by Luthans and Avolio (2003) in their development of authentic leadership theory. The contents of the special issue of *The Leadership Quarterly* and this book represent our own and others' efforts to build upon and extend their work. Below we provide a brief overview of the book and describe how each chapter contributes to the goal of advancing knowledge about authentic leaders and their development.

OVERVIEW

The chapters in this volume were chosen to cover a broad range of topics that we felt represented the state of the field with respect to what constitutes authentic leadership and its development. All of the chapters were reviewed by at least three scholars who voluntarily contributed their time and feedback to enhance the overall quality of the papers.

In Chapter 1, Chan, Hannah, and Gardner advance a theory of veritable authentic leadership. They propose that authenticity in leaders is an important *leadership multiplier*, as it provides the foundation for producing a virtuous cycle of performance and learning for leaders, followers, and organizations. Utilizing a social cognitive framework to guide their discussion, these authors examine how the leader's authenticity positively affects the intra- and inter-personal processes that occur in what Avolio (2005) referred to as constituting "the leadership system" in organizations.

In Chapter 2, Hannah, Lester, and Vogelgesang present a model for viewing moral leadership through the framework of the leader's moral self-concept. They propose that authentic leaders activate a working moral self-concept when faced with a moral dilemma, thus exercising moral agency. In addition, Hannah et al. assert that when leaders are perceived as morally authentic, virtuous, and altruistic, followers will afford them with greater influence and they will have more positive effects on organizations.

In Chapter 3, Hughes examines the roles of relational transparency and the use of humor within authentic leadership. The interactive effects of transparency and humor on follower outcomes such as positive emotions, trust in the leader, and creative performance are also considered. His focus on humor builds on recent interest in the leadership literature on how different styles and orientations toward humor affect leadership effectiveness (Cooper, in press).

Chapters 4–7 focuses on several specific theoretical perspectives, and how such theories help advance our understanding of the authentic leadership construct. In Chapter 4, Varella, Javidan, and Waldman suggest that authentic leaders may incorporate socialized forms of charismatic leadership, which they argue, are leadership manifestations that enhance the psychological and social capital of an organizational group. Varella et al. propose that authentic leaders promote the balanced development of social capital in their organizations, given their orientation toward socialized charismatic leadership.

In Chapter 5, Douglas, Ferris, and Perrewé examine how a leader's political skill and authenticity interact to influence followers' perceptions of authentic leadership. These authors argue that because leadership is a social phenomenon, leader political skill is an essential component in the study of authentic leadership. Furthermore, they assert that genuine, politically skilled leaders inspire trust, confidence, and authenticity as mechanisms to incur follower motivation, commitment, and productive work behavior.

In Chapter 6, Klenke advances a model of authentic leadership/followership that integrates cognitive, affective, conative, and spiritual antecedents and considers their influence at the group, organizational, and societal levels. Consistent with prior models of authentic leadership, her model is anchored in positive psychology (e.g., Gardner et al., 2005; Ilies, Morgeson, & Nahrgang, 2005; Luthans & Avolio, 2003). However, it extends prior authentic leadership theories by including a specific focus on conative and spiritual components of leadership.

Fry and Whittington extend our understanding of authentic leadership by discussing spiritual and legacy leadership in Chapter 7. These authors argue that understanding authentic leadership requires a focus on three key issues: (1) achieving agreement on universal or consensus values that are necessary for authentic leadership; (2) individual, group, and organizational level value congruence and consistency of values, attitudes, and behavior; and (3) the personal outcomes or rewards of authentic leadership. To address these issues and thereby enhance our understanding of authentic leadership, legacy leadership is introduced as a specific model within the spiritual leadership paradigm that has implications for authentic leadership theory, research, development, and practice.

Chapter 8 is a stand-alone chapter, in that it is provides a description of the status of leadership intervention research, and focuses on the very core of what constitutes how we conceive of "authentic leadership development." Reichard and Avolio provide a snapshot of the leadership field today in terms of the quality and quantity of leadership intervention research. These authors describe the type of interventions that have been conducted over the last 100 years within and between all of the major theories of leadership, the different settings in which such studies were conducted, and the quality of the research designs. Our aim for including this chapter was to provide a point in time estimate of what we know and what we need to learn about the causal impact of leadership interventions. These leadership interventions include what has been done to learn how to develop leadership, as well as how to experimentally manipulate it to test specific aspects of traditional and new genre theories of leadership. We believe that the next big growth areas and discoveries in the field of leadership will involve the emergence of a general theory of leadership development and in testing how to grow leadership. Thus we believe this chapter provides a strong foundation for future advances in leadership research and practice.

In Chapter 9, Chan outlines several important implications for measurement arising from the different theoretical models proposed by various authentic leadership scholars. He describes four theoretical lenses that scholars have used for studying authentic leadership and considers their implications for measurement. He goes on to identify several working assumptions regarding the nature of authentic leadership development interventions and offers useful suggestions for future efforts in measuring authentic leadership.

The next two chapters present two exploratory empirical studies that relate broadly to the area of authentic leadership. In Chapter 10, Pittinsky focuses on authenticity and leadership by studying "leader authenticity markers" (i.e., those features and actions of an individual leader which lead others to conclude that a leader is authentic) of African American political leaders, using a cohort of African Americans sampled from what he refers to as the "Hip Hop Generation." Using qualitative methods, seven authenticity markers for African American political leaders are identified, including experience of racism, policy positions, liberal party affiliation, speech patterns and mannerisms, experience of struggle, participation in the Black Church, and connection to historical African American events and to other African Americans. These markers are used as a basis for describing how fellow African Americans come to view an African American leader as authentic.

In Chapter 11, Dasborough and Ashkanasy report their findings of a qualitative and quantitative study on extensions to authentic leadership theory. They propose a significant extension to previous theoretical models of authentic leadership covered in the special issue and this volume, based on the nature of followers' emotional reactions to a leader's influence attempt. Specifically, they focus on follower attributions and emotional reactions to differentiate authentic from inauthentic leadership influence. In their exploratory study, Dasborough and Ashkanasy found that positive affect was associated with labeling of the leader's behavior as transformational and trustworthy. In contrast, negative affect was related directly to followers' intentions to comply with the leader's request. Hence, in line with ongoing work in positive psychology (Frederickson, 2001) and the original definition of authentic leadership provided by Luthans and Avolio (2003), Dasborough and Ashkanasy offer a useful connection between positive emotions and what constitutes authentic transformational leadership.

The last three chapters provide new directions for the study of authentic leadership. In Chapter 12, Youssef and Luthans propose a multi-level model to describe the processes by which organizational, leader, and employee resiliency can be developed, and have a positive impact on attitudinal and performance outcomes. The focus on resiliency represents an important addition to research on authentic leadership and its development, as it is one of the core characteristics oftentimes linked to world class leaders. This chapter builds on recent work by Luthans to quantify what he has called

PsyCap, which comprises optimism, resiliency, hope, and leader efficacy (Luthans, Luthans, & Luthans, 2004).

Most leadership research has been conducted on what constitutes the normal range of leadership functioning. Kolditz and Brazil extend the traditional leadership research focus by discussing their ongoing work to the study authentic leadership occurring "at the point of death," or what they call leadership "in extremis" contexts in Chapter 13. These authors propose that both men and women who lead others in life-threatening situations, will have to behave in ways that are indicative of authentic leadership in order to sustain performance with the least number of deaths. Perhaps there is no better place to depend on the authenticity of one's leader than in an environment where one's choices are life threatening.

In Chapter 14, Eigel and Kuhnert attempt to integrate Kegan's work on perspective-taking capacity and how one can conceptualize the moral growth of authentic leaders. Using a developmental perspective, the authors posit that leaders grow through a better understanding of what they have become and how others see them. The development in the leader's perspective-taking capacity at the highest level allows them to become the "authors" of their own destiny and the destiny of others. Such level 5 thinking provides leaders with the capacity to think about the way they think and to test and change the models of thinking which have guided their decisions.

Finally, in Chapter 15, the concluding chapter, we identify several emergent themes found in theory and research on authentic leadership development that reflect areas of convergence and divergence. Emerging areas of convergence include: a focus on the role of authentic leader and follower emotions and followers' emotional reactions to leader authenticity and inauthenticity; growing recognition of the importance of relational transparency to authentic leadership and followership; new insights regarding the developmental focus of authentic leadership; and explication of specific contextual influences on authenticity. Areas of divergence involve differences of opinion regarding the inclusion of a moral component and positive psychological capital as essential elements in models of authentic leadership. We discuss these themes and present our own perspective on these issues, including theoretical and philosophical arguments as to why we believe efforts to develop authentic leaders, and leaders in general, must devote attention to the leader's moral development, if true development is to occur. We conclude with suggestions of our own for advancing theory and conducting research on authentic leadership and its development.

NOTES

1. We wish to thank Adrian Chan and Sean Hannah for contributing to this brief review of the origins of modern conceptions of authentic leadership.

ACKNOWLEDGMENTS

We are grateful to all of the people who have supported this effort. Specifically, we extend our deep sense of appreciation to all of the authors who contributed their chapters to this volume. We are also grateful to James G. (Jerry) Hunt, for offering us this opportunity to publish the works from the GLI Summit in this monograph series. We appreciate the generous support provided by the sponsors of the inaugural GLI Summit, including the University of Nebraska-Lincoln, The Gallup Corporation, Howard and Rhonda Hawks, Connectivity Solutions, Peter Kiewit Sons, Inc., and *The Leadership Quarterly*. We thank the anonymous reviewers who provided quality feedback on the manuscripts submitted. Finally, we thank all the participants of the inaugural Gallup Leadership Institute (GLI) Summit and the doctoral students and staff at the GLI for their insights and suggestions. It was truly a collaborative effort.

REFERENCES

Avolio, B. J. (2005). *Leadership development in balance: Made/born*. Mahwah, NJ: Lawrence Earlbaum Associates.

Avolio, B. J., & Gardner, W. L. (2005). Authentic leadership development: Getting to the root of positive forms of leadership. *The Leadership Quarterly, 16*, 315–338.

Avolio, B. J., Gardner, W. L., Walumbwa, F. O., Luthans, F., & May, D. R. (2004). Unlocking the mask: A look at the process by which authentic leaders impact follower attitudes and behaviors. *The Leadership Quarterly, 15*, 801–823.

Cooper, C. D. (in press). Just joking around?: Employee humor expression as an ingratiatory behavior. *Academy of Management Review*.

Frederickson, B. L. (2001). The role of positive emotions in positive psychology: The broaden-and-build theory of positive emotions. *American Psychologist, 56*, 218–226.

Gardner, W. L., Avolio, B. J., Luthans, F., May, D. R., & Walumbwa, F. O. (2005). "Can you see the real me?" A self-based model of authentic leader and follower development. *The Leadership Quarterly, 16*, 343–372.

Goffman, E. (1959). *The presentation of self in everyday life*. Garden City, NY: Doubleday Anchor.

Halpin, A. W., & Croft, D. B. (1963a). The organizational climate of schools. *Administrator's Notebook, 11*, 1–4.

Halpin, A. W., & Croft, D. B. (1963b). *The organizational climate of schools.* Chicago: University of Chicago Press.

Halpin, A. W., & Croft, D. B. (1966). The organizational climate of schools. In: A. W. Halpin (Ed.), *Theory and research in administration* (pp. 131–249). New York: Macmillan.

Harter, S. (2002). Authenticity. In: C. R. Snyder & S. Lopez (Eds), *Handbook of positive psychology* (pp. 382–394). Oxford, UK: Oxford University Press.

Henderson, J. E., & Hoy, W. K. (1983). Leader authenticity: The development and test of an operational measure. *Educational and Psychological Research, 3*(2), 63–75.

Hoy, W. K., & Henderson, J. E. (1983). Principal authenticity, school climate and pupil-control orientation. *Alberta Journal of Educational Research, 29*(2), 123–130.

Ilies, R., Morgeson, F. P., & Nahrgang, J. D. (2005). Authentic leadership and eudaemonic well-being: Understanding leader–follower outcomes. *The Leadership Quarterly, 16,* 373–394.

James, W. (1890). *The principles of psychology.* New York: Holt.

Luthans, F., & Avolio, B. J. (2003). Authentic leadership: A positive developmental approach. In: K. S. Cameron, J. E. Dutton & R. E. Quinn (Eds), *Positive organizational scholarship* (pp. 241–261). San Francisco: Barrett-Koehler.

Luthans, F., Luthans, K. W., & Luthans, B. C. (2004). Positive psychological capital: Beyond human and social capital. *Business Horizons, 47*(1), 45–50.

McInnis, T. J. (1973). Authenticity and leadership: A study of the relationship between principals' self-perceived authentic behavior and leader behavior and teachers' perceptions of principals' self-perceptions. *Dissertation Abstracts International, 34*(5-A), 2227–2228.

Weigert, A. J. (1988). To be or not: Self and authenticity, identity, and ambivalence. In: D. K. Lapsley & F. C. Power (Eds), *Self, ego, and identity* (pp. 263–281). New York: Springer.

PART I:
ADVANCEMENTS TO AUTHENTIC LEADERSHIP DEVELOPMENT THEORY

VERITABLE AUTHENTIC LEADERSHIP: EMERGENCE, FUNCTIONING, AND IMPACTS

Adrian Chan, Sean T. Hannah and
William L. Gardner

ABSTRACT

*In this chapter we introduce the construct of the authenticity of a leader as
a logical extension of the authentic person. We provide an operational
definition of authenticity, and contrast the pseudo-authentic with the veritable authentic person. From a social cognitive lens, we propose that
authenticity is an emergent property of key processes and components of
the self-system. We then examine how the leader's authenticity positively
affects intra- and interpersonal leadership processes. We propose that
authenticity in leaders is an important leadership multiplier, and is foundational for producing a virtuous cycle of performance and learning for
leaders, followers and organizations.*

> The authentic self is the soul made visible.
>
> Sarah Ban Breathnach

In his thesis, Being and Nothingness (1943), the philosopher Jean Paul
Sartre (1905–1980) describes authenticity as a personal search for meaning,

Authentic Leadership Theory and Practice: Origins, Effects and Development
Monographs in Leadership and Management, Volume 3, 3–41

arguing that mankind, having been confronted with the meaninglessness of existence, embarks on a search for the true self. However, according to Sartre, individual authenticity is to be earned and emerges from its social context, under guidance of one's own conscience. Sartre's intimation that authenticity involves morality and a journey toward one's possible selves is a theme that will be elaborated throughout this chapter.

At first glance, the use of the word "authentic" in the definition of authentic leadership provided in the introduction of this book may appear to have been stretched beyond the meaning assigned to it by Sartre, and others (Erickson, 1995; Harter, 2002), of being true to oneself. While the core components of Authentic Leadership Theory (ALT) (e.g., self-awareness and self-regulation) reflect this adage, Luthans and Avolio (2003) also include additional, albeit desirable qualities (e.g., ethical standards, developmental focus, and positive psychological capacities) in their definition. As a result of these additions, it may seem difficult to find a person who fits their full definition of an authentic leader.

When one breaks down Luthans and Avolio's (2003) concept of an authentic leader into its constituent components, two underlying factors become apparent. First, the authenticity of the leader is predicated on the authenticity of the person (as it is traditionally defined). That is, the ability to behave authentically as a person is a necessary criterion for any leader hoping to be authentic in his/her leadership. Second, the leader who is authentic can achieve more than any other leader – in other words, authenticity serves as a key *leadership multiplier*. Hence, the extent that the leader is authentic as a person directly affects the efficacy of his/her given leadership style on followers, as defined by ALT. Cast in this manner, authentic leadership is no longer an impossible ideal, but a practical and achievable goal for many leaders. To this end, it is therefore imperative that the antecedents, components, and effects of authenticity are further explored within the general context of leadership, and with particular reference to ALT.

PURPOSE

We propose a deeper examination of the authenticity component of authentic leadership. We put forth an operational definition of authenticity, utilizing a social cognitive lens to identify the key processes and components of the self-system that foster authentic leadership, and how that system interacts in a given leadership environment. We recognize that leadership is a multilevel phenomenon (Ashforth, 1999; Yammarino, Dansereau, & Kennedy, 2001). However, we choose in this chapter to focus on the intrapersonal processes of the authentic leader, and limit our examination of the interpersonal aspects of authentic leadership to just the dyadic leader–follower relationship. Specifically, we address five major research questions: (1) What are the cognitive (including motivational) processes associated with authenticity? (2) How does authenticity become manifest through the leader's cognitive and behavioral self-regulation? (3) How is authenticity perceived, attributed, and internalized by the follower? (4) What are the follower-related outcomes? and (5) How does the authentic leader process and react to subsequent diagnostic feedback from the follower and the environment?

The above questions correspond to the five major components of our proposed theoretical framework for veritable authentic leadership. The major subprocesses proposed include: (1) the leader's self-clarity and meta-cognition over their self-system (self-awareness); (2) the leader's alignment of self-awareness and self-regulation through meta-cognitive oversight and agentic commitment to self; (3) the followers' cognitive processing of the leader's observed behavior and their resulting attributions and perceptions of leader authenticity; (4) the resulting proximal and veritable effects on the follower; (5) the self-verification and priming cues the leader processes from diagnostic feedback received through the follower feedback loop and various forms of performance and contextual feedback; and finally, (6) the formation and reinforcement of an authentic organizational culture (Figs. 1 and 2).

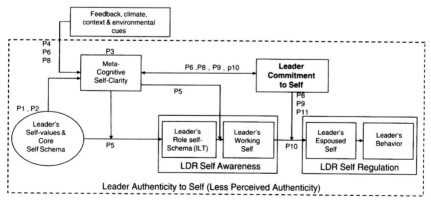

Fig. 1. Process Model of the Emergence of Authentic Behaviors.

Using this framework and lens, we advance a process model of authenticity to depict the intra- and interpersonal processes that occur in a leadership system, and how the leader's authenticity positively affects this system. We use the adjective "veritable" (i.e., true or genuine) to distinguish the true authentic leader from the *pseudo-authentic leader* who may temporally present him- or herself as authentic to followers, but does so for impression management purposes only. We also propose that authenticity in leaders is an important *leadership multiplier*, and is foundational for producing a virtuous cycle of performance and learning for leaders, followers and the organization.

WHAT IS AUTHENTICITY?

Discriminant Validity of the Leadership Authenticity Construct

Authenticity is not *sincerity.* Modern conceptions of authenticity are best understood by what it is not. Firstly, authenticity should not be confused with sincerity. Trilling (1972) best made this distinction clear in his definition of sincerity as "the absence of dissimulation or feigning or pretense" (p.13) in which there is "congruence between avowal and actual feeling" (p. 2). Insincerity is thus the *feeling* of a lack of incongruence in one's relations and interactions with others.

Authenticity, on the other hand, is a self-referential state of being (Sartre, 1943). It is more than a feeling, and has to do primarily with *being* one's true self. It is a state of being that is self-contained and does not require the presence of another for its reality to become manifest – unlike sincerity which is only manifest in one's relationships with others, one is authentic because one has *achieved* authenticity, and this state of being is the same whether one is alone or in a crowd. When applied to the leadership process, however, we will develop how this intrapersonal state of being positively influences the interpersonal follower–leader relationship.

Although we do acknowledge that being authentic has affective and perceptual implications, we stress that the essence of authenticity is a developmental achievement that is manifest in the wholesomeness of one's internal self. From the perspective of the self-system literature, to be authentic is to be "true to oneself"; the assumption being that there is a coherent phenomenological self (Kihlstrom & Klein, 1994) to which one can be true. Achieving coherence with this known and experienced self, and having the cognitive capabilities to maintain this coherence, is what is critical in defining what makes a person authentic.

Authenticity is not *impression management.* To be inauthentic is to betray one's own relationship with oneself. Berman (1970, p. 60) describes inauthenticity as "the determination of men to hide themselves not merely from others but from themselves." Behaviorally, this is manifest as hiding one's true thoughts, being phony, or saying what one thinks others want to hear, rather than what one really wants to say. However, this behavioral manifestation of inauthenticity is not to be confused with impression management (Gardner & Avolio, 1998; Leary & Kowalski, 1990; Rosenfeld, Giacalone, & Riordan, 2002). The behavioral manifestations, while similar, do arise from different causes.

In a social situation, the inauthentic person acts in deference to external information because of a lack of coherent internal information that he/she can draw upon, which may be due to causes such as a lack of self-awareness, or an inadequate commitment to the self. Taken away from the social setting, the inauthentic person is still intrinsically inauthentic, lacking the ability and/or motivation to be true to the self. Impression management, on the other hand, makes no assumption about the coherence of the self, and is primarily concerned with the manipulation of social information to achieve a particular image objective with a target or audience.

In fact, a person can have high levels of self-awareness and yet choose to use that awareness to further dramaturgically manipulate their external portrayal of the self. Although the inauthentic person may engage in impression management (e.g., as a defense mechanism to portray coherence), by itself impression management is an insufficient condition for determining the authenticity or inauthenticity of an individual. In fact, an authentic person may use impression management techniques to ensure that his/her true self is displayed to and perceived by others. What differentiates authentic leaders is whether the impression attempted is consistent with the self, or dramaturgical in nature.

Authenticity is not *self-monitoring.* The continuum of inauthenticity to authenticity appears to closely mirror that of self-monitoring (Snyder, 1987), with the high self-monitor displaying different behaviors according to what is perceived to be appropriate for the situation, while low self-monitors are more apt to listen inward for guidance on how to behave in a situation. High self-monitors report having multiple selves (Lester, 1997), while low self-monitors may initially appear more genuine and true to themselves.

Several things differentiate authenticity from self-monitoring. First, inauthenticity is characterized by false self-behavior (Lerner, 1993), while high self-monitors do not necessarily report or regard their behavior as false (Snyder, 1979). Although authenticity is a state of being, inauthenticity can be felt and experienced as an affect, measurable by self-reports (Harter, 2002). Self-monitoring focuses on behavioral flexibility across situations and not on the felt affect associated with behaviors. In addition, although Snyder's original definition of self-monitoring included the intention to display socially appropriate behavior (Snyder, 1979), self-monitoring scales do not measure either motive or intentionality (Briggs & Cheek, 1988).

Inauthenticity, on the other hand, arises out of a sense of false self that is "socially implanted" (Harter, 2002) against one's will and is often reported by the person. Hence, high self-monitors will adapt their behavior to the situation, believing strongly that they are presenting their most appropriate self for the situation at hand. On the other hand, the inauthentic person is aware that the self presented is phony and may judge it to be the product of situational pressures.

Second, authenticity includes a commitment to one's identity and values (Erickson, 1995). As such, this commitment aspect of authenticity is more state-like. On the other hand, self-monitoring is a personality attribute that becomes manifest as a preference for utilizing alternative sources of information when deciding on one's social behavior (i.e., context versus self-system; prototypical person for situation versus prototypical self for situation). Self-monitoring reflects a trait-like preference and proficiency for utilizing self-knowledge (low self-monitor) versus knowledge of others (high self-monitor) in social situations (Snyder, 1987). Authenticity is purely self-referential, to "exist wholly by the laws of its own being" (Trilling, 1972, p. 93). Put in another way, authenticity involves an agentic commitment to one's own laws. This intrapersonal *commitment to the self*, however the self is defined, constitutes another core characteristic of what it means to be authentic, and will positively affect the interpersonal processes that define leadership.

The final contrast between authenticity and self-monitoring is that the authentic person is concerned with the degree of self-referential expression, whereas the high self-monitor is concerned about the degree of social impression. Authenticity consists of knowing what being true to oneself means (self-awareness) and expressing oneself truly (self-regulation) – with discrepancies between the two resulting in feelings of inauthenticity (Lerner, 1993). Without fully invoking the admittedly important role of individual perceptual processes in order to retain the intrapersonal focus of this chapter, self-expression is here assumed to be accurately received by the external audience, resulting in perceived authenticity by others. Thus, faithful self-expression and perceived authenticity go hand in hand in the case of the authentic leader; there is no need for active impression management by the leader.

Conversely, the high self-monitoring leader is more concerned with making the appropriate social impression; that is, the goal is always to portray some level of the ideal group prototype (Hogg, 2001) or the leader's role-based prototypical self (Lord & Brown, 2004) that is deemed most appropriate for the social context. Hence, the high self-monitoring leader will have a higher propensity to engage in active impression management (Kilduff & Day, 1994).

We take the view that the authentic leader is not necessarily a low self-monitor, although we recognize that the overlap in personality traits associated with these constructs suggests that the authentic person may be predisposed to low self-monitoring. The reason for this seeming irony lies in the fact that authentic leaders are not given free rein for expressing their personalities, but are also bounded by their roles as leaders. Unlike authentic persons, authentic leaders are not only true to themselves, but also true to their roles as leaders, which include an element of being aware of social cues and followers' needs, expectations, desires and feedback (Day & Kilduff, 2003). Because the authentic leader is very self-aware (Gardner, Avolio, Luthans, May, & Walumbwa, 2005; Luthans & Avolio, 2003), he/she can react to environmental priming cues to make certain aspects of the true self more salient. This results in a *working self-concept* that is more adaptive and responsive to situational cues (Markus & Wurf, 1987).

Authentic leaders are not automatons driven by some homunculus that determines their behavior. In fact, the phenomenological self is too vast for any leader to access it at any given time (Kihlstrom & Klein, 1994). Hence, authentic leaders can remain true to themselves and yet display a range of behaviors that are well-adapted to the demands of the situation at hand depending on the part of the true self that is activated. Conversely, low self-monitors are less amenable to contextual priming cues at the self-awareness stage simply because of an inherent preference to defer to internal cues. This results in a less flexible working self-concept that carries itself through to self-regulation, eventually manifesting itself as behaviors that may be true to self, but "stubbornly so" and unheeding of situational demands. In this regard, low self-monitors tend to be less effective leaders (Day & Kilduff, 2003).

On the other hand, we also argue that authenticity adds incremental value to a leader who is also a high self-monitor. On his/her own, a high self-monitor is less receptive to internal priming cues at the self-awareness stage, and may instead allow situational cues to prime self-regulation mechanisms that conflict with the working self-concept. This produces behavior that is more appropriate for the situation, but not necessarily reflective of the "self-in-situation." When the high self-monitoring leader is also authentic, however, more aspects of the self become accessible due to higher levels of both self- and other-awareness. Consequently, more contextually applicable concepts associated with the self are activated, enabling the leader to be both adaptive and true to self in leadership episodes. What is critical is that this authentic temporal and role-based working self-concept is still a coherent part, albeit a subset, of the true self.

Authenticity develops in parallel to morality. As is further explained by Hannah, Lester, and Vogelgesang (2005) in this book, we propose that authenticity and morality are mutually reinforcing in that one cannot be authentically immoral or antisocial. Developmentally, the path to authenticity in a person gives rise to the ability for *postconventionalist* (Kohlberg, 1984) reflection and *self-authorship* (Kegan, 1994). These capacities not only increase one's pro-social orientation, but also the ability for self-regulation that is empathetic and relational.

Consistent with the notion of Leader Developmental Level (LDL) introduced by Eigel and Kuhnert (2005) in their contribution to this volume, we propose that the underlying cognitive processes that enable authenticity also produce high levels of moral capacity and agency. Such individuals are characterized by highly developed meta-cognitive ability, a heightened sense of self-awareness, a strong sense of one's core values and identity, and an efficient self-regulatory system. Authenticity is thus not a vacuous construct, and by logical extension, its antecedents produce higher levels of ethical, individually considerate leadership that is associate-building in its orientation. This logic supports Luthans and Avolio (2003) and May, Chan, Hodges, and Avolio's (2003) inclusion of these key leadership qualities in their authentic leadership construct.

In summary, the discussion so far indicates that the key components of authenticity include at least an affective component (feelings of being true to one's self), a cognitive component (self-awareness of one's true self and socially prescribed roles), a valance component (commitment to self), and a self-referential expression component that may be perceived by others. These components are summarized in Fig. 2.

AUTHENTICITY IN LEADERS: A SOCIAL COGNITIVE VIEW

Thus far, we have alluded to a social cognitive perspective in our conceptualization of authenticity. In line with this view, we view authenticity as an

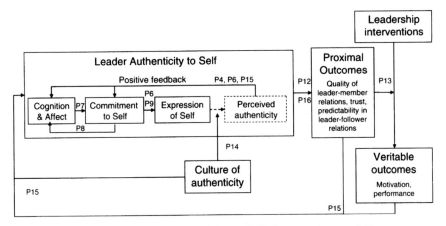

Fig. 2. Virtuous Cycle of Authenticity to Self, Interventions and Outcomes.

emergent property of various components and processes of the self-system. In particular, to illustrate the impact of the working self-concept, we chose the leader role as our focus. For the remainder of this chapter, we shift our discussion to authenticity as an emergent process in specific individuals, namely leaders, and further explicate the underlying constructs of authenticity presented thus far as key functions of the leadership process. In keeping with the intrapersonal focus of this chapter, we explicitly acknowledge, but choose for now to exclude the role that follower attributions and leader impression management may play in affecting how authenticity in the leader is perceived.

A social cognitive perspective of authenticity has two key features: (1) the presence and awareness of a core self within the self-system; and (2) the need for one's presentation of self to be aligned with one's core self. When defined this way, our operational definition of authenticity consists of the integrity of the self-system and the alignment of this self-system with public demonstrations and perceptions of the self by others. The proposed framework also provides for a third social cognitive variable, environmental influence, which is further developed in the discussion of priming cues and follower and environmental feedback mechanisms below.

Leaders, by virtue of their unique role demands, high visibility, and salience to followers, face additional challenges in being authentic to both themselves and to their roles as leaders. History is replete with examples of leaders, who under normal circumstances may be considered authentic, or at least not inauthentic people, but when called to face a leadership challenge, failed miserably and acted in the most inauthentic fashion.

For example, one could argue that abuse of Iraqi prisoners at the Abu Ghraib prison by military personnel, as well as the conduct of officers and noncommissioned officers – if charges that they condoned the beatings and humiliation of prisoners prove to be true – reflect an abdication of the moral responsibilities that accompany the role of leader. In other words, those responsible for the abuse behaved inauthentically as leaders, failing to display moral courage as they succumbed to pressures to combat terrorism at any costs. Similarly, the historical instances of groupthink documented by Janis (1972) and others (e.g., Esser, 1998; Turner & Pratkanis, 1998) suggest that such cases can arguably be seen as more than just the power of the group over the self – they can also be seen as failures of persons in leadership roles to behave authentically as leaders.

The power of the situation is but one of the many tensions that threaten to wrestle leaders away from acting true to themselves and to their leadership roles and responsibilities (Davis-Blake & Pfeffer, 1989; Mischel, 1973). The role of leader poses significant challenges. Not all authentic people can be leaders, much less authentic leaders. And not all authentic leaders behave authentically all the time. In fact, one must see oneself as possessing the attributes that one determines are needed in a given leadership situation in order to emerge authentically as a leader. Role conflict will result when authentic *persons* are asked to assume leadership roles that they believe require attributes not found in their true self and that they are unable to develop in time for expected performance. A more reserved police lieutenant, for example, may be very comfortable in leading officers through the processes involved in managing investigative resources, but may experience great inner conflict when asked to lead a Special Weapons and Tactics (SWAT) team.

We therefore, see authenticity as varying along a continuum from complete inauthenticity to full authenticity (Erickson, 1995). Rather than being dichotomously authentic or inauthentic, leader authenticity varies as a function of both internal and external factors. With regards to external factors, we agree with the assertion made by Luthans and Avolio (2003) that there are both trait and state components to a leader's authenticity. In their view, state components of authenticity are contingent on situational factors, and may be domain specific. In the next section, we first introduce the internal factors that we believe contribute to authenticity in leaders, and then turn our attention to the external influences.

SOCIAL COGNITIVE PROCESSES OF AUTHENTICITY

From a social cognitive perspective, we hold that authenticity is predicated on: (1) self-clarity regarding one's schematic self-system (to include values, beliefs, goals, roles, attributes and emotions); and (2) meta-cognitive ability and commitment to self to apply the true self-system to cognitive and behavioral self-regulation during leadership episodes. Below we advance a conceptual framework that delineates the emergence, structure, and functioning of this authentic self-system.

Veritable authenticity requires leaders to first have increased awareness of and self-clarity regarding their self-system. Referring to Fig. 1, the proposed framework posits that the leader's self-system is an interactive and multi-dimensional process composed of the leader's set of *core-self schema* and their collection of *leadership role self-schema.* Self-awareness is evidenced by the leader's ability and motivation to identify and assess the components of these schemas, and have meta-cognitive oversight with respect to the cognitive processing of self-information during leadership performances.

As originally defined, the self-awareness construct involves a cognitive state in which an individual focuses conscious attention on some aspect of the self (Duval & Wicklund, 1972); it says nothing about the degree of accuracy or inaccuracy of self-perceptions. As used here and by Gardner et al. (2005), however, self-awareness arises from self-reflection about one's values, beliefs, attributes, and motives. We believe that such self-reflection can help authentic leaders to know themselves and gain clarity and concordance with respect to their core values, identity, beliefs, emotions, motives, and goals. Moreover, as will be further elaborated, our framework proposes that distinct components of the leader's self-system will be activated at any given time through priming cues provided by the context, the followers, and personal introspection.

Our framework (Fig. 1) proposes that authentic leaders have a heightened capacity to effectively process self-information giving them strong abilities to: (1) access complex self-schemas and domain knowledge; (2) conduct centralized and peripheral cognitive processing of self-information; and (3) meta-cognitively select and activate (i.e., self-regulate) self-schema reflecting their beliefs, values, goals, roles, attitudes, and emotions in the activation of the working self-concept. The overriding driver of these processes, however, is the leader's strong and agentic commitment to be true to the self. As shown in Fig. 1, it is this driver that provides the motivation for deep and controlled meta-cognition and moderates the manifestation of self-awareness into self-consistent regulation. Below we elaborate on aspects of the self that make self-awareness and authentic self-regulation possible.

Cognitive Structure of the Authentic Self

Jones and Gerard (1967, p. 716) defined the *phenomenological* self as a "person's awareness, arising out of interactions with his environment, of his own beliefs, values, attitudes, the links between them, and their implications for his behavior." Such a definition views the self as both a memory store as well as a constructivist process. As a memory store, Kihlstrom et al. (1988, p. 150) stated that "the self is one of the richest, most elaborative knowledge structures stored in memory." As an emergent, constructed entity, the self affects current perceptions of reality, such "that memories of past actions and outcomes are available in integrated form to clarify current action possibilities" (Jones & Pittman, 1982, p. 232).

Drawing from this literature, our proposed framework offers a structuralist view where the leader's self-system involves the development and activation (instantiation) of selected self-schematic logogens held in long-term memory. In other words, the structure of one's self involves organized and accessible memories of one's self. The hypothetical constructs stored in the leader's self-schema (Markus, 1977) provide a framework for answering questions of existentialism ("Who am I?"), functioning ("How do I relate to different people/environments?"), self-attributions ("Am I friendly, moral, capable?"), and other key informational requirements. In sum, these self-hypotheses, to the extent that one has the ability and motivation to recall and process them, define the leader's phenomenological "self as known."

Building on the work of Markus (1977), Lord, Brown, and Freiberg (1999) proposed that there is a temporal dimension to the self-concept whereby one identifies not only a current *self-view*, but also holds a more distant image of a *possible self*. The ability to envision a possible self is unique to humans and is based on the ability to engage in mental time travel (Roberts & Dowling, 2002; Tulving, 1972). Because mental time travel techniques are largely context-based, they rely heavily on contextual episodic (autobiographical) memories. Such cases illuminate the interaction between semantic memories of one's self and episodic memory that will occur in leadership role episodes. Additionally, we assert that the clarity of one's possible authentic self, coupled with the drive to attain this possible self, can provide strong motivation for self-development toward authenticity. Although a full exploration is beyond the scope of this chapter, we propose that such motivation lies at the heart of authentic leadership development.

The Multidimensionality of the Self Structure

One's self-system is not a one-dimensional whole, but rather a complex, interconnected and multidimensional phenomenon (Hoyle, Kernis, Leary, & Baldwin, 1999). As shown in Fig. 1, our framework proposes that the authentic leader holds a core self of superordinate beliefs, values, attributes and other factors, as well as a leadership role-based self that contains the differentiated, role-based knowledge held in semantic memory. The cognitive processes, whereby portions of these domains are activated into a contextual working self-concept are examined further below as part of the discussion of the cognitive functioning of the authentic self. For parsimony, only the leader's role self-schema is shown in the model, but other role-based schemas held in the leader's memory, such as those associated with one's family roles and community roles, may be similarly activated (e.g., via spreading activation).

Due to the vast amount of self-information held in memory, some type of organization is necessary for cognitive functioning. Self-differentiation involves the ability to categorize one's self-concepts (self-knowledge) according to roles, situations, relationships, traits, states, emotions, and other categorical factors, creating multiple phenomenological selves (Markus & Wurf, 1987). Multiple selves can create more flexibility and resilience than a unified core self (Markus & Wurf, 1987), but excessive categorization may result in self-fragmentation, which may be characteristic of extremely high self-monitoring persons (Donahue, Robins, Roberts, & John, 1993).

Self-schemas are also thought to be defined at the individual, relational, and collective levels (Brewer & Gardner, 1996). Since leadership is at its core a pro-social and collective phenomenon (e.g., Bass & Steidlmeier, 1999), the term *authentic leader* – i.e., applying the attribute of *leader* to the authentic person – implies a pro-social leader who has high clarity of self, is motivated and able to regulate consistent with that self, and manages ongoing tensions between self and social/collective demands at various levels.

We know that developmentally, the complexity and strength of one's self-beliefs stored in long-term memory can be advanced by increasing the intensity and frequency of a person's exposure to trigger events, with more experienced (cognitively complex) individuals having better organized schemas and inter-concept linkages to make better sense of stimuli to acquire new knowledge (Bower & Hilgard, 1981; Hersey, Walsh, Read, & Chulef, 1990; Lurigio & Carroll, 1985). Experienced individuals can also, when called upon, consciously elect to spend more time deliberately processing new information without referring to learnt heuristics (Dollinger, 1984). This deliberate processing is critical to providing a feedback loop to the developmental process. Thus, we propose that increased levels and complexity of self-knowledge held in the leader's self-concept will create a reciprocal and cyclic heightening of self-awareness, and increased assimilation of future self-related feedback.

Based on the preceding discussion, we propose:

Proposition 1. The authentic leader's self emerges as a function of instantiation of core- and role-based self-schemas into an authentic working self during leadership episodes.

Proposition 2. Authentic leadership will be positively associated with the level (amount) and complexity of self-information held in a leader's episodic and semantic memory.

Cognitive Functioning of the Authentic Self

An important distinction is made in the proposed framework between the structure of the authentic self and the functioning of this self-system (Kihlstrom, Beer, & Klein, 2003; Kihlstrom et al., 1988; Kihlstrom & Klein, 1994). The latter comprises the activation, recall and processing of self-information from memory, and the resulting self-relevant beliefs, attitudes, perceptions, and other cognitions that emerge to drive the leader's self-awareness and self-regulation. We explore the cognitive functioning of the authentic self and its implications for our focus on veritable versus pseudo-authentic leadership below.

Self-concept clarity is the ability to report self-beliefs that are clear, confident, stable, and consistent; it has been recognized as an individual difference variable (Campbell, Assanand, & Di Paula, 2000; Campbell et al., 1996). The clarity of one's self-awareness, however, is confounded. Owing to cognitive limitations and attentional capacities, all self-relevant information is not accessible at any point in time. Additionally, individual biases alter the processing of that limited pool of information.

In light of these limitations, our framework (see Fig. 1), proposes that the phenomenological self displayed in a given leadership episode is a temporal entity – a subset of the leader's self-system, that becomes manifest in a contextual working self-concept (Markus & Wurf, 1987). The working self-concept is that part of one's domain of self-schema that is activated by stimuli (primes) from one's current environment, or by the self-activation of a more expert leader.

The various self-schemas that a person holds differ in the ease with which they can be activated (Markus, 1977), creating a highly salient core, and less accessible peripheral self-schemas. Research has shown that when individuals are focused on their self, the activation of core values increases (Verplanken & Holland, 2002). We propose that the values associated with and arising from authenticity are highly salient aspects of an authentic leader's core self-schema, and thus chronically accessible during working self-concept activation. This produces a strong *commitment to self* during leadership episodes. Hannah et al. (2005) propose that this value-laden commitment may be associated with the leader's internal virtues whereby they see self-consistent behavior as a moral issue and imperative.

Although this framework provides for context-based activation to form the leader's working self-concept, this is an acknowledgment of the role that context plays in the automatic and controlled triggering of the working self (Lord & Brown, 2001). It should not be confused with the controlled, conscious effort that the leader expends to address contextual factors as indicated in theories of self-monitoring or impression management. In these theories, one can be bankrupt in terms of the richness of one's working self-concept as a leader for the situation at hand, and still, with great effort and practice, conjure up a reasonably convincing leader role-play. Not that these are inherently bad – controlled processing is a feature of self-regulation. For example, anytime a leader encounters a novel leadership situation (a young commander giving a first speech to her soldiers), she employs such controlled processing.

Put another way, for a veritable authentic leader, the working self-concept is inherently a subset of the leader's self-system, and thus part of their true self. The authentic leader is aware of this activated self and carries it forward into self-regulation that is true to their self-system. Conversely, self-presentations by pseudo-authentic leaders (leaders who present themselves authentic for dramaturgical purposes only) entail some level of de-linkage between the true self-system and behavioral regulation, and hence varying levels of *self-distortion*. Like their veritable counterparts, pseudo-authentic leaders may appear authentic to their audiences. However, they can be distinguished by the manner in which they respond to environmental cues. For veritable authentic leaders, environmental cues exert their influence during the *self-awareness* process by activating context specific portions of the leader's core and role-based selves. In contrast, as will be further discussed, pseudo-authentic leaders may allow environmental cues to influence their self during the *self-regulation* process, by activating elements of a dramaturgical self that de-link and violate the working self.

Meta-Cognition and Self-Information Processing

Our framework proposes that veritable authentic leaders have heightened meta-cognitive abilities that provide them with an increased capacity to oversee the activation and implementation of their working self-concept. Meta-cognition (Brown, 1987; Flavell, 1979; Schraw & Dennison, 1994) is most broadly referred to as *thinking about your thinking.* Meta-cognition is commensurate with the top strata of Craik and Lockhart (1972)'s levels of processing approach (Velichkovsky, 2002), and has the two main functions of *monitoring* and *controlling* (regulation) human cognitions and processes (e.g., Metcalfe & Shimamura, 1994; Nelson & Narens, 1994). It thus serves both self-referential and executive-control functions that enable authentic leaders to process complex dilemmas and self-relevant information.

Increased meta-cognitive ability helps leaders to: (a) better assess and make meaning of self-relevant information during leadership episodes; (b) monitor and adjust their reasoning processes toward issue-specific outcomes, and (c) control the selection and activation of self-schemas to meet goals while also remaining true to themselves. Such oversight also allows personal biases and limitations to be identified, and thus scrutinized and controlled. Through the functions of monitoring and control, meta-cognitive capabilities also oversee the formation of intentions and other cognitions that support self-regulation, and thereby facilitate authentic behavior that is aligned with the leader's working self-concept.

Meta-cognition provides the authentic leader with heightened self-awareness through the dedicated and controlled processing of self-relevant information. When a person has both the *motivation* and *ability* to engage in meta-cognition, the amount of elaborative message-relevant thinking they apply increases, thereby determining whether a central (controlled cognitive effort), or less rigorous and peripheral (automatic or heuristic) mode of processing is utilized (Chaiken, 1980; Petty & Cacioppo, 1981, 1986). The level of processing ultimately determines the impact of a message on one's attitudes and beliefs, with controlled processing producing more persistent attitudes that are predictive of behavior (Petty & Cacioppo, 1986) and greater understanding and retention (Craik & Lockhart, 1972). We propose that controlled processing of self-information will lead to heightened self-concept clarity for authentic leaders and activation of commitment to self as a core value.

Additionally, although people seek accuracy, they are also *cognitive misers* and normally settle at a *sufficiency threshold* of processing once initial hypotheses are confirmed (Chaiken, 1980). To go beyond this threshold and initiate controlled processing, one must have sufficient motivation and ability. We propose that, for authentic leaders, this *motivation* comes from an agentic commitment to authenticity, whereas *ability* is derived from meta-cognitive self-clarity. In summary, meta-cognition will result in heightened self-concept clarity: the ability to report self-beliefs that are clear, confident, stable, and consistent (Campbell et al., 1996, 2000) and the emergence of this clear self into self-consistent regulation. This reasoning suggests:

Proposition 3. Authentic leadership will be associated with heightened levels of meta-cognitive ability and controlled processing of self-information, resulting in greater levels of self-concept clarity.

Functions of the Feedback Loop and Self-Information Processing

Our framework proposes that contextual feedback serves two purposes within the process of authentic leadership emergence. First, feedback serves to cue (cognitively prime) aspects of the leader's self during the self-awareness phase, resulting in the instantiation of selected self-schemas to form the working self-concept. Second, in response to the leader's subsequent behavior, contextual feedback serves a self-verifying control function. As shown in Fig. 1, contextual feedback is composed of follower verbal and non-verbal cues, follower performance and relational (e.g., trust) outcomes, and cultural/situational variables.

Self-schemas can be accessed into a working self-concept through either automatic or controlled cognitive processing (Lord & Brown, 2001). Research has shown, however, that with increased practice and familiarity, even complex and attention-intensive tasks may be executed through automatic processes (e.g., Logan & Klapp, 1991; Spelke, Hirst, & Neisser, 1976; Zbrodoff & Logan, 1986), suggesting that authenticity in one's activated working self-concept may become a habituated phenomenon.

Priming is an automatic process (e.g., Friedrich, Henik, & Tzelgov, 1991; Neely, Keefe, & Ross, 1989) occurring when an environmental cue (stimulus) automatically activates a meaning in semantic memory, and consequently cues meanings closely associated with it through spreading activation (Collins & Loftus, 1975). Primes have been shown to not only activate, but also inhibit activation of specific aspects of the self (Bargh, Chen, & Burrows, 1996; Higgins & Brendl, 1995), thus increasing or decreasing the accessibility of various aspects of self-schema in the working self-concept. Priming explains how a leader may develop a "trigger" or greater propensity to activate specific schemas and other inferences automatically based on stimuli in their environment.

By extension, we propose that an authentic leader who holds complex and clear core- and role-based self-schemas can habituate salient schemas, creating a propensity to instantiate authentic aspects of their self-system into an authentic working self-concept, and engage authentically during leadership episodes. Leaders will of course also call upon their schemas and scripts when making controlled processing judgments.

In summary, we propose that the temporal working self-concept is a multidimensional subset of the leader's domain of schematic self-knowledge, activated through environmental priming during the self-awareness process. Portions of this working self-concept may be implicit to the leader, but yet hold great influence over their cognitions and resulting behaviors.

Previously, we defined the authentic leader as holding a strong commitment to self, providing a pervasive *motive* for self-awareness and self-consistent regulation. Here, we propose that increased meta-cognitive capability will provide the *ability* to direct this motivation toward greater conscious oversight over both the activation of self-information and its use during self-regulation, supporting the following propositions:

Proposition 4. Contextual and follower feedback cues will prime selected aspects of the leader's domain of self-knowledge during leadership episodes.

Proposition 5. An authentic leader's increased meta-cognitive ability and commitment to authenticity will provide the ability and motivation to balance conflicting requirements from the environment, self-values and self-schema, resulting in the instantiation of core- and role-based schemas into an authentic working-self.

Contextual feedback serves a second *self-verifying* function for the leader. Relationally, how others perceive us serves as a primary determinant of our self-concepts. Such *reflected appraisals* (Mead, 1934) serve as a "sociometer" and are critical to effective self-regulation (Higgins & May, 2001; Tice & Baumeister, 2001). These feedback cues can be implicitly or explicitly processed by the leader and, as shown in Fig. 2, include follower verbal and non-verbal responses to the leader's displays of authenticity, follower proximal (e.g., trust) and performance outcomes, and cultural/situational variables.

We propose that an authentic leader's agentic commitment to self also includes an increased motive for self-verification (Swann, 1983), and thus, a propensity to transparently display one's true self. We further propose that this increased projection of the authentic self will lead to increased leader-relevant cueing from followers. Together, a commitment to self, heightened attention to self-relevant information, and meta-cognitive processing ability will increase the leader's capability to perceive and process self-verifying information from the environment.

This process produces a cycle of reinforcement for the leader's authentic self and the associated commitment to that self. In other words, because authentic leaders are true to themselves, they influence followers around them to respond to their authenticity. Part of this follower response will include authentic and other supportive behaviors (Gardner et al., 2005; Ilies, Morgeson & Nahrgang, 2005). Authentic followership in turn causes or verifies leaders to remain or become more authentic. Accordingly, we advance:

Proposition 6. Authentic leadership is positively associated with self-verification motives, leading to increasingly transparent displays of the self during leadership episodes.

Proposition 7. Increasingly transparent displays of the self by leaders produce increase in self-verification cueing from followers.

Proposition 8. Authentic leadership is positively associated with the perception and processing of self-verification cues, resulting in heightened reinforcement of leaders' self-concepts, and their commitment to authenticity.

Linking Leader Self-Awareness to Authentic Leader Self-Regulation

As the dual-headed arrow in Fig. 1 indicates, we view meta-cognitive processes and commitment to authenticity as interactive processes. Heightened meta-cognitive self-clarity provides the requisite ability for self-awareness, whereas a high level of commitment to self provides the motivation to self-regulate behaviors in accordance with the true self. Additionally, meta-cognition raises the salience of one's core values and beliefs, including one's commitment to authenticity. We have proposed that this elevated level of self-commitment, reciprocally provides the motivation for centralized deep processing, resulting in heightened meta-cognition of self-information.

Beyond this interaction, we also propose that a leader's *commitment to self*, as shown in Fig. 1, directly moderates the relationship between self-awareness and self-regulation, thus enabling authenticity. Specifically, higher levels of commitment to self foster behaviors that are consistent with the leader's activated role-based working self-concept. Research has shown that the most activated portions of one's self-concept serve as the greatest source of proximal regulation (e.g., Lord et al., 1999). In our proposed framework, the construct of commitment to self contains two major dimensions: a *cybernetic self-regulatory system*, and a *drive for attitude alignment*.

Markus and Wurf (1987) proposed that one's inter- and intrapersonal behaviors are regulated by cybernetic processes that compare one's self-views with either proximal goals or a more distal view of one's possible selves. Lord and Brown (2004) expanded this model into a cybernetic self-regulatory control system. They argue that activation of the working self-concept includes activation of one's *self-views*, *current goals*, and *possible selves* that, through comparative processes, create cognitive, affective and motivational forces to regulate behavior.

In this model, comparing one's self-view to *current goals* establishes salient standards and creates a largely affect-based response if a discrepancy is found, thereby eliciting proximal motivation to reestablish alignment. Comparing one's current self-view with one's possible selves, conversely, creates motivation for self-development. Lastly, comparing current goals to a possible self provides a more cognitive-based reaction and distal motivational forces. Any two of these three components can therefore initiate regulatory control processes that drive the leader's behavior, with any one of the components providing the standard and the other the feedback source (Lord & Brown, 2004). This cybernetic process can be either controlled or automatic and can activate powerful goal-relevant scripts that drive action (Lord & Kernan, 1987).

By extension from this line of research, we argue that an authentic leader holds a value-laden commitment to self that will manifest itself during activation of the working self-concept. This supports the value-laden description of authentic leadership provided by Luthans and Avolio (2003). Specifically, we propose that these values will be highly salient in the leader's self-view, current goals, and their vision of a possible (and authentic) self. The salience of these values, coupled with the heightened meta-cognitive self-clarity of the authentic leader, typically results in increased recognition of discrepancies in the leader's cybernetic system, creating powerful motivational forces to reduce the discrepancy and reestablish authenticity.

The cybernetic model suggests that if an authentic leader's current self-view is not aligned with the current goal of being authentic with associates, negative affective reactions and proximal motivational forces will produce a drive back toward authentic behavior. If the leader holds a vision of a possible self that is even more authentic than his/her current self, this cybernetic process will result in regulation toward self-development to achieve greater authenticity.

Lastly, if the leader's current goals are determined to be incompatible with achieving a highly authentic possible self, cognitive-based distal motivational forces will drive the adjustment of goals to put the leader on a path toward a possible, authentic self. Hence, we see in authentic leaders a high commitment to self, characterized by a drive toward being true to their own development as individuals and leaders in the long term, being true to their own performance of leadership responsibilities in the short- to mid-term, and being true to ensuring that both sets of objectives are compatible.

The second major dimension of the leader's commitment to self consists of a heightened propensity and need for alignment of object and behavioral attitudes. This dimension complements the first. People establish attitudes not only toward objects, but also toward specific behaviors, with both forms of attitudes requiring alignment to accurately predict the relationship between intentions and behaviors (Ajzen, 1991; Eagly & Chaiken, 1998). Hence, an authentic leader's commitment to self leads him/her to be behaviorally consistent – to "walk the talk" so to speak. For example, an authentic leader's attitude toward a possible promotion opportunity in another company may be very strong and positive (object attitude), but they may choose to forgo that opportunity because such behavior would betray a position espoused to followers of remaining loyal to and "growing with the company" (a values-based behavioral attitude that is salient in the leader's self-system).

The theory of planned behavior proposes that attitudes toward behavior are more predictive of behavior than are attitudes toward objects (Ajzen, 1991), suggesting that one's held beliefs may often not be acted upon. This can be a functional source of self-regulatory constraint, such as shown in the above example. Conversely it can be dysfunctional, as illustrated when a leader's desire to speak out against unethical accounting practices is not acted upon due to a behavioral attitude that resists "rocking the boat" and facing potential ridicule. We argue that attitude inconsistency often manifests itself in impression management or other forms of self-distortion, leading to cognitive dissonance (Festinger, 1957). As stated earlier, such cognitive dissonance, or inauthenticity, is typically experienced as negative affect. One can extrapolate that leaders must have a strong agentic commitment to self, and to their held object attitudes, to act authentically, even in the face of potential personal risk.

We propose that authentic leaders, as a consequence of their commitment to self, will tend to hold behavioral attitudes that are in alignment with their object attitudes, and will have a high propensity to hold true to those attitudes, making their behavior consistent, predictable, and coherent with their self-system. This predictability, as will be further discussed, elicits more consistent follower attributions and trust. This discussion suggests the following propositions:

Proposition 9. Heightened levels of meta-cognition among authentic leaders will increase the salience of core values, producing an emergent agentic commitment to authenticity.

Proposition 10. Increased commitment to authenticity provides the motive for controlled meta-cognition of self-relevant information, thereby creating greater alignment between one's object attitudes and associated behavioral attitudes.

Proposition 11. The activation of authenticity values and commitment in a leader's self-view, current goals, and possible selves will positively moderate the linkage between self-awareness and self-regulation, resulting in lower levels of cognitive dissonance.

IMPACT OF LEADERS WHO ARE AUTHENTIC TO SELF

Having explicated the *intra*personal processes of authentic leadership, we turn to discussion of the *inter*personal effects of such a leader in the leadership process. The framework provided in Fig. 2 proposes a self-reinforcing *virtuous cycle* of impact. The construct definitions comprising authenticity in leaders discussed thus far are encapsulated in the box spanning cognition and affect perceived authenticity. At the interpersonal level, authentic leaders positively impact the proximal outcomes of trust, predictability, and the overall quality of leader–follower relations. These proximal outcomes in turn positively moderate any leader-led interventions so as to multiply the veritable effects of such interventions. We call this a *leadership multiplying* effect.

At the same time, authentic leaders positively influence a culture of authenticity directly. This culture is indirectly reinforced through the beneficial impact of veritable outcomes of leader-led interventions as perceived by followers. Ultimately, both the culture and the veritable outcomes serve as self-verifying reinforcement for the leader to continue to be authentic, thereby perpetuating the virtuous cycle. The following sections elaborate on the components that contribute to this virtuous cycle.

Leadership Multiplier Effects

As indicated above, we posit that authenticity in leaders operates as a *leadership multiplier*. By this we mean that when leaders are perceived as authentic, their leadership interventions are more favorably received and the resultant impact multiplied. Gardner et al. (2005) proposed that authentic leadership leads to veritable, sustainable follower performance. We agree with this proposition and assert that it is the level of authenticity in leaders that provides the moderating effect between the two variables (see Fig. 2).

Leaders who are authentic to themselves are able to achieve this leadership multiplier effect because they display behaviors that engender trust and allow followers to easily and confidently infer authenticity from their actions. Such behaviors have two components that lend themselves to an easy inference of authenticity. First, they are consistent, thereby facilitating internal attributions to the leader by followers (Kelley, 1971). Such consistency in the leader's behavior is maintained through the various psychological and social mechanisms described above (e.g., self-verification and reinforcement).

The second component contributing to the attributed authenticity of such leaders is that their behavior is intrinsically authentic. By this, we mean that the leader's behaviors do not contradict the espoused values, espoused principles and other self-referential information that followers may infer about the leader from other sources. In other words, the observed behavior supports the leader's (inferred and espoused) commitment to be true to him- or herself (Erickson, 1995). Together these two components help followers to make accurate inferences about the authenticity of the leader and achieve a level of stability and predictability in their relationship.

A dramatic example of a leader who remained true to his values and secured the trust and devotion of followers as a result is provided by Aaron

Feurstein, the CEO of textile manufacturer Malden Mills. In one of the largest fires in Massachusetts history, the firm's plant in Lawrence burned to the ground. Immediately following this disaster, Mr. Feurstein pledged to continue paying workers their salaries and to rebuild in Lawrence rather than moving the plant overseas to reduce labor costs or declaring bankruptcy.

During an interview with *60 Minutes* correspondent Morley Safer, Feurstein quotes a Jewish proverb: "When all is in moral chaos, this is the time to be a 'mensch'." The word "mensch" is Yiddish for a "man with a heart." Although Feuerstein's efforts to avoid bankruptcy ultimately failed due to competitive pressures facing the U.S. textile industry, he succeeded in earning the trust and devotion of followers, who remain committed to him and stand behind him as he pledges to continue the fight for Malden Mills' future (Seeger & Ulmer, 2001; Ulmer & Seeger, 2000).

When followers are able to accurately infer that their leader is authentic, their working relationship with the leader becomes more manageable. Because leaders who are true to themselves are predictable, followers spend less time and energy trying to anticipate what such leaders' next moves will be. Instead, they quickly build up shared cognitions with the leader regarding his/her behavior and expectations of followers that constitute a psychological contract. Such shared cognitions guide followers by providing cues and standards for appropriate behavior that meet the expectations of the leader. Because such implicit roles and behavioral norms are quickly learned and shared, followers experience higher levels of psychological safety (Edmondson, 1999) and enhanced performance in organizations (Cannon-Bowers & Salas, 2001). These processes help to explain why the development of authentic leadership can produce the leadership multiplier effect described above, and thereby enhance the effectiveness of a leader and his/her associates.

When followers attribute authenticity to the leader, the overall level of trust in the leader–follower relationship is likewise elevated. Trust involves a "willingness to be vulnerable" (Butler & Cantrell, 1984; Rousseau, Sitkin, Burt, & Camerer, 1998). People who achieve authenticity engage in routine self-disclosure because they are comfortable revealing self-referential information (Kernis, 2002). Such acts of self-disclosure by a leader can be construed as a willingness to be vulnerable, thereby fostering higher levels of trust by followers.

Moreover, because such leaders display a commitment to core-self values, integrity is inferred. The trust literature defines integrity as one's commitment to a set of principles that is acceptable to the beholder. It is "... the degree to which the trustor's actions reflect values acceptable to the trustee," such as consistency and predictability (Brower, Schoorman, & Tan, 2000, p. 236). Given the consistency and predictability of behavior displayed by authentic leaders, such leaders are also likely to be seen as possessing integrity, which is a crucial foundation for trust-building (Butler & Cantrell, 1984).

The contribution of leader authenticity to heightened levels of trust among followers has important implications for resultant outcomes. For example, follower trust in a leader has been shown to mediate the relationship between leadership style and performance (Jung & Avolio, 2000) and, over time, trust in one's leader predicts future performance (Dirks & Ferrin, 2002). Additionally, trust is a key component in the quality of leader-member exchanges (LMX) (Graen & Uhl-Bien, 1995; Schriesheim, Castro, & Cogliser, 1999). LMX is in turn related to performance (Howell & Hall-Merenda, 1999; Scandura & Schriesheim, 1994) and moderates the effects of leadership interventions (Scandura & Graen, 1984).

Research indicates that emotions can be transmitted automatically to followers through emotional contagion processes (Cherulnik, Donley, Wiewel, & Miller, 2001; Hatfield, Cacioppo, & Rapson, 1994; Ilies et al., 2005; Pugh, 2001). As we discuss in more detail below, we assert that authenticity reduces the levels of cognitive dissonance and negative affect experienced by the leader, and thereby contributes to increases in well-being. Followers will detect and respond to these largely non-verbal emotion-based cues "given off" by the leader (Goffman, 1959). Positive affect can also be used to inform judgments about the leader's competence and status (Tiedens, 2000). Followers will use both affective and cognitive processing during role episodes with the leader, with affective processing normally occurring more quickly and spurring instantaneous responses unless it is overridden by cognitive processes (Lord & Harvey, 2002). Emotions can thus activate followers' scripts, often automatically, driving behavioral responses. For example, positive emotions have been shown to raise self-efficacy through arousal processes and thus increase engagement in tasks (Bandura, 1997).

Based on the above literature and reasoning, we assert that authenticity is a leadership multiplier. We propose that followers respond more favorably to interventions by authentic leaders because they are more likely to identify with and trust leaders who are true to themselves. Followers are also better able to predict the leader's style and make their own adjustments to the relationship for mutual benefit.

We also believe that followers prefer transparency in any leader–follower relationship as it leads to feelings of stability and predictability. Transparency is more likely to occur in leaders who self-disclose their values, beliefs, and intentions, and abide by them consistently, resulting in more accurate attributions by followers (Gardner et al., 2005). Additionally, the contagion effects of the leader's positive affect will likely result in a higher propensity for positive behavioral responses (Ilies et al., 2005). As an example of this multiplier effect, the level of perceived authenticity may determine whether a leader's use of individual consideration is perceived by followers as genuine concern or an attempt to gain their support for a needed initiative. Thus, we advance:

Proposition 12. Leader authenticity to self produces more consistent and predictable leader behavior, and thereby fosters higher levels of attributed integrity, trust, and positive affective responses among followers.

Proposition 13. Leader authenticity to self positively moderates the impact of any interventions initiated by the leader.

IMPACT OF ORGANIZATIONAL CULTURE ON AUTHENTICITY

Impact of Organizational Culture on Perceptions of Authenticity

Leaders are shapers of organizational culture. Schein (1992, p. 9) defines culture as, the "pattern of basic assumptions ... that has worked well enough to be considered valuable and therefore to be taught to new members as the correct way to perceive, think and feel in relation to those problems." For an authentic culture to exist, we propose that organizational members must perceive that: (1) they are asked, expected, and enabled to be authentic, (2) that such efforts will be rewarded and are part of the "way things are done around here," and (3) that they are inspired by a cadre of authentic exemplars.

When espoused values are observed to be associated with valued outcomes, the values undergo a process of cognitive transformation in followers to become a shared value or belief, and ultimately a shared assumption (Schein, 1992, p. 19). This shared assumption forms as a newly adopted organizing schema and goes through a process of *objectification* and *reification* (Augoustinos & Walker, 1995), by which individuals lose sight of the assumption's socially derived character and forget about its inception. Ultimately, the assumption becomes transformed into the member's institutionalized view of the organization. We propose that when authenticity is espoused by the leader, and members experience such authenticity as beneficial, it becomes taken for granted. When this occurs, there are not only priming effects, but top-down cognitive processing by members as they come to recognize, interpret and expect authentic acts of leadership. This reasoning suggests:

Proposition 14. Organizational culture moderates the extent to which authentic leader behaviors are interpreted as authentic by followers.

Cultural Effects on a Leader's Commitment to Authenticity

We have argued that authentic leaders use external cues to regulate their authenticity, such cues prime controlled or automatic meta-cognitive processes to regulate the self-system and secure self-verifying feedback, and promote self-clarity. We further propose that organizational culture can enhance the leader's commitment to be authentic.

Leaders are not only shapers of culture, but products of culture as well (Schein, 1992). Certain types of organizational cultures are toxic to the authenticity in leaders. In particular, an organizational culture that is low on psychological safety does not allow for creativity and self-development (Edmondson, 1999). On the other hand, learning organizations (Argyris, 1999) encourage learning and development at all levels. In such organizations, the less stable or trait-like portions of one's learning goal orientation (Button, Mathieu, & Zajac, 1996; Dweck, 1986) are enhanced by a culture that is perceived to be supportive (Potosky & Ramakrishna, 2002).

Efficacy beliefs regarding one's ability to be authentic may also be strengthened by aspects of the work culture, and enhanced by vicarious learning, enactive mastery and social persuasion (Bandura, 1997). Hence, a culture that strongly encourages role modeling and is positive and strengths-based, should enhance efficacy beliefs regarding authenticity (Gardner et al., 2005). With repetition, these cues will reinforce authentic behaviors that become habituated and serve as a powerful force for aligning the values and behavior of individuals with the authentic culture.

Proposition 15. Leader authenticity is increased at the intrapersonal level by agentic (valued) outcomes, at the interpersonal level by positive and self-verifying feedback from followers, and at the organizational culture level by norms that promote authenticity.

When leaders are confronted with inauthentic cultures characterized by ethical lapses and a lack of transparency, their efforts to remain true to themselves and promote a positive ethical culture will be challenged.

Consider, for example, United Nations Secretary-General Kofi Annan. In recent years, Mr. Annan's once stellar reputation has been tarnished by a series of scandals at the U.N. including widespread corruption in the now defunct oil-for-food program provided to Iraq and charges of sexual abuses to youths in the Congo by U.N. peacekeepers.

Ironically, these scandals overshadow the successes Mr. Annan has achieved in pursing the primary initiative he championed upon taking office in 1997, including sweeping steps to overhaul the U.N. bureaucracy and changes in personnel to increase accountability and transparency in the agency. Nonetheless, he plans to continue with these efforts by introducing initiatives, such as a freedom of information policy that will make U.N. records available to the media and public, protections for whistleblowers, and promotion criteria that will emphasis accomplishments over tenure (Bravin, 2005). It remains to be seen if his efforts to foster greater openness and higher ethical standards will be successful in creating a healthier organizational culture while restoring the U.N.'s external reputation.

DISCRIMINATING THE VERITABLE FROM THE PSEUDO-AUTHENTIC LEADER

Having outlined our framework, both at the intrapersonal level as shown in Fig. 1, and the expanded interpersonal level shown in Fig. 2, we now further delineate *pseudo-authentic* leaders from *veritable authentic* leaders.

Similar to discussions of personalized versus socialized charismatic leaders or pseudo-transformational versus authentic transformational leaders (e.g., Avolio & Gibbons, 1988; Bass & Steidlmeier, 1999; Klein & House, 1995), it is critical to differentiate actual from the perceived authenticity of leaders. Viewing Fig. 1, pseudo-authenticity would be defined as a de-coupling between the leader's self-awareness and their self-regulatory processes. We call such leaders pseudo-authentic because this de-coupling is not often readily detected by followers.

During self-regulation, pseudo-authentic leaders attempt to and often succeed at matching their espoused self (values, norms, goals, etc.) with their behavior, giving followers' an impression of authenticity. Although their regulation, as viewed by followers, appears to be authentic, this regulation is not aligned with the leader's true self. Pseudo-authenticity can occur when a leader is incapable of or not motivated to conduct an accurate and controlled self-assessment. It can also occur when a leader chooses to practice *self-distortion* through the use of impression management.

Interpersonal Effects of Inauthenticity or Pseudo-Authenticity

We propose that pseudo-authenticity can only be maintained over the short-term and only in contexts that include short, infrequent and structured leader–follower interfaces, high leader–follower distance, and a lack of organizational transparency. In longer-term relationships and in organizations that sponsor transparency, inclusion and interaction, a lack of true, veritable authenticity will eventually be uncovered leading to a *boomerang effect* (Gilbert & Jones, 1986). That is, a leader who is perceived as highly authentic may be more easily discredited than a less authentic leader when they experience a similar lapse in authenticity.

We propose that authentic leaders draw much of their direct follower affect through the self-presentation strategy of *exemplification* (Gardner, 2003; Jones & Pittman, 1982). That is, they elicit attributions of moral worth and culturally defined worthiness that serve to motivate others to emulate or model their exemplary conduct. However, there are two situations when this strategy can backfire. Jones and Pittman argue that exemplification elicits feelings of guilt from targets, in that they feel inadequate in comparison to the exemplifier and attempt to live up to the example set. Such guilt can easily turn into anger if targets discover that the exemplifier's conduct falls short of the espoused standard. They may feel that their guilt arose from manipulation and/or is unnecessary. Such anger may result in attempts to assail and "bring-down" the exemplifier. Retribution would be less likely among followers with lower moral expectations (and hence lower levels of experienced guilt) of their leaders.

Second, Jones and Pittman (1982) propose that exemplification is viewed by followers as a more one-dimensional, seamless whole than is the case for other self-presentational strategies, such as self-promotion. Whereas the displayed or inferred ability associated with self-promotion has some room to vary by context and task, targets will look at the exemplifier in an all-or-nothing fashion. Because exemplification is one-dimensional, it has a single possible point of failure. That is, a single failure to perform authentically or morally, depending upon the severity of the moral lapse, can easily undermine the power base from which the leader's influence is derived. This supports the earlier contention that to achieve veritable and sustained leadership performance, any significant de-coupling between one's self and one's behavior must be quickly reconciled. Thus, we advance:

Proposition 16. Higher levels of previously attributed authenticity will be associated with higher levels of damage to the leader–follower relationship upon later discovery of inauthentic behavior.

Intrapersonal Effects of Inauthenticity or Pseudo-Authenticity

By remaining true to the self, authentic leaders experience less dysfunctional cognitive disequilibrium such as poor self-esteem, negative affect and hope, than would otherwise be felt from incongruent behaviors (Harter, Marold, Whitesell, & Cobbs, 1996). Their consistent and transparent actions likewise elicit positive follower feedback that provides for self-verification and reinforcement of the self. We propose that viewing the positive, self-verifying effects of their leadership will also build leadership efficacy, self-esteem and other positive psychological capacities that contribute to well-being. Although beyond the scope of this chapter, Gardner et al. (2005) and Ilies et al. (2005) argue that the authentic leader will create a transparent and consistent "authentic relationship" that will likewise enhance the well-being of followers.

Because inauthentic leaders do not always display their true self during leadership episodes, followers are unable to provide self-verifying feedback to the leader. Instead, their feedback can only serve to reinforce or weaken the leader's dramaturgical self. We propose that this lack of self-verifying feedback will result in a dysfunctional repetitive process composed of a cyclic lowering of the leader's self-awareness, which is followed by increasingly inauthentic behavior, less self-verifying feedback, lower self-awareness, and so on. This process will continue so long as the leader receives reinforcing feedback for their dramaturgical self, lowering subsequent motivation to assess the true self and break from this cycle. As the antithesis of *authentic* leadership development, this negative development cycle shows the dark side of leadership development and could explain why societies and organizations may sometimes develop "damaged" leaders.

We also argue that inauthentic behavior that, by definition, is not aligned with one's attitudes will ultimately cause one to adjust one's attitudes to align with one's behaviors, thus restoring cognitive equilibrium (Festinger, 1957). Pertinent to inauthentic or pseudo-authentic behavior, Higgins and McCann (1984) found that attitudes expressed for strategic goals (e.g., impression management) may eventually become internalized. Because attitudes can be formed from one's schemas and heuristics (Eagly & Chaiken, 1998), such counter-attitudinal behavior creates a distortion of one's self-schemas driven by a desire to match counter-self behaviors. This by itself is not harmful if the feedback stimulus is consistently applied – this is how people grow and adapt to life.

However, in the case of the pseudo-authentic leader, because he/she overadapts to situational demands, the feedback stimuli is inconsistent and highly dependent on the situation, thereby leading to distortions of self-schemas in all directions. If left unchecked, this cycle would lead to a fragmentation of the self-system, a lack of self-awareness, and in the extreme case, some form of psychopathology. At less extreme levels, this cycle could nonetheless lead to inconsistent behaviors and inaccurate follower attributions, and thereby foster a dysfunctional leader–follower relationship. Perhaps such negative cycles account in part for the lapses of judgment exhibited by executives such as Michael Eisner of the Walt Disney Co. with his exorbitant salary and Martha Stewart's insider trading infractions that have disheartened and alienated their followers. Additionally, the cybernetic regulatory system (Lord & Brown, 2004) discussed earlier indicates that discrepancies between one's current self-views and current goals will result in negative affect and strong proximal motivation to reestablish equilibrium. Hence, the salience of an authentic leader's value-laden goals toward authenticity adds to the force of such disruptive dissonance.

Proposition 17. Inauthentic behavior will decrease self-verifying feedback and produce cognitive disequilibrium, resulting in a lack of self-clarity and lower levels of well-being.

Temporal Nature of Authenticity

The delineation of pseudo and veritable authenticity also requires discussion of the temporal versus static nature of the self. It should be evident from the discussion thus far that while authenticity in a person is a state of being, leadership authenticity is more temporal in nature, both proximally and distally, depending on which and how many aspects of the self are activated in the leader's working self-concept.

Critics of the authentic leadership construct have argued that no leader can be completely true to the self over time, or all the time. This is especially true when the leadership roles require an intimate involvement of the self. These arguments would be most cogent if the underlying assumption is that the self is a static entity, that is, a retrieval memory store, rather than an adaptive, dynamic system.

We are of the view that the authentic self is an evolving, learning entity. Although we have attempted to provide support to show that leaders have certain aspects of their selves that are more chronically accessible than others, and that heightened meta-cognitive ability produces greater self-concept clarity, we have also argued that the knowledge structures that make up the self are learned and continually developed over time.

In fact, Ibarra's (1999) qualitative study suggests that people are continually experimenting with provisional selves before appropriating them into a current or envisioned possible-self. Additionally, we have shown that the context will prime certain aspects of the self while inhibiting others, resulting in varying contextually-based working-selves. The distinction again lies in the fact that an authentic leader will remain consistent with whatever aspects of the true self are currently activated, while a pseudo-authentic leader will de-couple from that working self-concept during self-regulation either due to lack of commitment to self or an inability to achieve self-concept clarity.

FUTURE DIRECTIONS

Our proposed framework provides a social-cognitive approach to authenticity. We recommend that future research extend the framework into a developmental model focusing on: (a) trigger events and experiences that form the self-schemas in memory that foster authenticity, (b) the developmental processes that create heightened meta-cognitive ability over one's self-awareness and regulation, and (c) the processes by which the motivational forces underlying commitment to self are formed as core beliefs. Additionally, our desire for parsimony prevented a full discussion of emotions beyond the affect elicited from one's perceptions of authenticity, and the role of affect in cybernetic control processes. The role of affect and emotions in the development and application of authentic leadership should be further investigated.

Our proposed framework invites further inclusion of various dual-processing, or cognitive–affective models such as those outlined by Mischel and Morf (2003) in their treatment of the self as a psychosocial dynamic processing system. Affective processing, automatic activation of affect, schema-triggered affect, and other phenomenon may provide great explanatory power of how emotions may affect the leader's self-awareness processes and the manner in which emotions moderate; how that awareness is regulated into behavior.

Another area meriting further theoretical and empirical attention involves the effects of goals and motivational states on the functioning of the authentic self. As part of our discussion of cybernetic control systems, we proposed that authentic leaders will display less self-incongruent behavior in pursuit of their goals. Of potential utility, however, would be applications of Singer and Salovey's (1988) work to investigate the effects that goals exert on the self-domains leaders' choose to activate in given situations/contexts.

The result could be goal-directed, situational, and yet authentic behavior that is distinct from goal-directed impression management or self-monitoring behavior.

A FINAL WORD

Authentic leadership is a lifelong developmental phenomenon that involves acquiring greater self-awareness along with an unwavering commitment to and regulation of the self. It is manifested through the emergence of authenticity during leadership episodes, multiplying leadership effects on veritable performance. We have offered a social cognitive explanation of what it means to be an authentic leader, and provided an operational definition of authentic leadership for future investigation of this important construct.

REFERENCES

Ajzen, I. (1991). The theory of planned behavior. *Organizational Behavior and Human Decision Processes, 50,* 179–211.

Argyris, C. (1999). *On organizational learning* (2nd ed.). UK: Blackwell.

Ashforth, B. E. (1999). Leadership as an embedded process: Some insights from Sayles' managerial behavior. *The Leadership Quarterly, 10,* 21–25.

Augoustinos, M., & Walker, I. (1995). *Social cognition: An integrated introduction.* London: Sage.

Avolio, B. J., & Gibbons, T. C. (1988). Developing transformational leaders: A life span approach. In: J. A. Conger & R. N. Kanungo (Eds), *Charismatic leadership: The elusive factor in organizational effectiveness* (pp. 276–308). San Francisco: Jossey-Bass.

Bandura, A. (1997). *Self-efficacy: The exercise of control.* New York: Freeman.

Bargh, J. A., Chen, M., & Burrows, L. (1996). Automaticity of social behavior: Direct effects of trait construct and stereotype activation on action. *Journal of Personality and Social Psychology, 71,* 230–244.

Bass, B. M., & Steidlmeier, P. (1999). Ethics, character and authentic transformational leadership. *The Leadership Quarterly, 10,* 181–217.

Berman, M. (1970). *The politics of inauthenticity: Radical individualism and the emergence of modern society.* New York: Atheneum.

Bower, G. H., & Hilgard, E. R. (1981). *Theories of learning.* New Jersey: Prentice-Hall.

Bravin, J. (2005). Annan's next project: The U.N. *The Wall Street Journal,* January 17, 10.

Brewer, M. B., & Gardner, W. (1996). Who is this "we"? Levels of collective identity and self representations. *Journal of Personality and Social Psychology, 71,* 83–93.

Briggs, S. R., & Cheek, J. M. (1988). On the nature of self-monitoring: Problems with assessment, problems with validity. *Journal of Personality and Social Psychology, 54,* 663–678.

Brower, H. H., Schoorman, F. D., & Tan, H. H. (2000). A model of relational leadership: The integration of trust and leader-member exchange. *The Leadership Quarterly, 11*, 227–251.

Brown, A. D. (1987). Metacognition, executive control, self-regulation, and other more mysterious mechanisms. In: F. Weinert & R. Kluwe (Eds), *Metacognition, motivation, and understanding* (pp. 65–116). Hillsdale, NJ: Erlbaum.

Butler, J. K., & Cantrell, R. S. (1984). A behavioral decision theory approach to modeling dyadic trust in superiors and subordinates. *Psychological Reports, 55*, 19–28.

Button, S. B., Matheiu, J. E., & Zajac, D. M. (1996). Goal orientation in organizational research: A conceptual and empirical foundation. *Organizational Behavior and Human Decision Processes, 67*, 26–48.

Campbell, J. D., Assanand, S., & Di Paula, A. (2000). Structural features of the self-concept and adjustment. In: A. Tesser, R. B. Felson & J. M. Suls (Eds), *Psychological perspectives on self and identity* (pp. 67–87). Washington, DC: American Psychological Association.

Campbell, J. D., Trapnell, P. D., Heine, S. J., Katz, E. M., Lavallee, L. F., & Lehman, D. R. (1996). Self-concept clarity: Measurement, personality correlates, and cultural boundaries. *Journal of Personality and Social Psychology, 70*, 141–156.

Cannon-Bowers, J. A., & Salas, E. (2001). Reflections on shared cognition. *Journal of Organizational Behavior, 22*, 195–203.

Chaiken, S. (1980). Heuristic versus systemic information processing and the use of source versus message cues in persuasion. *Journal of Personality and Social Psychology, 39*, 752–766.

Cherulnik, P. D., Donley, K. A., Wiewel, T. S. R., & Miller, S. R. (2001). Charisma is contagious: The effect of leader charisma on observers' affect. *Journal of Applied Social Psychology, 31*, 2149–2159.

Collins, A. M., & Loftus, E. F. (1975). A spreading activation of semantic processing. *Psychological Review, 82*, 407–428.

Craik, F. I. M., & Lockhart, R. (1972). Levels of processing: A framework for memory research. *Journal of Verbal Learning and Verbal Behavior, 11*, 671–684.

Davis-Blake, A., & Pfeffer, J. (1989). Just a mirage: The search for dispositional effects in organizational research. *Academy of Management Review, 14*, 385–400.

Day, D. V., & Kilduff, M. (2003). Self-monitoring personality and work relationships: Individual differences in social networks. In: M. Barrack & A. M. Ryan (Eds), *Personality at work: Reconsidering the role of personality in organizations*. San Francisco: Jossey-Bass.

Dirks, K. T., & Ferrin, D. L. (2002). Trust in leadership: Meta-analytic findings and implications for research and practice. *Journal of Applied Psychology, 87*, 611–628.

Dollinger, M. J. (1984). Environmental boundary spanning and information processing effects on organizational performance. *Academy of Management Journal, 27*, 351–368.

Donahue, E. M., Robins, R. W., Roberts, B. W., & John, O. P. (1993). The divided self: Concurrent and longitudinal effects of psychological adjustment and social roles on self-concept differentiation. *Journal of Personality and Social Psychology, 64*, 834–846.

Duval, S., & Wicklund, R. A. (1972). *A theory of objective self-awareness*. New York: Academic Press.

Dweck, C. S. (1986). Motivational processes affecting learning. *American Psychologist, 41*, 1040–1048.

Eagly, A. H., & Chaiken, S. (1998). Attitude structure and function. In: D. T. Gilbert, S. T. Fiske & G. Lindzey (Eds), *Handbook of social psychology* (4th ed., Vol. 1, pp. 269–322). Boston: McGraw-Hill.

Edmondson, A. (1999). Psychological safety and learning behaviors in work teams. *Administrative Science Quarterly, 44*, 350–383.

Eigel, K. M., & Kuhnert, K. W. (2005). Authentic development: Leadership development level and executive effectiveness. In: W. L. Gardner, B. J. Avolio & F. O. Walumbwa (Eds), *Authentic leadership theory and practice: Origins, effects and development*. Oxford, UK: Elsevier Science.

Erickson, R. J. (1995). The importance of authenticity for self and society. *Symbolic Interaction, 18*(2), 121–144.

Esser, J. K. (1998). Alive and well after 25 years: A review of groupthink research. *Organizational Behavior and Human Decision Processes, 73*, 116–141.

Festinger, L. (1957). *A theory of cognitive dissonance*. Stanford, CA: Stanford University Press.

Flavell, J. H. (1979). Metacognition and cognitive monitoring: A new era of cognitive development inquiry. *American Psychologist, 34*, 906–911.

Friedrich, F. J., Henik, A., & Tzelgov, J. (1991). Automatic processes in lexical access and spreading activation. *Journal of Experimental Psychology: Human Perception and Performance, 17*, 792–806.

Gardner, W. L. (2003). Perceptions of leader charisma, effectiveness and integrity: Effects of exemplification, delivery and ethical reputation. *Management Communication Quarterly, 16*, 502–527.

Gardner, W. L., & Avolio, B. J. (1998). The charismatic relationship: A dramaturgical perspective. *Academy of Management Review, 23*, 32–58.

Gardner, W. L., Avolio, B. J., Luthans, F., May, D. R., & Walumbwa, F. O. (2005). "Can you see the real me?" A self-based model of authentic leader and follower development. *The Leadership Quarterly, 16*, 373–394.

Gilbert, D. T., & Jones, E. E. (1986). Exemplification: The self-presentation of moral character. *Journal of Personality, 54*, 593–615.

Goffman, E. (1959). *The presentation of self in everyday life*. Garden City, NY: Doubleday Anchor.

Graen, G. B., & Uhl-Bien, M. (1995). Relationship-based approach to leadership: Development of leader-member exchange (LMX) theory of leadership over 25 years: Applying a multi-level multi-domain perspective. *The Leadership Quarterly, 6*, 219–247.

Hannah, S. T., Lester, P. B., & Vogelgesang, G. R. (2005). Moral leadership: Explicating the moral component of authentic leadership. In: W. L. Gardner, B. J. Avolio & F. O. Walumbwa (Eds), *Authentic leadership and practice: Origins, effects, and development*. Amsterdam: Elsevier.

Harter, S. (2002). Authenticity. In: C. R. Snyder & S. Lopez (Eds), *Handbook of positive psychology* (pp. 382–394). Oxford, UK: Oxford University Press.

Harter, S., Marold, D. B., Whitesell, N. R., & Cobbs, G. (1996). A model of the effects of parent and peer support on adolescent false self behavior. *Child Development, 67*, 360–374.

Hatfield, E., Cacioppo, J. T., & Rapson, R. L. (1994). *Emotional contagion*. New York: Cambridge University Press.

Hersey, D. A., Walsh, D. A., Read, S. J., & Chulef, A. S. (1990). The effects of expertise on financial problem solving: Evidence for goal-directed problem solving scripts. *Organizational Behavior and Human Decision Processes, 46*, 77–101.

Higgins, E. T., & Brendl, M. (1995). Accessibility and applicability: Some "activation rules" influencing judgment. *Journal of Experimental Social Psychology, 31*, 218–243.

Higgins, E. T., & May, D. R. (2001). Individual self-regulatory functions: It's not "we" regulation, but it's still social. In: C. Sedikides & M. B. Brewer (Eds), *Individual self, relational self, collective self* (pp. 47–67). New York, NY: Psychology Press.

Higgins, E. T., & McCann, C. D. (1984). Social encoding and subsequent attitudes, impressions, and memory: "Context-driven" and motivational aspects of processing. *Journal of Personality and Social Psychology, 47*, 26–39.

Hogg, M. A. (2001). A social identity theory of leadership. *Personality and Social Psychology Review, 5*, 184–200.

Howell, J. M., & Hall-Merenda, K. E. (1999). The ties that bind: The impact of leader-member exchange, transformational and transactional leadership, and distance on predicting follower performance. *Journal of Applied Psychology, 84*, 680–694.

Hoyle, R. H., Kernis, M. H., Leary, M. R., & Baldwin, M. W. (1999). *Selfhood: Identity, esteem, regulation.* Boulder, CO: Westview Press.

Ibarra, H. (1999). Provisional selves: Experimenting with image and identity in professional adaptation. *Administrative Science Quarterly, 44*, 764–791.

Ilies, R., Morgeson, F. P., & Nahrgang, J. D. (2005). Authentic leadership and eudaemonic well-being: Understanding leader-follower outcomes. *The Leadership Quarterly, 16*, 343–372.

Janis, I. L. (1972). *Victims of groupthink.* Boston: Houghton Mifflin.

Jones, E. E., & Gerard, H. B. (1967). *Foundations of social psychology.* New York: Wiley.

Jones, E. E., & Pittman, T. S. (1982). Toward a theory of strategic self-presentation. In: J. Suls (Ed.), *Psychological perspectives on the self* (pp. 231–262). Hillsdale, NJ: Erlbaum.

Jung, D. I., & Avolio, B. J. (2000). Opening the black box: An experimental investigation of the mediating effects of trust and value congruence on transformational and transactional leadership. *Journal of Organizational Behavior, 21*, 949–964.

Kegan, R. (1994). *In over our heads: The mental demands of modern life.* Cambridge, Mass: Harvard University Press.

Kelley, H. H. (1971). *Attributions in social interaction.* New York: General Learning Press.

Kernis, M. H. (2002). Toward a conceptualization of optimal self-esteem. *Psychological Inquiry, 14*, 1–26.

Kihlstrom, J. F., Beer, J. S., & Klein, S. B. (2003). Self and identity as memory. In: M. R. Leary & J. P. Tangney (Eds), *Handbook of self and identity* (pp. 68–90). New York: Guilford.

Kihlstrom, J. F., Cantor, N., Albright, J. S., Chew, B. R., Klein, S. B., & Niedenthal, P. M. (1988). Information processing and the study of the self. In: L. Berkowitz (Ed.), *Advances in experimental psychology* (Vol. 21, pp. 145–178). New York: Academic.

Kihlstrom, J. F., & Klein, S. B. (1994). The self as a knowledge structure. In: R. S. Wyer & T. K. Srull (Eds), *Handbook of social cognition* (Vol. 1: Basic Processes, pp. 153–208). New Jersey: Erlbaum.

Kilduff, M., & Day, D. V. (1994). Do chameleons get ahead? The effects of self-monitoring on managerial careers. *Academy of Management Journal, 37*, 1047–1060.

Klein, K. J., & House, R. J. (1995). On fire: Charismatic leadership and levels of analysis. *The Leadership Quarterly, 6*, 183–198.

Kohlberg, L. (1984). *The psychology of moral development.* New York: Harper and Row.

Leary, M. R., & Kowalski, R. M. (1990). Impression management: A literature review and two-component model. *Psychological Bulletin, 107*, 34–47.

Lerner, H. G. (1993). *The dance of deception.* New York: Harper-Collins.

Lester, D. (1997). Multiple selves and self-monitoring. *Perceptual and Motor Skills, 84,* 938.

Logan, G. D., & Klapp, S. T. (1991). Automatizing alphabet arithmetic: Is extended practice necessary to produce automaticity? *Journal of Experimental Psychology: Learning, Memory and Cognition, 17,* 179–195.

Lord, R. G., & Brown, D. J. (2001). Leadership, value, and subordinate self-concepts. *The Leadership Quarterly, 12,* 133–152.

Lord, R. G., & Brown, D. J. (2004). *Leadership processes and follower self-identity.* Mahwah, NJ: Erlbaum.

Lord, R. G., Brown, D. J., & Freiberg, S. J. (1999). Understanding the dynamics of leadership: The role of follower self-concepts in the leader/follower relationship. *Organizational Behavior & Human Decision Processes, 78,* 167–203.

Lord, R. G., & Harvey, J. L. (2002). An information processing framework for emotional regulation. In: R. G. Lord, R. J. Klimoski & R. Kanfer (Eds), *Emotions in the workplace: Understanding the structure and role of emotions in organizational behavior* (pp. 115–146). San Francisco: Jossey-Bass.

Lord, R. G., & Kernan, M. C. (1987). Scripts as determinants of purposeful behavior in organizations. *Academy of Management Review, 12,* 265–277.

Lurigio, A. J., & Carroll, J. S. (1985). Probation officers' schemata of offenders: Context, development and impact on treatment decisions. *Journal of Personality and Social Psychology, 48,* 1112–1126.

Luthans, F., & Avolio, B. J. (2003). Authentic leadership: A positive developmental approach. In: K. S. Cameron, J. E. Dutton & R. E. Quinn (Eds), *Positive organizational scholarship* (pp. 241–261). San Francisco: Barrett-Koehler.

Markus, H. R. (1977). Self-schemata and processing information about the self. *Journal of Personality and Social Psychology, 35,* 63–78.

Markus, H. R., & Wurf, E. (1987). The dynamic self-concept: A social psychological perspective. *American Review of Psychology, 38,* 299–337.

May, D. R., Chan, A. Y. L., Hodges, T. D., & Avolio, B. J. (2003). Developing the moral component of authentic leadership. *Organizational Dynamics, 32,* 247–260.

Mead, G. H. (1934). *Mind, self, and society from the standpoint of a social behaviorist.* Chicago: University of Chicago Press.

Metcalfe, J., & Shimamura, A. P. (1994). *Metacognition: Knowing about knowing.* Cambridge, MA: MIT Press.

Mischel, W. (1973). Toward a cognitive social reconceptualization of personality. *Psychological Review, 80,* 253–283.

Mischel, W., & Morf, C. C. (2003). The self as a psycho-social dynamic processing system: A meta-perspective on a century of the self in psychology. In: M. R. Leary & J. P. Tangney (Eds), *Handbook of self and identity* (pp. 15–43). New York: Guilford.

Neely, J. H., Keefe, D. E., & Ross, K. L. (1989). Semantic priming in the lexical decision task: Roles of prospective prime-generated expectancies and retrospective semantic matching. *Journal of Experimental Psychology: Learning, Memory and Cognition, 15,* 1003–1019.

Nelson, T. O., & Narens, L. (1994). Why investigate metacognition? In: J. Metcalfe & A. P. Shimamura (Eds), *Metacognition: Knowing about knowing* (pp. 1–25). Cambridge, MA: MIT Press.

Petty, R. E., & Cacioppo, J. T. (1981). *Attitudes and persuasion: Classic and contemporary approaches.* Dubuque, IA: Brown.

Petty, R. E., & Cacioppo, J. T. (1986). The elaboration likelihood model of persuasion. In: L. Berkowitz (Ed.), *Advances in experimental social psychology* (pp. 123–205). New York: Academic Press.

Potosky, D., & Ramakrishna, H. V. (2002). The moderating role of updating climate perceptions in the relationship between goal orientation, self-efficacy and job performance. *Human Performance, 15*(3), 275–298.

Pugh, S. D. (2001). Service with a smile: Emotional contagion in the service encounter. *Academy of Management Journal, 44*, 1018–1027.

Roberts, P. W., & Dowling, G. R. (2002). Corporate reputation and sustained superior financial performance. *Strategic Management Journal, 23*, 1077–1093.

Rosenfeld, P., Giacalone, R. A., & Riordan, C. A. (2002). *Impression management: Building and enhancing reputations at work.* London: Thomson Learning.

Rousseau, D. M., Sitkin, S. B., Burt, R. S., & Camerer, C. (1998). Not so different after all: A cross-discipline view of trust. *Academy of Management Review, 23*, 393–404.

Sartre, J. P. (1943). In: H. E. Barnes (Trans.), *Being and nothingness: An essay on phenomenological ontology.* New York: Washington Square Press. (Reprint Edition, Aug 1993).

Scandura, T. A., & Graen, G. B. (1984). Moderating effects of initial leader-member ex change status on the effects of a leadership intervention. *Journal of Applied Science, 69*, 428–436.

Scandura, T. A., & Schriesheim, C. A. (1994). Leader-member exchange and supervisor career mentoring as complementary constructs in leadership research. *Academy of Management Journal, 37*, 1588–1602.

Schein, E. J. (1992). *Organizational culture and leadership* (2nd ed.). San Francisco: Jossey-Bass.

Schraw, G., & Dennison, R. S. (1994). Assessing metacognitive awareness. *Contemporary Educational Psychology, 19*, 460–475.

Schriesheim, C. A., Castro, S. L., & Cogliser, C. C. (1999). Leader-member exchange (LMX) research: A comprehensive review of theory, measurement, and data-analytic practices. *The Leadership Quarterly, 10*, 63–113.

Seeger, M. W., & Ulmer, R. R. (2001). Virtuous responses to organizational crisis: Aaron Feurestein and Milt Cole. *Journal of Business Ethics, 31*, 269–376.

Singer, J. A., & Salovey, P. (1988). Mood and memory: Evaluating the network theory of affect. *Clinical Psychology Review, 8*(2), 211–251.

Snyder, M. (1979). Self-monitoring processes. In: L. Berkowitz (Ed.), *Advances in experimental social psychology* (Vol. 12, pp. 85–128). New York: Academic Press.

Snyder, M. (1987). *Private appearances/public realities: The psychology of self-monitoring.* New York: W. H. Freeman.

Spelke, E., Hirst, W., & Neisser, U. (1976). Skills of divided attention. *Cognition, 4*, 215–230.

Swann, W. B., Jr. (1983). Self-verification: Bringing social reality into harmony with the self. In: J. R. Suls & A. G. Greenwald (Eds), *Psychological perspectives on the self* (Vol. 2, pp. 33–66). Hillsdale, NJ: Erlbaum.

Tice, D. M., & Baumeister, R. F. (2001). The primacy of the interpersonal self. In: C. Sedikides & M. B. Brewer (Eds), *Individual self, relational self, collective self* (pp. 71–88). New York, NY: Psychology Press.

Tiedens, L. Z. (2000). Powerful emotions: The vicious cycle of social status positions and emotions. In: N. M. Ashkanasy, W. J. Zerbe & C. E. J. Hartel (Eds), *Emotion in the workplace: Research, theory, and practice.* Westport, CT: Quorum Books.

Trilling, L. (1972). *Sincerity and authenticity.* Cambridge, MA: Harvard University Press.

Tulving, E. (1972). Episodic and semantic memory. In: E. Tulving & W. Donaldson (Eds), *Organization of memory* (pp. 381–403). New York: Academic Press.

Turner, M. E., & Pratkanis, A. R. (1998). Twenty-five years of groupthink theory and research: Lessons from the evaluation of a theory. *Organizational Behavior and Human Decision Processes, 73,* 105–115.

Ulmer, R. R., & Seeger, M. W. (2000). Communicating ethics and the Malden Mills disaster. In: G. L. Peterson (Ed.), *Communicating in organizations* (pp. 191–194). Boston, MA: Allyn & Bacon.

Velichkovsky, B. M. (2002). Heterarchy of cognition: The depths and the highs of a framework for memory research. *Memory, 10*(5–6), 405–419.

Verplanken, B., & Holland, R. W. (2002). Motivated decision making: Effects of activation and self-centrality of values on choices and behaviors. *Journal of Personality and Social Psychology, 82,* 434–447.

Yammarino, F. J., Dansereau, F., Jr., & Kennedy, C. J. (2001). A multiple-level, multidimensional approach to leadership: Viewing leadership through an elephant's eye. *Organizational Dynamics, 29*(3), 149–164.

Zbrodoff, N. J., & Logan, G. D. (1986). On the autonomy of mental processes: A case study of arithmetic. *Journal of Experimental Psychology: General, 115,* 118–130.

MORAL LEADERSHIP: EXPLICATING THE MORAL COMPONENT OF AUTHENTIC LEADERSHIP

Sean T. Hannah, Paul B. Lester and
Gretchen R. Vogelgesang

ABSTRACT

Authentic leadership is defined in large part by evidence of morality in the leadership influence process. A highly developed moral leader is expected to act in concert with his or her self-concept, to achieve higher levels of agency to make the "right" and "ethical" decisions. Moral leadership is developed through a highly developed self-concept, and supported by heightened abilities of meta-cognitive and emotional regulation. These cognitive structures and abilities help leaders to activate moral solutions cross-situationally during leadership episodes. Moreover, we posit that a leader who is perceived by followers as morally authentic and imbued by altruism and virtuousness will be afforded greater influence and have increased positive effects on followers and organizations.

Authentic Leadership Theory and Practice: Origins, Effects and Development
Monographs in Leadership and Management, Volume 3, 43–81
Copyright © 2005 by Elsevier Ltd.

The goal of this chapter is to clarify what we see as constituting moral leadership, with a particular focus on the moral component of authentic leadership. We draw from two key conceptual frameworks – moral agency (Bandura, 1999, 1991) and the self-concept (Kihlstrom, Beer, & Klein, 2003; Lord & Brown, 2004; Markus & Wurf, 1987) – and explore the various subcomponents of these frameworks to provide a roadmap to guide future research. We define the moral component of authentic leadership as the exercise of altruistic, virtuous leadership by a highly developed leader who acts in concert with his or her self-concept to achieve agency over the moral aspects of his or her leadership domain.

We argue here that the developmental experiences and processes that facilitate authenticity, such as heightened cognitive complexity and self-awareness in the leader, foster higher levels of moral reasoning and reflection, which in turn positively influence the leader and ultimately the followers' moral behavior. Such developed moral capacities increase the leader's ability to assume ownership, or "self-authorship" (Kegan, 1994), over a lifetime.

We begin this chapter with a broad ontological discussion of moral leadership and ethics with the purpose of clarifying their properties and providing construct definitions. Next, we introduce the agency framework and specifically link it to morality; our purpose here is to clarify how, with respect to authentic leadership, agency and morality are intertwined. We then present a model for viewing moral leadership through the framework of a moral self-concept that we propose authentic leaders activate when faced with a moral dilemma, albeit in varying degrees, to exercise their moral agency. Later, we discuss how leaders explicate their self-concepts as moral self-structures; here our intent is to not only elaborate how leaders develop and activate components of the self to act morally, but also how they clarify their moral behavior to themselves during the moral reasoning and decision-making process. Next, we outline moral and emotional self-regulation and explain how these concepts relate to authentic leadership, focusing on the role of the moral working self-concept. Our purpose here is to expand on the linkages between the moral self-concept, and how it results in consistent (and self-consistent) moral behaviors being exhibited by the authentic leader. Finally, we close by discussing the tangible influence that the authentic leader's moral decision making and behavior exert at the leader, follower, and organizational levels.

THE ONTOLOGICAL BASIS FOR AUTHENTIC MORALITY: THE MORAL SELF-CONCEPT AND MORAL AGENCY

The Moral Self-Concept as a Developed Entity

We propose that moral standards are primarily developed via cultural and societal influences and can be best explained via social learning theory/ processes (Bandura, 1977). Ethics are learned and part of one's culture, and thus morality is only generalizeable across cultures inasmuch as there are universal moral truths between cultures. Further, ethics are formed not only at the societal level, but also at the organizational, group, and individual levels through social learning, social enactment, and meaning-making processes (Bartunek, 1984; Bartunek & Moch, 1987; Weick, 1979).

We propose that the adaptability that allows the leader to develop morally and to execute moral control over the leadership influence process in large part stems from the plasticity of schemas and scripts that evolve over time through defining developmental "trigger events" (e.g., high-impact moral dilemmas) (Bandura, 2002; Kolb & Whishaw, 1998). As leaders internalize their environment and form their self-concept over the life span, a moral component is formed as part of, and developed in parallel with, that self-concept. A given leader's moral development will differ from that of other leaders in terms of its robustness and complexity. We will argue that such moral development depends largely upon both the quality and quantity of ethical experiences a leader faces through life-long learning and the moral meaning-making taken away from those experiences that end up shaping the leader's development (Kohlberg, 1981).

Kohlberg's (1981) model of cognitive moral development (CMD) similarly proposed that moral reasoning capabilities are malleable, and that life experiences or trigger events will move a person through various moral stages across the life span. Trigger events may be viewed as critical incidents in a given leader's life that result in deep introspection and a change in his or her implicit theories about the linkage between leadership and morality. Evidence of this state-like and developmental approach is provided by the positive correlations of age and education level with CMD levels (Rest, 1986).

Through such social learning processes, leaders not only form a global self-concept of themselves as leaders (Lord & Brown, 2004), but also form a specific dimension of the self-concept as it relates to their self-views of their own morality. In other words, a leader may consider him- or herself a "good" leader but not necessarily a "moral" leader. We propose that authentic leaders have a highly developed self-concept, with a particularly complex and evolved moral dimension. We view this moral dimension of the self-concept as a primary enabler behind moral perception and decision making. Specifically, if sufficiently developed and complex, this moral self-concept, as shown in Fig. 1, sets the conditions for leaders to make moral decisions through the activation of and concordance between their *current selves* (i.e., who they perceive themselves to be), *possible selves* (i.e., who they want to be), and *current goals* (i.e., what they want to accomplish proximally).

Viewed using the self-concept framework, morality is in part a function of one's memories as encoded and stored from one's moral experiences and reflections. As we explicate the construct of a moral leader, we must therefore look at: (1) the mental models and representations stored in semantic memory, which contain general schematic moral knowledge; and (2) the autobiographical moral experiences stored in episodic memory. The interaction of these memory structures ultimately drives the leader's moral behavior through both automatic and controlled processes (Ashcroft, 2002). Moreover, they include not only the knowledge one holds of oneself (e.g., the self-concept), but also one's knowledge of moral concepts (e.g., what is

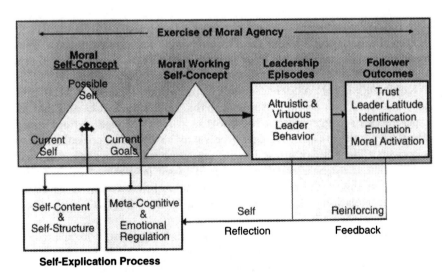

Fig. 1. A Model of Authentic-Moral Leadership.

morality?), and the hypotheses that are formed from interlinking concepts in memory to establish causality (Lord & Foti, 1986).

Agentic Morality

Agency is central to the linkages between authenticity and ethical leadership, representing the leadership processes that influence and control the leader's and followers' moral environment. Consistent with the theoretical frameworks of Bandura (1999) and Rottschaefer (1986), we define moral leadership agency as the exercise of control over a leader's moral environment through the employment of forethought, intentionality, self-reactiveness, and self-reflectiveness to achieve positive moral effects through the leadership influence process. As shown in Fig. 1, the influence of moral agency spans from the leader's self-concept, as just discussed, to follower outcomes.

Leaders *achieve* authenticity as they develop and become aware of a core moral self, and then manifest that true self in control of their environment through the exercise of moral agency. Below we argue that at the most basic levels of authentic leadership, moral agency ultimately leads to ownership; this ownership is not only reflected in the individual leader's behavior, but also in followers' behavior and outcomes derived from authentic leadership as a result of the leader's exercise of agency through followers, referred to as *proxy agency* (Bandura, 2000). In short, authentic leaders are moral agents who take ownership of, and therefore responsibility for, the end results of their moral actions and the actions of their followers.

We believe that leaders with heightened levels of complex moral domain content held in long-term memory will have an increased propensity for agentic control over their moral experiences. One's moral reasoning, however, is linked to moral conduct through self-regulatory mechanisms where moral agency is employed (Bandura, 2002; Rottschaefer, 1986). We must point out that individuals who employ cognitive reasoning processes to determine what is right and wrong may still fail to act morally for a variety of reasons including enormous external pressures to make the "wrong" decision.

Moral agency in our model spans from personal agency, whereby leaders manifest their authentic moral-self during leadership episodes, through to proxy agency to positively influence followers through their manifestation of morality. This agency over the self and the environment is further reinforced by the leader's altruism and virtue, as discussed later in this chapter.

Central Components of Moral Agency

Having outlined the basis for moral agency in authentic leadership, we turn our attention to further explain the moral agency construct. Agency is embedded in *social cognitive theory* (SCT) (Bandura, 1999, 2001), which models the capacity for individuals to exercise control over the nature and quality of their lives. Through reciprocal interactions between leaders, their behavior, and the environment, leaders become both producers and products of their moral environment. Specifically, they exercise the agentic capacities of: (1) *intentionality* (acts of agency are done intentionally), (2) *forethought* (agents anticipate likely consequences of actions and select courses of action that produce desired outcomes and avoid detrimental ones), (3) *self-reactiveness* (the ability to self-motivate and self-regulate), and (4) *self-reflectiveness* (the capability to reflect upon oneself and the adequacy of one's thoughts and actions) (Bandura, 2001). The moral component of agency also includes both *refrain power*, which is viewed as an inhibition against acting immorally, and *proactive power*, or the ability to proactively behave morally (Bandura, 1991). We view these agentic capacities as central components of authentic leadership and draw on them throughout the remainder of this chapter.

Taken together, it appears that the link between authenticity and moral agency is, as suggested by Chan, Hannah, and Gardner (2005), a question of ability and motivation. By this we mean that authentic leaders have not only the ability to think morally by employing the agentic capacities of forethought, self-reaction, and self-reflection, but they also have the motivation to behave morally through the use of intentionality and the employment of refrain and proactive power. And, as we discuss below, choosing to become a moral agent has many positive outcomes for not only the leader and follower, but also for the organization.

Influences of Moral Agency

Authentic leadership theory (Gardner, Avolio, Luthans, May, & Walumbwa, 2005) holds that a leader with high levels of self-awareness and commitment-to-self behaves in a manner consistent with his or her true self. Through processes of self-regulation and self-determinism (Deci & Ryan, 1985; Ryan & Deci, 2003), the authentic leader obtains a level of self-concordance (Sheldon & Elliot, 1999) by satisfying inherent needs; this in turn increases leader well-being. We propose that a highly developed moral self-concept facilitates self-determinism in moral behavior. External requirements will often challenge the leader's self-concept and strain his or her authenticity and morality. We propose that moral leaders, through higher levels of agentic ownership, will be more likely to reach a level of self-concordance or balance. Agentic moral leaders achieve this balance by: (1) positively altering the moral environment through the exercise of proxy agency and (2) internalizing and integrating the processes of self-determination (Deci & Ryan, 1995) to achieve equilibrium with the altered environment through personal agency.

Agency and efficacy are highly intertwined (Bandura, 2001) and we believe that *moral* efficacy will help explain why one leader will act upon his or her moral judgments while another will fail to do so. Similarly, Kohlberg (1969) proposed that moral reasoning does not link directly to moral conduct, but that there are *ego-strength* factors that may limit moral conduct. These factors are self-reflective in nature (including perceived lack of competence regarding the intelligence, physical, or problem-solving capabilities to achieve moral ideals) and are thus related to efficacy beliefs.

Virtuousness and Altruism as Qualities of Agency

Any moral behavior that is not supported by genuine virtue and moral altruism (as a motivational concept) is by definition *inauthentic*. In short, we must differentiate impression-management behaviors from the concept of authenticity. Additionally, any behaviors that are reinforced primarily through external or organizational controls that are not consistent with or that betray the leader's self-concept are also inauthentic. When discussing *authentic* leadership, therefore, we must separate calculative or socially imposed moral behaviors from moral behaviors that stem from higher levels of leader moral development, genuine virtue, and altruistic motivation to help others.

Virtuousness
Leaders with highly developed moral capacity exercise agency over their moral domain, with their actions supported by a sense of virtuousness. An agentic sense of morality requires a leader to view him- or herself as a moral actor behaving in concordance with his or her true self. The moral content held in the self-concept must therefore support such a self-view when accessed by the leader through self-reflection. Altruism and virtue are activated as part of the moral working self-concept (Markus & Wurf, 1987) and are exhibited during leadership episodes as behaviors, as shown in Fig. 1.

Virtues are defined here as a "psychological process that consistently enables a person to think and act so as to yield benefits to him- or herself and society" (McCullough & Snyder, 2000). They are embedded and nurtured in culture in a similar fashion as ethics and morality, rather than simply being deduced through reasoning (Jordan & Meara, 1990; Sandage & Hill, 2001). Though often confused with values, virtues reference the integration of moral discussion and action into life (Prillenltensky, 1997), or in essence, the exercise of moral agency.

Virtues are based on the understanding of rational, connected thought. Such thought can be on a level internal to an individual, such as the ability to reason, or on a universal level, such as the laws and rationality that govern the universe (Aurelius, 2002). More recent research has centered upon six core virtues: wisdom, courage, humanity, justice, temperance, and transcendence (e.g., Peterson & Seligman, 2004). These core virtues are conceptualized as moral strengths that offer resiliency in meeting the challenges of life (Sandage & Hill, 2001), or as embodied traits of character (Cohen, 1994; Nicholas, 1994). We believe these core virtues are highly salient in the self-concept of the authentic leader; and through cybernetic self-regulatory processes, these virtuous core values drive leaders to positively influence their leadership domain. Over time, consistently virtuous behavior will make a leader's virtue appear as a *predisposition* to act in ways that produce recognizable human excellence, as proposed by Yearley (1990).

Virtuousness as an Enabler of Commitment-to-self
To fully understand our conception of moral behavior, it is critical to recognize the construct of *commitment-to-self*, which is inherent to authentic leadership (Chan et al., 2005). This commitment is reflective of both moral development and personal virtue. By definition, authenticity is self-referential and "exists wholly by the laws of its own being" (Trilling, 1972). A commitment to the self is inherently virtuous and is a key characteristic of what it means to be authentic. As suggested by Chan et al. (2005), authenticity involves both owning one's personal experiences (thoughts, emotions, needs, and wants) and then behaving in accordance with the true self. This commitment to one's identity and values (Erickson, 1995) is what translates knowledge of oneself into self-regulation, which lies at the core of what we call authentic leadership.

An authentic leader, therefore, has both internally and externally focused virtues and ethical processes. Internal virtue sponsors commitment-to-self and a willingness to conduct moral behavior consistent with one's beliefs, regardless of the social costs of such virtuousness. These internal moral processes then enable external ethical processes associated with moral leadership to sponsor altruistic behavior toward others. We propose that these external processes will become manifest in the morally uplifting leader proposed by Burns (1978) and Bass (1985, 1998).

Altruism

In continuing to highlight the difference between calculative or externally reinforced moral behaviors from authentic moral behaviors, we introduce the construct of altruism. In contrast to egoism, altruism involves the motivation to increase another person's welfare (Batson, 1998). Batson suggests that theories of pro-social behavior based upon behavioral social learning, norms and roles, exchange or equity, attributions, esteem enhancement/maintenance, or moral reasoning fail to fully explain anomalous acts of prosocial behavior or anomalous failures to act prosocially. We argue that these anomalous acts must be driven by high levels of virtuousness and agency held core to the leader's self-concept.

Batson (1998) suggests that empathy can create pro-social emotions such as sympathy, compassion, and tenderness toward individuals that, as proposed in the *empathy-altruism hypothesis*, will lead to altruistic motivation (see Batson, 1991 for an overview of the empathy-altruism hypothesis and supporting empirical studies). We propose that authentic leaders will hold moral ownership (agency) and altruistic empathy salient in their self-concept. Through activation of these aspects in their working self-concept, authentic leaders raise their levels of moral engagement through heightened propensity to form moral intentions. If sufficiently strong, such engagement can extend beyond the leader's personal realm and motivate him or her to intervene during unethical situations that are witnessed, but do not directly affect him or her. Included among these situations are acts of charity, "bystander" engagement, and other altruistic behavior.

We propose that moral leaders who are also authentic will hold heightened levels of virtue and altruism. Together, these levels will build their capacities for *forethought, intentionality, self-reflectiveness* and *self-reactiveness*, and foster increased levels of personal and proxy moral agency with their followers.

Thus far, we have presented authentic leadership as a process that: (1) emanates from a leader; (2) is driven by the abilities and motives inherent in a highly developed moral self-concept; and (3) is fueled by leader virtue and an altruistic desire to exercise agentic control over the leadership domain. The *authenticity* of this process can be assessed by aligning the moral self-concept, altruistic intentionality as activated in the working self-concept, and resulting behavior as modeled in Fig. 1. This leads us to our first set of propositions:

Proposition 1a. More as opposed to less morally attuned leaders will incorporate higher levels of altruism and virtue into their core self-concept.

Proposition 1b. Leaders who incorporate higher levels of altruism and virtue in their core self-concept will exercise higher levels of moral agency over their leadership domain.

Proposition 1c. Moral leaders who are also authentic will reach higher levels of self-concordance, through the exercise of agency, by achieving better alignment between their self-concept, their working self-concept, and self-consistent moral behaviors.

THE MORAL SELF

In this section, we explicate the structure and functioning of the dynamic moral self-concept and describe how it enables and drives moral agency and virtuous leadership. We view the self as an elaborate and highly accessible memory structure containing one's domain of self-knowledge (Kihlstrom & Klein, 1994; Markus, 1977), organized into schematic structures, and interlinked to form a multidimensional self-concept. The increased salience and accessibility of self-relevant information causes it to be processed more efficiently and competently than other forms of information (Markus & Wurf, 1987). Self-knowledge is more salient and familiar than other knowledge structures, and thus more easily activated during processing (Markus, 1977), producing what is known as the self-reference effect (Rogers, 1977). Through the social learning processes outlined previously, leaders acquire *meta-knowledge* about themselves (such as "I know how to influence others to act morally") that is integrated into their self-concept (Kihlstrom et al., 2003). Meta-knowledge can be accessed through both controlled and automatic procedures during moral processing, such as when a leader analyzes options for action when facing a moral dilemma.

The influence of meta-knowledge on leaders' subsequent moral processing is critical. The more robust and central moral knowledge is held within the leader's self-concept, the more likely the leader will be to activate this knowledge and be guided by its moral content to make decisions during leadership role episodes. Later in this chapter we will define how portions of this self-knowledge become activated in a given situation into a *working self-concept* (Markus & Wurf, 1987) to guide the leader's exercise of self-regulatory agency over moral experiences.

The Structure and Content of Moral Self-Concepts

As we refine our understanding of leaders' moral self-concepts, we must look at not only the domain of moral content held in long-term memory, but also the way that this content is structured. Ultimately, both will impact the activation of the moral-self during leadership episodes into a morally laden working self-concept. Fig. 1 displays a self-explication process that will affect the moral self-concept. Specifically, we propose that leaders will have differing levels of ability to explicate (activate, become aware of, and employ) their moral self-concept during leadership episodes dependent upon: (1) the robustness and complexity of moral *self-content*; (2) the accessibility provided by the *structure* of that content; (3) *meta-cognitive ability* to process this activated content domain during moral dilemmas; and (4) heightened awareness of and ability to control *emotions* during moral processing.

Researchers have made theoretical distinctions between the *contents* and the *structure* of the self-concept (Altrocchi, 1999; Campbell, Assanand, & Di Paula, 2003). *Content* refers to the beliefs held in one's self-schemas and can be divided into knowledge components (e.g., Who am I as a moral being?) and evaluative components (e.g., What are my feelings about my level of morality?) (Campbell et al., 1996). *Structure* then refers to the organization of these contents into mental models or representations (e.g., schemas) that affect both moral processing and behavior when activated through either automatic or controlled processes. The overall composition of long-term memory is critical because leaders may make moral judgments automatically, calling upon implicit memory, stored schemas, and heuristics to drive processing without explicit control during evaluative episodes (Ashcroft, 2002; Schacter, 1987).

Content of the Moral Self

The ability of leaders to explicate their moral-self is predicated on the quantity and quality of moral content held in memory. Moral content is created through the formation of well-developed schemata by increasing the pure magnitude and accessibility of stored moral knowledge held in long-term memory. Such content is stored, however, not only as schemas held in semantic memory, but also in episodic (autobiographical) memories that can be activated during moral dilemmas. In other words, highly developed leaders have knowledge structures that not only illuminate how they should act in a present situation, but also how they acted in previous situations and the outcomes of those actions. Both types of knowledge structures influence: (1) the decision a leader will make based upon agentic *forethought* and (2) the ultimate behavior displayed by the leader based upon agentic *intentionality*. Additionally, as they guide perceptual processes, they impact both, (3) agentic *self-reflectiveness*, and (4) *self-reactiveness* during moral processing.

Development of such a robust content of self-schema parallels the development process as outlined by multistage theories of CMD (Kohlberg, 1976, 1981; Piaget, 1948). Kohlberg (1981) proposes that at *postconventionalist* (transcendent) levels of cognitive moral development, individuals are more enlightened and strive for universal values and principles. They transcend the norms and authority of groups or individuals to seek what they deem as proper through their own self-regulatory processes. We have proposed that authenticity is measured on a continuum and developed in parallel to moral capacity. This capacity, as represented by higher postconventionalist levels, enables the leader to conduct complex assessments of moral information against a robust domain of moral content to achieve optimal moral solutions. As leader-moral schemas develop, they contain more viable and accessible moral information, thereby increasing the probability that the leader will make a positive moral decision.

The number and types of events experienced by leaders will affect the content of their self-schema. Leaders are captive to the information they can retrieve from memory during processing. Therefore, greater robustness of moral content will raise leaders' efficacy in the moral meaning-making process *because they simply know more*, and feel prepared to face moral dilemmas. Likewise, greater robustness of moral content will influence the leader's *quality* of agentic *self-reflectiveness* insofar as such a leader has more knowledge to process, assess, and select from when making moral decisions. This of course assumes that the leader chooses to self-reflect.

Additionally, memory development research has shown that more experienced and thus cognitively richer individuals have multifaceted and better organized schemas. The linkages between concepts allow individuals to make better sense of information and acquire new knowledge (Bower & Hilgard, 1981; Hersey, Walsh, Read, & Chulef, 1990; Lurigio & Carroll, 1985), thus spending more time interpreting new information (Dollinger,

1984). Research on attitudes (e.g., Eagly & Chaiken, 1998) also informs us that the comprehensiveness of one's beliefs will determine the extremity or polarity of one's attitudes during moral processing. With respect to morality and leadership, this polarity should be viewed as the limits of information a leader will be able to access in guiding moral behavior – be it his or her own behavior or the behavior of others.

In their work with adolescents, Swanson and Hill (1993) called this increased ethical information capacity *meta-moral knowledge*, which they defined as all the knowledge and beliefs about morality that are stored in a person's long-term memory. This view is similar to Rest's (1986) assertion that moral knowledge is a specific domain or component of stored general knowledge that can be automatically or intentionally accessed during cognitive moral processing. Swanson and Hill found that increased levels of meta-moral knowledge were accompanied by higher levels of moral reasoning and increased moral behavior.

Thus, we propose:

Proposition 2. Holding altruistic motivation constant, leaders with more as opposed to less developed content in their leader-moral schemas and episodic memories are more likely to exhibit positive moral reasoning and conduct.

Structure of the Moral Self

We turn now to *self-structure* as the next construct in the self-explication process shown in Fig. 1. Beyond the sheer moral content held in long-term memory, the way that content is *structured* in memory will also affect the leader's moral reasoning process. Self-complexity and self-concept clarity are both subsumed under this structural view of the epistemological approach to the self (Campbell & Lavallee, 1993). Self-*structure* is then further delineated into measures of *pluralism* and measures of *unity* (Campbell & Lavallee, 1993; Zajonc, 1960). Pluralism reflects the diversity of the self and has been operationalized as self-complexity (Bieri et al., 1966; Linville, 1985, 1987; Woolfolk, Gara, Allen, & Beaver, 2004), self-differentiation (Zajonc, 1960), and self-concept compartmentalization (Showers, 1992). These constructs are similar in that they all assess the number of self-aspects a person holds in memory and the level of redundancy between the contents (self-knowledge) contained in each of those aspects (Campbell & Lavallee, 1993).

Self-concept Unity

Self-concept *unity* references the extent to which one holds coherent, integrated selves continuous across various roles and situations (Block, 1961). Unity has been operationalized as self-concept differentiation (a somewhat misleading title) (Donahue, Robins, Roberts, & John, 1993), self-concept clarity (Campbell et al., 1996), and self-discrepancy (Higgins, 1987). Note that pluralism and unity are not by definition related to one another. A person can have few or many self-aspects (low or high pluralism), but these aspects can be either highly correlated (high unity) or independent (low unity) (Campbell et al., 2003).

Most contemporary theorists view the self as a multidimensional cognitive structure (Kihlstrom et al., 1988; Kihlstrom & Klein, 1994; Lord & Brown, 2004; Markus & Wurf, 1987). We posit that authentic leaders have complex selves, but hold a central unified self-structure of core beliefs (high unity) that transcend the situation. In other words, we view authentic leader behavior, as it relates to core self-aspects, as being fairly consistent from one situation to the next. Thus, the variance in morally inconsistent behavior is marginalized because an authentic leader with high unity in the moral domain acts morally both within and across environments/situations. This consistency is due to the chronic activation of core moral meta-knowledge into the working self-concept across numerous situations (e.g., as father, leader, friend, etc.). Tying this assertion back to the agency framework, we see this consistent moral behavior manifested through the (proper) use of both *refrain* and *proactive* powers as leaders interact with their environment and organizational members.

Complexity of the Moral-self

The construct of *self-complexity* (Woolfolk et al., 2004) is the second component of self-structure and is used to assess the pluralism aspects of the self. We assert that cognitively complex leaders develop broader knowledge sets within the moral leadership domain, and this knowledge is integrated by underlying principles that are readily accessible (Ericsson & Charness, 1994). Hence, such leaders are able to exercise greater agentic forethought, self-reflection, and self-reaction during moral processing.

Cognitive complexity is defined as the capacity to construe social behavior in a multidimensional way (Bieri et al., 1966). Hence, the capacity to change cognitive information is necessary for both moral complexity development and for the expansion of the breadth of information available for altruistic moral judgments. Furthermore, self-complexity has been dichotomized by some researchers into the categories of *positive* and *negative* complexity

(Woolfolk et al., 2004). Therefore, a distinction can be made between leaders who have high representations of attributes with positive (e.g., I am "virtuous, and empathetic") as opposed to negative connotations (e.g., I "lack conviction" and I am "easily swayed") in their self-concepts. The implication is that leaders with positive as opposed to negative self-complexity may exhibit different responses when processing moral issues.

Cognitive complexity enables the leader to view moral dilemmas through multiple lenses to determine optimal moral solutions. As society becomes more complex, thereby making it more difficult for moral patterns to emerge, cognitive complexity becomes more important (Kegan, 1994). Hunt and Vitell (1986) likewise posit that individuals may use multiple lenses in forming moral judgments. By reviewing moral issues through multiple lenses over the life span, authentic leaders develop and reinforce various moral schemas, thus enhancing over time their level of moral complexity. Moral leaders have a developed capacity to analyze moral issues through various logic-based lenses such as *deontological* (laws, rules, duties, or norms), *teleological* (utilitarian, consequence, or goal-based), and *areteological* (the inherent virtuousness of a moral actor or issue) lenses.

We suggest that authentic leaders analyze and arbitrate between these logic frameworks or sources of analysis to achieve the best moral fit. Such analysis is incorporated into the leader's views on agentic self-reflectiveness, self-reactiveness, and forethought to help narrow decision making. We further propose that the influence of these three classes of ethical frameworks may vary in differing contexts and dilemmas. Initial empirical support has been found for this assertion in the work of May and Pauli (2002). For instance, although a moral dilemma about whether or not to call in sick to watch a mid-afternoon baseball game on television may have little estimated harm for others (low teleological impact), such behavior may violate the virtuousness of an authentic leader (high areteological impact). Nevertheless, we propose that as leaders achieve higher levels of moral complexity (and are imbued by agency), these leaders will exhibit a greater propensity to use many – if not all – of these lenses to assess moral dilemmas.

Moral Self-clarity

Self-concept clarity is the next component of self-structure that will affect the leader's ability for moral self-explication. Self-concept clarity reflects the unity aspects of the self, and refers to "the extent to which self-beliefs (e.g., perceived personal attributes) are clearly and confidently defined, internally consistent, and stable" (Campbell et al., 1996). As with complexity, self-concept clarity is a structural phenomenon. It is distinct from the *contents* of the self-structure, and reflects instead the belief that a leader has in the level of clarity they hold *over* that content area. Additionally, it is important to note that *self-awareness* has often been used erroneously to represent the level of accuracy of self-knowledge. As originally conceptualized, however, self-awareness is an attentional state, referring to those times that an individual directs his or her conscious attention to some aspect of the self (Duval & Wicklund, 1972). Although attentional states are distinct from evaluative clarity, they often lead to self-assessment, such as is reflected in cybernetic control processes (Carver & Scheier, 1982) or self-discrepancy theory (Higgins, 1987); such self-assessment may result in enhanced self-clarity if sufficient time and motivation are available for cognitive expenditure.

Self-concept clarity is conceptualized to have both trait and state properties (Campbell et al., 1996; Conley, 1984). The linkages proposed between self-concept clarity and the activation of self-evaluation portions of the working self-concept (Campbell et al., 1996) are informative to the understanding of the self-reflectiveness component of moral agency. For example, Campbell et al. (1996) have established preliminary linkages between self-concept clarity and state-like attention to the self. Additionally, self-attention (such as self-consciousness) has also been shown to result in a more clearly articulated self-schema (Kernis & Grannemann, 1988; Nasby, 1989), and higher awareness of internal states (Setterlund & Niedenthal, 1993), which together may raise the salience and articulation of core moral content in the leader. Using an agency lens, high self-awareness may influence an authentic leader's ability to self-reflect upon and activate their core moral values and beliefs and to be in tune with their internal states.

Our discussion of the explication of the moral-self has described how the sheer *content* of the moral meta-knowledge a leader possesses – as developed through social learning and developmental trigger events and stored into self-concept structures – will affect the capacity and ability for authentic leadership. We further discussed how that content is *structured* in its complexity, and how the clarity and confidence the leader holds over that content will affect the activation and processing of moral information during leadership role episodes. This discussion provides support for our next set of propositions.

Proposition 3a. More as opposed to less authentic leaders will possess higher levels of complexity of moral content stored in long-term memory, more self-concept clarity over that content, and such content will reflect higher unity as it relates to core moral aspects.

Proposition 3b. Higher levels of moral content, moral complexity and unity, and self-concept clarity will enhance the leader's ability to explicate his or her moral self during leadership role episodes, leading to improved moral reasoning and behaviors.

Moral Processing Ability

Thus far, we have described the central role of a highly developed moral self-concept in the exercise of agency by an authentic leader. Additionally, the robustness of the *content* and *structure* of the self-concept was presented to explore what may differentiate a highly developed authentic leader from a less-developed inauthentic leader. As shown as the second part of the self-explication process in Fig. 1, we now propose that leaders will have differing levels of ability to process the domain content of moral self-knowledge. Specifically, we posit that leaders will possess varying levels of: (1) meta-cognitive abilities and motivation to process and explicate this moral information through dedicated and controlled processing and (2) abilities for emotional regulation. As suggested by the double arrows in Fig. 1, we propose that the capacity for meta-cognition and emotional regulation interacts with the leader's moral content and structure to enable the leader to explicate his or her moral self-concept (current self, current goals, and possible self).

Depth of Moral Processing

The level or *depth* at which a moral dilemma is processed will result in higher understanding and retention of experiences, as well as higher abilities for personal and interpersonal reference (Craik & Lockhart, 1972). Meta-cognitive processing (Brown, 1987; Flavell, 1987) is the pinnacle of processing depth (Velichkovsky, 2002); it fulfills the two main functions of *monitoring* and *control* (regulation) of human cognitions and processes (Metcalfe & Shimamura, 1994; Nelson & Narens, 1990). Meta-cognition is critical to moral processing and regulation of complex moral dilemmas – in short, meta-cognition allows leaders to *think about their thinking*, and thus possibly change the content of *what* they think. As proposed by Flavell (1979), meta-cognition allows for self-transformation and interpretation of the self-concept, which we propose facilitates more transparent processing of self-referential information during moral dilemmas. Further, Swanson and Hill (1993) found that the self-referential and executive-control functions of meta-cognition have a significant relationship with moral reasoning and moral actions, suggesting that meta-cognition influences moral agency.

Such *meta-moral ability*, which we view as a leader's ability to monitor and control his or her moral thinking, enables an authentic leader to monitor and adjust his or her moral reasoning processes toward issue-specific outcomes. Further, meta-moral ability allows a leader to control the selection and activation of moral content (schemas) during mental processing. Given the earlier discussion of script-based and automatic moral processing and behaviors, it is critical to note the significant role played by meta-cognition. Individuals can usually recall what strategies they use for task performance, but the meta-cognitive process used to select those strategies may often be implicit (Gollwitzer & Schaal, 1998; Reder & Schunn, 1996).

Dual-processing models such as the elaboration likelihood model (ELM) (Petty, Cacioppo, & Goldman, 1981; Petty & Cacioppo, 1986) and the heuristic–systematic model (Chaiken, 1980) provide additional insight into the conditions under which a moral dilemma may be processed via a deeper and controlled mode, commonly referred to as a central or systematic mode. These models state that both motivation and ability are required to increase the amount of elaborative message-relevant thinking a person applies. Paralleling the agency framework, deep processing allows for meta-cognitive introspection and may alter leaders' schemas based on new information received. Street and colleagues (Street, Douglas, Geiger, & Martinko, 2001) applied the elaboration concept to moral processing and found that deep or systematic processing resulted in greater recognition of moral issues versus peripheral processing.

Finally, we concur with Chan et al.'s (2005) assertion that authentic leaders possess heightened levels of meta-cognitive ability gained through developmental cognitive experiences throughout their lifetime. We have also proposed that authentic leaders develop a heightened sense of ownership or agency over their moral experiences and are intent on achieving virtuousness in moral solutions. Together these attributes provide the *ability* and *motivation* for deep elaboration and meta-cognitive self-explication and processing of moral dilemmas. This reasoning suggests the following proposition:

Proposition 4. More as opposed to less authentic leaders possess higher meta-cognitive abilities and agentic motivation to exercise centralized processing of moral dilemmas, resulting in greater self-explication and recognition of and effective processing of those dilemmas.

MORAL EMOTIONS AND
MORAL SELF-REGULATION

Moral Emotions

It is important to recognize that moral processing is not confined to "cold" cognitive processes, as "hot" affective processes have also been shown to strongly influence the self-system, cognitive processing, and self-regulation (Mischel & Morf, 2003). We propose that moral challenges and dilemmas are often affect-laden and that a highly developed authentic leader will have a heightened ability to regulate these influences during moral processing. Specifically, as proposed by Gardner et al. (2005), authentic leaders may possess a higher level of *emotional intelligence* (Goleman, Boyatzis, & McKee, 2002; Salovey, Mayer, & Caruso, 2002), which provides them with a greater capacity to analyze and regulate their emotions. Hence, they are more likely to invoke attentional processes to assess their emotions during moral processing.

Because moral dilemmas are inherently affect-laden, leaders will often use affect as information just as they use any other criteria to influence attitude change (Albarracin & Kumkale, 2003). Additionally, returning to the dual processing models previously discussed, research has found (e.g., Tiedens & Linton, 2001) that negative mood states may lead to systematic processing, whereas positive mood states may lead to less effective heuristic processing. More specific to moral leadership, Camacho, Higgins, and Luger (2003) applied the concept of regulatory focus (Higgins, 1997) to moral evaluations, discovering that when a person perceived a fit violation, they experienced cognitive disequilibrium and expressed more guilt (Tangney, 2003). When participants experienced a good regulatory fit, however, they were more likely to assess their past actions as morally right. The authors also found that the "feeling right" of achieving fit is transferred to future evaluations of rightness. Leaders must recognize that regulatory fit affects what *feels* right or wrong, and transfers this feeling to what people experience as *being* right or wrong.

Because self-aware leaders display higher levels of emotional intelligence, they are able to better understand the activation and influence of emotions upon their cognitive processes and decision making during moral leadership episodes. Viewed through an agency lens, emotional intelligence would most likely manifest itself in an authentic leader's ability to perceive, understand, and control strong emotions experienced during moral processing to ensure that both refrain and proactive powers to behave ethically are effectively employed.

Given the demonstrated influence of affect on moral processing, we propose that a highly developed and self-aware authentic leader who is imbued with emotional intelligence will be more likely to effectively understand and control emotions in his or her moral processing during leadership episodes. This leads us to the following propositions.

Proposition 5a. More as opposed to less morally developed authentic leaders possess a greater capacity for emotional regulation.

Proposition 5b. Leaders with a greater capacity for emotional regulation will more effectively perceive, monitor, and control emotions during moral processing, leading to more virtuous and altruistic moral solutions.

To summarize, we propose that moral capacity is developed in parallel with authenticity. As leaders experience robust moral trigger events, they encode a vast amount of meta-moral knowledge (content) that they can draw upon during future moral reasoning to achieve more virtuous and altruistic moral solutions. Inasmuch as developmental trigger events occur over various permutations of roles and contexts, leaders will structure that content into more complex schemas that allow for greater breadth of analysis and less polarized processing. As leaders subsequently behave morally, achieve success, and reflect upon that success, they increase their self-concept clarity and self-unity, which they can employ cross-situationally as moral leaders. In essence, the end result of these processes is a core moral self that is chronically activated into the moral leader's temporal working self-concept. The process of self-explication is enabled through the leader's meta-cognitive abilities and emotional regulation. Ultimately, it is this moral working self-concept, activated during leadership role episodes, that lies at the heart of authentic leadership and enables the leader to exercise the facets of moral agency over his or her leadership domain. We turn now from the self-concept to this *working* self-concept and the self-regulation inherent in the exercise of moral agency.

Moral Self-Regulation

Leaders
***Who** they are is **how** they are.* Any useful framework for moral leadership must bridge the moral self-concept to moral behavior, and so we turn now to focus on the *self-reactiveness* facet of moral agency. Specifically, having

explored the agentic moral self and how individuals explicate this moral-self during leadership episodes, we now define how a highly developed moral self-concept manifests into moral self-regulation.

The domain content and complexity of the moral self-concept is vital as leaders tend to make decisions and act in a fashion consistent with their self-schemas (Lord & Brown, 2004). Specifically, we propose that activation of core moral domains in the leader's self-concept will manifest into a morally laden *working self-concept* (Markus & Wurf, 1987) that drives moral behavior during leadership role episodes. This working self-concept comprises the part of the leader's self-concept and domain knowledge activated by internal and external primes in the current environment during leadership episodes.

Activation of a moral working self-concept can be triggered externally, by environmental cues (e.g., another leader framing an issue in moral terms), or internally, by a more experienced and morally aware leader who has a heightened attention to and propensity for recognizing and processing moral dilemmas. Critical to moral leadership, Markus and Wurf (1987) propose that when self-focused aspects of this working self-concept are activated, people attend to goal-related actions and diagnostic, self-relevant information processing. As indicated in our discussion of self-concept unity, authentic leaders will have a greater propensity to activate a moral working self-concept as they hold a core set of beliefs that are chronically activated cross-situationally. A morally self-schematic leader will thus be driven by these activated beliefs into goal-directed and diagnostic cybernetic control processes (Carver & Scheier, 1982) toward moral self-regulation.

Specifically, schema activation heightens peoples' awareness to attend to schema-relevant and consistent information and to discount schema-inconsistent information (Dutton & Jackson, 1987). Therefore, once an authentic leader becomes confident in his or her moral self-concept, he or she will come to rely upon those salient moral concepts to guide moral behavior. Such self-schemas must be fairly robust and stable to guide such vital functions.

Three theoretical considerations/findings are important here: (1) Rest, Narvaez, Thoma, and Bebeau's (2000) proposition that cognitive moral development levels reflect varying levels of moral schema development; (2) the findings that individuals prefer to use the highest moral development stage available to them (Trevino, 1992); and (3) the positive relations found between cognitive moral development and moral behavior (Rest, 1994). Therefore, we again propose that levels of schematic moral development will result in higher instances of moral behavior, regardless of whether these schemas are activated through automatic or controlled processes.

As these schemas impact moral behavior through either automatic or controlled cognitive processing (Lord & Brown, 2004), it is important to note that even complex and attention-intensive events, such as moral processing can become less demanding or even automatic for an experienced leader over time (Logan & Klapp, 1991; Spelke, Hirst, & Neisser, 1976; Zbrodoff & Logan, 1986). Moral self-regulation may be driven by schema-based automatic processes such as scripts, which provide habituated ways for a leader to respond in specific domains, thus allowing cognitive resources to be redirected to more complex processing, or toward unique or unfamiliar events (Abelson, 1981; Gioia & Poole, 1984; Schank & Abelson, 1977). Such scripts constitute a form of temporal event-driven schemas that we propose can be predictive of moral behavior. As a leader uses strategies and behaviors that are repeatedly successful, they become habituated and integrated in memory for later use as standardized responses (Gioia & Poole, 1984; Hair, Anderson, & Tatham, 1987; Wofford & Goodwin, 1994) through priming processes and spreading activation (Collins & Loftus, 1975). Scripts can influence why one leader's automatic response to workers who arrive extremely late to the office may be to publicly berate them, while another leader's response is to first inquire as to the reason and possibly offer empathy if there is justification. Due to these schema and script activation processes, the development of a leader's moral domain content is critical to promoting moral self-regulation.

The influence of learned self-schemas and scripts upon moral leadership is also supported by the work of Wofford and colleagues (Wofford & Goodwin, 1994; Wofford, Goodwin, & Whittington, 1998). Their findings show that as individuals experience leadership role episodes, they develop schemas and scripts that can be defined as either more transformational or transactional in orientation. Similar to authentic leadership theory, transformational leadership theory has an inherent moral component (Bass, 1985), which has been discriminated in empirical testing (Turner, Barling, Epitropaki, Butcher, & Milner, 2002). We propose that leaders will differentially develop moral leadership styles based upon their learned experiences and successful prior performances as they apply to current and/or future anticipated performance challenges, which in turn will largely define their moral leadership behaviors.

Additional insight into the process of schema-activated moral self-regulation can be gained by review of the *integrated self-schema model* (ISSM) (Peterson, 1994; Stahlberg, Peterson, & Dauenbeimer, 1999).

A self-dimension would be classified as schematic when a leader rates it as being highly important to his or her identity (Markus, 1977). The ISSM has shown that in areas of the self-concept where people are highly elaborated (self-schematic), they tend to have a self-consistency (self-verifying) motive to confirm their self-beliefs, even if those beliefs confirm a negative aspect of their self-schema. In areas where people are less elaborated (aschematic), they tend to show a motive toward self-enhancing information, regardless of its accuracy. As alluded to previously, this model is based upon the proposition that highly schematic self-information is central and highly salient in the cognitive system (Kihlstrom et al., 2003), and is therefore interlinked with many other knowledge structures, which could be greatly disrupted by inconsistent information or dissonance. Higgins, Van Hook, and Dorfman (1988) demonstrated this dependence and found that priming one self-aspect led to automatic activation of many other linked self-aspects. Aschematic dimensions, conversely, are less central in the self-structure.

In summary, the ISSM informs us that if a leader is highly self-schematic on (and has high unity over) core moral aspects of his or her self-concept, the leader will be driven toward self-consistent moral action based upon a self-verification motive (Swann, 1983, 1987). That is, the leader will not be driven to achieve self-enhancement at the cost of immorality. For example, if a leader is highly self-schematic as being empathetic to disabled employees, he or she will likely behave extremely altruistically toward those employees to verify that self-schema.

The theoretical linkages described above suggest the following proposition:

Proposition 6. More as opposed to less authentic leaders are more self-schematic on salient and core moral dimensions, resulting in a higher propensity to activate altruistic and virtuous moral working self-concepts, schemas, and scripts, and thus are more likely to engage in moral behavior to obtain self-verification.

Moral Goals and Self-regulation

As we explore further the processes of agentic self-reactiveness and moral self-regulation, it is important to discuss the interactions between goals, the self-concept, and goal-directed moral behaviors. As previously noted, Lord, Brown, and Freiberg (1999) proposed that there is a temporal dimension to the self-concept whereby leaders identify not only with their current *self-view*, but also with a more distant image of a *possible self* (Markus & Wurf, 1987). Expanding this model into a self-concept-based cybernetic regulatory control system, Lord and Brown (2004) argue that the leader's working self-concept arises from activation of portions of the self-concept, including his or her *current self-views*, *current goals*, and *possible selves* (as modeled in Fig. 1). Through comparative processes, these components of the working self-concept create motivational forces to regulate behavior by eliciting proximal motivation to reestablish alignment when any discrepancy is found. Any two of these three components can therefore initiate regulatory control processes that drive the leader's moral behavior, with any one of the components providing the standard and the other the feedback source (Lord & Brown, 2004).

Underlying these effective cybernetic control processes is a heightened level of self-awareness, previously stated as an inherent attribute of an authentic leader (Avolio, Gardner, Walumbwa, Luthans, & May, 2004; Gardner et al., 2005). Self-awareness theory has shown that self-focused attention leads to comparisons between one's personal standards and current self-views, leading to a motive to reduce any discrepancies found (Duvall & Wicklund, 1972). We propose that due to the high level of moral development reflected in their self-concept, and an enhanced ability to explicate their selves, authentic leaders possess a more efficient and influential cybernetic system that drives goal-directed moral behavior. Additionally, through capabilities for *forethought* (Bandura, 1997), these leaders can better envision a possible moral-self that drives their goals toward further moral development.

Proposition 7. Leaders with more as opposed to less developed moral self-concepts will be more likely to activate a morally laden working self-concept and execute goal-directed moral behavior through cybernetic self-regulatory processes.

EFFECTS OF AUTHENTIC LEADERS ON FOLLOWERS

The focus of this chapter thus far has been devoted to developing a framework for authentic leadership based upon the leader's self-concept and the linkages between that self-concept and the ability and motivation to exercise moral behavior through moral agency. We have concentrated our attention on the internal processes of the leader and stressed the activation of complex moral domains in the leader's working self-concept during role episodes. We have also shown how this working self-concept is laden with salient altruism, virtuousness, and activated moral goals that drive authentic moral behavior during leadership episodes. The remainder of this paper focuses on authentic leadership as an influence *process* and the external manifestations of moral leadership.

As modeled on the right of Fig. 1, we propose that as the leader transparently exemplifies moral behavior and displays authentic altruism and virtue during leadership episodes, attributions by and influences upon the follower will result in positive outcomes. Proposed follower outcomes of authentic moral leadership include: (1) greater trust in the leader; (2) higher power and latitude afforded to the leader; (3) increased social identification with the leader and emulation of his or her moral actions; and (4) activation of the follower's moral working self-concept. As previously noted, our view is that authentic leaders are moral actors who are likely to enforce, reinforce, and foster moral behavior within their span of organizational control. And, while we have thus far primarily focused on the *leader*, the outcomes of authentic leadership are largely manifested through their effects on the *follower* through the exercise of proxy agency.

The Bottom-Up View

There is little in leadership that is private anymore. Hence, followers are much more likely to recognize gaps between a leader's espoused values and intentions and their behaviors (Avolio, Kahai, & Dodge, 2000). Inconsistent leader behavior can result in the follower perceiving a break from their psychological contract with the leader, resulting in a downward spiral of progressively higher levels of distrust. Such distrust can eventually block the leader's efforts to initiate any positive change in the leader/follower relationship (May, Gilson, & Harter, 2004). Indeed, the more authentic the leader is perceived to be, the quicker the leader's authenticity may unravel if followers witness inconsistent and unethical leader behavior. Thus, hypocritical leadership may contribute to follower cynicism and distrust, as well as unethical follower behavior (Trevino, Hartman, & Brown, 2000).

We propose that authentic leaders will establish a strong base of trust and referent power with their followers. When authentic leaders are faced with an ethical challenge as distinguished by the dimensions of moral intensity (Jones, 1991; May & Pauli, 2002), we expect that they and their followers will proceed with a more open discussion. Furthermore, the exercise of moral discussion is posited to produce a deeper understanding of the issues and foster moral development by the leaders and their followers. Before going too deeply into the impacts on followers, however, it is important to describe how followers view moral leaders, the concepts that influence these views, and how leaders activate and change these views.

Highly moral leaders will likely see themselves, and be seen by others, as prototypical leaders with a defined role to emerge as a central leader of a given group. *Leader categorization theory* (Lord, Foti, & De Vader, 1984; Lord & Mayer, 1991) explains this emergence using an information-processing approach. The theory holds that both leaders and followers develop a schema of what they deem to be a prototypical leader, or an *implicit leadership theory (ILT)*. When a leader's ILT and associated behavior matches followers' ILTs, the outcome is increased influence and support afforded by followers (Hollander, 1992). And, as previously discussed, the leader will use his or her own ILT to envision a *possible-self* through agentic forethought that will guide their moral development and goal-directed behaviors (Lord & Brown, 2004).

A contrary view, however, is offered by Michael Hogg and his associates (Hogg, 2001; Hogg, Hains, & Mason, 1998). These authors assert that leader emergence and influence are not a function of matching a schematic implicit theory, but rather involve a process of matching the prototypical attributes of the group. Due to the influence of social identification, whereby individuals identify with social groups to achieve greater self-categorization (Tajfel, 1978) or self-esteem (Hogg & Abrams, 1988; Tajfel, 1972), Hogg et al. (1998) posit that when a group sees the leader's attributes as prototypically representative of the group members' attributes, they are more likely to support the leader in his or her emergence and influence (Hogg, 2001).

There is preliminary evidence that group prototypicality effects may diminish the effects of individual-level prototypicality (such as ILT) on leadership outcomes (Hogg et al., 1998). As discussed at the outset of this chapter, however, morality (as a component of humane orientation) is a recurring attribute in leadership across contexts and theories, and is thus proposed to be central to the prototypes envisioned by both leaders and groups (Bass, 1997; House, Hanges, Javidan, Dorfman, & Gupta, 2004).

Although the debate of whether ILTs or group prototypicality have greater effects at the *interpersonal* level has yet to be resolved, we propose that at the *intrapersonal* level, leaders with higher levels of authentic morality will see themselves as prototypical to both their own and their followers' ILTs. Insofar as moral leaders increase the moral identity of the group, they will also increase their prototypicality within that group, thereby further reinforcing both their own and other moral actors' emergence as group leaders. Over time, development of such a cycle would foster and reinforce a moral organizational culture.

Research has also shown that leaders' self-identities can shape followers' self-identities and schemas (Gardner & Avolio, 1998; Lord & Brown, 2004; Lord et al., 1999). Not only can leaders impact the self-concepts of followers, there is initial evidence that this process may be interactive and reciprocal. Building on earlier investigations into the influence followers exert on leader behaviors (Hollander, 1992; Lord et al., 1999; Shamir, House, & Arthur, 1993), Dvir and Shamir (2003) showed that followers' level of development (operationalized as self-actualization needs, internalization of moral values, collectivist orientation, and other factors) predicted transformational leadership exhibited by their officers. This dynamic of the leadership process suggests that leaders' moral self-concepts may be influenced not only by their own supervisors, personal experiences, and development, but also by their followers. Fig. 1 reflects the follower impact on a leader's self-concept through a reinforcing feedback loop. As shown, leaders will use follower feedback, along with their own self-reflections on leadership episodes, as input for meta-cognitive processing to make meaning of and adapt their self-concepts to the new self-knowledge gained from these experiences.

Proposition 8a. More as opposed to less authentic leaders will be more likely to match both their own and followers' implicit leadership theories, resulting in higher levels of leadership emergence.

Proposition 8b. Inasmuch as moral leaders raise the valance and salience of moral aspects of the group's identity, they will increase the emergence of moral organizational leaders.

Activation of Moral Domains in Follower's Working Self-Concepts

A moral leader can elicit heightened moral behaviors in followers through the activation (priming) of moral domains in followers' working self-concepts. Research has supported the importance of emphasizing the consequences of moral behavior to moral decision making (Dubinsky & Loken, 1989; Ferrell & Gresham, 1985; Hunt & Vitell, 1986). An authentic leader who is highly developed and self-schematic on moral dimensions will not only be able to self-activate moral schemas, but also promote follower engagement by raising followers' perceptions of the *moral intensity* of the ethical dilemma (Jones, 1991). Followers' perceptions can thus be shaped by illuminating the *magnitude of consequences, probability of effect, concentration of effect*, and similar elements of a moral issue. Moreover, ample research has shown that by increasing moral intensity, a leader can motivate followers to act morally (e.g., Butterfield, Trevino, & Weaver, 2000; Davis, Johnson, & Ohmer, 1998; Flannery & May, 2000; May & Pauli, 2002; Singhapakdi, Vitell, & Kraft, 1996).

In a similar vein, moral intensity can be raised through moral issue-framing (Butterfield et al., 2000; Jones, 1991; Watley & May, 2004). Issue framing concerns the way information about an issue or situation is presented and ultimately interpreted by the presenter and the target audience. Butterfield and his colleagues have proposed that if moral language is used in framing an issue, then it is more likely to trigger (prime) followers' moral scripts and therefore enhance their level of moral awareness, especially in morally ambiguous contexts. This activation process suggests our next proposition:

Proposition 9. Consistent and transparent leader exemplification of altruism and virtue during leadership episodes will enhance activation of a morally laden working self-concept within followers.

Dyadic Effects of Authentic Moral Leadership

We believe that authentic leaders who make exemplary moral decisions will elicit emulation of such behavior by followers. Specifically, we predict the development of: (1) follower emulation of the leader's conduct; (2) stronger bonds of trust between the leader and follower; (3) a higher degree of transparency across the organization; (4) stronger social identification and buy-in by followers; and (5) greater leader latitude to make difficult and potentially unpopular decisions. Below, we discuss each outcome in further detail.

Emulation of Exemplary Leader Conduct

We suggest that authentic leaders who make exemplary moral decisions will elicit similar behavior from followers through emulation processes (Jones & Pittman, 1982). Organizations are social entities and followers are quickly socialized into the organizational environment, responding to both implicit and explicit social norms of their peers (Schneider, Smith, & Paul, 2001). As described by Trevino and colleagues (2000), ethical leaders must find ways to infuse their ethics and values into the organization in order to guide future actions by organizational members. As followers learn vicariously by watching leaders behave within the organizational context, they are more likely to emulate that leader's actions and, in turn, internalize the shared ethics and values (Trevino et al., 2000). In short, when leaders consistently display high levels of moral conduct, they set a positive ethical standard to be followed across the organization. Provided that an authentic leader attenuates unethical behavior as it occurs and develops a collective ethical culture, followers are likely to emulate such behavior when faced with an ethical dilemma because ethical behavior is now the norm to which they have been socialized (Lord & Brown, 2004).

Similarly, Heifetz (1994) theorized that leaders can use their various powers to motivate followers to decrease the gap between their values-conflicts. Leaders do this first by exercising their expert and position power, then through participatory methods, such as helping followers become more adaptive and reflective when facing competing values. We suggest that because authentic leaders have reputations for ethical leadership, they secure high levels of follower-attributed credibility and trust that in turn promote follower acceptance of their expert power. Along with their obvious referent power and participatory style, such leaders will also encourage the development of followers' moral capabilities. Heifetz proposed that leaders could create tensions to ensure that followers identify and eliminate their values-conflicts. Authentic leaders can help create such tensions through open moral discussions, and by exemplifying contrasting personal examples of higher-level moral development.

Trust

As the authentic leader's ethical behavior is infused into organizational norms, trust between the leader and followers rises. Such trust has proven to be an important component in predicting various attitudinal, behavioral, and performance outcomes, such as job satisfaction, organizational commitment, involvement, and justice (Dirks & Ferrin, 2002). As followers come to attribute consistency to the authentic leader's moral actions, they become more willing to openly communicate with the leader. In the process, they become empowered to assume moral agency and make their own moral decisions without having to contemplate how the leader will respond. Mayer and Gavin (1999) suggest that followers who do not trust their leaders will divert energy toward "covering their backs," thus adding support to the argument that many organizational-level moral failures can be directly tied to a lack of trust between leaders and followers. If trust between leaders and followers solidifies, most moral failures can be avoided because an unethical decision would run counter to the organizational culture.

Transparency

Another likely outcome of morally positive decisions by authentic leaders is organizational and operational transparency. Authentic leaders are described as promoting transparency with regards to information sharing in their relationships with others, which is therefore expected to foster greater trust and positive interactions (Avolio et al., 2004). By organizational and operational transparency, we mean that the decisions concerning the structure of the organization and its operations are more readily accessible to followers and disseminated widely. For transparency to have a maximum effect, few – if any – secrets (whether positive or negative in nature) should be kept between the leader and his or her followers (Kernis, 2002). The positive effects of transparency will become manifest in part through open discussions of moral dilemmas. We assert that moral leaders are open and invite participation in their deliberations on moral issues. Evidence of the power of such transparent discussions is provided by Rest and Thoma's (1986) study of 23 ethics training programs. Their results revealed that programs with and without dilemma discussions had average effect sizes of 0.41 and 0.09, respectively.

Stronger Social Identity

As ethical decision making becomes the norm within an organization, it exerts a positive influence in followers with respect to their social identity. In short, the organization – over time – becomes *known* for making ethically sound decisions that are reflected in not only the conduct of the authentic leader, but also within followers. This social identity ultimately influences *who they are* because they can identify with doing what is right; moral decision making becomes a tangible outcome, rather than an elusive goal.

Together, prior research suggests that leaders can harness the motivational forces that provide a propensity for organizational members to align their self-concept with the organization's identity (Hogg, 2001; Hogg & Abrams, 1988; Tajfel, 1978) by enhancing the salience of the organization's moral identity. If followers are sufficiently motivated to align with an organization's values, and provided the organization rewards moral actions that reflect these values, followers will be more likely to become moral agents. Such followers would in turn further reinforce that positive environment through social identification processes.

Leader Latitude

Because authentic leaders display consistency in aligning their espoused values with their actions, we believe that followers will reward such leaders with idiosyncratic credits (Hollander, 1992). Specifically, due to chronic activation of core moral aspects in their working self-concepts, authentic leaders will continually accrue idiosyncratic credits as a result of the cross-situational consistency of their moral actions. Such idiosyncratic credit is a critical enabler for future leader decision making. If a leader has established a high level of credibility among followers, he or she will possess sufficient latitude to make very difficult, often unpopular decisions. Authentic leaders are also well positioned to bring about change as a function of followers' attributions of competence, loyalty, and trust that have accrued from prior events.

In summary, as authentic leaders display transparency and consistently exemplify altruism and virtue through their actions, perceiver attribution processes will yield positive follower outcomes. Additionally, positive follower behaviors will provide reinforcing feedback to further bolster the leader's moral self-concept. This reasoning suggests our final proposition.

Proposition 10. Consistent and transparent leader exemplification of altruism and virtue during leadership episodes will yield higher levels of follower trust, moral-emulation, moral social-identification, and latitude afforded to the leader.

IMPLICATIONS

The current model attempts to provide a general framework to guide future research on the moral component of authentic leadership by integrating theories of the self-concept (such as moral self-complexity, self-concept clarity, and meta-knowledge), along with the tenets of agency (including altruism, virtue and self-regulatory processes), and by modeling the positive effects of a morally authentic leader on followers and organizations. Inherent in the manifestation of moral leadership is the exercise of personal agency and proxy agency, whereby the leader is both a product of and a producer of the moral context. Future research is needed to investigate how the leader influences – and is influenced by – the context as it pertains to the moral component of authenticity, including the contextual effects on the social learning and developmental processes discussed earlier. Additionally, the propensities of leaders to activate core moral domains cross-situationally in their working self-concept during leadership episodes should be further reviewed as measures of both inter- and intrapersonal authenticity. Potential moderators that influence how various contexts may either bolster or strain the moral leader's ability to be true (authentic) to his or her core ethical beliefs likewise merit investigation.

REFERENCES

Abelson, R. P. (1981). The psychological status of the script concept. *American Psychologist, 36,* 715–729.

Albarracin, D., & Kumkale, G. T. (2003). Affect as information in persuasion: A model of affect identification and discounting. *Journal of Personality and Social Psychology, 84,* 453–469.

Altrocchi, J. (1999). Individual differences in pluralism in self-structure. In: J. Rowan, & M. Cooper (Eds), *The plural self: Multiplicity in everyday life* (pp. 168–182). London, UK: Sage.

Ashcroft, M. H. (2002). *Cognition* (3rd ed.). New Jersey: Prentice-Hall.

Aurelius, M. (2002). Meditations: A new translation. In: G. Hays (Ed.), *Meditations: A new translation.* New York: Random House.

Avolio, B. J., Gardner, W. L., Walumbwa, F. O., Luthans, F., & May, D. R. (2004). Unlocking the mask: A look at the process by which authentic leaders impact follower attitudes and behaviors. *The Leadership Quarterly, 15,* 801–823.

Avolio, B. J., Kahai, S. S., & Dodge, G. (2000). E-leadership and its implications for theory, research and practice. *The Leadership Quarterly, 11,* 615–670.

Bandura, A. (1977). *Social learning theory.* Englewood Cliffs, NJ: Prentice-Hall.

Bandura, A. (1991). Social cognitive theory of moral thought and action. In: W. M. Kurtines, & J. L. Gewirtz (Eds), *Handbook of moral behavior and development* (Vol. 1, pp. 45–103). Hillsdale, NJ: Erlbaum.

Bandura, A. (1997). *Self-efficacy: The exercise of control.* New York: Freeman.

Bandura, A. (1999). Moral disengagement in the perpetuation of inhumanities. *Personality and Social Psychology Review, 33,* 193–209.

Bandura, A. (2000). Exercise of human agency through collective efficacy. *Current Directions in Psychological Science, 9,* 75–78.

Bandura, A. (2001). Social cognitive theory: An agentic perspective. *Annual Review of Psychology, 52,* 1–26.

Bandura, A. (2002). Social cognitive theory in cultural context. *Journal of Applied Psychology, 51,* 269–290.

Bartunek, J. M. (1984). Changing interpretive schemes and organizational restructuring: The example of a religious order. *Administrative Science Quarterly, 29,* 355–372.

Bartunek, J. M., & Moch, M. K. (1987). First order, second order, and third order change and organizational development interventions: A cognitive perspective. *Journal of Applied Behavioral Science, 23,* 483–500.

Bass, B. M. (1985). *Leadership and performance beyond expectations.* New York: Free Press.

Bass, B. M. (1997). Does the transactional-transformational leadership paradigm transcend organizational and national boundaries? *American Psychologist, 52,* 130–139.

Bass, B. M. (1998). *Transformational leadership: Industry, military, and educational impact.* Mahwah, NJ: Lawrence Erlbaum.

Batson, C. D. (1991). *The altruism question: Toward a social psychological answer*. Hillsdale, NJ: Erlbaum.

Batson, C. D. (1998). Altruism and prosocial behavior. In: D. T. Gilbert, S. T. Fiske, & G. Lindsey (Eds), *Handbook of social psychology* (4th ed., Vol. II, pp. 282–316). Boston: McGraw-Hill.

Bieri, J., Atkins, A., Briar, S., Leaman, R., Miller, H., & Tripodi, T. (1966). *Clinical and social judgment: Discrimination of behavioral information*. New York, NY: Wiley.

Block, J. (1961). Ego-identity, role variability, and adjustment. *Journal of Consulting and Clinical Psychology, 25*, 392–397.

Bower, G. H., & Hilgard, E. R. (1981). *Theories of learning*. New Jersey: Prentice-Hall.

Brown, A. D. (1987). Metacognition, executive control, self-regulation, and other more mysterious mechanisms. In: F. E. Weinert, & R. H. Kluwe (Eds), *Metacognition, motivation, and understanding* (pp. 65–116). Hillsdale, NJ: Erlbaum.

Burns, J. M. (1978). *Leadership*. New York: Harper & Row.

Butterfield, K. D., Trevino, L. K., & Weaver, G. R. (2000). Moral awareness in business organizations: Influences of issue-related and social context factors. *Human Relations, 53*, 981–1018.

Camacho, C. J., Higgins, T. E., & Luger, L. (2003). Moral value transfer from regulatory fit: What feels right is right and what feels wrong is wrong. *Journal of Personality and Social Psychology, 84*, 498–510.

Campbell, J. D., Assanand, S., & Di Paula, A. (2003). The structure of the self-concept and its relation to psychological adjustment. *Journal of Personality, 71*, 140.

Campbell, J. D., & Lavallee, L. F. (1993). Who am I? The role of self-concept confusion in understanding the behavior of people with low self-esteem. In: R. F. Baumeister (Ed.), *Self-esteem: The puzzle of low self-regard* (pp. 3–20). New York: Plenum.

Campbell, J. D., Trapnell, P. D., Heine, S. J., Katz, E. M., Lavallee, L. F., & Lehman, D. R. (1996). Self-concept clarity: Measurement, personality correlates, and cultural boundaries. *Journal of Personality and Social Psychology, 70*, 141–156.

Carver, C. S., & Scheier, M. F. (1982). Control theory: A useful conceptual framework for personality—social, clinical, and health psychology. *Psychological Bulletin, 92*, 111–135.

Chaiken, S. (1980). Heuristic versus systemic information processing and the use of source versus message cues in persuasion. *Journal of Personality and Social Psychology, 39*, 752–766.

Chan, A. Y. L., Hannah, S. T., & Gardner, W. L. (2005). Veritable authentic leadership: Emergence, functioning, and impacts. In: W. B. Gardner, B. J. Avolio, & F. O. Walumbwa (Eds), *Authentic leadership theory and practice. Origins, effects, and development*. Elsevier.

Cohen, E. D. (1994). What would a virtuous counselor do? Ethical problems in counseling clients with HIV. In: *Aids: Crisis in professional ethics* (pp. 149–176). Philadelphia: Temple University Press.

Collins, A. M., & Loftus, E. F. (1975). A spreading activation of semantic processing. *Psychological Review, 82*, 407–428.

Conley, J. J. (1984). The hierarchy of consistency: A review and model of longitudinal findings on adult individual differences in intelligence, personality, and self-opinion. *Personality and Individual Differences, 5*, 11–25.

Craik, F. I. M., & Lockhart, R. (1972). Levels of processing: A framework for memory research. *Journal of Verbal Learning and Verbal Behavior, 11*, 671–684.

Davis, M. A., Johnson, N. B., & Ohmer, D. G. (1998). Issue contingent effects on ethical decision making: A cross-cultural comparison. *Journal of Business Ethics, 17*, 373–389.

Deci, E. L., & Ryan, R. M. (1985). *Intrinsic motivation and self determination in human behavior.* New York: Plenum.

Deci, E. L., & Ryan, R. M. (1995). Human autonomy: The basis for true self-esteem. In: M. H. Kernis (Ed.), *Efficacy, agency, and self-esteem* (pp. 31–49). New York: Plenum Press.

Dirks, K. T., & Ferrin, D. L. (2002). Trust in leadership: Meta-analytic findings and implications for research and practice. *Journal of Applied Psychology, 87,* 611–628.

Dollinger, M. J. (1984). Environmental boundary spanning and information processing effects on organizational performance. *Academy of Management Journal, 27,* 351–368.

Donahue, E. M., Robins, R. W., Roberts, B. W., & John, O. P. (1993). The divided self: Concurrent and longitudinal effects of psychological adjustment and social roles on self-concept differentiation. *Journal of Personality and Social Psychology, 64,* 834–846.

Dubinsky, A. J., & Loken, B. (1989). Analyzing ethical decision making in marketing. *Journal of Business Research, 19*(2), 83–107.

Dutton, J. E., & Jackson, S. E. (1987). Categorizing strategic issues: Links to organizational action. *Academy of Management Review, 12,* 76–90.

Duval, S., & Wicklund, R. A. (1972). *A theory of objective self-awareness.* New York: Academic Press.

Dvir, T., & Shamir, B. (2003). Follower development characteristics as predicting transformational leadership: A longitudinal field study. *The Leadership Quarterly, 14,* 327–344.

Eagly, A. H., & Chaiken, S. (1998). Attitude structure and function. In: D. T. Gilbert, S. T. Fiske, & G. Lindzey (Eds), *Handbook of social psychology* (4 ed., Vol. 1, pp. 269–322). Boston: McGraw-Hill.

Erickson, R. J. (1995). The importance of authenticity for self and society. *Symbolic Interactions, 18*(2), 121–144.

Ericsson, K. A., & Charness, N. (1994). Performance: Its structure and acquisition. *American Psychologist, 49,* 725–747.

Ferrell, O. C., & Gresham, L. G. (1985). A contingency framework for understanding ethical decision-making in marketing. *Journal of Marketing, 49,* 87–96.

Flannery, B. L., & May, D. R. (2000). Prominent factors influencing environmental activities: Application of the environmental leadership model (elm). Special issue: Leadership for environmental and social change. *The Leadership Quarterly, 5,* 201–221.

Flavell, J. H. (1979). Metacognition and cognitive monitoring: A new era of cognitive development inquiry. *American Psychologist, 34,* 906–911.

Flavell, J. H. (1987). Speculations about the nature and development of metacognition. In: F. E. Weinert, & R. H. Kluwe (Eds), *Metacognition, motivation and understanding* (pp. 21–29). Hillside, NJ: Lawrence Erlbaum Associates.

Gardner, W. L., & Avolio, B. J. (1998). The charismatic relationship: A dramaturgical perspective. *Academy of Management Review, 23,* 32–58.

Gardner, W. L., Avolio, B. J., Luthans, F., May, D. R., & Walumbwa, F. O. (2005). "Can you see the real me?" A self-based model of authentic leader and follower development. *The Leadership Quarterly, 16*(3).

Gioia, D. A., & Poole, P. P. (1984). Scripts in organizational behavior. *Academy of Management Review, 9,* 449–459.

Goleman, D., Boyatzis, R. E., & McKee, A. (2002). *Primal leadership: Realizing the power of emotional intelligence.* Boston: Harvard Business School Press.

Gollwitzer, P. M., & Schaal, B. (1998). Metacognition in action: The importance of implementation intentions. *Personality and Psychology Review, 2,* 124–136.

Hair, J. F., Anderson, R. E., & Tatham, R. L. (1987). *Multivariate data analysis.* New York: Macmillan.

Heifitz, R. A. (1994). *A leadership without easy answers.* Cambridge, MA: Belknap/Harvard University Press.

Hersey, D. A., Walsh, D. A., Read, S. J., & Chulef, A. S. (1990). The effects of expertise on financial problem solving: Evidence for goal-directed problem solving scripts. *Organizational Behavior and Human Decision Processes, 46,* 77–101.

Higgins, E. T. (1987). Self-discrepancy: A theory relating self and affect. *Psychological Review, 94,* 319–340.

Higgins, E. T. (1997). Beyond pleasure and pain. *American Psychologist, 52,* 1280–1300.

Higgins, E. T., Van Hook, E., & Dorfman, D. (1988). Do self-attributes form a cognitive structure? *Social Cognition, 6,* 177–206.

Hogg, M. A. (2001). A social identity theory of leadership. *Personality and Social Psychology Review, 5,* 184–200.

Hogg, M. A., & Abrams, D. (1988). *Social identifications: A social psychology of intergroup relations and group processes.* London, UK: Routledge.

Hogg, M. A., Hains, S. C., & Mason, J. (1998). Identification and leadership in small groups: Salience, frame or reference, and leader stereotypicality effects on leader evaluations. *Journal of Personality and Social Psychology, 75,* 1248–1263.

Hollander, E. P. (1992). Leadership, followership, self, and others. Special issue: Individual differences and leadership. *The Leadership Quarterly, 3,* 43–54.

House, R. J., Hanges, P. J., Javidan, M., Dorfman, P. W., & Gupta, V. (2004). *Culture, leadership, and organizations: The globe study of 62 societies.* Thousand Oaks, CA: Sage.

Hunt, S. D., & Vitell, S. J. (1986). A general theory of marketing ethics. *Journal of Macromarketing, 6,* 5–16.

Jones, E. E., & Pittman, T. S. (1982). Toward a theory of strategic self-presentation. In: J. Suls (Ed.), *Psychological perspectives on the self* (pp. 231–262). Hillsdale, NJ: Erlbaum.

Jones, T. M. (1991). Ethical decision making by individuals in organizations: An issue-contingent model. *Academy of Management Review, 16*(2), 366–395.

Jordan, A. E., & Meara, N. M. (1990). Ethics and the professional practice of psychologists: The role of virtues and principles. *Professional Psychology: Research and Practice, 21,* 107–114.

Kegan, R. (1994). *In over our heads: The mental demands of modern life.* Cambridge, MA: Harvard University Press.

Kernis, M. H., & Grannemann, B. D. (1988). Private self-consciousness and perceptions of self-consistency. *Personality and Individual Differences, 9,* 897–902.

Kernis, M. H. (2002). Toward a conceptualization of optimal self-esteem. *Psychological Inquiry, 14,* 1–26.

Kihlstrom, J. F., Beer, J. S., & Klein, S. B. (2003). Self and identity as memory. In: M. R. Leary, & J. P. Tangney (Eds), *Handbook of self and identity* (pp. 68–90). New York: Guilford.

Kihlstrom, J. F., Cantor, N., Albright, J. S., Chew, B. R., Klein, S. B., & Niedenthal, P. M. (1988). Information processing and the study of the self. In: L. Berkowitz (Ed.), *Advances in experimental psychology* (Vol. 21, pp. 145–178). New York: Academic.

Kihlstrom, J. F., & Klein, S. B. (1994). The self as a knowledge structure. In: R. S. Wyer, & T. K. Srull (Eds), *Handbook of social cognition* (Vol. 1). New Jersey: Erlbaum.

Kohlberg, L. (1969). Stage and sequence: The cognitive-developmental approach to socialization. In: D. A. Goslin (Ed.), *Handbook of socialization theory and research* (pp. 347–480).
Chicago: Rand McNally.

Kohlberg, L. (1976). Moral stages and moralization. In: T. Lickona (Ed.), *Moral development
and behavior* (pp. 31–53). New York: Holt, Rinehart and Winston.

Kohlberg, L. (1981). *The philosophy of moral development*. San Francisco, CA: Harper Row.

Kolb, B., & Whishaw, I. Q. (1998). Brain plasticity and behavior. *Annual Review of Psychology,
49*, 43–64.

Linville, P. W. (1985). Self-complexity and affective extremity: Don't put all your eggs in one
basket. *Social Cognition, 3*, 94–120.

Linville, P. W. (1987). Self-complexity as a cognitive buffer against stress-related illness and
depression. *Journal of Personality and Social Psychology, 52*, 663–676.

Logan, G. D., & Klapp, S. T. (1991). Automatizing alphabet arithmetic: Is extended practice
necessary to produce automaticity? *Journal of Experimental Psychology: Learning,
Memory and Cognition, 17*, 179–195.

Lord, R. G., & Brown, D. J. (2004). *Leadership processes and follower self-identity*. Mahwah,
NJ: Erlbaum.

Lord, R. G., Brown, D. J., & Freiberg, S. J. (1999). Understanding the dynamics of leadership:
The role of follower self-concepts in the leader/follower relationship. *Organizational
Behavior and Human Decision Processes, 78*, 167–203.

Lord, R. G., & Foti, R. J. (1986). Schema theories, information processing and organizational
behavior. In: H. M. Sims, & D. A. Gioia (Eds), *The thinking organization: Dynamics of
organizational social cognition* (pp. 20–48). San Francisco: Jossey-Bass.

Lord, R. G., Foti, R. J., & De Vader, C. L. (1984). A test of leadership categorization theory:
Internal structure, information processing and leadership perceptions. *Organizational
Behavior and Human Performance, 34*, 343–378.

Lord, R. G., & Mayer, K. J. (1991). *Leadership and information processing: Linking perceptions
and performance*. Cambridge: Unwin Hyman Ltd.

Lurigio, A. J., & Carroll, J. S. (1985). Probation officers' schemata of offenders: Context,
development and impact on treatment decisions. *Journal of Personality and Social Psychology, 48*, 1112–1126.

Markus, H. R. (1977). Self-schemata and processing information about the self. *Journal of
Personality and Social Psychology, 35*, 63–78.

Markus, H. R., & Wurf, E. (1987). The dynamic self-concept: A social psychological perspective. *Annual Review of Psychology, 38*, 299–337.

May, D. R., Gilson, R. L., & Harter, L. M. (2004). The psychological conditions of meaningfulness, safety and availability and the engagement of the human spirit at work.
Journal of Occupational and Organizational Psychology, 77, 11–37.

May, D. R., & Pauli, K. P. (2002). The role of moral intensity in ethical decision making–a
review and investigation of moral recognition, evaluation, and intention. *Business &
Society, 41*, 84–117.

Mayer, R. C., & Gavin, M. B. (1999). Trust for management and performance: Who minds the
shop while the employees watch the boss? Paper presented at the Academy of Management Meetings, Chicago, IL.

McCullough, M. E., & Snyder, C. R. (2000). Classical sources of human strength: Revisiting an
old home and building a new one. *Journal of Social and Clinical Psychology, 19*, 1–10.

Metcalfe, J., & Shimamura, A. P. (1994). *Metacognition: Knowing about knowing.* Cambridge, MA: MIT Press.

Mischel, W., & Morf, C. C. (2003). The self as a psycho-social dynamic processing system: A meta-perspective on a century of the self in psychology. In: M. R. Leary, & J. P. Tangney (Eds), *Handbook of self and identity* (pp. 15–43). New York: Guilford.

Nasby, W. (1989). Private and public self-consciousness and articulation of the self-schema. *Journal of Personality and Social Psychology, 56,* 117–123.

Nelson, T. O., & Narens, L. (1990). Metamemory: A theoretical framework and new findings. In: G. H. Bower (Ed.), *The psychology of learning and motivation: Advances in research and theory* (Vol. 26, pp. 125–173). San Diego, CA: Academic Press.

Nicholas, M. W. (1994). *The mystery of goodness and the positive moral consequences of psychotherapy.* New York: Norton.

Peterson, C., & Seligman, M. E. P. (2004). *Character strengths and virtues: A handbook and classification.* New York, NY: Oxford University Press.

Peterson, L. E. (1994). *Self-concept and information processing.* Essen, Germany: Blaue Eule.

Petty, R. E., & Cacioppo, J. T. (1986). The elaboration likelihood model of persuasion. In: L. Berkowitz (Ed.), *Advances in experimental social psychology* (pp. 123–205). New York: Academic Press.

Petty, R. E., Cacioppo, J. T., & Goldman, R. (1981). Personal involvement as a determinant of argument-based persuasion. *Journal of Personality and Social Psychology, 41,* 847–855.

Piaget, J. (1948). *The moral development of a child.* Glencoe, IL: Free Press.

Prillenltensky, I. (1997). Values, assumptions, and practices: Assessing the moral implications of psychological discourse in action. *American Psychologist, 52,* 517–535.

Reder, L. M., & Schunn, C. D. (1996). Metacognition does not imply awareness: Strategy choice is governed by implicit learning and memory. In: L. M. Reder (Ed.), *Implicit memory and metacognition* (pp. 45–78). Mahwah, NJ: Erlbaum.

Rest, J. R. (1986). *Moral development: Advances in research and theory.* New York: Praeger.

Rest, J. R. (1994). Background, theory and research. In: J. R. Rest, & D. Narvaez (Eds), *Moral development: Advances in theory and research* (pp. 59–88). New York, NY: Praeger.

Rest, J. R., Narvaez, D., Thoma, S. J., & Bebeau, M. J. (2000). A neo-Kohlbergian approach to morality research. *Journal of Moral Education, 29,* 381–395.

Rest, J. R., & Thoma, S. J. (1986). Education programs and interventions. In: J. R. Rest (Ed.), *Moral development: Advances in theory and research* (pp. 59–88). New York, NY: Praeger.

Rogers, T. B. (1977). Self-reference in memory: Recognition of personality items. *Journal of Research in Personality, 1,* 295–305.

Rottschaefer, W. A. (1986). Learning to be a moral agent. *Personalist Forum, 2,* 122–142.

Ryan, R. M., & Deci, E. L. (2003). On assimilating identities to the self: A self-determination theory perspective on internalization and integrity within cultures. In: M. R. Leary, & J. P. Tangney (Eds), *Handbook of self and identity* (pp. 253–272). New York: Guilford.

Salovey, P., Mayer, J. D., & Caruso, D. R. (2002). The positive psychology of emotional intelligence. In: C. R. Snyder, & S. J. Lopez (Eds), *Handbook of positive psychology* (pp. 159–171). Oxford, UK: Oxford University Press.

Sandage, S. J., & Hill, P. C. (2001). The virtues of positive psychology: The rapprochement and challenges of an affirmative postmodern perspective. *Journal for the Theory of Social Behavior, 31*(3), 241–260.

Schacter, D. L. (1987). Implicit memory: History and current status. *Journal of Experimental Psychology: Learning, Memory and Cognition, 13*(3), 501–518.

Schank, R. C., & Abelson, R. P. (1977). *Scripts, plans, goals and understanding: An inquiry into human knowledge structures.* Hillsdale, NJ: Erlbaum.

Schneider, B., Smith, D. B., & Paul, M. C. (2001). P-e fit and the attraction-selection-attrition model of organizational functioning: Introduction and overview. In: M. Erez, U. Kleinbeck, & H. Thierry (Eds), *Work motivation in the context of a globalizing economy* (pp. 231–246). Mahwah, NJ: Erlbaum.

Setterlund, M. B., & Niedenthal, P. M. (1993). Who am I? Why am I here? Self-esteem, self-clarity, and prototype matching. *Journal of Personality and Social Psychology, 65,* 769–780.

Shamir, B., House, R. J., & Arthur, M. B. (1993). The motivational effects of charismatic leadership: A self-concept based theory. *Organizational Science, 4,* 1–17.

Sheldon, K. M., & Elliot, A. J. (1999). Goal striving, need satisfaction, and longitudinal well-being: The self-concordance model. *Journal of Personality and Social Psychology, 76,* 482–497.

Showers, C. J. (1992). Compartmentalization of positive and negative self-knowledge: Keeping bad apples out of the bunch. *Journal of Personality and Social Psychology, 62,* 1036–1049.

Singhapakdi, A., Vitell, S. J., & Kraft, K. L. (1996). Moral intensity and ethical decision-making of marketing professionals. *Journal of Business Research, 36,* 245–255.

Spelke, E., Hirst, W., & Neisser, U. (1976). Skills of divided attention. *Cognition, 4,* 215–230.

Stahlberg, D., Peterson, L. E., & Dauenbeimer, D. (1999). Preferences for and evaluation of self-relevant information depending on the elaboration of the schema involved. *European Journal of Social Psychology, 29,* 489–502.

Street, M. D., Douglas, S. C., Geiger, S. W., & Martinko, M. J. (2001). The impact of cognitive expenditure on the ethical decision-making process: The cognitive elaboration model. *Organizational Behavior and Human Decision Processes, 86,* 256–277.

Swann, W. B., Jr. (1983). Self-verification: Bringing social reality into harmony with the self. In: J. R. Suls, & A. G. Greenwald (Eds), *Psychological perspectives on the self* (Vol. 2, pp. 33–66). Hillsdale, NJ: Erlbaum.

Swann, W. B., Jr. (1987). Identity negotiation: Where two roads meet. *Journal of Personality and Social Psychology, 53,* 1038–1051.

Swanson, H. L., & Hill, G. (1993). Metacognitive aspects of moral reasoning and behavior. *Adolescence, 28,* 711–735.

Tajfel, H. (1972). *The context of social psychology: A critical assessment.* London: Academic Press.

Tajfel, H. (1978). Social categorization, social identity and social comparison. In: H. Tajfel (Ed.), *Differentiation between social groups: Studies in the social psychology of intergroup behaviour.* London: Academic Press.

Tangney, J. P. (2003). Self-relevant emotions. In: M. R. Leary, & J. P. Tangney (Eds), *Handbook of self and identity* (pp. 384–400). New York: Guilford Press.

Tiedens, L. Z., & Linton, S. (2001). Judgment under emotional certainty and uncertainty: The effects of specific emotions on information processing. *Journal of Personality and Social Psychology, 81,* 973–988.

Trevino, L. K. (1992). Moral reasoning and business ethics: Implications for research, education, and management. *Journal of Business Ethics, 11,* 445–459.

Trevino, L. K., Hartman, L. P., & Brown, M. (2000). Moral person and moral manager: How executives develop a reputation for ethical leadership. *California Management Review, 42*, 128–142.

Trilling, L. (1972). *Sincerity and authenticity.* New York: Harcourt Brace Jovanovich.

Turner, N., Barling, J., Epitropaki, O., Butcher, V., & Milner, C. (2002). Transformational leadership and moral reasoning. *Journal of Applied Psychology, 87*, 304–311.

Velichkovsky, B. M. (2002). Heterarchy of cognition: The depths and the highs of a framework for memory research. *Memory, 10*(5/6), 405–419.

Watley, L. D., & May, D. R. (2004). Enhancing moral intensity: Personal and consequential information in ethical decision-making. *Journal of Business Ethics, 50*, 105–126.

Weick, K. E. (1979). *The social psychology of organizing* (2nd ed.). New York: McGraw-Hill.

Wofford, J. C., & Goodwin, V. L. (1994). A cognitive interpretation of transactional and transformational leadership theories. *The Leadership Quarterly, 5*, 161–186.

Wofford, J. C., Goodwin, V. L., & Whittington, J. L. (1998). A field study of a cognitive approach to understanding transformational and transactional leadership. *The Leadership Quarterly, 9*, 55–84.

Woolfolk, R. L., Gara, M. A., Allen, L. A., & Beaver, J. D. (2004). Self-complexity: An assessment of construct validity. *Journal of Social and Clinical Psychology, 23*, 463–474.

Yearley, L. H. (1990). *Mencius and aquinas: Theories of virtue and conceptions of courage.* Albany: State University of New York Press.

Zajonc, R. B. (1960). The process of cognitive tuning in communication. *Journal of Abnormal and Social Psychology, 61*, 159–167.

Zbrodoff, N. J., & Logan, G. D. (1986). On the autonomy of mental processes: A case study of arithmetic. *Journal of Experimental Psychology: General, 115*, 118–130.

DEVELOPING TRANSPARENT RELATIONSHIPS THROUGH HUMOR IN THE AUTHENTIC LEADER–FOLLOWER RELATIONSHIP

Larry W. Hughes

ABSTRACT

Relational transparency is necessary in a new age of leadership during which followers have nearly the same access, via technology and the Internet, to the same information as most of their leaders. Followers also demand to know the mission and goals of their leaders and are more skeptical of leaders' motives, especially in the wake of so many ethical dilemmas surrounding corporate activities. The relationally transparent, authentic leader may be able to employ humor to emphasize his or her transparency, but must do so in a way that is both tactful and appropriate. Organizational outcomes are discussed.

When the sea was calm,
  all ships alike
  Showed mastership in floating.

— William Shakespeare

Authentic Leadership Theory and Practice: Origins, Effects and Development
Monographs in Leadership and Management, Volume 3, 83–106
Copyright © 2005 by Elsevier Ltd.
All rights of reproduction in any form reserved

The preceding quotation was remarkably apt for corporations during the late 1990s when it seemed like getting rich was no more difficult than establishing a website. Organizational leaders were lauded as heroes and rewarded lavishly for steering their firms and investors to initial public offerings and stock prices that rivaled long-lived, blue-chip giants. However, when the waters became choppy in early 2001, and following the terrorist attacks later that year, it was all that many of these companies could do to keep from capsizing in the wake of the bursting bubble. Sometimes the leaders of these companies were found to be wholly lacking in the face of adversity. Authentic leaders are posited to be more effective captains especially when handling rough seas that require openness, high moral character, and transparency.

The origin of the modern discussion of transparency is found in Kernis (2003), who offered four critical components of authenticity, one of which is proposed to be relational in nature. Gardner, Avolio, Luthans, May, and Walumbwa (2005) referred to this as relational transparency, which is openness of information and idea sharing, appropriate self-disclosure and the evoking of higher levels of trustworthiness. It has also been cast as a critical component of authentic leadership development theory (Avolio, 2005; Gardner et al., 2005).

Relational transparency has been defined along two dimensions: (1) openness to information and ideas (Butler, 1991) and (2) appropriate self-disclosure that is based upon self-awareness (Avolio, Luthans, & Walumbwa, 2004). Relational transparency is self-disclosure comprised of an expression of any or all of four aspects of self-disclosure: goals/motives, identity, values, and emotions (GIVE). GIVE is activated by events occurring externally to one's self-awareness.

In conjunction with the role of relational transparency in the discussion of effective authentic leadership, humor is a construct that allows us to say things that we could not get away with saying otherwise. Consider, for example, the medieval court jester. The jester was allowed to say nearly anything he wished to ... provided that it was funny. Evidence of this is seen in various publications of and about that era. For example, in Shakespeare's (1962) *Love's Labor's Lost*, Costard, considered ignorant by many of the characters in the comedy, was able to speak candidly with the other characters through his use of humor. From a less dramaturgical perspective, a transparent follower may be able to employ an appropriate style of humor delivery to provide important feedback to her or his leader that might otherwise remain unsaid (Zinsser, 1995). Thus, humor is also proposed as an effective method of delivering a transparent message.

Humor is defined here by its theory of use, which can be one of three general theories of humor: arousal/affect, cognitive/perceptual, or superiority/behavioral. Affective humor theory considers attempts to reduce emotional tension via laughter (Berlyne, 1969; Freud, 1963); cognitive humor theory juxtaposes two contrasting objects or situations for which resolution results in laughter (Koestler, 1964; Meyer, 1997; Suls, 1983); and superiority theory asserts that an attempt to elicit laughter involves making someone or something the butt of a joke (Gruner, 1997; cf. Vinton, 1989).

In this chapter, I explore the importance of relational transparency and humor to authentic leadership, as well as their interactive effects on follower outcomes, including positive emotions, trust in the leader, and creativity.

AUTHENTICITY AND AUTHENTIC LEADERSHIP

Kernis (2003, p. 13) defined authenticity as "unobstructed operation of one's true, or core, self in one's daily enterprise." Four underlying components comprise authenticity in the Kernis model. These have been recast by Gardner et al., (2005) as (1) self-awareness, (2) balanced information processing, (3) authentic behavior, and (4) relational transparency. All four are essential to the discussion of authentic leadership. However, self-awareness and relational transparency are most critical to understanding the discussion presented in this chapter.

To be authentic, one must know, accept, and remain true to oneself regardless of environmental contingencies. For leaders who attempt to achieve greater self-awareness, authenticity is continuous and ranges from more to less authentic rather than existing in a dichotomous state in which we either are or are not authentic (Erickson, 1995).

Authenticity in leadership is an increasingly common topic of discussion in both the academic (Luthans & Avolio, 2003) and applied literatures (e.g., George, 2003). Avolio and colleagues (Avolio, 2005; Avolio, Gardner, Walumbwa, Luthans, & May, 2004; Gardner et al., 2005; Luthans & Avolio, 2003) have recognized the emergence of authentic leadership as a root construct of leadership. This means that nearly any style of leadership may operate upon this construct. Therefore, an authentic leader can be transformational, transactional, directive or participative, and be defined as an authentic leader. For example, the authentic transactional leader is self-aware and relationally transparent, but employs contingent rewards to motivate followers. In contrast, the authentic transformational leader may be equally self-aware and relationally transparent, but individually considerate and intellectually stimulating in eliciting follower performance.

George (2003) observed that authentic leaders are genuine and have intentions to not only serve others through their leadership, but also to empower their followers. Authentic leaders lead in a manner that their peers, followers, and other stakeholders recognize as authentic. Because such leaders are more transparent, are more open, and self-disclose more, they evoke higher levels of follower trust through personal identification with their followers (Gardner et al., 2005). Authentic leaders act according to their values, build relationships that enable followers to offer diverse viewpoints, and build social networks with followers. Authentic leaders also recognize followers' talents and see their job as one in which they nurture followers' talents into strengths (Luthans & Avolio, 2003).

RELATIONAL TRANSPARENCY

Transparency as a topic is emerging concurrently with the discussion of leader authenticity in the post-9/11 business literature. Authors of both popular and academic publications caution against the previously covert nature of managerial decision-making in which leaders possess information to the exclusion of followers (cf. Gardner et al., 2005; Pagano & Pagano, 2004).

Examples of academic discussions encompassing the notion of transparency include Brown and Starkey's (2000) suggestion that self-reflection and an identity-focused dialogue among organization members aids in establishing organizational identity and organizational learning processes. Another example is that of Jones and George (1998), who suggested that a free sharing of information and knowledge, contributing to unconditional or relational trust, leads to interpersonal cooperation and teamwork. Furthermore, Popper and Lipshitz (2000) explicitly identify what we are calling transparency, as well as leadership, as two factors that aid in the development of organizational learning. Also, Avolio (2005) discusses transparency as an important component of life-long leadership development.

Gardner et al., (2005) assert that authentic leaders will be "relatively transparent in expressing their true emotions and feelings to followers [when appropriate], while simultaneously regulating such emotions to minimize displays of inappropriate or potentially damaging emotions" (p. X). In other words, within relational transparency lies the commitment of a leader to help a follower to see the leader's true self. The leader attempts to establish the ultimate goal of trust, among other outcomes, through appropriate disclosure. Self-disclosure, is the expression of true emotions (Kernis, 2003), regulated to minimize inappropriate displays or potentially damaging effects (Gardner et al., 2005).

Although transparency in its most generic form may be revealed to have various elements, relational transparency is of greatest interest in this discussion of authentic leadership. Relational transparency "is relational in nature, inasmuch as it involves valuing and achieving openness and truthfulness in one's close relationships" (Kernis, 2003, p. 15) and occurs when a leader displays high levels of openness, self-disclosure, and trustworthiness in leader–follower relationships (Gardner et al., 2005).

In relational transparency, self-disclosure is comprised of the expression of the four aspects of self-disclosure: goals/motives, identity, values, and emotions (GIVE). These self-aspects are frequently activated by important events that are external to one's self-awareness. Therefore, the knowledge that makes one self-aware becomes manifested in behavior, or relational transparency. Also important to this discussion is the relevance of the information shared or the disclosures between leaders and followers.

The Dimensions of GIVE

The words "know thyself" have been etched over the portals of historical edifices throughout time. For example, "Gnothi se auton" was displayed over the entry of the Sun God Apollo's Oracle of Delphi temple in ancient Greece. "Temet Nosce" is the Latin version that admonishes its readers to look within themselves for answers to their questions. Plutarch and Socrates have also been attributed as offering this admonition to their acolytes. Today, it is used to discuss authenticity and authentic leadership (Harter, 2002).

In order to share oneself transparently, one must first be self-aware. Kernis (2003) described the awareness component of authenticity as that which involves "having awareness of, and trust in, one's motives, feelings, desires, and self-relevant cognitions" (p. 13). Self-awareness is a means to an end. It is a process by which persons come to reflect on their own unique values, identity, emotions, and goals and motives (Gardner et al., 2005). Authentic leaders are highly self-aware regarding their beliefs and values, which they act upon during interactions with followers and other organizational stakeholders (Gardner et al., 2005). Importantly, self-awareness is not the final step of a journey, but the journey itself along which a person tries to develop an understanding of his or her core values, purpose, and strengths (Luthans & Avolio, 2003).

Goals and Motives

Lord, Brown, and Freiberg (1999) presume the context of the working self-concept (Markus & Wurf, 1987) in their definition of goals: "contextualized schema that direct current information processing" (p. 180). For the authentic leader, his or her possible self will reflect "the leader's role as an agent for positive change with respect to themselves and others" (Gardner et al., 2005, p. X). Authentic leaders will transparently share their motives for pursuing specific organizational goals. There should be no secret as to why followers are asked to perform specific functions in the course of their work.

Identity

Identity is defined as "a theory (schema) of an individual that describes, interrelates, and explains his or her relevant features, characteristics, and experiences" (Schlenker, 1985, p. 68). Gardner et al., (2005) suggest that, for authentic leaders, identification is the process by which the role of leader is encompassed into one's interpersonal identity. Furthermore, follower identification is the process by which people come to define themselves as followers (Gardner & Avolio, 1998). Enactment of both forms of identification is operative when leaders and followers form an authentic relationship between them through private and public interactions characterized by openness, appropriate self-disclosure, and trustworthiness (Avolio, 2005; cf. Schlenker, 1985).

For example, if as a leader I share information with my followers about my passion for wallpapering and how this activity allows me to express myself (i.e., identity), the disclosure might be interesting or perhaps resonate with followers who also decorate. However, the disclosure is not particularly relevant and is not expected to have salience in developing an authentic leader–follower relationship.

Values

In the context of authentic leadership, values are defined as "conceptions of the desirable that guide the way social actors select actions, evaluate people and events, and explain their actions and evaluations" (Schwartz, 1999, pp. 24–25). As normative standards for behavior and evaluation, values are applied across situations (Schwartz, 1992) and provide a basis for actions that conform both to the needs of the overall community and individuals within it (Lord et al, 1999). Values, once internalized, become integral to one's self-system. However, they are learned through socialization for the benefit of serving groups. Therefore, authentic leaders learn values through socialization, but once their value systems are internalized, they are true to their values, to themselves, and resist social, situational, and environmental pressures to compromise these values (Erickson, 1995).

For example, if I disclose my opinion about an unpopular work-related issue despite the potential for being criticized, such as an impending reengineering of technology that is not being integrated in the spirit of the organization's social processes, the disclosure is highly relevant and relational transparency is expected to manifest.

Emotions

Self-awareness goes beyond the simple knowledge of one's goals and motives, identity, and values. It also includes the knowledge of one's emotions, which has been offered as a determinant of effective leadership (Avolio, 2003). With regard to relational transparency, authentic leaders are hypothesized to express their true emotions to followers, but also regulate them to ensure that these displays are appropriate. However, this emotional intelligence does not simply encompass emotional self-awareness, but also an understanding of, over time, the causes and effects of emotions on cognitive processes and decision-making. Essentially, as authentic leaders become more self-aware, their relationships will become more open and, subsequently, an appropriate sharing of thoughts and feelings will occur.

HUMOR

... so Batman and Robin asked Superman, "was Wonder Woman surprised to see you?" and he said, "No, but the Invisible Man sure was!"
– Anonymous U.S. Marine at a Fairfax, Virginia tavern (1986)

The preceding punch line of an interminable, but well told joke is the product of incongruity humor, a cognitive-perceptual form of humor that is also a primary theory of humor in the topic's broad and eclectic history.

There are a variety of techniques for eliciting humor. Although scholars widely differ on specific techniques, Berger (1992) offers a typology of 45 techniques for the elicitation of humor. This considerable list appears to contain the vast majority of common techniques for eliciting humor, such as sarcasm, satire, slapstick, and parody, to name a few.

But what does humor have to do with authenticity, and specifically relational transparency? Relational transparency is self-disclosure along the GIVE dimensions, but humor is simply clowning around by those who are at play. Or is it?

Zinsser (1995) provided examples of literary humorists who performed acts of courage by attempting to convey serious material in a manner that heightened a truth to a level at which its stark reality is revealed. Along the way the humorist also hopes that it will be seen as funny. Examples include the late Erma Bombeck's views on parenting, George Will's acerbic, but cerebral and witty social commentary, and Garrison Keillor's parodies of everything leaving itself open to criticism!

For example, a leader can heighten a truth to a level of revelation because humor helps organization members create psychological distance between themselves and difficult issues. A categorical example of this is the gallows humor of workers on the frontline of an otherwise emotional issue. Specifically, paramedics may heighten the level of reality about death, dying, injury, and illness to cope with the visceral mess they face daily. Similarly, teachers may joke about children bullying other children in situations that might elicit tears from people who do not see its effects on a daily basis. This does not mean that paramedics and teachers are callous and lack compassion and empathy, but that their roles place them at the center of such matters and expose them to a high emotional cost, without providing a release valve that still allows them to work.

Conceptualization of Humor

A scientist could invest her career reading about humor in hundreds of books, countless articles in academic and popular publications, and in scores of research studies devoted to its study (cf. Roeckelein, 2002). This work would span academic disciplines as diverse as literatures in communication, psychology, anthropology, and possibly more. Even in the management sciences, humor and its effects have been studied (e.g., Avolio, Howell, & Sosik, 1999; Cooper, in press; Rizzo, Booth-Butterfield, & Wanzer, 1999; Vinton, 1989).

Rosaline, in Shakespeare's (1962) *Love's Labor's Lost*, aptly summarized the elusive and ephemeral nature of humor when she said "A jest's prosperity lies in the ear/of him that hears it/never in the tongue/of him that makes it" (p. 42). But the definition of humor is as elusive as its nature. Scholars, in their repeated attempts to develop taxonomies of humor, have inadvertently confused and confounded the discussion.

Many behavioral scientists have attempted to tackle the humor construct, but most theories are simply descriptive and taxonomic accounts that explain the effects of humor, but not why it occurs. A review of the scientific literature on humor reveals that attempts to establish an overarching theory of humor have largely been abandoned for more focused, specific efforts on behalf of researchers. Many definitions of humor use laughter and other humor outcomes to explain humor (cf. Roeckelein, 2002). This tautological approach lacks rigor in defining precisely what humor is. In lieu of establishing an overarching definition of humor, it may be more easily defined by how it is viewed in a theoretical sense. Eysenck (1942; cf. Nias, 1981) offered a typology that is not only an enduring, pithy psychological model, but has been used repeatedly in the last 60 years of humor research.

Eysenck's (1942) model offers a merger of the affective, cognitive, and conative theories of humor (Fig. 1). Another dimension included in the model is the orectic, which is a combination of the affective and conative theories. Other leading theorists have elaborated upon this model, but retained its basic features. See Table 1 for a contrast of the three theories. For example, Lefcourt and Martin (1986) identified a typology of three humor theories: arousal, incongruity and superiority. Raskin (1985) summarized various humor theories into three categories: psychoanalytical (e.g., Freud, 1963); cognitive-perceptual, and social-behavioral.

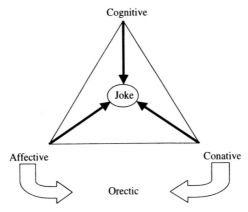

Fig. 1. Eysenck's (1942) Humor Typology (Adapted from Nias, 1981).

Table 1.   Modern Typologies of Humor Theories.

Eysenck (1942)	Raskin (1985)	Lefcourt and Martin (1986)
Affective	Psychoanalytical	Arousal
Cognitive	Cognitive-perceptual	Incongruity
Conative	Social-behavioral	Superiority
Orectic		

The first two theories – affective/arousal and cognitive/incongruity – are helpful in explaining why jokes are funny. However, conative/superiority theory is offered here as an explanation of humor. In fact, Gruner (1997) considers superiority theory to be the only explanatory basis for humor, because all humor has some element of superiority to it. Gruner said that every joke, riddle or pun contains a target, or a butt, and challenges anyone to provide a joke, even a so called harmless joke, that can withstand dissection. The three types of humor theory are discussed below.

Arousal Theories
Arousal theories focus on *why* things are funny and are those in which humor induced laughter reduces built-up tension. These are also known as affect theories of humor. Early work serving as the basis of more modern conceptualizations of arousal theories include Joubert's physio-psychological theory of laughter, Descartes' discussion of the physiological and psychological aspects of affect-based humor, and McDougall's relief theory (Roeckelein, 2002). Modern discussions include Freud's theory of humor; Berlyne's notion of a relationship between physiological arousal and subjective pleasure; and Apter's reversal theory, which concerns the meta-motivational states that define one's sense of humor (Lefcourt, 2001).

Incongruity Theories
Incongruity or cognitive-perceptual theory tells us *what* it is about humor that makes it funny, specifically, with regard to jokes. Early thinkers who discussed the cognitive theories included Cicero, Locke, Kant, and Schopenhauer (Eysenck, 1942). The work of these philosophers led to the current, central premise of incongruity theory that things that one finds funny must be somewhat unexpected or inappropriate, or perhaps illogical or ambiguous (Meyer, 1997). Koestler (1964) offered the term bisociation, which occurs when cognitive elements are salient when two normally disparate and

incompatible frames of reference, such as ideals or situations, are brought together unexpectedly. This dual perception is what makes a good joke funny.

Suls (1977, 1983) further argued that simple incongruity does not elicit humor without the joker offering resolution to the dissonance. In other words, simple juxtaposition of two seemingly incompatible situations is not necessarily funny without explanation. For example, the punch line of a joke makes sense of information provided earlier. Common examples of bisociation are jokes that present several clerics of disparate faiths walking into a tavern. The collection of clergy of different faith is incongruous as is the presentation of them walking into a tavern. A punch line, provided later, will resolve these incongruities and, hopefully, make us laugh.

Superiority Theories

Gruner (1997) argues that the fragile nucleus of humor depends on either a sense of our own superiority or on a sense of the inferiority of others, an argument that reaches us as far back as Plato and Aristotle. It was Hobbes who said that laughter occurs when "a sudden glory [arises] from some sudden conception of some eminency in ourselves; by comparison with the infirmity of others, or with our own formerly" (Berlyne, 1969, p.801). From the perspective of superiority theory, every other theory is merely descriptive of humor as a phenomenon and encompassed as sub-theories of superiority.

Superiority theory holds that actors derive pleasure as the result of someone else's misfortune. This pleasure occurs without the actor experiencing cognitive dissonance or fear of social censure. Most humor techniques, or specific uses of humor, fall under this category. Berlyne (1969) offers several examples, including absurdity, facetiousness, parody, sarcasm and satire.

Can We have Fun at Work?

Work in itself does not have to be laborious, joyless, brutally repetitious, isolated in its performance, and, in general, deformative of human beings.

– O'Hare (1992)

In *Animals, Inc.*, authors Tucker and Allman (2004) discuss organizational issues from the perspective of the barnyard. This slim volume is an example of how an author can heighten truth to a level of absurdity (e.g., farm animals engaging in discussion) in order to deliver conventional wisdom without hundreds of pages of admonition.

Theoretical and empirical work in the organization sciences has revealed positive effects of humor at work. Avolio et al. (1999) studied the moderating influence of humor on leadership and organizational outcomes in the banking and insurance industries. They found that usage of humor (high vs. low) in different leadership styles along the full range model moderated the influence on different performance outcomes (individual and unit). For instance, transformational leadership was significantly and positively related to use of humor and to both performance outcomes, whereas contingent reward was positively related to use of humor, but negatively related to both performance outcomes. An avoidant leadership style was negatively related to use of humor and to both levels of performance outcomes.

Kahn (1989) proposed humor as a tool for organizational change. Vinton (1989) found that humor alleviated status differentials and workplace tension between organization members. Humor has also been found to enhance employee perceptions of manager effectiveness (Rizzo et al., 1999). Other conceptual articles have supported the notion that humor is essential and important in organizations. For example, Cooper (in press) offers a discussion of how humor behavior enhances the effects of ingratiation. Other scholars have proposed the value of humor to improve work group performance (Duncan, 1982; Duncan, Smeltzer, & Leap, 1990) and as a management tool (Malone, 1980).

Geuens and De Pelsmacker (2002) suggest that leader's can use humor as an effective means of persuasion. Humor can also be a sturdy bridge between managers and employees, thus helping them to identify with each other and share perspectives of their organization (Fox & Amichai-Hamburger, 2001). Kahn (1989) argued that our ability, as an organization member, to psychologically align ourselves with the detached perspective offered by humor, depends partly on our already sufficient detachment from a situation, which allows us to perceive its humor without bias.

So, what does this have to do with transparency? In any form of communication, a target audience receives a sender's message, but noise in the communication process sometimes impedes the delivery of a message. One way to mitigate noise is to select a form of delivery that circumvents it. However, care must be taken in choosing a style of delivery or the message will be interpreted as either too bold, or perhaps too subtle, resulting in misunderstanding. Due to this potential dilemma, a sender may elect to not offer a message at all for fear of being misunderstood. Therefore, the true value of humor lies in the sender's ability to employ it to say something that might otherwise have been left unsaid (Zinsser, 1995).

How can Humor be Used to Elicit Transparency?

According to Plato, laughter is directed at those who violate the precept "know thyself" provided that they are weak and innocuous (Berlyne, 1969). However, I propose here that possessing a sense of humor is the essence of knowing oneself and sharing one's authentic self, transparently, with followers.

Previously presented was Gruner's (1997) argument that all humor can be classified under superiority theory. At its most fundamental, humor results from, as Hobbes said, a sudden glory of seeing our superiority in relation to someone else or of us in our former naiveté. Therefore, two ways by which a humorous message can be delivered is through self or other derogation, or making fun of ourselves or someone else.

Humor is not always employed in order to elevate oneself in relation to others. For example, putdown humor has been found to have a socializing effect in temporary groups provided that certain "rules" of its use are observed (Lennox-Terrion & Ashforth, 2002). Furthermore, Vinton (1989) suggested that self-directed ridicule is well used by leaders who wish to communicate to followers that he or she has a sense of humor and can laugh at him or herself. Self-directed humor makes a powerful statement to followers, and thus enables followers to see leaders as accessible rather than remote, capable of adopting detached perspectives on themselves, and worthy of emulation (Kahn, 1989). If leaders can laugh at themselves, they create conditions that are more relational and thus communication is proposed to become more transparent.

BENEFITS OF TRANSPARENCY AND HUMOR TO FOLLOWERS

There are a variety of outcomes, beneficial for followers of authentic leaders who are relationally transparent. Gardner et al., (2005) and Avolio et al., (2004) have presented several outcomes that have been offered as sharing a consistent linkage with authenticity. Three in particular are trust, engagement, and well-being. Here, I will expand upon the trust discussion as specifically influenced by transparency and will also highlight other outcomes, including positive emotions and creative performance.

Positive Emotions

Ekvall (1996) found that there is emotional safety in organizational relationships in which ideas and opinions are shared and communication is
open and straightforward. In other words, people can find positive meaning
in their connectedness with others and positive meaning evokes positive
emotions (Fredrickson, 1998). Gardner et al. (2005) suggest that interpersonal intimacy results from relational transparency. By evoking personal
meaning in a relationship with followers, manifested in the openness and
appropriate self-disclosure that defines relational transparency, a leader may
evoke positive emotions in followers. However, the relational benefits of the
authentic leader–follower relationship do not simply accrue for the follower.
When leaders succeed in achieving transparency, they give something and
get something in return in the leader–follower relationship. In the transparent relationship, the situation is win-win.

Emotions are a conscious or unconscious multi-component response tendency that evolves and manifests over relatively short time segments (Fredrickson, 1998), and are comprised of the personal meaning found in the
person–environment relationship (Lazarus, 1991). Emotions have an object,
or signify some *thing* (e.g., occurrence). Emotions also involve an appraisal
process that triggers response tendencies, such as subjective experiences,
physiological changes, and facial expressions (e.g., the Duchenne smile;
Fredrickson, 1998).

Recently, Fredrickson (1998, 2002, 2003) Fredrickson and Joiner (2002)
discussed positive emotions within the emerging body of knowledge known
as positive psychology. Fredrickson (1998) has discussed four categories of
positive emotions – joy, interest, contentment, and love – that contain other
similar emotions. Love has been proposed as a core category containing a
symbiosis of the other three categories.

Fredrickson (2002, 2003) argues that positive emotions should not be
viewed from the traditional perspective that emotions are simply urges to act
in particular ways or specific action tendencies (e.g., fight-or-flight). Instead,
distinct theories should be developed for each of the positive and negative
categories of emotions. Although appropriate for the discussion of negative
emotions and responses, specific actions have not been linked to positive
emotions (e.g., joy); instead, positive emotions are more appropriately
viewed as feeling states than specific, physiological responses to stimuli
(Fredrickson, 2003). In response to the observed need for theory, Fredrickson (1998, 2002, 2003) has offered a model of thought-action tendencies that
are elicited by positive emotions. Negative emotions are local feeling states

that *narrow* response repertoires to specific actions. Conversely, positive emotions are hypothesized as global feeling states that *broaden* response repertoires.

Fredrickson's broaden-and-build theory suggests that thought-action repertoires can be developed, or built, to strengthen personal resources (i.e., physical, intellectual, social, and psychological; Fredrickson, 2003). *Broadening* of thought-action repertoires enables people to explore novel approaches to thought and action, or the broadening of attention and cognition. The *build* component refers to the person's ability to develop their various personal resources (e.g., intellectual, psychological, physical, and social). The hypotheses that reciprocal relationships between positive emotions, broadened cognitions, and positive meaning trigger upward spirals toward emotional well-being have been supported empirically (Fredrickson & Joiner, 2002).

When thought-action repertoires are developed, the outcomes result in "upward spirals toward optimal individual and organizational functioning" (Fredrickson, 2003, p. 163). This is accomplished, to some extent, through a broadening of the cognitive context (Isen, 1987), which produces flexible and creative patterns of thought (Fredrickson & Joiner, 2002). These broadened mindsets have long-term benefits in the building of personal and enduring resources (Fredrickson, 2003).

One implication of Fredrickson's (2002) broaden-and-build theory is that leaders can evoke global, positive emotions in followers by *broadening* their thought–action repertoires and further aid followers' in *building* their personal resources in order to mitigate future occurrences of negative emotions (Fredrickson, 2003). I propose that the authentic leader can accomplish this by behaving in a relationally transparent manner.

Follower Trust in Leader

Trust is an important proximal outcome of the leader–follower relationship. Relational authenticity is posited to produce greater trust in interpersonal relationships (Kernis, 2003) and leaders who are relationally transparent are predicted to achieve high levels of follower trust (Avolio et al., 2004; Gardner et al., 2005).

Organizational relationships in which ideas and opinions are brought forward and shared, and communication is open and straightforward, foster high levels of trust (Ekvall, 1996). This assertion is well supported in the organizational literature (Argyris, 1962; Butler, 1991; Farris, Senner,

& Butterfield, 1972; Hart, Capps, Cangemi, & Caillouet, 1986; Mayer, Davis, & Schoorman, 1995). Butler (1991; see also Butler & Cantrell, 1984) conducted a series of studies to develop a scale to measure conditions of trust in a specific target person (e.g., leader). Results revealed that openness predicts trust across several samples of students and working adults. Jennings (1971) and Gabarro (1978) likewise found that integrity and openness were the most critical determinants of followers' trust in a leader.

A variety of trust definitions exist in the management literature. One definition describes trust as the willingness of an individual to be vulnerable to the actions of another person or group (Mayer et al., 1995) in situations that involve some degree of risk (Deutsch, 1958). In addition to risk, factors like benevolence, competence, and honesty are typically perceived as being indicative of trust (Mayer et al., 1995). In this vein, trust can be addressed on personal level by considering the psychology of the individual.

Cummings and Bromiley (1996, p. 303) raised the level of analysis distinction in their definition based on the assumption that trust is socially embedded within interactions among organization members. Leadership is likewise viewed as a social influence process that is dependent upon trusting relationships for maximum effectiveness. The rationale for this definition of trust rests on the socially embedded, subjective, and optimistic nature of most interactions within and between people. This definition considers *why* people trust and *why* trust declines or increases (Tyler & Kramer, 1996).

Rousseau, Sitkin, Burt, and Camerer (1998, p. 395) suggest that trust is one party's willingness to be vulnerable, based on a positive expectation that the other party intends to perform an action that benefits the first party. Jones and George (1998) advanced a two-factor theoretical discussion in support of the socio-emotional perspective of trust. *Conditional* trust is defined as a transactional trust state in which all parties are willing to transact provided that the other behaves in an appropriate manner, acceptable to the other party. On the other hand, *unconditional* trust occurs when the so-called "pretense of suspending belief" has occurred and is based more on confidence in the other party than on the transactional nature of the relationship (Jones & George, 1998, p. 535). It is this unconditional form of trust that a leader endeavors to create in the authentic leader–follower relationship. However, this occurs through conditional means.

By developing a conditional trust relationship, fertile ground is provided for an unconditional trust relationship. By sharing information, and being vulnerable through self-disclosure, the authentic leader establishes the first link of a reciprocal chain of trust. In time, and through consistency of behavior, and congruence between espoused and enacted values, the authentic leader–follower relationship becomes established.

Creative Performance

Transparency and humor have been posited here as important causal agents impacting followers' positive emotions and trust in leader. I also propose that both can mediate the more distal relationships between the two independent variables and follower creative performance.

Creativity and individual creative processes are not new topics in the behavioral sciences. Both have been studied extensively, but little within the realm of the leader–follower relationship (Mumford, Scott, Gaddis, & Strange, 2002). This is surprising because innovation and creative performance is an important and inimitable core competency for the attainment of a sustainable competitive advantage (Hambrick & Fredrickson, 2001; Lei & Slocum, 2005).

Bass (1985) discussed the effects of organizational culture and climate on openness and trust and subsequent follower performance. Recently, Mumford et al. (2002) synthesized research papers on creativity as related to leadership published since 1990. Jaussi and Dionne (2003) contributed to the literature with their study of the effects of unconventional leader behavior on followers' creative performance at both the individual and group levels of analysis. Unconventional leader behavior was determined to be a construct distinct from transformational leadership and explained additional variance in group cohesion.

Other studies explore leaders' contributions to problem construction and follower efficacy beliefs and resultant creativity (Redmond, Mumford, & Teach, 1993); the positive effects of transformational leadership on group fluency and flexibility (Sosik, Avolio, & Kahai, 1998); and the combined, mediating roles of flow and anonymity between transformational leadership and creativity in the context of a group decision support system (Sosik, Kahai, & Avolio, 1999).

Positive Affect and Creativity
Ekvall (1996) found that members who were emotionally involved in an organization's operations and goals were also more creative. Those who were more playful and who worked in climates in which humor and light mood were fostered were also more innovative. These positive outcomes are posited to produce thought patterns that are both flexible and creative

(Fredrickson, 1998; Fredrickson & Joiner, 2002). Empirical support for this assertion has been offered by Isen (1993;cf. Isen, Johnson, Mertz, & Robinson, 1985) who suggested that positive affect tends to promote exploration and enjoyment of new ideas and possibilities. Ruch (1993) asserts that humor has a positive influence on exhilaration, which influences creativity. Furthermore, participants exposed to comedic humor have been shown to possess higher levels of positive affect and are subsequently more creative on performance tasks (Humke & Schaefer, 1996; Isen, Daubman, & Nowicki, 1987).

Creativity and Trust
Fukuyama (1995) argues that individual creativity is empowered by trust. Ekvall (1996) supported this powerful statement empirically. Findings revealed that openness and trust lead to creativity at work when ideas and opinions are brought forward and shared, and communication is open and straightforward. Amabile and colleagues (Amabile, 1983; Amabile, Goldfarb, & Brackenfield, 1990) have suggested that in order to be creative, individuals need freedom to take risks. Willingness to take risks is a component of the trust construct (Mayer et al., 1995; Meyerson, Weick, & Kramer, 1996) thus making trust an antecedent to creativity. Furthermore, because trust is hypothesized to be an outcome of relational transparency, the indirect relationship of the latter to creativity is noted.

Through the verbal expression of trust, leaders can convince followers that they possess the capability for creativity (Tierney & Farmer, 2002). Avolio (1999) cited evidence that transformational leaders stimulate their followers' efforts toward innovation and creativity. They do so by challenging assumptions and looking at new and routine problems from new and alternative perspectives. Furthermore, trust in the leader can have "dramatic, positive effects on a team's effort" (p. 120).

IMPLICATIONS FOR RESEARCH AND PRACTICE

Humor and relational transparency are challenging topics to study in organizational settings. Both are ephemeral, highly context-driven and the effects often reside in the eye of the beholder. Duncan et al., (1990) warned that despite longevity as a theoretical discussion, humor lacks a clear operational definition and many scholars elect to focus within the seemingly boundless theory of humor on variables that can be measured. For example, in Avolio et al., (1999), humor was operationalized as a leader's "use of humor" and measured based upon existing and valid tools. Similarly, relational transparency lies, in part, in the eye of the beholder. Moreover, it is likely to overlap conceptually with similar constructs such as information clarity and content.

With the growing understanding of the relationships of humor and transparency to authentic leadership, care must be taken in applying them to the workplace. It is possible that the organizational context is likely to mediate followers' receptiveness to both practices. In the spirit of Rousseau and Fried (2001), context should be established in the emerging study of these constructs whether or not humor manifests in different responses and outcomes depending upon industry and geographic placement.

For example, Avolio et al. (1999) found, as discussed previously, that the effects of transformational leadership on individual and unit performance were positively moderated by use of humor. This study occurred in a large financial institution, which is stereotypically serious and we might expect that its members would respond differently to attempts at humor or self-disclosure than, say, those employees of a software development company or a governmental agency. Because the study of humor in organizations has not yet considered the impact of context on outcomes, future research endeavors should consider the role of context.

In addition to the organizational context, humor and relational transparency in differing national cultures is another important area for future research. In other organizations, conditions such as power distance and affective differences may dictate the appropriate use of humor and relational transparency. A joke that is typically funny in one culture may not likely elicit the same degree of laughter if told within the context of another culture (McCullough, 1993). We suggest that the implications of these potential differences on cross-cultural leader–follower relationships may influence trust relationships, as well as cultural appropriateness.

DEVELOPMENT OF AUTHENTIC LEADERS

One goal of this chapter is to contribute to the central theme of this book: developing authentic leaders. Here, the causal agents for positive and trusting leader–follower relationships are humor use and relational transparency. Do we suggest that leaders try to be funnier? Or that they bare their souls to their followers? No. However, like any other aspect of authentic leadership development, leaders should be made aware of the effects of these independent variables on important follower outcomes, such as higher levels of positive emotions, greater trust in the leader, and creativity and innovation. Furthermore, leaders should understand their own capability to behave in a relationally transparent manner and, perhaps, use humor in an appropriate manner in order to leverage its effects.

For example, humor may enhance the enjoyment of positive life experiences (Lefcourt, 2001) and research supporting this notion includes studies in which greater levels of humor were associated with a more positive self-concept (i.e., higher self-esteem) and greater positive affect in response to both positive and negative life events (Martin, Kuiper, Olinger, & Dance, 1993). Both findings contribute to the creation of a positive culture, or institution, which Seligman (2003) identifies as the third pillar of positive psychology, which supports the first two, which are positive emotions and positive traits and abilities.

By continuing to study and also sharing with leaders the important interactive effects of relational transparency and humor, researchers can encourage them to consider these variables in their personal, life-long, leadership development programs. In the quest for self-awareness, leaders who assess their own sense of humor will discover and understand their strengths and limitations. Furthermore, by educating leaders about the process of self-awareness, they will also discover what a relationally transparent disclosure is. By disclosing, appropriately, along the dimensions of GIVE, and leveraging their effort with an appropriate style of humor delivery, the leader is likely to find that the resultant interactive effects have powerful effects on both individuals and organizations.

REFERENCES

Amabile, T. M. (1983). *The social psychology of creativity.* New York: Springer.

Amabile, T. M., Goldfarb, P., & Brackfield, S. C. (1990). Social influences on creativity: Evaluation, coaction, and surveillance. *Creativity Research Journal, 3*, 6–21.

Argyris, C. (1962). *Interpersonal competence and organizational effectiveness.* Homewood, IL: Dorsey.

Avolio, B. J. (1999). *Full leadership development: Building the vital forces in organizations.* Thousand Oaks, CA: Sage.

Avolio, B. J. (2003). Examining the full range model of leadership: Looking back to transform forward. In: D. Day & S. Zaccarro (Eds), *Leadership development for transforming organizations: Grow leaders for tomorrow* (pp. 71–98). Mahwah, NJ: Erlbaum.

Avolio, B. J. (2005). *Leadership development in balance: Made/Born.* Mahwah, NJ: Erlbaum.

Avolio, B. J., Gardner, W. L., Walumbwa, F. O., Luthans, F., & May, D. R. (2004). Unlocking the mask A look at the process by which authentic leaders impact follower attitudes and behaviors. *The Leadership Quarterly, 15,* 801–823.

Avolio, B. J., Howell, J. M., & Sosik, J. J. (1999). A funny thing happened on the way to the bottom line: Humor as a moderator of leadership style effects. *Academy of Management Journal, 42,* 219–227.

Avolio, B. J., Luthans, F., & Walumbwa, F. O. (2004). Authentic leadership: Theory-building for veritable sustained performance. Working Paper, Gallup Leadership Institute, University of Nebraska-Lincoln.

Bass, B. M. (1985). *Leadership and performance beyond expectations.* New York, NY: Free Press.

Berger, A. (1992). *An anatomy of humor.* New Brunswick, NJ: Transaction Publishers.

Berlyne, D. (1969). Laughter, humor, and play. In: G. Lindzey & E. Aronson (Eds), *Handbook of social psychology,* (Vol. 3, pp. 795–852). Reading, MA: Addison-Wesley.

Brown, A. D., & Starkey, K. (2000). Organizational identity and learning: A psychodynamic perspective. *Academy of Management Review, 25,* 102–120.

Butler, J. K. (1991). Toward understanding and measuring conditions of trust: Evolution of a conditions of trust inventory. *Journal of Management, 17,* 643–663.

Butler, J. K., & Cantrell, R. S. (1984). A behavioral decision theory approach to modeling dyadic trust in superiors and subordinates. *Psychological Reports, 55,* 19–28.

Cooper, C. D. (in press). Just joking around?: Employee humor expression as an ingratiatory behavior. *Academy of Management Review.*

Cummings, L. L., & Bromiley, P. (1996). The organizational trust inventory (OTI): Development and validation. In: R. Kramer & T. Tyler (Eds), *Trust in organizations: Frontiers of theory and research* (pp. 302–330). Thousand Oaks, CA: Sage.

Deutsch, M. (1958). Trust and suspicion. *Journal of Conflict Resolution, 2,* 265–279.

Duncan, W. J. (1982). Humor in management: Prospects for administrative practice and research. *Academy of Management Review, 7,* 136–142.

Duncan, W. J., Smeltzer, L. R., & Leap, T. L. (1990). Humor and work: Applications of joking behavior to management. *Journal of Management, 16,* 255–278.

Ekvall, G. (1996). Organizational climate for creativity and innovation. *European Journal of Work and Organizational Psychology, 5,* 105–123.

Erickson, R. J. (1995). Our society, our selves: Becoming authentic in an inauthentic world. *Advanced Development, 6,* 27–39.

Eysenck, H. J. (1942). The appreciation of humor: An experimental and theoretical study. *British Journal of Psychology, 32,* 295–309.

Farris, G., Senner, E., & Butterfield, D. (1972). Trust, culture and organizational behavior. *Industrial Relations, 12,* 144–157.

Fox, S., & Amichai-Hamburger, Y. (2001). The power of emotional appeals in promoting organizational change programs. *Academy of Management Executive, 15,* 84–94.

Fredrickson, B. L. (1998). What good are positive emotions? *Review of General Psychology, 2,* 300–319.

Fredrickson, B. L. (2002). Positive emotions. In: C. R. Snyder & S. J. Lopez (Eds), *Handbook of positive psychology* (pp. 120–134). New York: Oxford University Press.

Fredrickson, B. L. (2003). Positive emotions and upward spirals in organizations. In: K. S. Cameron, J. E. Dutton & R. E. Quinn (Eds), *Positive organizational scholarship* (pp. 163–175). San Francisco, CA: Berrett-Koehler.

Fredrickson, B. L., & Joiner, T. (2002). Research report: Positive emotions trigger upward spirals toward emotional well-being. *Psychological Science, 13*, 172–175.

Freud, S. (1963). In: J. Strachey (Ed.), *Jokes and their relation to the unconscious.* New York, NY: Norton, (Original work published 1905).

Fukuyama, F. (1995). *Trust: The social virtues and the creation of prosperity.* New York, NY: Free Press.

Gabarro, J. J. (1978). The development of trust influence and expectations. In: A. G. Athos & J. J. Gabarro (Eds), *Interpersonal behavior: Communication and understanding in relationships* (pp. 290–303). Englewood Cliffs, NJ: Prentice-Hall.

Gardner, W. L., & Avolio, B. J. (1998). The charismatic relationship A dramaturgical perspective. *Academy of Management Review, 23*(1), 32–58.

Gardner, W. L., Avolio, B. J., Luthans, F., May, D. R., & Walumbwa, F. O. (2005). Can you see the real Me?: A self-based model of authentic leader and follower development. *The Leadership Quarterly, 16*(3), 343–372.

George, B. (2003). *Authentic leadership: Rediscovering the secrets to creating lasting value.* San Francisco, CA: Jossey-Bass.

Geuens, M., & De Pelsmacker, P. (2002). The role of humor in the persuasion of individuals varying needs for cognition. *Advances in Consumer Research, 29*, 50–56.

Gruner, C. R. (1997). *The game of humor: A comprehensive theory of why we laugh.* New Brunswick, NJ: Transaction Publishers.

Hambrick, D. C., & Fredrickson, J. W. (2001). Are you sure you have a strategy? *Academy of Management Executive, 15*, 48–59.

Hart, K. M., Capps, H. R., Cangemi, J. P., & Caillouet, L. M. (1986). Exploring organizational trust and its multiple dimensions: A case study of General Motors. *Organization Development Journal, 4*, 31–39.

Harter, S. (2002). Authenticity. In: C. R. Snyder & S. Lopez (Eds), *Handbook of positive psychology* (pp. 382–394). Oxford, UK: Oxford University Press.

Humke, C., & Schaefer, C. (1996). Sense of humor and creativity. *Perceptual and Motor Skills, 82*(2), 544–546.

Isen, A. M. (1987). Positive affect, cognitive processes and social behavior. *Advances in Experimental Social Psychology, 20*, 203–253.

Isen, A. M. (1993). Positive affect and decision making. In: M. Lewis & J. M. Haviland (Eds), *Handbook of emotions* (pp. 261–277). New York, NY: Guilford Press.

Isen, A. M., Daubman, K. A., & Nowicki, G. P. (1987). Positive affect facilitates creative problem solving. *Journal of Personality and Social Psychology, 52*, 1122–1131.

Isen, A. M., Johnson, M. M., Mertz, E., & Robinson, G. F. (1985). The influence of positive affect on the unusualness of word associations. *Journal of Personality and Social Psychology, 48*, 1413–1426.

Jaussi, D. S., & Dionne, S. D. (2003). Leading for creativity: The role of unconventional leader behavior. *The Leadership Quarterly, 14*, 475–498.

Jennings, E. E. (1971). *Routes to the executive suite.* New York, NY: McGraw-Hill.

Jones, G. R., & George, J. M. (1998). The experience and evolution of trust: Implications for cooperation and teamwork. *Academy of Management Review, 23*, 531–546.

Kahn, W. (1989). Toward a sense of organizational humor: Implications for organizational diagnosis and change. *Journal of Applied Behavioral Science, 25*, 45–63.

Kernis, M. H. (2003). Toward a conceptualization of optimal self-esteem. *Psychological Inquiry, 14*, 1–26.

Koestler, A. (1964). *The act of creation.* New York, NY: Macmillan.

Lazarus, R. S. (1991). *Emotion and adaptation.* New York, NY: Oxford.

Lefcourt, H. M. (2001). *Humor: The psychology of living buoyantly.* New York, NY: Kluwer Academic/Plenum Publishers.

Lefcourt, H. M., & Martin, R. A. (1986). *Humor and life stress: Antidote to adversity.* New York, NY: Springer.

Lei, D., & Slocum, J. W. (2005). Strategic and organizational requirements for competitive advantage. *Academy of Management Executive, 19,* 31–45.

Lennox-Terrion, J., & Ashforth, B. E. (2002). From 'I' to 'we': The role of putdown humor and identity in the development of a temporary group. *Human Relations, 55,* 55–88.

Lord, R. G., Brown, D. J., & Freiberg, S. J. (1999). Understanding the dynamics of leadership: The role of follower self-concepts in the leader/follower relationship. *Organizational Behavior & Human Decision Processes, 78,* 167–203.

Luthans, F., & Avolio, B. J. (2003). Authentic leadership development. In: K. S. Cameron, J. E. Dutton & R. E. Quinn (Eds), *Positive organizational scholarship* (pp. 241–258). San Francisco, CA: Berrett-Koehler.

Malone, P. B. (1980). Humor: A double-edged tool for today's managers? *Academy of Management Review, 5,* 357–360.

Markus, H. R., & Wurf, E. (1987). The dynamic self-concept: A social psychological perspective. *American Review of Psychology, 38,* 299–337.

Martin, R. A., Kuiper, N. A., Olinger, L. J., & Dance, K. A. (1993). Humor, coping with stress, self-concept, and psychological well-being. *Humor: International Journal of Humor Research, 6,* 89–104.

Mayer, R. C., Davis, J. H., & Schoorman, F. D. (1995). An integrative model of organizational trust. *Academy of Management Review, 20,* 709–735.

Meyer, J. C. (1997). Humor in member narratives: Uniting and dividing at work. *Western Journal of Communication, 61,* 188–209.

Meyerson, D., Weick, K. E., & Kramer, R. (1996). Swift trust and temporary groups. In: R. Kramer & T. Tyler (Eds), *Trust in organizations: Frontiers of theory and research* (pp. 166–195). Thousand Oaks, CA: Sage.

McCullough, L. S. (1993). A cross-cultural test of the two-part typology of humor. *Perceptual and Motor Skills, 76*(3, pt 2), 1275–1281.

Mumford, M. D., Scott, G. M., Gaddis, B., & Strange, J. (2002). Leading creative people: Orchestrating expertise and relationships. *The Leadership Quarterly, 13,* 705–750.

Nais, D. K. B. (1981). Humor and personality. In: R. Lynn (Ed.), *Dimensions of personality: Papers in honour of H. J. Eysenck* (pp. 287–313). Oxford, UK: Pergamon.

Pagano, B., & Pagano, E. (2004). *The transparency edge: How credibility can make or break you in business.* New York: McGraw-Hill.

Popper, M., & Lipshitz, R. (2000). Organizational learning. *Management Learning, 31,* 181–196.

Raskin, V. (1985). *Semantic mechanisms of humor.* Boston, MA: Reidel Publishing Co.

Redmond, M. R., Mumford, M. D., & Teach, R. J. (1993). Putting creativity to work Leader influences on subordinate creativity. *Organizational Behavior and Human Decision Processes, 55,* 120–151.

Rizzo, B. J., Booth-Butterfield, M., & Wanzer, M. B. (1999). Individual differences in managers' use of humor: Subordinate perceptions of managers' humor. *Communication Research Reports, 16,* 360–369.

Roeckelein, J. E. (2002). *The psychology of humor: A reference guide and annotated bibliography.* Westport, CT: Greenwood Press.

Rousseau, D. M., & Fried, Y. (2001). Location, location, location: Contextualizing organizational research. *Journal of Organizational Behavior, 22*(1), 1–13.

Rousseau, D. M., Sitkin, S. B., Burt, R. S., & Camerer, C. (1998). Not so different after all: A cross-discipline view of trust. *Academy of Management Review, 23,* 393–404.

Ruch, W. (1993). Exhilaration and humor. In: M. Lewis & J. M. Haviland (Eds), *Handbook of emotions* (pp. 605–616). New York, NY: Guilford Press.

Schlenker, B. R. (Ed.) (1985). *The self and social life.* New York: McGraw-Hill.

Schwartz, S. H. (1992). Universals in the content and structure of values: Theoretical advances and empirical tests in 20 countries. In: M. P. Zanna (Ed.), *Advances in experimental social psychology* (Vol. 25, pp. 1–65). San Diego, CA: Academic Press.

Schwartz, S. H. (1999). A theory of cultural values and some implications for work. *Applied Psychology an International Review, 48,* 23–47.

Seligman, M. E. P. (2003). Forward: The past and future of positive psychology. In: C. L. Keyes & J. Haidt (Eds), *Flourishing* (pp. xi–xx). Washington, DC: APA.

Shakespeare, W. (1962). In: J.D. Wilson, (Ed.), *Love's labour's lost.* Cambridge, MA: Cambridge University Press. (Original work published 1631)

Sosik, J. J., Avolio, B. J., & Kahai, S. S. (1998). Inspiring group creativity: Comparing anonymous and identified electronic brainstorming. *Small Group Research, 29,* 3–31.

Sosik, J. J., Kahai, S. S., & Avolio, B. J. (1999). Leadership style, anonymity, and creativity in group decision support systems: The mediating role of optimal flow. *Journal of Creative Behavior, 33,* 227–257.

Suls, J. (1977). Cognitive and disparagement theories of humor: A theoretical and empirical synthesis. In: A. J. Chapman & H. C. Foot (Eds), *It's a funny thing, humor* (pp. 41–44). Oxford, UK: Pergamon Press.

Suls, J. (1983). Cognitive processes in humor appreciation. In: P.E. McGhee & J.H. Goldstein (Eds), *Handbook of humor research: Basic issues* (pp. 39–57). New York, NY: Springer-Verlag

Tierney, P., & Farmer, S. M. (2002). Creative self-efficacy Its potential antecedents and relationship to creative performance. *Academy of Management Journal, 45,* 1137–1149.

Tucker, K. A., & Allman, V. (2004). *Animals Inc.: A business parable for the 21st century.* New York, NY: Warner Business Books.

Tyler, T., & Kramer, R. (1996). Whither trust? In: R. Kramer & T. Tyler (Eds), *Trust in organizations: Frontiers of theory and research* (pp. 1–15). Thousand Oaks, CA: Sage.

Vinton, K. L. (1989). Humor in the workplace It is more than telling jokes. *Small Group Behavior, 20,* 151–166.

Zinsser, W. K. (1995). *On writing well.* New York, NY: Harper Collins.

THE DIFFERENTIAL EFFECTS OF SOCIALIZED AND PERSONALIZED LEADERSHIP ON GROUP SOCIAL CAPITAL

Paul Varella, Mansour Javidan and David Waldman

ABSTRACT

In this chapter, we suggest that authentic leaders incorporate socialized forms of charismatic leadership to enhance the social capital of organizational groups. We consider the differential effects of socialized and personalized charismatic leadership on groups. We propose that authentic leaders promote the balanced development of social capital, as they incorporate qualities of socialized charismatic leadership. In contrast, the influence of personalized charismatic leaders operates to restrict group social capital. Propositions about how these alternative forms of charismatic leadership produce such variations in group social capital are advanced. Further, we propose relationships between social capital and group and organizational performance.

In this chapter, we revisit the neo-charismatic contributions to the authentic leadership school (Luthans & Avolio, 2003), examine current understanding

Authentic Leadership Theory and Practice: Origins, Effects and Development
Monographs in Leadership and Management, Volume 3, 107–137
Copyright © 2005 by Elsevier Ltd.

about why charismatic leaders may have positive and negative influences over followers, and explore theories of group social capital. Our goal is to identify the conditions under which charisma *is* conducive to authentic leadership by exploring the concept of charismatic leadership and its impact as a group level phenomenon, using group social capital as an interpretive lens.

To offer a fresh look into the duality that surrounds charisma, we also connect leadership to group level theories, instead of relying on the dyadic focus that is predominant in the neo-charismatic literature. This approach is consistent with recommendations that charismatic leadership researchers move beyond studies of the effects of leaders on individual followers to examine the impact on the group as a whole (Beyer, 1999; Sosik, Avolio, & Kahai, 1997; Yukl, 1999). To do so, we use theories of group social capital (Adler & Kwon, 2002; Burt, 1992; Coleman, 1988; Portes, 1998) and examine the interplay between leadership and the group dynamics of followers. We elaborate on how leaders influence their followers in groups, and introduce propositions on how charisma influences the group dynamics that reshape their social capital.

SOCIALIZED CHARISMATIC LEADERSHIP AND THE AUTHENTIC LEADER

One important goal here is to explore the differential effects of positive and negative charismatic leadership. We rely on the argument that there are two types of charismatic leadership: socialized and personalized (House & Howell, 1992). Our intention is to use these contrasting views of charisma to examine the impact on group dynamics among followers. We use this framework to provide insight into three characteristics of authentic leadership: (1) transparency, openness, and trust, (2) guidance toward worthy objectives; and (3) an emphasis on follower development (Gardner, Avolio, Luthans, May, & Walumbwa, 2005).

We argue that socialized charismatic leadership (SCL) pertains to leaders who use their inspirational power to move organizations and groups to accomplish shared, worthy goals that promote the progress of the entire organization. Conversely, personalized charismatic leadership (PCL) involves a pattern of leadership that builds charismatic relationships for leaders' self-aggrandizement, which serves to maximize one's personal over the interests of the group, and goes against current operational definitions of authentic leadership (Gardner et al., 2005).

The differentiation of socialized from personalized charisma follows recent concerns about the effects of charismatic leadership (Beyer, 1999; Gardner, 2003; Howell & Avolio, 1992; Yukl, 1999). Our reading of such concerns is that charismatic leadership falls along a continuum, from the positive socialized form to the manipulative, negative personalized charismatic leader, which may parallel the continuum for authentic to inauthentic leadership suggested in this edited book. This continuum is defined by the motivation for power that different charismatic leaders have and by the values they espouse (Klein & House, 1998; McClelland, 1985), or, more specifically, the integrity of their values (House, Hanges, Javidan, Dorfman, & Gupta, 2004).

SCL includes mechanisms of self-control and activity inhibition over the leader's power motive (McClelland, 1985), and is focused on and motivated by a desire to serve the collective good. House and Howell (1992) defined activity inhibition in terms of the degree of restraint applied in the use of power. In other words, it involves the unconscious motive to use one's influence in socially desirable ways for the betterment of the collective entity, rather than for personal gain. SCL harnesses and directs power toward goals and objectives that will benefit the larger entity (House & Howell, 1992).

In contrast, PCL builds on motives for personal gain. Such leaders use power to achieve their personal goals and tend to be self-centered or narcissistic, exploitative, and manipulative in their relationship with others (Kets de Vries, 1993; Maccoby, 2004). They orchestrate events and their aftermath to symbolize their own perceived greatness (Gardner & Avolio, 1998), and will cultivate followers' allegiance to themselves, rather than the organization and its vision. The upshot is that while the public behaviors arising from SCL and PCL may oftentimes look similar, the underlying motives are quite different and result in divergent, long-term consequences.

However, capturing a leader's motivations involves practical and methodological challenges (McClelland, 1985). In that regard, Sully, Waldman, House, and Washburn (2005) discuss *values-based leadership* as a form of charismatic leadership. Sully et al., suggested that outstanding leaders show charismatic qualities, at the same time that they articulate beliefs in the importance of performance, determination, integrity and ethics, justice, openness, imagination, courage, and responsibility to others.

By assessing the values a leader espouses, we may be able to determine the extent to which the power motivation of a charismatic leader is of the socialized variety. Such assessments would, in turn, facilitate the identification of more positive charismatic relationships between leaders and followers (Gardner, 2003). Here again there is an overlap with the *positive moral perspective* construct that is posited to be an inherent quality of authentic leadership (Avolio & Gardner, 2005; Luthans & Avolio, 2003).

In addition, one may explore on the followers' side what Luthans, Avolio, Walumbwa, and Li (2005) refer to as psychological capital. Specifically, we would expect that followers working with SCL to have higher, sustainable psychological capital over time, which involves higher levels of optimism, hope, resiliency, and efficacy. In the short term, both PCL and SCL may generate similar levels of psychological capital, but as personalized charismatics begin to show "their true colors" we suspect that the psychological capital of followers will drop precipitously. In sum, we argue that PCL is not conducive to the development of authentic leadership or authentic followership; whereas, positive manifestations of SCL are indeed highly relevant to authentic leadership, authentic followership, and sustainable, veritable performance.

Charismatic Manifestations

Charismatic leadership theories (e.g., Conger, 1989; Conger & Kanungo, 1998; House, 1977; Shamir, House, & Arthur, 1993; Waldman & Yammarino, 1999) conceptualize a particular type of leadership as behavioral patterns combined with follower attributions, whose variation is a matter of degree; charisma is not viewed as an all-or-none phenomena (Beyer, 1999). Further, although uncertainty and turbulence in an organization's external context is seen as a moderating factor (Waldman, Ramírez, House, & Puranam, 2001), charismatic leadership is considered relevant even in the absence of a crisis (Bass, 1997; Conger & Kanungo, 1998). We assume that presence of charisma is indeed a matter of degree, and that it includes a relation between followers and leaders (Klein & House, 1998; Shamir et al., 1993; Waldman & Yammarino, 1999). The charismatic relationship involves idiosyncratic leader behavior and attributions from the followers (Conger & Kanungo, 1998). We describe the nature of these behaviors and attributions below.

The conventional view in the charismatic leadership literature is that such leadership will result in generally positive and beneficial consequences. Indeed, much of the theory and empirical research on charismatic leadership points to a number of positive consequences, such as higher performance ratings, more satisfied and motivated employees, and high effectiveness ratings by subordinates and superiors, especially when it is a component of transformational leadership (Judge & Piccolo, 2004; Lowe, Kroeck, & Sivasubramaniam, 1996). However, some recent work recommends caution in understanding the outcomes of charismatic leadership, in what may be considered inauthentic in some instances (Bass & Steidlmeier, 1999; Conger, 1990; Graham, 1991; Howell & Avolio, 1992).

Another important difference between SCL and PCL is the extent of consensus among followers that arises and their responses to the leader. PCL tends to engender diverse perceptions and attributions regarding the leader's charisma (Klein & House, 1998). Some followers may be quite attracted to the leader's actions and accomplishments. They may trust the leader and feel secure in terms of their own positions as long as they remain loyal. Conversely, other followers may not be so enamored and this, in our view, may be connected to a greater variation in followers' psychological capital. Followers may attribute personalized goals to the leader, especially in the absence of a shared collective vision. They may also display a lack of trust in his or her actions and motives, which would draw down optimism, hope, resiliency, and efficacy. Thus, we would expect a greater degree of consensus among the followers of the SCL due to a stronger belief in shared values and vision.

BEHAVIORAL AND PERSONAL QUALITIES OF CHARISMATIC LEADERS

Table 1 includes a summary of the differences between SCL and PCL. We focus on four behavioral or personal qualities of charismatic leaders. In our discussion, we will describe how these qualities are displayed differentially by authentic charismatic leaders, in their manifestation of socialized versus personalized charismatic leadership.

Visionary and Persuasive

Many writers agree that charismatic leadership involves proficient communication of a new vision for the organization over a period of time (Conger & Kanungo, 1998; House & Aditya, 1997; Nanus, 1992; Sashkin & Fulmer, 1988). The vision in charismatic leadership is based on strongly held beliefs and values by the leader, and it is emotionally appealing to followers. The vision communicates a better and more attractive future and encourages followers to accept change while postponing their personal gains. It also

Table 1.   Development of Authentic Leaders: Socialized vs. Personalized
Charismatic Leadership.

Behaviors and Personal Qualities	Socialized Charismatic Leaders	Personalized Charismatic Leaders
Visionary and persuasive	• Strong commitment to a shared vision • Involving people in developing shared vision • Emphasis on ideas and attractiveness of the vision	• Commitment to the leader's vision, rather than shared vision • Intimidation for non-conforming people • Emphasis on attraction to, and reverence for, the leader more than the vision
Superior assessment of the environment (internal and external) and discontent with the status quo	• Balanced processing and goals (group vs. the organization) • Incorporate external opportunities in their ideas • View challenges as opportunities to improve the collective	• Greater emphasis on external threats, rather than opportunities • Strong promotion of "us vs. them" • Characterizes challenges as external threats and rallying points for defending the group
Unconventional action w/ boundaries	• Unconventional actions are linked to the enhancement of the broader social unit	• Unconventional actions become instrumental for the leaders' image and personal advantage
Self-confidence	• Confidence to include diverse and different perspectives to enhance individual and collective self awareness • Confidence in the group or organization for attaining the shared vision • Displays emotional stability, resiliency, optimism, and hope	• Personal projection and lack of tolerance for diversity of opinions or ideas • Confidence primarily in the leader's own personal ability to take the group to a better future • Leader is impetuous and narcissistic

encourages followers to subsume their self-interests for the greater collective good.

We propose that SCL reflects an emphasis on the development of a shared vision. According to Senge (1990), a leader's vision becomes shared when it builds upon the desire of followers to pursue a common and important undertaking, and when it connects to their individual visions and goals. Nanus (1992) suggested that it can be a worthwhile endeavor for major constituents (e.g., employees, internal and external customers, and so forth) to get involved in vision formulation in order to ensure that it is truly shared – advice that is likely to be heeded in the case of SCL.

Conversely, leaders who display personalized charisma are not so concerned about building a shared vision, although they may want followers to believe it is shared in the beginning, at least to gain compliance. Instead, PCL involves a leader who articulates his or her own vision, and how that vision can alleviate uncertainty and fear that followers might have about the environment or their future. Overall, with PCL, more emphasis is placed on the leader as an extraordinary person, rather than the actual vision. Conversely, the authentic charismatic leader is likely to de-emphasize their accomplishments and prowess in favor of giving credit to the group of followers.

Superior Assessment of the Environment and Discontent with the Status Quo
Charismatic leaders provide a convincing case that identifies problems with the status quo, reasons for change, and the rationale for a better future and ways of attaining that future. A superior assessment by the leader of external environmental pressures, in combination with an appropriate understanding of the internal realities, will enhance follower perceptions of the leader's credibility and elicit their support (Bass, 1985; Conger & Kanungo, 1998). Socialized charismatics frame the environment as one that offers opportunities to the group. In contrast, personalized charismatics depict the environment as posing more threats than opportunities, and in so doing, present it in "us versus them" terms. As such, the leader's ideas and vision become a rallying point for defending the group. Authentic leaders take a more positive approach, and therefore as a "root construct" underlying SCL, we would expect them to focus more on the "we" then the "they".

Unconventional Action Within Accepted Boundaries
Charismatic leadership often involves actions that might be considered unconventional in nature. In the case of SCL, such actions are taken to promulgate the group's goals and vision. In contrast, personalized charismatics tend to take such actions for their own self-aggrandizement and image-building purposes (Gardner & Avolio, 1998; Maccoby, 2004). As an example of the former, Herb Kelleher of Southwest Airlines once challenged the leader of a competitor to an arm-wrestling contest to settle a dispute between their firms, as opposed to the more conventional means of settling the dispute in a legal court (Daft, 2002). In line with other SCL behavior by Kelleher, his actions were meant to symbolize the value of taking quick and

even unconventional behavior to solve problems, rather than to display his own physical prowess. He lost!

While PCL may also reflect unconventional acts, the underlying intention for such behavior is different. Personalized charismatics aim to prop up an image of grandeur, so that followers will be in awe of them. For instance, Frank (1997) describes how a highly charismatic leader reshaped an under-performing division of American Express Financial Advisors. Within 5 years of his appointment, Mr. John R. Hantz turned the Detroit office into the best producing region of the company. He was described as someone who mesmerized employees with an unusual approach that tied financial success to personal growth.

Mr. Hantz, however, appeared to be driven more by his personal interests than interests of the organization. At the same time he was asking for sacrifices from followers, he found himself a "Gatsby-like mansion in a posh enclave, affordable on his $1.3 million salary, much more than others in a similar position earned. He owned a black Ferrari" (Frank, 1997, p. 1). Soon after the Detroit office of American Express Financial Advisors became a top producer, Mr. Hantz announced that he had formed his own money-management firm. The new firm was staffed by fellow defectors from American Express, a quarter of the Detroit region's staff. Such violations of trust are common among inauthentic charismatic leaders.

Self-Confidence

Charismatic leadership is characterized by high levels of leader self-confidence, which helps to elicit respect for the leader, and reduces the uncertainties and anxieties experienced by followers. Leader self-confidence increases followers' comfort levels, especially during times of ambiguity and environmental uncertainty (Javidan, 1991; Waldman & Yammarino, 1999). Despite the common denominator of self-confidence, the self-confidence displayed in socialized and personalized charismatic leaders can be quite divergent. For example, SCL reflects confidence in the group's ability to attain the shared vision, and as such, helps build the confidence of group members. In line with authentic leadership theory, such leadership builds the efficacy of followers to take on yet another challenge fostering over time greater hope, optimism, and resiliency.

Conversely, PCL focuses confidence building more on the direction provided by the leader, as he or she is portrayed as the one individual who can deliver a better future for the group, as opposed to spreading responsibility for securing that future throughout the group. As such, SCL channels the confidence from the leader to build up confidence within the group (Collins,

2001; Shamir et al., 1993). In contrast, PCL involves leaders who are narcissistic and even thin-skinned when faced with criticism or threats to their self-confidence (Maccoby, 2004). Authentic leaders are expected to be higher on positivity and not to be narcissistic at all.

Connections to Authentic Leadership

Scholars have begun to explore the dimensions of what constitutes authentic leadership. May, Chan, Hodges, and Avolio (2003) describe how authentic leaders display transparency in linking inner desires, expectations, and values to daily activities. Luthans and Avolio (2003) define authentic leadership as "a positive construct, descriptive words include genuine, reliable, trustworthy, real, and veritable" (p. 243). Thus, the essence of authentic leadership includes the notion that leaders portray high moral standards when facing challenges. Moreover, such leaders embrace a wide scope of concerns and many different perspectives, in an effort to acknowledge the usual incongruent needs of diverse stakeholders.

The key dimensions of an authentic leadership include: transparency, openness and trust, guidance toward worthy objectives, and an emphasis on follower development (Gardner et al., 2005). From these dimensions, it appears that PCL is not congruent with the root construct of authentic leadership. PCL engenders mixed levels of trust, and personalized charismatics are more concerned with their own objectives rather than those of the broader organization. Further, they place a heavy emphasis on controlling the group of followers, instead of developing them and their psychological capital as well as social capital. Followers adhere to the personality of the leader, instead of the organizational vision that he or she promotes. Unequivocally, we are talking about an inauthentic leader.

On the other hand, SCL develops charismatic relationships that are based on inspiring members toward a worthy vision; one that is not only transparent to the followers, but with a new direction, which followers feel empowered to pursue. Socialized charismatic leaders attach the self-concept of followers to a positive new vision of the future (Shamir et al., 1993). Under these conditions, SCL is much more open and develops trustworthiness within the followers, promotes a shared positive vision of the future, and empowers followers to work toward that future. We view these facets as being consistent with the tenets of authentic leadership as described by Avolio and colleagues (e.g., Avolio & Gardner, 2005; Avolio, Gardner, Walumbwa, Luthans, & May, 2004; Gardner et al., 2005; Luthans & Avolio, 2003).

Now, the question is to explore how such different forms of leadership evolve in groups. Social capital theory offers a useful framework to the understanding of such developments. Our intention is to explain how authentic leaders may help to develop their followers as they enhance the psychological and social capital of the group, through socialized charismatic relationships. At the same time, we offer a model that helps explain when charismatic leadership becomes inauthentic, i.e., when PCL influences group dynamics. Before we can suggest such connections, it is important that we clearly define the concept of social capital.

SOCIAL CAPITAL

Social capital is a sociological concept defined in different and sometimes contradictory terms. Despite divergent viewpoints, there seems to be a general consensus on the basic notion of social capital as the "ability of actors to secure benefits by virtue of membership in social networks or other social structures" (Portes, 1998, p. 6). The general notion of *capital*, when applied in the *social* context, invokes the idea that social units possess supportive goods, assets, or processes that facilitate the productive function.

This idea suggests that the term does not relate to specific individuals; instead, it refers to a social unit in which individuals are embedded. As such, social capital is generally associated with social networks, groups, organizations, communities, and even countries. The notion is that, social units hold a specific kind of capital that becomes a factor of socio-economic production. Consequently, we see social capital as the collection of assets, values, behaviors and processes, which members of a group of followers jointly exchange as they foster collaboration and support among themselves toward the achievement of their collective socio-economic goals. This is distinguished from psychological capital, which is an individual level factor, which could contribute to the growth of social capital in groups (Luthans et al., in press).

The level of group social capital is an intangible attribute emerging from the relationships among members, which helps them to pursue collective goals. Group members can access such capital because of their membership, but they do not own it individually. As Portes (1998) describes it: "Whereas economic capital is in people's bank accounts and human capital is inside their heads, social capital inheres in the structure of the relationships. To possess social capital, a person must be related to others, and it is those others, not himself, who are the actual source of his or her advantage". (p. 7)

It is generally accepted that social capital comes from two characteristics of social units: (1) the cognitive/relational dimensions and (2) the structural dimensions (Adler & Kwon, 2002; Koka & Prescott, 2002; Nahapiet & Ghoshal, 1998). The former is related to the social psychological dimensions of the relationships among group members, as illustrated by group norms, values, identification, and trust (Portes, 1998). The latter, is associated with the structure of the social networks and how social ties are distributed in space and time, the nature of these connections, and the assets that such connections are able to link (Burt, 1992; Lin, Cook, & Burt, 2001). We start with the cognitive dimensions.

Cognitive Social Capital in Groups: A Behavioral Perspective

There are some specific attributes of groups that are associated with high levels of social capital. A group with high levels of cognitive social capital provides a rich array of opportunities to its members, as they benefit from the resources at its disposal. We suggest that such a group would tend to exhibit the following attributes.

Physical Proximity
It is largely through social interaction that social capital develops (Burt, 1992, 1997; Coleman, 1988; Lin et al., 2001). Membership interaction offers the opportunity for members to share perspectives, exchange information, and collaborate, thus, developing the social ties that foster social capital (Putnam, 2000). Higher levels of social interaction combined with positive feedback and feelings generate higher levels of social capital. We expect two sets of behaviors to emerge in such groups. First, in the organizational context, functional groups with higher levels of social capital will have frequent personal interactions. Members will manifest enjoyment in teamwork and portray a higher density of exchanges with colleagues. Meetings will be held more regularly, and joint actions are more frequent.

Second, there will be a higher frequency of social and informal encounters outside the work environment. Closed networks will enhance the generation of social capital because more frequent encounters make social capital more encompassing for a group (Coleman, 1988). In this way, members have reinforcing connections (i.e., they have a chance to interact with group members in more than one setting or fashion, which also makes the connections denser). Similar to formal gatherings, social encounters represent a strong source and manifestation of social capital levels. Increased social intercourse is particularly important for social capital in organizational groups because social contact has been reduced by day-by-day pressures of modern life (Putnam, 1995, 2000). Therefore, if members of formal work groups voluntarily use their non-work time to engage in frequent social interactions, they will foster high levels of social capital.

Psychological Proximity
Aligned with the above argument, in regards to physical proximity, some researchers view network architecture and frequency of contact as the surrogate measures of social capital (Lin, 2001). While physical proximity and contact is a necessary condition, it is by no means sufficient. The emotional connections to colleagues in the work environment are also critical to the development of social capital in formal groups. Members of a group with high levels of social capital will display behaviors that portray a shared appreciation of psychological proximity. They show concern for and look after each other. Portes (1998) defined this phenomenon as bounded solidarity, describing how members of a group with high social capital are willing to help each other because of a process of shared identification and common objectives (van Knippenberg & Hogg, 2003). This, in our view, will contribute even further to the individual psychological capital displayed by each member, and in turn, it also fosters group levels of social capital.

We expect two sets of behavior in such groups. First, members in a high social capital group are more inclined to offer help to other group members. They offer material and psychological support to help achieve collective objectives. Second, members of the group appreciate and take advantage of the fact that they can count on others. Hence, high levels of social capital are associated with the propensity to reach out for help and support. Group members are more inclined to ask for and rely on the support of their colleagues in performing their own tasks, which we would expect to coincide with a more transparent climate and culture linked with authentic charismatic leadership. In sum, in addition to frequency of contact, high social capital groups enjoy deep and high quality interpersonal relationships.

Strong Norms that Support Social Capital
Groups with high levels of social capital exhibit strong and specific norms and values. They achieve what Portes (1998) called enforceable trust, and what Coleman (1988) referred to as obligations and sanctions within an appropriable organization. These norms create an ambience of trustworthiness and empowerment, where members not only trust each other but

also feel empowered to deal with non-conforming behaviors. The following is an explanation of the four supportive norms of social capital.

Reciprocity and Willingness to Delay Repayments
Members are willing to engage and maintain their reciprocity exchanges through an informal and unwritten chit system whereby favors, information, or any other form of assistance is backed by a norm of reciprocity (Portes, 1998). Additionally, members have little doubt about contributing without immediate repayment because they believe other members will offer reciprocal help when later, they need support from the group (Portes & Sensenbrenner, 1993). Membership actions could be interpreted as "irrational" behaviors because there might be no apparent increase in the individual's utility. However, the overall social group's rationality persists because if the group's utility is not increased, the group will have no reason to exist (Granovetter, 1985). There is an expectation that the aggregate value of the contributions of all members will be larger than the sum of the individual inputs and this is largely based on the relational trust levels built up in such groups.

Remedies for Non-Conforming Members
The unspecified time for repayment of the collaborative actions from members, and the sense of protection that social capital offers to them, could potentially result in free riding, since those who benefit from current offerings of the group could refuse to contribute back, when called upon for their support. To prevent this outcome, along with expectations of reciprocity, groups develop norms to enforce their rules and to penalize free riders (Coleman, 1988; Portes, 1998; Putnam, 2000; Zhou & Bankston, 1996).

Trust is the common underlying factor in the group's dynamics and is sustained through the existence of mechanisms to punish dysfunctional behavior. Ostracism, alienation, and loss of reputation are possible examples of such mechanisms. Individual members are motivated to abide by the group's rules due to their desire to sustain the benefits of good standing within the group, and their desire to avoid being ostracized and blacklisted.

Conformity to Group Pressures
Norms not only work as controls for deviant behaviors but also limit individual expression and freedom (Portes & Sensenbrenner, 1993; Zhou & Bankston, 1996). Members are expected to conform to the group's expectations and to suppress actions that challenge or contradict group norms

and values. Such restrictions may even limit the abilities of members to build strong ties with those outside the group's boundaries because such ties may be in conflict with the group's values, which could lead to destructive in- and out-group relationships, which we would expect to find in PCL.

Meticulous Processes for Admission and Socialization of New Members
Embracing new individuals to a group represents a major challenge to the norms that are agreed upon by all existing members. New individuals and ideas may challenge the status quo inside the group (Portes, 1998). Therefore, groups with high social capital tend to devise membership selection and socialization processes that ensure acculturation of the new members to group norms. They take hiring decisions seriously and spend much time, both individually and as a group, to ensure that the new hires are compatible with the group.

The presented cognitive social capital parallels the construct of group cohesion (Evans & Dion, 1991; Griffin, 1997). Still, social capital offers an opportunity to evaluate group phenomena in more detail. This detailed framework also helps us to understand the leadership influences over group performance, as we differentiate between intra-group and inter-group actions. Next, we discuss the structural dimensions of social capital that relate to the inter-group phenomenon.

Structural Social Capital of Groups: A Social Network Perspective

External Connections
Groups need to develop external reach to ensure the diversity of ideas and availability of resources required for their long-term survival (Adler & Kwon, 2002). Burt (2001a) has convincingly demonstrated that spanning over structural holes across different clusters in a social network is a major source of added value for organizational groups. As he puts it, group cohesion might be necessary for realization of value, but external connections are necessary for adding value to such units. Consequently, despite the enhanced internal dynamics that groups enjoy from the cognitive dimensions of social capital, they cannot isolate themselves from their broader environment. The external environment is an important source of resources and diversity (Burt, 1997).

The network positions that usually offer high levels of social capital are positions with a high degree of centrality (Burt, 1992; Tsai & Ghoshal, 1998). Network centrality is the socio-metric concept of being at the centre of the social connections within a network of relationships (Scott, 2000); it is the degree to which a group is linked to other groups of the organization. For example, a group in a central position would have the largest number of external connections. Such a structure would suggest that the members of the more central group would develop extensive connections to other members of the organization and use them as sources of advantage. Hence, for the group membership to benefit from the positive intra-group dynamics of its cognitive social capital, they must be well connected within the social structure of an organization.

To summarize, organizational groups with high levels of social capital include members that have a higher propensity to: offer and seek help and support, engage in frequent personal interaction, hold social encounters outside the work environment, use reciprocal exchanges with delayed repayments, assign remedies for non-conforming members, conform to group expectations, socialize new members meticulously, and actively seek connections outside the closer network of immediate colleagues.

Organizational Consequences of Social Capital

Our understanding of the positive influences of social capital in the organizational context can be enhanced if we use it as a metaphor for group advantage (Burt, 2001b). Initially, there are advantages that result from the relationships, synergies, and collaboration among members of a group, as they make available to their peers the resources that they control (Bourdieu, 1986). Subsequently, social capital reduces transactional costs because it helps to control behaviors that could be harmful to the group (Portes & Sensenbrenner, 1993; Putnam, 2000). In other words, social capital reduces transactional costs due to enforceable trust within the membership (Coleman, 1988; Portes, 1998). Finally, social capital facilitates the development of intellectual capital inside groups or organizations (Nahapiet & Ghoshal, 1998), as it reduces the barriers of information flow (Szulanski, 1996). However, there are also risks associated with the development of social capital.

There is much debate about the negative consequences that social capital can cause in groups, since it is possible that the processes that generate social capital may also promote outcomes that hinder optimal socio-economic processes (Adler & Kwon, 2002; Portes, 1998; Portes & Landolt, 1996). Negative consequences come from the fact that high social capital groups have objectives that relate primarily to their membership (Coleman, 1988). Even though individuals engage in behaviors that generate high social capital and, consequently, facilitate collective action, there might be group-specific behaviors that are accepted among members but cause negative externalities to the broader organization (Gabbay & Leenders, 1999; Portes, 2000). That is, the group could profit, but the overall organization might suffer. We suspect that the authentic charismatic leader would be more cognizant of this occurring, and would work to make social groups open and transparent to avoid such build up that would reduce the advantages of developing larger cohesive networks.

The negative influence of social capital development in groups can be reinforced by the strengthening of bounded solidarity and the consequent constraining of the membership's diversity of thought. Questioning the group's norms and values can be unpleasant and unacceptable. The discomfort in voicing differing opinions happens because members find protection in their group, and they may face sanctions or censure if they decide to behave differently from the group's expectations (Pennings & Lee, 1999; Portes, 1998).

Groupthink, enforced compliance, lack of creativity, and inability to access needed external resources are the resulting unintended, but serious, consequences for the survival of organizations. Adler and Kwon (2002) describe how those consequences generate organizations that resemble a collection of compartmentalized, inward groups.

In sum, we come to two important conclusions. First, the relationship between cognitive social capital and group performance may take the shape of an inverted-u curve, if the propensity of strong, cohesive group development is not monitored carefully (Frank & Yasumoto, 1998; Fukuyama, 2000; Gabbay & Leenders, 1999; Leenders & Gabbay, 1999; Pennings & Lee, 1999; Uzzi & Gillespie, 1999). In other words, groups may have too or too much cognitive social capital, and both conditions are limiting. The former generates disconnected groups, with limited synergies and loss of opportunities for effective collaborative action (Adler & Kwon, 2002). The latter causes too much in-group pressure, conformity and isolation, thus, groups do not accommodate change and diversity. Hence, the appropriate social capital development calls for a balanced development of the cognitive underlying processes.

The second conclusion is that besides the development of cognitive social capital, groups have to develop connections to other groups within the organization (Burt, 2001b). This is a condition that can be more difficult to attain, if the cognitive social capital is too strong (Portes, 1998; Portes & Sensenbrenner, 1993). Too much cognitive social capital and limited external reach, via the group's external connections, will generate an unfavorable social context, where social capital actually restricts the development of the group. Thus, we contend that social capital development has to evolve in a balanced way so that the cognitive dimensions are positive, and the external reach is present.

Based on the discussion up to now, we draw some conclusions. First, formal organizational groups have varying degrees of social capital, and their performance is partly based on the level and nature of the social capital they hold. Second, charismatic leadership can occur in socialized and personalized forms, which may influence followers and groups in a differential manner. Now, we turn to the examination of how charismatic leadership can help develop balanced social capital within an organizational group.

THE SOCIAL CAPITAL CONSEQUENCES OF CHARISMATIC LEADERSHIP

The earliest reference we could find on the relationship between leadership and group social capital was the work of Hanifan (1916), who reported on how a new school-district manager used his leadership capabilities to promote and employ social capital to enhance the socio-economic conditions of a rural community. To our knowledge, the literature has remained largely silent on this topic. We venture now into this territory. Our overall thesis is that both SCL and PCL will promote the development of social capital in groups. However, as shown in Table 2, the precise nature of that social capital will vary. In turn, the nature of the social capital that develops will have differential effects on group and organizational performance.

We now proceed to describe the model illustrated in Fig. 1 and the propositions that can be formed on its basis. Although the model of relationships between leadership, social capital, and outcomes is a single one, in the illustration we decided to include two alternative paths. The first one indicates the relationships when leaders are charismatic and have a highly socialized power motive and would, as noted above, be more likely to be called authentic. The second model illustrates an alternative path, the one where leaders are charismatic but have a personalized power motive, and thus over time would be labelled more inauthentic.

We believe that SCL fosters psychological proximity by building group norms and values stressing identity with the ideas and vision of the group. Individuals that identify with their groups show emotional involvement and commitment to the group (Tajfel & Turner, 1986; van Knippenberg &

Table 2. Development of Balanced vs. Restrictive Social Capital.

	Balanced Social Capital	Restrictive Social Capital
Group social capital dimensions	Authentic leadership promoted by SCL	Inauthentic leadership promoted by PCL
Physical proximity	• Positive reinforcement for members' interaction • Non-hierarchical interactions	• Coercive pressure to remain physically close • Hierarchy is often stressed
Psychological proximity	• Identification with the ideas and vision of the group • Tailored to enhancing social needs of members • Builds positive feelings of member psycological capital • Commitment to working with other team members in a cooperative manner	• Strong dependency on, and identification with, the leader vs. the group • Member fears of being left out and facing external threat alone • Little concern for member psycological capital
Underlying norms	• Emphasis on fairness and positive reinforcements for adherence to norms • Encouragement to contribute toward the shared vision • Shared leadership among group members • Encouragement of emergence of new leaders	• Emphasis on favoritism and negative reinforcement or ostracism for disobeying norms • Pressures for conformity to the leader's vision and desires • Impedes emergence of new leaders
External reach	• Open to outside information, ideas, and groups • Supportive and collaborative with outside individuals and groups	• Closed to the outside world • Suspicious of, and often competitive with, outsiders

Hogg, 2003), and are perceived to share the same fate with their peers (Ashforth & Mael, 1989; Chattopadhyay, Tluchowska, & George, 2004). Consequently, SCL fosters a commitment to working together as a team, and the building of member psychological capital. Such leaders also promote physical proximity by triggering personal interaction and social encounters.

In addition, SCL encourages the development of norms of reciprocity, the control of deviant behaviors, and the meticulous screening of new members. The result is the building of a shared vision among group members. Vision enhances the sense of community because it provides a strong identity to the group. Finally, SCL encourages the group of followers to connect to other groups and individuals in the broader organization. In total, we characterize

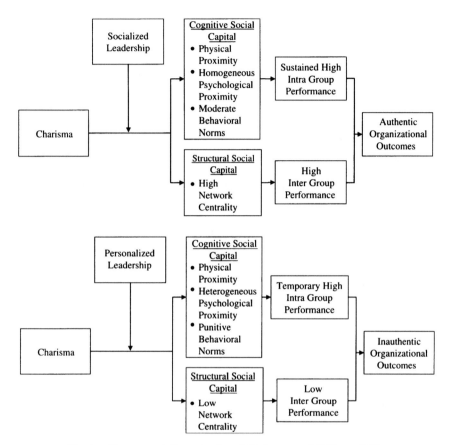

Fig. 1.   Group and Organizational Outcomes of SCL vs. PCL.

the effects of SCL in terms of balanced social capital. Below, we describe the formation of this type of social capital in more detail.

The distinctive realistic assessment of the environment in SCL enhances the leader's credibility due to the ability to support specific contentions with facts and evidence. SCL helps the group understand the environmental forces that influence them, and why and how the leader's ideas will address the challenges of external adaptation and internal integration. Heightened environmental awareness, along with the building of a shared vision, provide for a stronger sense of identity and psychological proximity within the group. Followers develop a favorable self-image strengthened by the association with the leader and the group (House & Howell, 1992; Javidan, 1991;

Shamir et al., 1993), which should result in more authentic followers, as noted by Gardner et al. (2005). Specifically, Gardner et al. (2005) argue that there is a reciprocal relationship between authentic leadership and followership, and we see SCL as building more authentic followers, and in the extreme would develop them into leaders; we could call that authentic, transformational leadership. Ultimately, these followers would view their fellow group members as distinct from outsiders (Coleman, 1988), and that would have to be balanced so as not to form strong in-group versus out-group bias.

Enhanced psychological proximity further facilitates the development of physical proximity, as group members enjoy more interpersonal encounters and a high-interaction work environment. The new vision and persuasion from the leader will introduce an additional reinforcement for interpersonal contact and a potential trigger for social encounters and development. Members are willing to donate their personal time for activities that go beyond their professional duties, since they appreciate the association with the leader and the collegial group (Portes, 1998).

A persuasive vision also encourages a norm of reciprocity because it implies individual sacrifice for the betterment of the overall group (Bass, 1985). It motivates the members to collaborate and delay personal gratification, in the interest of the collective good. Kouzes and Posner (1993) found that when asked to define credibility in behavioral terms, most people responded that credible leaders "walk the talk" and "practice what they preach". In addition, SCL stresses positive reinforcement and encouragement as the means to engender individual conformity toward the group's norms, and facilitate the group's remedies to correct deviant behaviors. Further, SCL promotes meticulous scrutiny for group membership, to ensure that new recruits are in tune with the group's vision and norms.

As shown in Table 2 balanced social capital is also characterized by the equilibrium achieved between the internally oriented dimensions of social capital on the one hand (e.g., physical and psychological proximity), and external reach, on the other. Excessive internal focus leads to group isolation and inwardness. If a group develops too much psychological proximity and stresses the norms of conformity to group pressures and remedies against non-conforming behaviors, the members of the group will become inward looking and will suffer sanctions for reaching outside the group, as described below. On the other hand, too much external reach may dilute internal ties because of the excessive energies dedicated to building and maintaining relations with outsiders.

Therefore, besides the positive cognitive process inside the group, SCL has the broader organizational well-being in mind. Accordingly, social charismatic leaders will promote the social positioning of their followers inside the social structure of the organization. Thus, we can expect that groups under SCL will occupy more centralized positions in the social network. As explained above, central positions for groups represent a higher degree of social connections with the other groups within the organization (Scott, 2000). Linkages between the leader's social network and the followers' social position become, therefore, a determinant of leadership influences (Sparrowe & Liden, 1997).

For instance, leaders will promote and facilitate the connections of their followers to other key players in the organization, important suppliers, valuable customers (internal or external), among others. It is through processes along these lines that the group progresses and works toward the goal of the broader organization.

In sum, we propose that SCL promotes a difficult, yet important balance in terms of the formation of internal ties and external reach.

Proposition 1. Socialized charismatic leadership favors the development of inclusive, permeable groups that foster internal cohesion at the same time that they are well connected to other groups in the organization. These groups will develop balanced social capital as their leaders promote internal collaboration, as well as external connections to other groups and ideas.

On the other hand, PCL is characterized by the development of punitive internal group pressures and norms, and the consequent isolation from the rest of the organization, which leads to the generation of restrictive social capital. This form of social capital is characterized by groups that are inwardly focused, hierarchical, emotionally dependent on the leader, and non-collaborative with individuals and entities in their broader context. Groups with this type of social capital are cohesive, but intolerant or non-supportive of diverse thought and new ideas.

PCL builds on the manipulation of followers to gain their support and to reduce the group's external reach. For example, PCL introduces a strong, favorable image of the leader, while simultaneously playing upon group member fears of being left out and having to face external threats alone, which as noted above would draw down both the psychological capital of individuals and the social capital of the group. Thus, restrictive social capital becomes a powerful instrument of behavioral control, and personalized charismatics will use it to exert influence over followers and to sway them to work toward their self-centered objectives.

Kets de Vries (1993) explored the psychological basis for personalized charisma, pointing largely toward emotional insecurities. Such insecurities are likely to result in two phenomena that will restrict the social capital of the group. First, PCL will discourage communication, and especially collaboration or cooperation, with outside individuals or entities. Personalized charismatics view such behavior as occurring outside of their control, and thus feel threatened by it. Second, they are likely to do little, if anything, to develop new leadership potential within the group. Such leaders will see the development of leadership potential as threatening to their own status as the group's leader, which is an anathema to authentic leadership (Avolio & Gardner, 2005).

PCL actively reduces the external social connections of followers and, consequently, will reduce the network centrality of the group of followers (Scott, 2000). By reducing the social connections to other groups inside or around the organization, PCL not only enhances the leader's control over followers but also concentrates the social linkages. In so doing, the personalized leader enhances personal social capital (Burt, 1997), but at the expense of the group of followers.

In sum, PCL tends to favor imposed obedience, limited dissent, strong internal cohesion, and compliance to the leader's ideas. Personalized charismatic leaders do not support diversity of thought and ideas; instead, they instil norms that restrict communication or collaboration with outsiders. They also do not encourage the ongoing development of leadership talent within the group. At the same time, they present a favorable personal image and assure safety and belongingness to followers in return for their loyalty. It is likely their own authentic leadership development will be stifled as will followers', as neither over time is getting to know themselves any better due to fear and lack of transparency. Thus, our next proposition.

Proposition 2. Personalized charismatic leadership engenders the development of insular, inward looking groups that isolate themselves from other units in an organization. These groups develop restrictive social capital, as the leaders favor internal collaboration and cohesion at the expense of external connections to other groups and ideas.

Effects on Group and Organizational Performance

The implications of our propositions are substantial for groups and organizations. Fig. 1 illustrates graphically the relationship between PCL versus

SCL and group and organizational performance. As we will show below, SCL has the greatest potential to enhance the social capital of the group and positively affect the whole organization through inter-group connections.

We contend that both the restrictive social capital developed by PCL, as well as the balanced social capital developed by SCL, have the potential to positively affect group performance in the short term. For example, based on the majority of prior research (e.g., Evans & Dion, 1991; Guzzo & Dickson, 1996), we would expect that the cohesion resulting from both forms of social capital would have a positive effect on group performance, largely driven by the membership commitment to the goals of the group. Further, Zaccaro, Gualtieri, and Minionis (1995) obtained results suggesting that cohesion can improve team decision-making, especially when the team is under time pressure.

On the other hand, we also contend that balanced social capital will result in greater group performance over time. SCL tends to develop a shared and unifying vision, while simultaneously developing external connections and allowing for the influx of necessary information into the group. In the long term, the resulting balanced social capital should allow the group to continually adapt and improve its processes, decision-making, and so forth.

In contrast, the restrictive social capital resulting from PCL may have deleterious long-term effects on the group. We propose two dilemmas that can damage the long-term performance of the group. First, the lack of external reach may limit the group's ability to adapt to a changing environmental context. Second, over time, there is likely to be a polarization within the group. As noted earlier, we expect a gradual heterogeneous response among followers over time, in terms of reactions of group members toward PCL. Some members will work closely with the leader, while others will feel unease with the leader's actions.

Proposition 3. The restrictive social capital fostered by personalized charismatic leadership will result in short-term intra-group performance equal to that of the balanced social capital of the socialized charismatic leader. However, over the long term, the balanced social capital fostered by socialized charismatic leadership will engender better intra-group performance, as compared to restrictive social capital.

As shown in Fig. 1, we further expect inter-group performance to suffer with restrictive social capital, which is likely to hamper inter-group connectiveness and the firm's ability to adapt to environmental shifts. Under such conditions, short-term, localized goals may be attained at the expense of the long-term progress of the group and the organization. The overall organization will suffer due to the development of a fragmented network of independently working teams (Adler & Kwon, 2002). The proposition here is that group norms and loyalty inside specific units may evolve more strongly toward the immediate group, than they would to the larger organization. As a result, some groups engage in activities that further their own interests at the expense of the overall organization.

In contrast, balanced social capital is likely to enhance inter-group synergies, reduce transaction costs, and promote a free flow of information across organizational units. Thus, an important consequence is the development of organization-wide intellectual capital, as information flow and ability to use it become the drivers of new knowledge creation (Nahapiet & Ghoshal, 1998; Vera & Crossan, 2004). Further, it is clear in organizations that the actions and performance of groups may need to be coordinated if performance at the organizational level is to be realized. Specifically, inter-group cooperation and cohesion will lead to agreement regarding organizational goals and values, and in turn, performance that is oriented toward common goals (Kotter & Heskett, 1992; Yukl, 2002). In sum, we expect that:

Proposition 4. As compared to restrictive social capital, the inter-group performance fostered by balanced social capital will result in more effective performance at the organizational level.

These propositions show the group process through which leaders develop authentic leadership and followership. They explain how authentic charismatic leaders operate under transparency, openness, and trust; guide followers toward worthy objectives; and emphasize the development of followers. The conclusion is clear: if charisma is to be conducive to, and congruent with, authentic leadership, its manifestation will evolve through SCL processes.

Further, the alternative path of PCL illustrates how charisma may not lead to authentic leadership or its outcomes. Examples include: expressing fear of being left out of group processes instead of trusting to be a contributing follower; fostering individual compliance; instead of self-development; mythicizing the leader and not promoting succession; and attaining the leader's personal advantages, before considering the progress of the group and the organization.

ADDITIONAL CONSIDERATIONS

Contingencies and Contexts

We suggest that socialized and personalized charismatic leadership may be somewhat fluid in nature, changing over time for particular leaders. More-over, the tendency may be to shift from a socialized power motive to a more personalized power motive, rather than vice versa. Kets de Vries (1993) discussed how such tendencies may actually be associated with aging proc-esses and a leader's fear of losing strength, power, and even virility as he or she grows older. These fears could cause an otherwise socialized charismatic to resort to manipulation and image building to maintain power, while gradually losing genuine concern for the greater good of the unit or organi-zation. As a result, some followers may eventually reject the influence of a leader who they initially accepted (Shamir & Howell, 1999). In any event, an ethnographic/case study approach might be beneficial to examine the po-tentially fluid nature of socialized versus personalized charisma over time and the effects on the formation of social capital.

For the most part, this chapter focuses on leadership at the group or unit level, although we do recognize above the cross-level effects on individual psychological capital that coincides with authentic charismatic leadership. However, it is becoming clear that charismatic leadership at the CEO level may also be necessary to ensure inter-group cooperation on the part of units in order to enhance overall organizational performance. Thus, it may be essential for CEOs to establish and implement a vision stressing how the goals of one group are not to be accomplished at the expense of another. CEO leadership of this nature is likely to have an effect on the nature of social capital that will develop within groups, independent of group leaders, by directly influencing the greater organizational culture (Collins, 2001; Kotter & Heskett, 1992; Waldman & Yammarino, 1999).

Conclusions

As explained earlier, a key purpose of this chapter is to examine the potential impact of authentic and inauthentic charismatic leadership, not on the individual members of the group, but on the texture of the group itself. Our interest is the effect of charismatic leaders on the dynamics of relationships among group members, as well as the impact on individual members over time as specifically linked to the concept of their psychological capital. Our premise is that there are group-level phenomena that go beyond the cumulative effect on individual members (Beyer, 1999; Yukl, 1999). We have used the concept of social capital to embark on such a conceptualization. Through our propositions, we have argued that the attributes of two forms of charismatic leadership, personalized and socialized, can have differential effects on how they shape the social capital of groups. The effect can be largely positive, through balanced social capital, or largely negative, through restrictive social capital.

Looking at leadership from the perspective of social capital is a new way of exploring it. The extant literature, "in looking for the effects of charismatic leadership, focuses on how individual followers respond to such leaders" (Beyer, 1999, p. 309). The approach proposed here examines how charismatic leaders can affect relationships among followers. Such an approach requires fundamentally different methodologies. Instead of just examining the impact of leaders on the psychological well-being and performance of individual members, we need group-level methodologies that measure the impact of leaders on the dynamics of the relationships among members. Indeed, over time we suspect there will be reciprocal effects on individual psychological capital and group social capital.

We also suggest that areas of study should move beyond the individual and focus on different types of groups at different organizational levels. While we have used formal groups as our level of analysis, additional work is needed to fine-grain our understanding of the impact of charismatic leadership in different types of organizational groups and group attributes that mediate such processes. In short, the cross-fertilization of both streams of research offers a rich opportunity to develop propositions on how socialized and personalized manifestations of charisma evolve, and how they can affect a group's social capital in different ways.

In looking for an explanation of the conditions under which charisma would be conducive to authentic leadership, we suggest utilization of a multi-level examination. It started with an individual level of analysis of some personal dimensions of leaders. Subsequently, we connected our individual level of analysis to the group-level phenomenon of the social capital of the group. With that, we suggested how authentic leaders might influence inter- and intra-group processes that have consequences for the whole organization.

Through the multi-level analysis we can conclude that authentic leadership can be developed by socialized charismatic leaders, and that group-level phenomena will mediate the consequent authentic outcomes. However, our model does not exhaust all aspects and issues surrounding charisma, psychological capital, group social capital, and authentic leadership. For example, it would be quite interesting to explore how the social capital of the leader, and the group to which the leader is connected, might explain his/her charisma. Some authors have equated charisma to network centrality and an individual's social capital (Bourdieu, 1980, 1999; Pfeffer, 1992). This approach suggests that it may be possible to see charisma using resource dependency theory (Pfeffer & Salancik, 1978), which is still unexplored. Finally, the question remains open as to how a non-charismatic leader can generate the desired authentic leadership outcomes. Progress on both fields, charismatic, and authentic leadership, may help us into understanding such issues.

REFERENCES

Adler, P. S., & Kwon, S. (2002). Social capital: Prospectus for a new concept. *Academy of Management Review, 27*, 17–40.

Ashforth, B. E., & Mael, F. (1989). Social identity theory and the organization. *Academy of Management Review, 14*, 20–39.

Avolio, B. J., & Gardner, W. L. (2005). Authentic leadership development: Getting to the root of positive forms of leadership. *The Leadership Quarterly, 16*, 315–338.

Avolio, B. J., Gardner, W. L., Walumbwa, F. O., Luthans, F., & May, D. R. (2004). Unlocking the mask: A look at the process by which authentic leaders impact follower attitudes and behaviors. *The Leadership Quarterly, 15*, 801–823.

Bass, B. M. (1985). *Leadership and performance beyond expectations.* New York: Harper.

Bass, B. M. (1997). *Does the transactional-transformational leadership paradigm transcend organizational and national boundaries? American Psychologist, 52*, 130–139.

Bass, B. M., & Steidlmeier, P. (1999). Ethics, character, and authentic transformational leadership. *The Leadership Quarterly, 10*, 181–217.

Beyer, J. (1999). Taming and promoting charisma to change organizations. *The Leadership Quarterly, 10*, 307–330.

Bourdieu, P. (1980). *Symbolic capital.* The logic of practice (1st ed.). Cambridge, UK: Polity Press.

Bourdieu, P. (1986). The forms of capital. In: J. G. Richardson (Ed.), *Handbook of theory and research for the sociology of education* (pp. 241–258). New York: Greenwood Press.

Bourdieu, P. (1999). Scattered remarks. *European Journal of Social Theory, 2*(3), 334–340.

Burt, R. S. (2001a). The social capital of structural holes. In: M. F. Guillén, R. Collins, P. England & M. Meyer (Eds), *The new economic sociology: Developments in an emerging field.* New York: Russell Sage Foundation.

Burt, R. S. (2001b). Structural holes versus network closure as social capital. In: N. Lin, K. Cook & R. Burt (Eds), *Social capital theory and research* (pp. 31–56). New York: Aldine de Gruyter.

Burt, R. S. (1992). *Structural holes: The social structure of competition.* Cambridge, MA: Harvard University Press.

Burt, R. S. (1997). The contingent value of social capital. *Administrative Science Quarterly, 42*, 339–365.

Chattopadhyay, P., Tluchowska, M., & George, E. (2004). Identifying the in group: A closer look of the influence of demographic dissimilarity and employee social identity. *Academy of Management Review, 29*, 180–202.

Coleman, J. S. (1988). Social capital in the creation of human capital. *American Journal of Sociology, 94*, 95–120.

Collins, J. C. (2001). *Good to great: Why some companies make the leap and others don't*. New York: Harper Business.

Conger, J. A. (1989). *The charismatic leader: Behind the mystique of exceptional leadership*. San Francisco: Jossey-Bass.

Conger, J. A. (1990). The dark side of leadership. *Organizational Dynamics, 19*, 44–55.

Conger, J. A., & Kanungo, R. A. (1998). *Charismatic leadership in organizations*. Thousand Oask, CA: Sage.

Daft, R. L. (2002). *The leadership experience* (2nd ed.). Cincinnati, OH: South–Western.

Evans, C. R., & Dion, K. L. (1991). Group cohesion and performance: A meta-analysis. *Small Group Research, 22*, 175–186.

Frank, K. A., & Yasumoto, J. Y. (1998). Linking action to social structure: Social capital within and between subgroups. *American Journal of Sociology, 104*(3), 642–686.

Frank, S. E. (1997). Leaving home: How rising star quit at American Express and took staff along: Charismatic Detroit leader of financial – advice unit faced sharp questions – an aborted autonomy plan. *Wall Street Journal*, pp. A1. Dec. 2, 1997 (Eastern edition) Retrieved March 21, 2003, from Proquest database.

Fukuyama, F. (2000). Social capital and civil society. *IMF Working Paper, WP/00/74*, 1–18.

Gabbay, S. M., & Leenders, R. T. (1999). Corporate social capital: The structure of advantage and disadvantage. In: R. T. Leenders & S. M. Gabbay (Eds), *Corporate social capital and liability* (pp. 1–16). Norwell, MA: Kluwer Academic Publishers.

Gardner, W. L. (2003). Perceptions of leader charisma, effectiveness, and integrity. *Management Communication Quarterly, 16*(4), 502–527.

Gardner, W. L., & Avolio, B. J. (1998). The charismatic relationship: A dramaturgical perspective. *The Academy of Management Review, 23*, 32–58.

Gardner, W. L., Avolio, B. J., Luthans, F., May, D. R., & Walumbwa, F. O. (2005). "Can you see the real me?" A self-based model of authentic leader and follower development. *The Leadership Quarterly, 16*, 373–394.

Graham, J. W. (1991). Servant–leadership in organizations: Inspirational and moral. *The Leadership Quarterly, 2*, 105–119.

Granovetter, M. S. (1985). Social structures and economic action: The problem of embeddedness. *American Journal of Sociology, 91*, 481–510.

Griffin, M. A. (1997). Interaction between individuals and situations: Using HLM procedures to estimate reciprocal relationships. *Journal of Management, 23*, 759.

Guzzo, R. A., & Dickson, M. W. (1996). Teams in organizations: Recent research on performance and effectiveness. *Annual Review of Psychology, 47*, 307–338.

Hanifan, L. J. (1916). The rural school community center. *Annals of the American Academy of Political and Social Science, 67*, 130–138.

House, R. J. (1977). A 1976 theory of charismatic leadership. In: J. G. Hunt & L. L. Larson (Eds), *Leadership: The cutting edge* (pp. 189–207). Carbondale: Southern Illinois University Press.

House, R. J., & Aditya, R. N. (1997). *The social scientific study of leadership: quo vadis? Journal of Management, 23*, 409–473.

House, R. J., Hanges, P. J., Javidan, M., Dorfman, P. W., & Gupta, V. (2004). *Culture, leadership, and organizations : the GLOBE study of 62 societies.* Thousand Oaks, CA: Sage.

House, R. J., & Howell, J. M. (1992). Personality and charisma. *The Leadership Quarterly, 3,* 81–108.

Howell, J. M., & Avolio, B. J., (1992). The ethics of charismatic leadership: Submission or liberation? *Academy of Management Executive, 6,* 43–54.

Javidan, M. (1991). Leading a high-committed high-performance organization. *Long Range Planning, 24*(2), 28–36.

Judge, T. A., & Piccolo, R. F. (2004). Transformational and transactional leadership: A meta-analytic test of their relative validity. *Journal of Applied Psychology, 89,* 755–768.

Kets de Vries, M. F. R. (1993). *Leaders, fools, and imposter: Essays on the psychology of leadership.* San Francisco: Jossey-Bass.

Klein, K. J., & House, R. J. (1998). Further thoughts on fire: Charismatic leadership and level of analysis. In: F. Dansereau & F. J. Yammarino (Eds), *Leadership: The multiple-level approaches* (pp. 45–52). Stamford, CT: JAI Press.

Koka, B. R., & Prescott, J. E. (2002). Strategic alliances as social capital: A multidimensional view. *Strategic Management Journal, 23,* 795–816.

Kotter, J. P., & Heskett, J. L. (1992). *Corporate culture and performance.* New York: Free Press.

Kouzes, J., & Posner, B. (1993). *Credibility: How leaders gain and lose it, and why people demand it.* San Francisco: Jossey-Bass.

Leenders, R. T., & Gabbay, S. M. (1999). *Corporate social capital and liability.* Boston: Kluwer Academic.

Lin, N. (2001). Building a network theory of social capital. In: N. Lin, K. Cook & R. S. Burt (Eds), *Social capital: Theory and research* (pp. 3–30). Hawthorne, NY: Aldine de Gruyter.

Lin, N., Cook, K., & Burt, R. (2001). *Social capital: Theory and research.* Hawthorne, NY: Aldine de Gruyter.

Lin, N., Fu, Y., & Hsung, H. (2001). The position generator: Measurement techniques for investigations of social capital. In: N. Lin, K. Cook & R. S. Burt (Eds), *Social capital: Theory and research* (pp. 57–84). Hawthorne, NY: Aldine de Gruyter.

Lowe, K. B., Kroeck, K. G., & Sivasubramaniam, N. (1996). Effectiveness of correlates of transformational and transactional leadership: A meta-analytic review of the MLQ literature. *The Leadership Quarterly, 7,* 385–425.

Luthans, F., & Avolio, B. J. (2003). Authentic leadership: A positive development approach. In: K. S. Cameron, J. E. Dutton & R. E. Quinn (Eds), *Positive organizational scholarship: Foundations of a new discipline* (pp. 241–261). San Francisco: Berrett-Koehler.

Maccoby, M. (2004). Narcissistic leaders: The incredible pros, the inevitable cons. *Harvard Business Review, 82*(1), 92–101.

May, D. R., Chan, A. L. Y., Hodges, T. D., & Avolio, B. J. (2003). Developing the moral component of authentic leadership. *Organizational Dynamics, 32,* 247–260.

McClelland, D. C. (1985). *Human motivation.* Glenview, IL: Scott, Foresman.

Nahapiet, J., & Ghoshal, S. (1998). Social, capital intellectual capital, and the organizational advantage. *Academy of Management Review, 23,* 242–266.

Nanus, B. (1992). *Visionary leadership.* San Francisco: Jossey-Bass.

Pennings, J. M., & Lee, K. (1999). Social capital of organization: Conceptualization, level of analysis, and performance implications. In: R. T. A. J. Leenders & S. M. Gabbay (Eds), *Corporate social capital and liability* (pp. 43–67). Boston: Kluwer Academic.

Pfeffer, J. (1992). *Managing with power: Politics and influence in organizations.* Boston, MA: Harvard Business School Press.

Pfeffer, J., & Salancik, G. R. (1978). *The external control of organizations.* New York: Harper and Row.

Portes, A. (1998). Social capital: Its origins and applications in modern sociology. *Annual Review of Sociology, 24,* 1–24.

Portes, A. (2000). The two meanings of social capital. *Sociological Forum, 15*(1), 1–12.

Portes, A., & Landolt, P. (1996). The downside of social capital. *The American Prospect, 26,* 18–22.

Portes, A., & Sensenbrenner, J. (1993). Embeddedness and immigration: notes on the social determinants of economic action. *American Journal of Sociology, 98,* 1320–1350.

Putnam, R. D. (1995). Tuning in, tuning out: The strange disappearance of social capital in America. *Political Science and Politics, 28*(4), 664–683.

Putnam, R. D. (2000). *Bowling alone: The collapse and revival of American community.* New York: Simon & Schuster.

Sashkin, M., & Fulmer, M. (1988). Toward an organizational leadership theory. In: G. Hunt, B. R. Baliga, H. P. Dachler & C. A. Schriesheim (Eds), *Emerging leadership vistas* (pp. 51–65). Lexington, MA: Heath.

Scott, J. (2000). *Social network analysis: A handbook* (2nd ed.). Thousands Oaks, CA: Sage.

Senge, P. M. (1990). *The fifth discipline: The art and practice of the learning organization.* New York: Doubleday.

Shamir, B., House, R. J., & Arthur, M. B. (1993). The motivational effects of charismatic leadership: A self-concept based theory. *Organizational Science, 4,* 1–17.

Shamir, B., & Howell, J. M. (1999). Organizational and contextual influences on the emergence and effectiveness of charismatic leadership. *The Leadership Quarterly, 10,* 257–283.

Sosik, J. J., Avolio, B. J., & Kahai, S. S. (1997). Effects of leadership style and anonymity on group potency and effectiveness in a group decision support system environment. *Journal of Applied Psychology, 82,* 89–103.

Sparrowe, R. T., & Liden, R. C. (1997). Process and structure in leader-member exchange. *Academy of Management Review, 22,* 522–552.

Sully, M., Waldman, D. A., House, R. J., & Washburn, N. (2005). Understanding values-based leadership and transformation in firms: A study of CEOs in 16 countires. Paper presented at the Meeting of The Academy of Mangement, Honolulu.

Szulanski, G. (1996). Exploring internal stickiness: Impediments to the transfer of best practice within the firm. *Strategic Management Journal, 17,* 27–43.

Tajfel, H., & Turner, J. C. (1986). The social identity theory of intergroup behavior. In: S. Worchel & W. Austin (Eds), *Psychology of intergroup relations* (pp. 7–24). Chicago: Nelson-Hall.

Tsai, W., & Ghoshal, S. (1998). Social capital and value creation: The role of intrafirm networks. *Academy of Management Journal, 41,* 464–476.

Uzzi, B., & Gillespie, J. J. (1999). Corporate social capital and the cost of financial capital: An embeddedness approach. In: R. T. Leenders & S. Gabbay (Eds), *Corporate social capital and liability* (pp. 446–459). Boston: Kluwer Academic.

van Knippenberg, D., & Hogg, M. A. (2003). A social identity model of ledership effectiveness in organizations. *Research in Organizational Behavior, 25,* 243–295.

Vera, D., & Crossan, M. (2004). Strategic leadership on organizational learning. *Academy of Management Review, 29,* 222–240.

Waldman, D. A., Ramírez, G., House, R. J., & Puranam, P. (2001). Does leadership matter?: CEO leadership attributes and profitability under conditions of perceived environmental uncertainty. *Academy of Management Journal, 44*, 134–144.

Waldman, D. A., & Yammarino, F. J. (1999). CEO charismatic leadership: Levels-of-management and levels-of-analysis effects. *Academy of Management Review, 14*, 266–285.

Yukl, G. (1999). An evaluation of conceptual weaknesses in transformational and charismatic leadership theories. *The Leadership Quarterly, 10*, 285–305.

Yukl, G. (2002). *Leadership in organizations* (5th ed.). Upper Saddle River, NJ: Prentice-Hall.

Zaccaro, S. J., Gualtieri, J., & Minionis, D. (1995). Task cohesion as a facilitator of team decision making under temporal urgency. *Military Psychology, 7*, 77–93.

Zhou, M., & Bankston, C. L. (1996). Social capital and the adaptation of the second generation: The case of Vietnamese youth in New Orleans. In: A. Portes (Ed.), *The new second generation* (pp. 197–220). New York: Russell Sage Foundation.

LEADER POLITICAL SKILL AND AUTHENTIC LEADERSHIP ☆

Ceasar Douglas, Gerald R. Ferris and
Pamela L. Perrewé

ABSTRACT

We examine the important role of leader political skill in authentic leadership. Authentic leaders are individuals who hold true to their fundamental moral character and values. However, we must remember that leadership is a social phenomenon. Thus, we see leader political skill as an essential component in the study of authentic leadership because politically skilled leaders inspire trust, confidence, and authenticity as mechanisms to incur follower motivation, commitment, and productive work behavior.

In summary, we examine the pivotal role played by political skill in the leadership process, discuss the implications of leader authenticity, and examine how such a perspective can advance our understanding of leadership.

☆ An earlier version of this paper was presented at the UNL Gallup Leadership Institute Summit, Omaha, Nebraska, June 10–12, 2004. In: W.L. Gardner, B.J. Avolio & F.O. Walumbwa (Eds.), *Authentic leadership: Origins, development, and effects* (Vol. 3 of the *Monographs in Leadership Management* series, J.G. Hunt, Senior editor). Oxford, UK: Elsevier Science.

Authentic Leadership Theory and Practice: Origins, Effects and Development
Monographs in Leadership and Management, Volume 3, 139–154

Political perspectives on organizations have been around for half a century, with serious scholarship being undertaken within the past couple of decades. However, the study of leadership was largely ignored with respect to political perspectives until relatively recently. Indeed, just within the past couple of years, *The Leadership Quarterly* published an article taking a political perspective on leadership (Ammeter, Douglas, Gardner, Hochwarter, & Ferris, 2002), and a special issue on political perspectives on leadership (Volume 15, Number 4). Because there are different views or definitions of the term "political," we should mention that we characterize the term not in a negative, but in a neutral to positive way, and quite similar to the effective exercise of influence.

Therefore, we see leader political skill as subject matter quite relevant to the topic of "authentic leadership." Because we deal in images and our perceptions of reality, what is actually authentic may be more of a socially constructed reality than an objective one. Gardner (1995, p. 60) discussed the construction and manipulation of leader images, and suggested that ". . .it is no longer clear to audience members whether they are being exposed to an authentic individual, speaking her actual words, or to a personage created by media advisors." The fact of the matter is that whereas we desperately want to believe that our leaders are sincere and genuine in their statements, we simply do not know – good actors can feign authenticity through the effective execution and delivery of apparent sincerity. These issues project two important perspectives on authentic leadership, one as the product of follower perceptions and another as an unobservable construct.

Political skill is emerging as a key set of competencies for effective leadership (Ahearn, Ferris, Hochwarter, Douglas, & Ammeter, 2004; Ferris, Davidson, & Perrewé, 2005; Treadway et al., 2004). Also, the concept of authentic leadership is quickly gathering momentum and generating interest (e.g., Avolio & Gardner, 2005). What is important is the intuitive conflict between the construct of authentic leadership and what is necessary to maintain viable leadership effectiveness. Authentic leaders, leaders who are true to their core beliefs and values, may fail to generate follower trust and commitment (Eagly, 2005), hence limiting their effectiveness as leaders. We believe that leader political skill helps authentic leaders become effective leaders. However, these two constructs, albeit compatible in many respects, have not been brought together previously. Yet, in doing so, such integration has the potential to contribute meaningfully to a more informed understanding of leader effectiveness in organizations today. Indeed, this is the purpose of the present chapter.

BACKGROUND THEORY AND RESEARCH

Nature of Political Skill

A political view of organizations has been advocated by some scholars for over two decades, and it generally assumes that job performance and effectiveness at work are determined as much or more by shrewdness, savvy, and positioning as by intelligence and hard work (e.g., Luthans, Hodgetts, & Rosenkrantz, 1988; Mintzberg, 1983). Pfeffer (1981) and Mintzberg (1983) independently proposed political perspectives on organizations, and they argued that political skill was needed to be successful. Mintzberg viewed political skill as involving influence, which is accomplished through the use of manipulation, negotiation, and persuasion.

In an effort to capture the essential nature of the construct, political skill has been defined as: "The ability to effectively understand others at work and to use such knowledge to influence others to act in ways that enhance one's personal and/or organizational objectives" (Ahearn et al., 2004, p. 311). Thus, politically skilled individuals combine social astuteness with the ability to adjust their behavior to different and changing situational demands in a manner that inspires support and trust, appears to be sincere, and effectively influences others.

Leaders high in political skill not only know precisely what to do in different social situations at work, but also how to do it in a manner that disguises any ulterior, self-serving motives, and appears to be sincere. Furthermore, political skill is distinct from general mental ability, and related to personality traits and other interpersonally oriented constructs such as self-monitoring and emotional intelligence, but not so highly as to raise a concern about construct redundancy. In terms of its derivation, we borrow from others who have suggested the usefulness of taking an integrative dispositional-situational approach to personality (e.g., Murtha, Kanfer, & Ackerman, 1996) and social effectiveness (e.g., Buck, 1991). Specifically, we believe political skill is at least partially dispositional, but we also believe political skill can be developed and shaped through a combination of formal and informal developmental experiences.

Leader Political Skill

Organizations today have moved away from the simplistic – mechanistic or linear – to arrangements saddled with uncertainty and unpredictability (Regine & Lewin, 2000), making the decisions made by leaders much more complex and relying more on social influence than command and control. Although it has been viewed in many ways, we believe leadership is best characterized as a social influence process, and as such, leaders are effective to the extent to which they influence followers to meet or exceed standards of performance, as well as inspire followers to engage in extra-role behavior that contributes to the effectiveness of the unit. Like former President Harry Truman once said: "A leader is a man who has the ability to get other people to do what they don't want to do and like it" (Matthews, 1988, p. 195).

Leaders possessing political skill are socially astute, accurate observers of others, and keenly attuned to diverse social situations. They comprehend social interactions, and accurately interpret their behavior, as well as that of others, in social settings. Furthermore, they have strong powers of discernment, and high self-awareness. We argue that leader political skill is one of those key skills that is critical to leadership effectiveness and agree with Zaccaro (2002) who stated, "… successful social influence by the leader requires the mastery of a range of skills and the ability to select and apply them to the appropriate situation" (p. 45). Further, Bolman and Deal (1991) indicated that political skill gives leaders power, and Kotter (1985) argued that effectiveness demands a sophisticated type of leader social/political skill that can inspire and mobilize people to work together to accomplish critical goals and objectives.

Leaders also can become more effective by networking, coalition building, and social capital creation by working with and through others (e.g., Boyatzis, 1982; Brass, 2001; Luthans et al., 1988), which is facilitated by political skill. House (1995) argued that networked, well-positioned leaders are able to acquire more resources for their units, and thus are valued more by their teams. The compilation of friendships, connections, and alliances with influential others allows leaders to leverage their social capital to help facilitate change efforts for increased effectiveness. Additionally, leader social capital has increased reputational benefits for the leader, which are believed to favorably influence follower reactions (Ammeter et al., 2002).

Ciampa (2005) argued that Chief Executive Officers (CEOs) today need to possess a unique blend of what he calls "management savvy, political intelligence, and personal style." These are qualities captured in the construct of political skill.

Authentic Leadership

Webster's dictionary defines authentic as: (1) authoritative, (2) worthy of acceptance, and (3) not imaginary or false. When we think of the first two definitions together with leadership, the terms are seemingly redundant. However, the third definition in combination with leadership raises an interesting question; when is a leader imaginary or false? This is a question that only the leader can fully answer.

In the broader sense, authentic leadership is viewed in the context of leader actions and follower development, where leader transparency and worthy objectives guide follower development (Gardner, Avolio, Luthans, May, & Walumbwa, 2005). Shamir and Eilam (2005) provide a more narrow view of authentic leaders, seeing them as original, true to themselves, motivated and guided by values and convictions. At issue here is the distinction between authentic leadership as a function of leader behaviors and follower perceptions, and authentic leadership as an unobservable construct.

At the base of authentic leadership are two questions, who is the leader, and is the leader being true to him/herself? The answer to these questions lies within the leader's self-concept. Self-concept is a collection of self-schema (Markus & Wurf, 1987) that defines our own mental representation of who we are (Kihlstrom & Cantor, 1984), becomes more complex and differentiated through our experiences (London, 1994), and shifts from the personal "I" to the collective "We" (Ellemers et al., 2004). We argue that self-concept is important to leader authenticity because it influences one's behavior, and is influenced by others and social situations.

The view that we have of ourselves in social situations operates on a continuum between two opposing positions; our self as a unique being and our self as a group member (Brewer & Gardner, 1996; Markus & Kitayama, 1991). Leader authenticity may operate along a similar continuum. If the leader closely identifies with the followers, then he/she will remain focused on follower issues; if not, the leader may briefly support the follower's position only to refocus on his/her own self-interest at a later time. In either case, the leader does not independently choose a path of action; this decision is shaped by follower perceptions and expectations.

Follower perceptions and expectations contribute to the leader's working self-concept, which is the current self-concept consisting of stable core self-conceptions and self-conceptions that are based on prevalent circumstances (Markus & Wurf, 1987). The stable core represents the leader's foundation, who he or she really is (*actual selves*), while the other self-conceptions reflect who the leader is capable of being (*possible selves*). Leader authenticity greatly depends on social interaction, hence follower interaction. In the next section, we discuss the implications of leader – follower interaction for authentic leadership.

Follower Influence on Authentic Leadership

Follower perceptions affect leader authenticity through the images followers associate with leadership. Hogg (2001) suggested that follower perceptions of leadership are derived from that of the prototypical group member. In other words, leader imagery is based on the follower's perception of the ideal group member. Thus, the leader at some level must adopt or reinforce the group prototype to effectively lead the group. Engle and Lord (1997) found that managers who relied on their own perceptions of leadership, as compared with those of their subordinates, received less favorable evaluations. This study points to the need for congruence between leader and follower perceptions. Moreover, leaders will adjust to the group prototype as they seek to improve relationships.

Leaders shape, and are shaped by, their interactions with others, and their self-concept aids in defining and reacting to those encounters (Markus & Wurf, 1987). The development of one's self-concept emerges from resolving crises and dilemmas that are intertwined with key interpersonal relationships (London, 1994). Higgins (1985) argued that a portion of our self-concepts stems from characteristics that others believe we should have, and indicated that discrepancies between this and our actual self-concepts were related to anxiety. In this situation, follower expectations may produce leader anxiety, which in turn prompts the leader to reduce the discrepancy between the conflicting views of his/her self-concept by adopting behaviors that meet other's expectations.

Authentic leaders need the ability to consider multiple perspectives or issues and make assessments in a balanced manner (Avolio & Gardner, 2005); they must be cognizant of follower views of leadership and have the capacity to make the necessary adjustments. Henderson and Hoy (1983) linked authentic leadership to one's ability to exhibit a "salience of self over role," where the leader is focused on follower needs more than role requirements. Importantly, modifications must extend beyond situation-based impression management or chameleon-like behaviors. These behaviors prompt leaders to make situation-based (role required) adjustments potentially causing them to appear less authentic. If leaders choose to remain true to themselves and role requirements, then follower perceptions will cast the leaders as ineffective and out of touch with their needs.

In summary, to be authentic and effective, leaders must be viewed as making the transition from the "I" position, based on leader needs and role requirements, to the "We" position, striving for congruence between leader behavior and follower needs. Successful authentic leaders do not change who they are, but rather they modify their presentations based on leader – follower interactions.

MODEL OF LEADER POLITICAL SKILL AND AUTHENTIC LEADERSHIP

Leaders who are high in political skill know precisely what to do in different social situations at work (e.g., selecting the most situationally appropriate behaviors), and also know exactly how to do it with a sincere, engaging manner that disguises any ulterior motive, which in turn, inspires believability, trust, and confidence (Dirks & Ferrin, 2002; Mayer, Davis, & Schoorman, 1995; McAllister, 1995). The political skill of leaders appears to be similar in nature to House and Aditya's (1997) characterization of leader style, as the manner in which leaders express particular behaviors that contribute to follower interpretation and subsequent effectiveness of those behaviors.

Thus, we argue that leader political skill provides the social astuteness and behavioral flexibility and adaptability necessary to effectively address the needs and aspirations of followers in ways that favorably influence their work reactions and behavior, and affect the climate of the work unit. Further, we believe leader political skill influences followers' trust in the leader, perceptions of leader credibility, and leader reputation, which, ultimately, will be associated with effectiveness (e.g., Ahearn et al., 2004; Hall, Blass, Ferris, & Massengale, 2004; Treadway et al., 2004). Finally, the networking ability aspect of leader political skill has been found to be particularly influential in explaining variance in leader effectiveness (Douglas & Ammeter, 2004).

Leadership implies, if not explicitly assumes, influence, and we suggest that leader political skill articulates precisely how the influence process operates in work settings to bring about desired outcomes. Therefore, we propose the working conceptualization presented in Fig. 1 to describe how leader political skill interacts with authentic leadership to influence follower performance and reactions.

In Fig. 1, we provide an overview of the relationship between leader authenticity and leader political skill within organizations. As the figure indicates, leader authenticity and leader political skill interact and directly affect follower perceptions of trust in leadership, leader creditability, and leader reputation. Follower perceptions directly influence leader

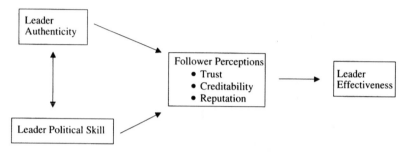

Fig. 1. Leader Political Skill and Authentic Leadership.

effectiveness, and these perceptions evolve over time and through multiple encounters. Specifically, the model recognizes that authentic leadership exists on a continuum, where we are thinking that some leaders are more authentic than inauthentic (Avolio & Gardner, 2005; Bass & Steidlmeier, 1999; Gardner et al., 2005). The variance in both leader authenticity and leader political skill has both direct and indirect effects on follower perceptions of trust in leadership, leader creditability, and leader reputation.

The interaction between leader authenticity and leader political skill is depicted in Fig. 2. We believe that leaders represented in each of the four quadrants will have a distinct effect on follower perceptions. Leaders occupying quadrant 1 (low authenticity and low LPS) will never generate positive perceptions of trust in leadership, creditability, and reputation. Here, inauthentic leaders fail to generate positive perceptions because they do not reveal any true core values or convictions and lack the political skill to make their actions believable.

Leaders in quadrant 2 (high authenticity and low LPS) will struggle in early encounters, but will develop positive perceptions in the long run. Authentic leaders face the difficulty of being true to oneself while adjusting to situational demands and follower expectations. In the absence of political skill, it is the authentic leader's consistency that leads to positive perceptions over time.

Quadrant 3 leaders (low authenticity and high LPS) may have a positive initial influence on follower perceptions, but these perceptions will fade through time. Leaders possessing high levels of political skill are adept in responding to situational demands, which contribute to initial positive perceptions. However, over time inauthentic leaders appear opportunistic or manipulative because their goal is mastering the situation instead of remaining true to oneself. As a result, followers eventually recognize the leader's inconsistent behavior and downgrade previous positive perceptions.

2. High Authenticity Low LPS	4. High Authenticity High LPS
1. Low Authenticity Low LPS	3. Low Authenticity High LPS

Fig. 2. The Interaction between Leader Authenticity and Leader Political Skill (LPS).

Finally, quadrant 4 leaders (high authenticity and high LPS) will produce positive initial and lasting perceptions of trust in leadership, leader creditability, and leader reputation. Political skill enables leaders to smoothly make the transition from "I" to "We", and authenticity allows leaders to enhance trust, creditability and reputation through consistent behavior.

DISCUSSION

Leaders who possess political skill are perceived as having high levels of integrity, authenticity, sincerity, and genuineness. They are, or appear to be, honest, open, and forthright. This dimension of political skill strikes at the very heart of whether influence attempts will be successful, because it focuses on the perceived intentions of the behavior exhibited. The perceived intentions or motives of a leader are important, and may alter the interpretation and labeling of behavior.

For example, what appears to be helping behavior (e.g., such as offering to help with a project) is labeled as "citizenship," if the intentions are seen as positive, and "political," if the intentions are perceived as instrumental or self-serving, whereby the actor expects to get something out of it (e.g., Bolino, 1999; Ferris, Bhawuk, Fedor, & Judge, 1995). Influence attempts will be successful only to the extent to which the leader is perceived as possessing no ulterior motive (e.g., Jones, 1990).

Leaders high in apparent sincerity can inspire trust and confidence in and from those around them because their actions are not interpreted as

manipulative or coercive. Their tactics often are seen as subtle, and their
motives do not appear self-serving. They have the ability to disguise ulterior
motives so they appear to others as being "straight shooters." In Rudolph
W. Giuliani's (2002) book, *Leadership*, Giuliani portrays himself as a
"straight shooter" with an aggressive style that can be characterized as
"what you see is what you get." The leadership that he displayed on and
around the events of September 11, 2001, earned him the title "America's
Mayor." Giuliani is an example of someone who is politically skilled and
appears to others to be authentic – and he well may be authentic.

In order to be effective, leaders need to influence others, and political skill
is an essential quality that facilitates the influence process. Partisan politics
always has been an arena for influence, whether it be face-to-face persuasion, or coalition or network building to muster sufficient support to push
through, or block, legislation. Therefore, political skill is important in politics, and may well be the single most important characteristic that distinguishes the truly effective political leaders.

Politicians operate in a world of reputation creation and management,
where there is more interpretation of fact than reality, and the politician's
ability to promote ideas with the proper "spin" is critical to success, and
even survival. As such, politics provides an arena not that different from the
way influence done in organizations, or life in general, and political skill is
critically important in all these contexts.

We are coming off a presidential election year, during which newspapers
and magazines were full of stories about the political candidates, and the
undercurrent of much of this news was the basic question: What characteristics do we look for in a President? Although there are many answers to
this question, depending on who you ask, there are some interesting sim-
ilarities we found across media accounts. Indeed, looking back over recent
elections, it appears that the American public seems to want a President who
looks and acts presidential, which involves style, temperament, likability,
and authenticity, or at least the appearance of these qualities (e.g., Gibbs,
2004).

If political candidates are perceived as insincere or phony, we do not like
them, nor will we want to elect them; yet if they dazzle us with charisma, we
tend to like them, and will probably vote for them. So, liking is important to
candidates, because then we probably trust them more, and experience
more of a comfort level with them. Politically skilled candidates understand this well, and are skillful at managing impressions that lead to
favorable outcomes. Because politics has a reputation for phoniness, candidates who succeed are often the ones who appear most sincere, genuine,

and authentic – that is, the what-you-see-is-what-you-get sort of person. This is a key competency of the politically skilled, and it can make the difference in an election.

RESEARCH IMPLICATIONS

Contributions to Theory and Research

The concepts of authentic leadership and leader political skill have interesting implications for theory and research because, at the surface level, these terms appear to be contradictory. However, from a closer view, we can see some common ground.

Authentic leaders are individuals who hold true to their moral character and values. However, we must remember that leadership does not take place in a vacuum, but instead it is a social phenomenon. A leader's identity is socially constructed and refined through years of interaction in social and organizational settings (Gardner & Avolio, 1998). Therefore, a portion of the leader's identity is anchored by this "working self-concept" (Markus & Wurf, 1987), which describes who the leader is during social encounters. Following from this we see that an authentic leader, in fact, may be a leader politician, or one who is adept at political skill. In this case, a necessary part of the leader politician identity would require the leader to be political in most social settings. Leader authenticity is a valuable attribute in that it provides a sense of stability for followers. We indicate that authenticity has direct and indirect effects on follower perceptions of trust in leadership, leader creditability, and leader reputation.

Indirectly, authenticity influences follower perceptions through the use of leader political skill. If an individual's self-identity includes political behavior, then as a leader this individual will exhibit greater ease in utilizing political skill. Directly, authenticity affects follower perceptions by creating an image of consistency. Consistent presentations reinforce existing follower schema, which allows followers to develop patterns of expected behavior that lead to more stable perceptions over time.

Leader political skill is the use of influence to enhance one's personal or organizational agendas. We believe that when used effectively, political skill will generate positive perceptions in the short run. However, as time passes, if there is no consistency in direction or purpose in the leader's actions, the leader's effectiveness and image will suffer. If the leader is consistently self-serving in his/her actions, follower perceptions will be more favorable than if the leader acts inconsistently. Trust, reputation, and creditability are all anchored by the concept of behavior predictability. That is, we believe followers are better prepared to respond to a consistently self-serving leader than one who is politically inconsistent.

Conceptual Issues

Additionally, we believe there are other construct validity challenges not only for political skill, but also for the broad set of social or interpersonal constructs that have emerged in the literature over the years. Ferris, Perrewé, and Douglas (2002) discussed this proliferation of social constructs, and the need for each to more precisely delineate their individual uniqueness and identity, at the same time acknowledging that there might be some degree of covariation with other constructs. We observe the ongoing development of constructs like social intelligence, social skill, emotional intelligence, social competence, self-monitoring, and interpersonal acumen, to name but a few, and we see natural overlap among these.

The point here is that we need to empirically examine the relationships among some of these constructs. In the case of political skill, it is perhaps most critical to demonstrate that it is indeed different than social skill, primarily because the two sometimes are used interchangeably in discussion. Scholars in this area have argued that social skill and political skill are, in fact, different (Luthans et al., 1988; Peled, 2000). Peled argued that social skill refers to "the ease and comfort of communication between leaders and their employees, peers, superiors, and clients" (p. 27). Alternatively, Peled suggested that political skill refers to "the manager's ability to manipulate his/her inter-personal relationships with employees, colleagues, clients, and supervisors to ensure the ultimate success of the project" (p. 27).

Future research should empirically validate such claims and demonstrate that although perhaps related at a modest level, social and political skills represent separate and unique constructs. Work also is needed to demonstrate the construct delineation between political skill and Zaccaro's (2002) conceptualization of social intelligence.

Measurement Issues

Although most of the research on political skill has focused on data gathering from the job incumbent, we would encourage research to expand by including the perceptions of a target person's political skill from his or her superiors, peers, and subordinates. Self-report measurement of interpersonally focused constructs, like political skill, can be useful and enlightening (e.g., Riggio & Riggio, 2001). However, we must be able to demonstrate some consistent level of political skill agreement across sources (e.g., superiors, peers, and subordinates) to have a greater confidence in the measure's ability to tap a meaningful element of interpersonal effectiveness.

CONCLUSION

We have argued in this chapter that political skill is a foundational component of effective leadership, with particular relevance to authentic leadership. Possessing the intuitive savvy and style to know what to do when, and how to execute such behaviors in convincing, genuine, and sincere ways is a key to leadership performance and effectiveness. People want to trust and have a comfort level with their leaders and perceive them as authentic, and the "real thing." However, as noted recently, "... even the claim for authenticity can be manufactured (good actors know how to feign sincerity), while many 'authentic' individuals simply look awkward or amateurish when setting under klieg lights" (Gardner, 1995, p. 60).

Therefore, we see leader political skill as an essential category in the study of authentic leadership because politically skilled leaders inspire trust, confidence, and authenticity as mechanisms to incur follower motivation, commitment, and productive work behavior. Further, we see political skill as an element quite consistent with the increasingly important and popular movement toward "positive organizational behavior" recently articulated by Luthans (Luthans, 2002a, b; Luthans & Youssef, 2004).

Finally, the individual who does not embody his or her values in every day life may not be viewed as authentic. The issue of embodiment raises the question of whether the person is authentic. In other words, does the leader truly embody the message of which he or she speaks? The leader who does not embody his or her message is not authentic and will eventually be found out (Gardner, 1995). However, the authentic leader who leads an exemplary life but lacks political skill, will not be able to inspire trust and confidence in others, and will not be an effective leader. Thus, the combination of authenticity in leadership coupled with political skill is likely the best recipe for leader success.

The political skill construct is quite early in its evolution, but we have been encouraged by the conceptual and empirical research to date. We see leader political skill as a potentially new and important stream of research that has the potential to lead us in productive directions in our quest to develop a more informed understanding of the dynamics of leadership.

REFERENCES

Ahearn, K. K., Ferris, G. R., Hochwarter, W. A., Douglas, C., & Ammeter, A. P. (2004). Leader political skill and team performance. *Journal of Management, 30*, 309–327.

Ammeter, A. P., Douglas, C., Gardner, W. L., Hochwarter, W. A., & Ferris, G. R. (2002). Toward a political theory of leadership. *The Leadership Quarterly, 13*, 751–796.

Avolio, B. J., & Gardner, W. L. (2005). Authentic leadership development: Getting to the root of positive forms of leadership. *The Leadership Quarterly, 16*, 315–338.

Bass, B. M., & Steidlmeier, P. (1999). Ethics, character, and authentic transformational leadership behavior. *The Leadership Quarterly, 10*, 81–217.

Bolman, L. G., & Deal, T. E. (1991). *Reframing organizations: Artistry, choice, and leadership.* San Francisco: Jossey–Bass.

Bolino, M. G. (1999). Citizenship and impression management: Good soldiers or good actors? *Academy of Management Review, 24*, 82–98.

Boyatzis, R. E. (1982). *The competent manager: A model for effective performance.* New York: Wiley.

Brass, D. J. (2001). Social capital and organizational leadership. In: S. J. Zaccaro, & R. J. Klimoski (Eds), *The nature of organizational leadership* (pp. 132–152). San Francisco: Jossey–Bass.

Brewer, M. B., & Gardner, W. L. (1996). Who is this "We"? Levels of collective identity and self representations. *Journal of Personality and Social Psychology, 71*, 83–93.

Buck, R. (1991). Temperament, social skills, and the communication of emotion: A development-interactionist view. In: D. G. Gilbert, & J. J. Connolly (Eds), *Personality, social skills, and psychopathology: An individual difference approach* (pp. 85–105). New York: Plenum Press.

Ciampa, D. (2005). Almost ready: How leaders move. *Harvard Business Review, 83*(1), 46–53.

Dirks, K. T., & Ferrin, D. L. (2002). Trust in leadership: Meta-analytic findings and implications for research and practice. *Journal of Applied Psychology, 87*, 611–628.

Douglas, C., & Ammeter, A. P. (2004). An examination of leader political skill and its effect on ratings of leader effectiveness. *The Leadership Quarterly, 15*, 537–550.

Eagly, A. H. (2005). Achieving relational authenticity in leadership: Does gender matter? *The Leadership Quarterly*, in press.

Ellemers, N., de Gilder, D., & Haslam, S. A. (2004). Motivating individuals and groups at work: A social identity perspective on leadership and group performance. *Academy of Management Review, 29*, 459–478.

Engle, E. M., & Lord, R. G. (1997). Implicit theories, self-schema, and leader-member exchange. *Academy of Management Journal, 40*, 988–1010.

Ferris, G. R., Bhawuk, D. P. S., Fedor, D. B., & Judge, T. A. (1995). Organizational politics and citizenship: Attributions of intentionality and construct definition. In: M.J. Martinko (Ed.), *Advances in attribution theory: An organizational perspective* (pp. 231–252). Delray Beach, FL: St. Lucie Press.

Ferris, G. R., Davidson, S. L., & Perrewé, P. L. (2005). *Political skill at work*. Palo Alto, CA: Davies-Black Publishing.

Ferris, G. R., Perrewé, P. L., & Douglas, C. (2002). Social effectiveness in organizations: Construct validity and directions for future research. *Journal of Leadership & Organizational Studies, 9*, 49–63.

Gardner, H. (1995). *Leading minds: An anatomy of leadership*. New York: Basic Books.

Gardner, W. L., & Avolio, B. J. (1998). The charismatic relationship: A dramaturgical perspective. *Academy of Management Review, 23*, 32–58.

Gardner, W. L., Avolio, B. J., Luthans, F., May, D. R., & Walumbwa, F. O. (2005). Can you see the real me? A self-based model of authentic leader and follower development. *The Leadership Quarterly, 16*, 373–394.

Gibbs, N. (2004). What becomes a president most? *Time*, February 2, 33–39.

Giuliani, R. W. (with Kurson, K.). (2002). *Leadership*. New York, NY: Miramax Books.

Hall, A. T., Blass, F. R., Ferris, G. R., & Massengale, R. (2004). Leader reputation and accountability in organizations: Implications for dysfunctional leader behavior. *The Leadership Quarterly, 15*, 515–536.

Henderson, J. E., & Hoy, W. K. (1983). Leader authenticity: The development and test of an operational measure. *Educational and Psychological Research, 3*, 63–75.

Higgins, E. T. (1985). Self-concept discrepancy theory: A psychological model for distinguishing among different aspects of depression and anxiety. *Social Cognition, 3*, 51–76.

Hogg, M. A. (2001). A social identity theory of leadership. *Personality and Social Psychology Review, 5*, 184–200.

House, R. J. (1995). Leadership in the twenty-first century. In: A. Howard (Ed.), *The changing nature of work* (pp. 411–450). San Francisco: Jossey-Bass.

House, R. J., & Aditya, R. N. (1997). The social scientific study of leadership: Quo vadis? *Journal of Management, 23*, 409–473.

Jones, E. E. (1990). *Interpersonal perception*. New York: W. H. Freeman.

Kihlstrom, J. F., & Cantor, N. (1984). Mental representations of the self. *Advanced Experimental Social Psychology, 17*, 1–47.

Kotter, J. P. (1985). *Power and influence: Beyond formal authority*. New York: Free Press.

London, M. (1994). *Self and interpersonal insight: How people gain understanding of themselves and others in organizations*. New York: Oxford University Press.

Luthans, F. (2002a). Positive organizational behavior: Developing and managing psychological strengths for performance improvement. *Academy of Management Executive, 16*, 57–75.

Luthans, F. (2002b). The need for and meaning of positive organizational behavior. *Journal of Organizational Behavior, 23*, 695–706.

Luthans, F., & Youssef, C. M. (2004). Human, social, and now positive psychological capital management: Investing in people for competitive advantage. *Organizational Dynamics, 33*, 143–160.

Luthans, F., Hodgetts, R. M., & Rosenkrantz, S. A. (1988). *Real managers*. Cambridge, MA: Ballinger.

Markus, H. R., & Wurf, E. (1987). The dynamic self-concept: A social psychological perspective. *American Review of Psychology, 38*, 299–337.

Markus, H. R., & Kitayama, S. (1991). Culture and the self: Implications for cognition, emotion, and motivation. *Psychological Review, 98*, 224–253.

Matthews, C. (1988). *Hardball: How politics is played told by one who knows the game*. New York: Harper & Row.

Mayer, R. C., Davis, J. H., & Schoorman, F. D. (1995). An integrative model of organizational trust. *Academy of Management Review, 20,* 709–734.

McAllister, D. J. (1995). Affect- and cognition-based trust as foundations for interpersonal cooperation in organizations. *Academy of Management Journal, 38,* 24–59.

Mintzberg, H. (1983). *Power in and around organizations.* Englewood Cliffs, NJ: Prentice-Hall.

Murtha, T. C., Kanfer, R., & Ackerman, P. L. (1996). Toward an interactionist taxonomy of personality and situations: An integrative situational-dispositional representation of personality traits. *Journal of Personality and Social Psychology, 71,* 193–207.

Peled, A. (2000). Politicking for success: The missing skill. *Leadership and Organization Development Journal, 21,* 20–29.

Pfeffer, J. (1981). *Power in organizations.* Boston: Pitman.

Regine, B. & Lewin, R. (2000). Leading at the edge: How leaders influence complex systems. *Emergence: A Journal of Complexity Issues in Organizations and Management, 2,* 5–23.

Riggio, R. E., & Riggio, H. R. (2001). Self-report measurement of interpersonal sensitivity. In: J. A. Hall, & F. J. Bernieri (Eds), *Interpersonal sensitivity: Theory and measurement* (pp. 127–142). Mahwah, NJ: Lawrence Erlbaum.

Shamir, B., & Eilam, G. (2005). What's your story?: A life-stories approach to authentic leadership development. *The Leadership Quarterly,* in press.

Treadway, D. C., Hochwarter, W. A., Ferris, G. R., Kacmar, C. J., Douglas, C., Ammeter, A. P., & Buckley, M. R. (2004). Leader political skill and employee reactions. *The Leadership Quarterly, 15,* 493–513.

Zaccaro, S. J. (2002). Organizational leadership and social intelligence. In: R. E. Riggio, S. E. Murphy, & F. J. Pirozzolo (Eds), *Multiple intelligences and leadership* (pp. 29–54). Mahwah, NJ: Lawrence Erlbaum.

THE INTERNAL THEATER OF THE AUTHENTIC LEADER: INTEGRATING COGNITIVE, AFFECTIVE, CONATIVE AND SPIRITUAL FACETS OF AUTHENTIC LEADERSHIP

Karin Klenke

ABSTRACT

In this chapter, I present a theoretical model of authentic leadership and followership which integrates cognitive, affective, conative, and spiritual antecedents and explores their effects on group, organizational and societal outcomes. Like other models of authentic leadership, the framework described here is theoretically anchored in positive psychology. However, unlike other models, this framework includes a specific focus on the spiritual components of leadership.

INTRODUCTION

The primary goal of this chapter is to build on existing conceptualizations of authentic leadership (Avolio, Gardner, Walumba, Luthans & May, 2004;

Authentic Leadership Theory and Practice: Origins, Effects and Development
Monographs in Leadership and Management, Volume 3, 155–182
© **2005 Published by Elsevier B.V..**

Avolio & Gardner, 2005; Bass & Steidlmeier, 1999; Ilies, Morgeson, & Nahrgang, 2005; Gardner, Avolio, Luthans, May, & Walumbwa, 2005; Luthans & Avolio, 2003; May, Chan, Hodges, & Avolio, 2003; Price, 2003) by developing an integrated model of authentic leadership that enlarges the existing theoretical framework. To do so, I anchor the construct of authentic leadership in a constellation of cognitive, affective, conative and spiritual antecedents which are then linked to group and organizational level outcomes. More specifically, the model extends the current discussions of authentic leadership by delineating four individual level antecedents of authentic leadership that result in several multilevel organizational outcomes. As Luthans and Avolio (2003) point out, one of the initial intents of defining authentic leadership and followership as constructs is to make it multidimensional and multilevel. Consequently, the model presented here takes levels of analysis issues into account as reflected in the proposed organizational level outcomes.

The model is derived from various bodies of theory including transforming and transformational leadership (Bass, 1985; Bass & Avolio, 1994; Burns, 1978, 2003), motivation (Maslow, 1954, 1971), complexity and chaos theory (Marion & Uhl-Bien, 2001), and cognitive and moral development theories (Kohlberg, 1976; Rest, 1999). In addition, like the other models of authentic leadership development reviewed here, this framework incorporates constructs from positive psychology and positive organizational behavior (Frederickson, 2003; Luthans, 2002; Seligman, 1998; Seligman & Csikentmihalyi, 2000). Fig. 1 depicts the model, which is explicated in the remainder of the chapter.

MODEL PARAMETERS

Contextual Factors

Authentic leadership, like other types of leadership, is shaped by context. In my 1996 book entitled *Women and Leadership: A Contextual Perspective (Klenke, 1996)*, I argued that leadership is context dependent and must be context sensitive in order to be effective. Leaders are tenants of context, which may be historical or contemporaneous, textual or embedded in images, organizational (i.e., political system or grassroots organization) or methodological. Context operates in such a way as to provide opportunities or constraints for leaders and followers from which interactions with followers may be predicted. Therefore, contextual factors set the boundaries

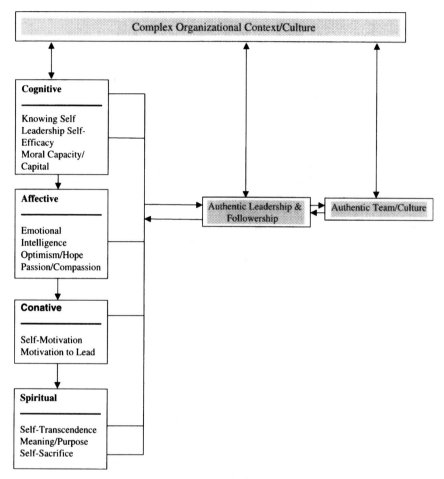

Fig. 1. Authentic leadership: Cognitive, Affective, Conative and Spiritual
        Antecedents of Authentic Leadership.

within which leaders and followers interact and determine the demands and
constraints placed on them as they contextualize their actions, attitudes,
emotions, and moral choices.

More recently, Osborn, Hunt, and Jauch (2002) reiterated the importance
of context, while Luthans and Avolio (2003) note that the greater variance
in leadership development is due to state-like characteristics *and* context.
Since leadership is embedded in context, authentic leadership may be most

fruitfully conceptualized from a systems perspective where leaders, followers and contextual factors converge to provide the fabric from which organizationally important and meaningful outcomes emerge. Contextual factors, whether as independent or moderating variables, are recursive in that context shapes and is shaped by authentic leadership and followership.

A number of contextual factors have been proposed as being particularly salient for authentic leaders and their followers. For example, Gardner et al. (2005) identify organizational power and politics, structure, gender and culture as contextual factors relevant to the study of the authentic leadership process. In addition, Avolio and Gardner (2005) suggested uncertainty and an ethical and positively oriented, strengths-based climate/culture as moderators of the authentic leadership–performance relationship. More specifically, these authors include the moderating role of a positive organizational context within the authentic leadership–performance link, acknowledging the opportunity for authentic leadership to be sustained and integrated into the context which they see as varying in terms of turbulence, uncertainty and challenge.

As depicted in Fig. 1, one of the contexts in which authentic leadership and followership are embedded is the complex organization, characterized by complexity, chaos, and uncertainty. Complexity, chaos and uncertainty serve as the cornerstone of the so-called "new" science which views organizations as complex, dynamic, nonlinear, co-creative and far-from-equilibrium systems (Wheatley, 1992). Social scientists now realize that most of the world is nonlinear and organic, characterized by uncertainty and unpredictability (Regine & Lewin, 2001). In particular, Regine and Lewin (2001) suggest that instead of restructuring the organization, leaders in complex, adaptive systems push their organizations into a degree of chaos by creating uncertainty and ambiguity. Leading in an interconnected dynamic system requires a different type of leadership, leadership that debunks the myths of autonomy, control, and omniscience, leadership that invites paradox (Klenke, 2003) and fosters network construction, leadership that considers follower behavior critical for fitness of the system or what Marion and Uhl-Bien (2001) term complex leadership. It is in the context of organizations as dynamic, interactive systems that I situate authentic leadership and followership.

In the framework offered here, I also view time as a salient contextual factor because not only do some of the behaviors of authentic leaders and followers change over time but, more importantly, the process of authentic leader and follower development spans a time horizon. Treating time as a contextual factor is consistent with one of the fundamental premises of authentic leadership development (ALD) proposed by Avolio and Gardner (2005) which posits that both leaders and followers develop over time as the relationship between them becomes more authentic. ALD is not only time-dependent at the individual level of analysis but also at the organizational level. For example, organizational longevity as a contextual variable offers leaders and followers opportunities to accrue a wide range of leadership experiences which may lead to greater authenticity in both parties.

Cognitive Antecedents of Authentic Leadership

Leader and follower cognitions play critical roles in authentic leadership. Wofford and Goodwin (1994), in their cognitive interpretation of transactional and transformational leadership theories, maintain that the immediate source of leader behavior is the activation of meta-cognitive processes, which are defined as higher level cognitive systems that regulate moment-to-moment cognitions or scripts. Meta-cognitions, or the knowledge of one's own cognitive processes, according to the authors, guide the internal context which, in turn, influences leaders' thoughts and behaviors. Applied to authentic leadership, research on the role of cognition in current models of leadership and their associated findings suggest that leadership factors reside not only in the minds of leaders but also in the minds of the followers and in the social context in which leaders and followers interact (Lord & Emrich, 2000). For example, Meindl, Ehrlich, and Dukerich (1985) characterize leadership as a "large cause" in the mind of the followers who attribute organizational successes and failures to their leaders.

Self-Knowledge and Leadership Self-Efficacy
Knowing oneself and being oneself are essential qualities of authentic leadership (May et al., 2003). "Know thyself" was the inscription on a frieze above the Oracle of Delphi, which has been ascribed to Socrates and to whom the concept of personal authenticity may go back to. "Know thyself" appears in the works of Ovid and Cicero, christian writings and eastern sacred texts. Abraham Maslow, Warren Bennis, and Stephen Covey, among others, have carried on the tradition. Sources of self-knowledge reside in early childhood experiences, feedback from classmates, teachers and supervisors, emulation of admired others and the lessons of experience. Badaracco (1997) states that leaders know about themselves from their "defining moments", events in which they are presented with dilemmas or difficult

choices and learned from the decisions made and the actions taken about their values, motivations, priorities, abilities and shortcomings.

Self-knowledge, as understood here, relates to self-awareness that several scholars (e.g., Avolio et al., 2004; Gardner & Avolio, 2005; Ilies et al., 2005) treat, as the starting point for interpreting what constitutes ALD. It not only includes the cognitive capacity of leaders and followers to assess their strengths and weaknesses but also self-knowledge in the existential sense of "verstehen" (Heidegger, 2002; Husserl, 1970). According to Heidegger, verstehen (understanding) is not a specific process of cognition; rather it is an existential, fundamental moment that belongs to the Dasein's existence. Both Heidegger and other existentialists like Husserl and Sartre stress the existential underpinnings of knowledge.

Leader and Follower Self-Efficacy
One of the focal elements relating to knowing oneself is the extent to which leaders and followers perceive themselves as self-efficacious individuals. Self-efficacy plays a pivotal role in leadership research and has been defined as beliefs in one's capabilities to mobilize the motivation, cognitive resources, and courses of action to meet given situational demands (Bandura, 1986, 1997). Bandura (1982) argues that self-efficacy arises from the gradual acquisition of complex cognitive, social, linguistic and/or physical skills through experience. As a result, individuals appear to weigh, integrate, and evaluate information about their capabilities and then regulate their choices and efforts accordingly.

By extension, leadership self-efficacy represents a leader's or follower's self-perceived capabilities for the general leadership tasks of direction setting, gaining followers' commitment and overcoming obstacles. More specifically, it refers to a person's judgment that he or she can successfully exert leadership by setting the direction for a work group, building relationships with followers in order to gain their commitment to change goals, and by working with them to overcome obstacles to change (Paglis & Green, 2002). McCormick (2001), also working within the theoretical framework of Bandura's social cognitive theory and adapting the self-regulation model, defines leadership self-efficacy as an individual's perceived capability to perform the cognitive and behavioral functions necessary to regulate group process in relation to goal achievement. The author treats leadership self-efficacy as a focal construct that affects the goals leaders select, their motivation, development of functional leadership strategies, and the skillful execution of these strategies.

More recently, self-efficacy, like some other constructs in this model such as emotional intelligence (Druskat & Wolff, 2001), has also been examined beyond the individual level of analysis as a group-level variable labeled collective efficacy or group potency (Guzzo, Yost, Campbell, & Shea, 1993). At the group level of analysis, collective efficacy has been conceptualized as being analogous to self-efficacy and, like the latter, positively predicts group performance (Prussia & Kinicki, 1996). For example, Chen and Bliese (2002) found that leadership is a more proximal predictor of collective efficacy than self-efficacy since leaders' actions toward the group represent an attempt to enhance group processes and facilitate the development of collective self-efficacy. The results of this study indicate that leadership climate, particularly at the executive level, is an immediate predictor of collective efficacy suggesting a discontinuous relationship between self- and collective efficacy.

However, clear agreement does not exist among group efficacy researchers regarding the operational definition of the construct and its appropriate level of analysis. For example, Jung and Sosik (2003) note that if group members share homogeneous perceptions about the effectiveness of their group, collective efficacy should be considered as a group-level phenomenon. On the other hand, if group members' perceptions differ, the construct should be treated as an individual-level phenomenon. This leads to my first proposition.

Proposition 1. Authentic leaders and followers who reciprocally encourage, nurture, and stimulate each others' development toward increasing authenticity may build work units or teams in which authenticity is discernible as a collective attribute of the group, similar to the distinction between self- and collective efficacy.

Authenticity as a collective attribute may be achieved by establishing norms for group self-awareness, building team spirit around positive psychological capacities or creating an affirmative environment in which positive psychological capabilities are recognized and rewarded.

Moral Capacity

According to Kanungo and Mendonca (1996), the moral development of the leader embraces individual, familial and spiritual dynamics of personality. Schulman (2002) posits that moral motives are as primary, powerful and emotionally intense as aggressive or acquisitive ones. Bass and Steidlmeier (1999), from the literature on transformational leadership, assert that it is clear that there are many points of congruence between the "authentic moral sage" and the "authentic transformational leader" since both engender virtue in self, others and society through example and virtuous conduct.

Although both Kohlberg's (1976) and Piaget's (1965) moral development theories are cognitively based, they offer little insight into the more specific constructs of moral motivation and moral capacity. Instead, they look for universals or stages in children's conceptions of justice and propriety as they age, conceptions which rarely have been found to correlate with measures of moral action such as helping or honesty (Schulman & Mekler, 1994). However, Kegan (1982) has made the specific connection between moral capacity, and/or what he refers to as perspective-taking capacity and moral decision-making and actions. Eigel and Kuhnert in this edited book, use Kegan's framework to show how his ideas about perspective-taking capacity can be tied to both authentic leadership, ALD and moral decision-making actions, as does the chapter by Hannah, Lester, and Vogelgesang. Earlier work in this area has also shown how moral decision-making involves more than cognitive processing (e.g., Sangharakshita, 1990; Wilber, 1991), acknowledging the emotional aspects of moral reasoning at the post-conventional level.

The ability to sustain authentic moral acts in the face of adversity requires leaders and followers to deal effectively with difficult moral issues. Burns (1978) notes that leaders need a sufficient level of moral capacity to make decisions that benefit not only themselves but their followers as well. Moral capacity builds the leader's moral capital, which has been defined as excellence of character or the possession and practice of a variety of virtues appropriate within particular socio-cultural contexts (Sison, 2003). Moral capital is what makes a person good as a human being.

May et al. (2003) argue that authentic leaders not only exhibit a high level of moral capacity, but also display moral resilience or the ability to positively adapt in the face of significant adversity or risk. They assert that authentic leaders develop and draw upon reserves of moral capacity, efficacy, courage, and resiliency to address ethical issues and achieve authentic and sustained moral actions (Avolio & Gardner, 2005). This leads to my second proposition.

Proposition 2. Authentic leaders and followers exhibit higher levels of moral capital compared to their less authentic counterparts.

Affective Antecedents of Authentic Leadership

Until recently, the role emotions play in leadership has received little or no attention in leadership theory and research, although, as Humphrey (2002) notes, leadership theorists never abandoned their belief in the importance of emotions during the "cognitive revolution" in leadership research (Lord & Emrich, 2000). However, it is only recently that research regarding the centrality of emotions as a key issue in leadership has generated a substantive empirical and theoretical body of work. For example, George (2000) suggests that transformational leadership is essentially an emotional process. Likewise, Ashkanasy and Tse (2000) see transformational leadership as the management of emotions where leaders display emotions, attempt to evoke emotions in their followers, and demonstrate that emotions influence leadership outcomes. In part sparked by the concept and popularity of emotional intelligence (Goleman, 1995; Goleman, McKee, & Boyatzis, 2002), attention to emotions in leadership and the leader's ability to manage complex emotional and social dynamics has become more prominent in recent writings on leadership.

In the affective category, three specific constructs are proposed as integral elements of authentic leadership: emotional intelligence or EI, dispositional optimism/hope and passion/compassion.

Emotional Intelligence
The potential importance of emotional intelligence for leadership has recently been described by a number of scholars (Gardner et al., 2005; Ilies et al., 2005; Bass, 2002; Mayer, Caruso, & Salovey, 2000; Michie & Gooty, 2005; Sosik & Megarian, 1999). Emotional intelligence refers to the leader's ability to recognize the meanings of emotions and their relationships, and to reason and problem-solve on the basis of them (Mayer et al., 2000; Mayer, Salovey, Caruso, & Sitarenios, 2001, 2003). The EI construct has generated a vigorous debate over the nature and different models of emotional intelligence (e.g., Davies, Stankov, & Roberts, 1998; Ciarocchi, Chan, & Caputi, 2000; Mayer et al., 2000) which is, however, beyond the scope of this chapter.

Focal elements of EI include self-awareness, emotional management, self-motivation, and empathy and relationship management. Although research linking emotional intelligence and leadership is limited (e.g., Barbuto & Burbach, 2004; Hartsfield, 2003; Sosik & Megerian, 1999), there is sufficient preliminary evidence to support the hypothesis that authentic leaders are emotionally intelligent leaders. The emotionally intelligent, authentic leader is able to identify his or her emotions in a given context, uses them to facilitate thinking, and understands and manages his or her emotions effectively and in a context-sensitive manner. Finally, authentic leaders and followers need self-awareness to know what is happening with their own emotions, maintain a positive state, keep distressing emotions out of the way and prime positive emotions in others (London & Maurer, 2004). The following proposition is derived from the extant literature on leadership and EI.

Proposition 3. Authentic leaders and followers display higher levels of emotional intelligence compared to their less authentic counterparts.

Hope and Dispositional Optimism
Dispositional optimism and hope are constructs derived from a larger body of psychological theories, collectively known as positive psychology (Frederickson, 2003; Peterson, 2000; Seligman, 1998, 1999; Seligman & Csikentmihalyi, 2000; Snyder, 1994, 2000), which is rapidly gaining momentum in organizational behavior and leadership. Until the advent of positive psychology much of contemporary social science research has produced vocabularies of deficiency and pathology, instead of creating "textured vocabularies of hope" – stories, theory, evidence, and illustrations that provide humanity new guiding images of relational possibility (Ludema, Wilmot, & Srivastra, 1997, p. 1016). The authors defined textured vocabularies of hope as "linguistic constructions that create new images, illuminate fresh avenues for moral discourse and expand the range of practical and theoretical resources available for the construction of healthy social and organizational relationship" (p. 1021). Thus, reminiscent of Maslow (1954) who first introduced the term "positive psychology" 50 years ago, Seligman and Csikentmihalyi (2000) describe the purpose of positive psychology as beginning "to catalyze a change in the focus of psychology from preoccupation only with the worst things in life to also building positive qualities" (p. 5). In fact, Maslow, in the final chapter of *Motivation and Personality* laid out a research agenda proposing the investigation of "new" and "central" psychological constructs such as growth, self-sacrifice, optimism, courage, humility, and actualization of potential which is evident in current research on positive psychology and positive organizational scholarship (Cameron, Dutton, & Quinn, 2003; Luthans & Avolio, 2003).

Hope is a fundamental attribute of humanness and the essence of human coping. It is often portrayed as having moral, spiritual or religious dimensions. Napoleon once stated, "leaders are dealers in hope." In the leadership literature, hope has been a dominant feature in several leadership theories (Avolio et al., 2004; Bass, 1988; Gardner, 1993). Luthans and Avolio (2003), for example stated, "the force multiplier throughout history has often been attributed to the leader's ability to generate hope" (p. 253).

Snyder (1994) defines hope as "the sum of mental willpower and way-power [the mental road map that guides hopeful thought] that you have for your goals" (p. 5). More specifically, according to the author, as a mul-tidimensional construct, hope is composed of a sense of agency, or sense of willpower, the motivated determination to begin and maintain the effort to achieve goals and pathways, a sense of waypower, the belief in one's ability to generate and implement alternative successful plans and actions to meet the desired goals. Thus, hope refers to the perceived capability to derive pathways, and motivate oneself via agency thinking to use those pathways (Snyder, 2002). Like self-efficacy theory, hope theory also emphasizes goals, but they may be enduring, cross-situational, situational goal-directed thoughts, or all three (Snyder, 2002).

In the context of leadership, Snyder and Shorey (2005) posit that high hope leaders are effective when they clearly conceptualize goals and forge subgoals to complex goals that are large and temporally distant. These subgoals are the pathways (strategies or action plans) through which high hopeful leaders are able to facilitate the attainment of overarching super-ordinate goals. By doing so, the hopeful leader sparks the agency thinking of his or her followers and models hope for them.

Authentic leaders not only generate hope, which reflects the future-oriented dimension of authentic leadership but also look at the glass as half-full and model optimism for their followers (Luthans, Luthans, Hodgetts, & Luthans, 2001). Similar to hope theory, a number of theorists (e.g., Carver & Scheier, 2002, 2003) assume that optimism is a goal-based process that operates whenever an outcome is perceived as having sub-stantial value. According to Carver and Scheier (2003), definitions of optimism rest on people's expectations of the future which connects opti-mism with the expectancy-valence models of motivation. In contrast to hope, however, which includes a moral/ethical dimension, the opti-mism construct does not imply moral or ethical values (Shorey, Rand, & Snyder, 2005).

In the leadership literature, a positive relationship between transforma-tional leadership and optimism has been established in several studies (Chemers, Watson, & May, 2000; Wolff, Pescosolido, & Druskat, 2002). Similarly, McColl-Kennedy and Anderson (2002) reported that transfor-mational leadership style had a 0.44 relationship with group members' optimism. These results are consistent with earlier findings that transfor-mational leaders score higher on optimism than other types of leaders (Spreitzer & Quinn, 1996). In addition, McColl and Anderson found that feelings of optimism have a significant influence on performance.

Based on this body of research and the theoretical grounding of authentic leadership in the positive psychology movement, I offer the following two propositions:

Proposition 4a. Authentic leaders and followers are more likely to generate hope than their less authentic counterparts and in doing so reinforce each other's future orientation.

Proposition 4b. Authentic leaders and followers exhibit a greater ability to express optimism than their less authentic counterparts.

Compassion/Passion

The great world faiths, including Christianity, Hinduism, Buddhism, Confucianism, Judaism, and Islam, at their core, agree on the importance of compassion. Compassion means to feel *with* others, to enter their point of view and realize that they have the same fears and sorrows as oneself. The essential dynamic of compassion is summed up by the golden rule enunciated by Confucius who taught his disciples to get into the habit of *shu* or "likening to oneself." They had to look into their own fears, discover what gave them pain, and then rigorously refrain from inflicting this suffering upon other people. Armstrong (2005) argues that atrocities such as Auschwitz, the Gulag, and the regime of Saddam Hussein could not have taken place if people were properly educated in the golden rule; in other words, if they practiced compassion. Dutton and her associates (Dutton, Frost, Worline, Lilius, & Kanov, 2002) are studying how organizations deal with pain and compassion and report that compassionate organizations have a direct impact on how quickly and effectively people are able to recover from tragic events.

When asked, many business leaders say that passion – the burning desire to lead, serve the customer, or support a cause or product is what drives them. When that passion fades, they question the meaning of work (Goleman, McKee, & Boyatzis, 2002). With regard to compassion, Cassell (2001) asserts that at its core, compassion is a process of connecting by identifying with another person. Himmelfarb (2001) makes the case that compassion, once a private "duty," has now become a public responsibility. Authentic leaders are not only optimistic and hopeful but passionately and compassionately understood that there is always grief in the workplace and share pain, brokenness, fear and anguish with those they lead. This leads to my fifth proposition.

Proposition 5. Authentic leaders and followers practice compassion and are more passionately involved in their interactions with each other, their organizations, and society than their less authentic counterparts.

Conative Components of Authentic Leadership

In addition to cognition and affect, the proposed model in Fig. 1 acknowledges the role of conation or motivation in authentic leadership which represents the third facet of the conceptualization of authentic leadership advanced here. Deci and Ryan (2000) proposed self-determination theory (SDL) which incorporates the importance of needs in specifying the conditions for psychological growth, integrity and well-being, concepts that are consistent with models of authentic leadership and followership presented in this volume. Intrinsically (or self-motivated) behavior, according to Deci and Ryan, is part of the self, cultural values, and emotional regulations that become part of the self through integrative processes. Further, SDL postulates that the process and content of goal pursuits make a difference for performance and well-being. For example, Pinder (1998) has demonstrated that intrinsic motivation involves positive emotions such as feelings of enjoyment, challenge and flow which has been described as an optimal psychological experience characterized by positive affect and arousal (Csikentmihalyi, 1997). Like flow (Csikentmihalyi, 1975, 1990), SDL begins with a focus on intrinsic or self-motivation.

Shamir, House, and Arthur (1993) describe how charismatic leaders exert motivational effects through linking followers' self-concepts to organizational visions and goals to encourage followers to internalize the importance of supporting and achieving these goals. Authentic leaders are motivated to satisfy the needs of followers by demonstrating self-motivation and the motivation to lead, which are the two specific constructs that make up this class of antecedents: an intra-individual antecedent, self-motivation, and an inter-individual antecedent, motivation to lead. The propositions regarding the motivational facets of authentic leadership are consistent with the fundamental premise postulated by Avolio and Gardner (2005) that authentic leaders and followers are characterized by a deep sense of self which manifests itself conatively through self-motivation and the motivation to lead.

Self-motivation
In a discussion of self-regulation, Latham and Locke (1991) echo Bandura (1986, 1997) in noting that self-motivation and goal setting together are "foremost a discrepancy-inducing process" (p. 233). In other words, people choose self-motivation by purposely creating disequilibrium in their environment. To facilitate this process, they create extremely challenging goals that are far beyond any previous set. The "discrepancy" between the existing reality and the envisioned probability is clearly a decision to

accommodate the conditions prevailing in complex organization. This leads to my sixth proposition.

Proposition 6. Authentic leaders and followers exhibit higher levels of self-motivation compared to their less authentic counterparts and, in the process of pursuing increasing authenticity, display more autonomous self-regulatory styles than less authentic leaders and followers.

Motivation to Lead

Chan and Drasgow (2001) introduced a new construct, called the motivation to lead (MTL), as a broad framework for understanding the role of individual differences in leadership behaviors. Their key assumption is that non-cognitive ability variables such as personality and values relate to leader behaviors through MTL. The authors defined MTL as an individual-difference construct that affect a leader's decision to assume leadership training, roles, and responsibilities and that it affects his or her intensity of effort at leading and persistence as a leader. The MTL construct does not imply that individuals are motivated to lead by birth, but that MTL can be learned and changed through experience. This research also shows that personality, socio-cultural values, leadership self-efficacy, and past leadership experience are antecedents to MTL, whereas general cognitive ability is unrelated to MTL.

Chan and Drasgow's general theory of MTL is relevant to authentic leadership because it begins to integrate the process of leader development and leadership performance. In addition, the theory assumes that leadership skills and leadership styles are learned and developed over time, an assumption underlying most conceptualizations of authentic leadership and followership development.

With authentic leaders, the self-motivation and the motivation to lead combine into a single motive pattern to produce outcomes desirable for leaders and followers. Authentic leaders, motivated intra-individually by self-motivation and inter-individually by the motivation to lead, set high goals for themselves and their followers and by doing so build a shared context.

Proposition 7. Authentic leaders and followers will both display higher levels of motivation to lead.

Spiritual Components of Authentic Leadership

The role of spirituality in leadership and the workplace has generated a lot of attention in both the popular press and the research literature, which is reflected in the recent spurt of articles (e.g., Gunther, 2001; Thompson, 2000; Ashmos & Duchon, 2000; Mitroff & Denton, 1999) that speak to the growing interest in spirituality in the corporate world. In addition, research shows the core benefits of organizational transformation are not merely economic, but that the non-material, spiritual aspects of transformation may be the most profound for individuals, organizations and society (Neal & Banner, 1999; Milliman, Czaplewski, & Ferguson, 2003).

Spirituality allows individuals to find a new personal centering that binds them with a higher reality and creates an experience of joy and security thereby providing coherence to the human existence despite the many competing and conflicting forces that impacts their lives (Piedmont, 1999). Theoreticians have noted an innate capacity of humankind to transcend immediate experiences in order to find a more integrative, synthetic understanding of life. For example, according to James (1994/1902) the core spiritual experience is the recognition of a transcendent reality that provides meaning to one's existence and answers the personal questions we ask of life. The spiritual dimension underscores not only virtuous behavior but an attitude of openness to the transcendent meaning of the human existence.

Fry (2003) proposed a theory of spiritual leadership which the author defines as "comprising the values, attitudes, and behaviors that are necessary to motivate one self and others so that they have a sense of spiritual survival through calling and membership" (p. 694–695). The author contends that spiritual leadership taps into the fundamental needs of leaders and followers, a proposition that also under girds authentic leadership and followership. Finally, authentic leader and follower development, like spiritual development, may be time dependent (i.e., take place either over a period of time) (Avolio & Gardner, 2005; Gardner et al., 2005; Helminiak, 1987) or may be triggered by specific events such as crisis situations or spiritual markers such as conversion experiences.

The three dimensions of spirituality, applied to authentic leaders and follower – transcendence, meaning/purpose or meaningfulness and self-sacrifice – have been incorporated in this model.

Transcendence
According to Fairholm (1998), this spiritual dimension underscores not only virtuous behavior but also an attitude of openness to the transcendent meaning of human existence. Self-transcendence, as defined by Cloninger, Przybeck, Svarkic, and Wetzel (1994), includes components such as creative self-forgetfulness, transpersonal identification, and spiritual acceptance. Bateman and Porath (2003) posit that transcendent behavior is

self-determined behavior that overrides constraining environmental factors and effects extraordinary positive change. The authors also note that such behavior serves the increasing need not to be victims or mere survivors of change but to create constructive, high impact change.

Carey (1992) argues that authentic leadership implies self-transcendence that comes only with genuine self-enlightenment and is the product of reflection and introspection. Piedmont (1999) refers to spiritual transcendence as the capacity of individuals to stand outside their immediate sense of time and place and develop a more holistic and interconnected perspective recognizing a synchronicity to life and developing a sense of commitment to others. In other words, transcendent individuals recognize the limitedness of their perspective, which is anchored in a specific time and place, to consider encompassing visions of life that are more holistic and interconnected. I believe that the concept of transcendence resonates well with definitions of authentic leadership and followership development.

Michie and Gooty (2005) argue that self-transcendent values and positive other-directed emotions are important determinants of authentic leadership. Along with other scholars (e.g., Bass & Steidlmeier, 1999; Luthans & Avolio, 2003), these authors assert that authentic leaders are engaged in self-transcending behaviors that are consistent with high-end, other regarding values that are shaped and developed through the leaders' life experiences, leading to the eighth proposition.

Proposition 8. Authentic leaders and followers commit to self-transcendent values more than their less authentic counterparts and in doing so, their behaviors become more consistent and authentic over time.

Meaning/purpose

Frankl (1963) identifies meaning as a central factor enabling people to endure torture and injustice. Sosik (2000) defines personal meaning "as that which makes one's life most important, coherent, and worthwhile" (p. 61). Building on Frankl's purpose-in-life (PIL) concept, Sosik posits that PIL is a positive attitude toward possessing a future-oriented, self-transcendent goal in life which can be described in terms of the depth (strength) and type (content) of meaning associated with PIL. Wong (1998) reports that a sense of personal meaning leads to a reduction of individual and collective stress, while Conye (1998) suggests that it also enhances group effectiveness. Irving and Klenke (2004) suggest that a sense of personal meaning when woven into the leader's meta-narrative, defined as an integrated life story, enhances leadership effectiveness. Bennis (1999) notes that without meaning, the human condition denigrates when he states:

> What's missing at work, the root cause of the affluenza syndrome, is meaning, purpose beyond one's self, wholeness, integration .... The underlying cause of organizational dysfunctions, ineffectiveness, and all manner of human stress is the lack of a spiritual foundation in the work place (quoted in Preface to Mitroff & Denton, 1999, xi).

Meaning and purpose are embedded in many definitions of spirituality. Tepper (2003) defines spirituality as the extent to which an individual is motivated to find meaning and purpose in his or her existence. Many of the negative work experiences such as downsizing, isolation, lack of sense of community or trust have been cited to account for the search for greater meaning in workplaces (Cash & Gray, 2000). These negative experiences create a hunger for a deeper meaning in life, a need for finding an anchor, and a desire for greater integration of the spiritual and work identities (Thompson, 2000), leading to the ninth proposition.

Proposition 9. Authentic leaders and followers strive to find an over-arching meaning and purpose in their lives that connects them with a deeper sense of individual and collective self.

Self-sacrifice
Historical leaders such as Mahatma Gandhi, Mother Teresa and Martin Luther King demonstrated self-sacrificial leadership; contemporaneously, business leaders, especially during economic downturns and crises such as 9/11 made selfless contributions that have fueled the interest in the role of sacrifice in leadership (Halverson, Holladay, Kazama, & Quiñones, 2004). For example, Howard Lutnick, described as the notoriously hard-edged and demanding CEO of Cantor Fitzgerald who lost 627 employees when terrorists flew airplanes into the twin towers of the World Trade Center, gave of self and millions of dollars in bonuses (although he briefly reneged on his promise) to the families of the employees who lost their lives. Michie and Gooty (2005) make a distinction between sacrificial and egocentric leaders. Although Howard Lutwick before the 9/11 attack probably fit the profile of an egocentric leader better, his case nevertheless shows that under extraordinary circumstances, even inauthentic leaders may also engage in sacrificial behaviors.

Self-sacrificial leadership goes beyond an individual's motivation to help others, or selflessness (Cialdini, Brown, Luce, Lewis, & Neuberg, 1997). It has been defined as "the total/partial abandonment, and permanent/temporary postponement of personal interests, privileges, and welfare in the: (1) division of labor (by volunteering for more risky and arduous tasks); (2) distribution of rewards which involves giving up one's fair and legitimate share of organizational rewards; and/or (3) voluntarily refraining from using position power and privileges" (Choi & Mai-Dalton, 1998, 1999). Self-sacrifice promotes the image of leaders, especially when confronted with external threats or crises, who deny themselves personal privileges or share pain and hardship with their followers. Many political and grassroots leaders have given up their freedom by spending time in prison to demonstrate their commitment to causes they stand for (House & Shamir, 1993).

Several authors (e.g., Avolio & Locke, 2002; Burns, 1978; Bass & Steidlmeier, 1999) have suggested that leaders may willingly sacrifice for the collective good of their work group, organization, or society at large. For example, van Knippenberg and van Knippenberg (2005) argued that being self-sacrificial is probably one of the most direct ways for a leader to state that he or she considers the group's welfare to be important and explicitly shows his or her commitment to the well-being of the collectivity. Moreover, the authors suggest that a leader's self-sacrificing behavior will create pressure on followers to do as is done to them, thereby prescribing what kind of behavior is expected in the light of the group's common cause.

Proposition 10. Authentic leaders and followers will engage in self-sacrificing behaviors in situations that challenge and test their deep sense of self and require them to be true to it al all costs without compulsion or conflict.

Spiritually authentic leaders and followers draw from the selfless ground of the human experience; they recognize the emotional labor involved in the tasks and responsibilities of leadership, and consider suffering and sacrifice an integral component of authentic leadership. The question of whether self-sacrificing leadership leads to greater authenticity of leaders and followers or enhances performance is an empirical issue that has not been addressed.

Outcomes of Authentic Leadership

In this model of authentic leadership that integrates cognitive, affective, conative and spiritual facets, the emergent construct is defined by a set of antecedents that capture the positive psychological capital of leaders and followers related to the conceptualization of authentic leadership presented here. This model postulates a multi-dimensional and multi-level conceptualization of authentic leadership that includes group and organizational level variables as consequences of leader and follower authenticity. This approach is consistent with Rousseau's (1985) argument that theories must be built with explicit description of the levels to which generalization is appropriate.

Culture is the construct that serves as the connective tissue that links group, organizational, and community/society level variables. Leadership and culture have always been intertwined (Schein, 1985). One of the most decisive functions of leadership is the creation, the management, and sometimes the destruction of organizational culture. This assumption is reflected in several contemporary theories including transformational (e.g., Bass & Avolio, 1994), charismatic (e.g., Shamir & Howell, 2000) and visionary (e.g., Sashkin & Sashkin, 2003) leadership.

At the team level, I would expect that authentic leaders develop teams characterized by clear, elevating goals, a results-driven structure, competent team members, unified commitment and a collaborative climate (Larson & LaFasto, 1989). If a team shares the belief that these characteristics enhance leader and follower authenticity at the collective level, the team can then develop norms for authentic behaviors that can be derived from these characteristics, resulting in the emergence of a more authentic culture. A pattern of such underlying assumptions can then form the foundation for the team's culture-oriented toward authentic leadership and followership development.

Embedded Organizational Context

Situating authentic leadership and followership in the organizational context recognizes that leadership effects are constrained by more broad forces than the structure of individual tasks and the interaction between leaders and followers (Tosi, 1991). Bass and Avolio (1994) in their discussion of transformational leadership in the organizational context argued that like the leaders themselves, organizations can also be characterized as exhibiting qualities of transformational leadership. Extending this argument to authentic leadership and followership, Gardner et al. (2005) suggest that authentic leaders and followers create "proximal" organizational climates that are more inclusive, caring, engaging, and more oriented toward developing strengths. They build an organizational culture where hope and optimism flourish, where leaders and followers individually and collectively develop and nurture a culture of care, and pursue transcendent values toward a democratic and egalitarian society, at home and abroad. Furthermore,

Luthans and Avolio (2003) assert that the development of authentic leaders and followers at the individual level must coincide with the development of the person's positive psychological capacities *and* a positive, highly developed organizational context and culture for leadership development.

IMPLICATIONS FOR LEADERSHIP THEORY, RESEARCH AND PRACTICE

The model of authentic leadership explicated in this chapter adds to existing theoretical frameworks by offering a perspective designed to integrate cognitive, affective, conative and spiritual components of authentic leadership and followership. Previous research has shown that affective processes continually interact with cognitive processes, and affective reactions are likely to be essential for understanding how leadership schemata develop and change over time (Lord & Emrich, 2000). However, unless we fully understand how motivation and spirituality, which both contain affective and cognitive elements, factor into the model and interact with the other antecedents, we are faced with conceptual gaps in the theory of authentic leadership and its development.

Like other perspectives on authentic leadership and followership (e.g., Avolio & Gardner, 2005; Gardner et al., 2005; Ilies et al., 2005), the framework offered here anchors the antecedents in the positive psychology movement that recently gained momentum and is emerging as a new discipline (Cameron et al., 2003). More specifically, the model contributes to the theoretical development of authentic leadership and followership in several ways.

First, as Seligman and Csikentmihalyi (2000) point out there are several levels of analysis that require attention resulting from the inclusion of positive psychology. They include: (1) the subjective level that includes positive subjective experiences such as well-being, contentment and satisfaction (focused on the past and hope and optimism anchored in the future), along with flow and happiness in the present; (2) the micro, individual level with positive traits and qualities such as the capacity for love, courage, aesthetic sensibility, forgiveness and wisdom; and (3) the group or macro level encompassing positive civic virtues such as civility, tolerance and work ethic (Luthans et al., 2001).

On the other hand, the model presented here also differs from other perspectives in several significant ways. Instead of focusing on the dynamics of the development of authenticity in leaders and followers, this model calls for more focused attention to group and organizational level consequences of authentic leadership and followership. The proposed model also includes a spiritual component that links authentic behavior to self-transcendence, meaningfulness and self-sacrifice. In addition, the model specifies the importance that a complex organization context plays in authentic leadership processes.

Apart from its theoretical contributions, the model offers a researchable framework from which numerous research questions and testable hypotheses can be derived. I recommend the need for multilevel studies collecting data on authentic leaders and the groups or teams they lead, as well as focusing on how collective constructs such as efficacy can be used in examining the intervening processes in groups that result in sustainable growth and performance. Future research also needs to focus on providing "thick descriptions" (see Glaser & Strauss, 1967; Locke, 2001) of the lived experiences of authentic leaders and followers. Historiography, rhetorical, and narrative analyses can be employed to elucidate specific characteristics of authentic leadership. For example, Shamir and Eilam (2005) recommend examining the process by which followers judge the authenticity of leaders' life stories as a qualitative approach. Such stories are often created for self-knowledge, self-representation, and self-expression and are less concerned with the construction of reality and more about meanings ascribed to life events.

Future research may want to cast a wider net regarding the context in which we study authentic leaders – authentic leaders are found among artists, caregivers of the terminally ill as well as in other cultures. In sum, by mapping the internal theater of the authentic leader – personal victories, resilience of spirit, transformative relationships with followers, a chemistry of passionate engagement that shapes meaning and identity and trigger events that promote authentic leadership and followership development – quantitatively and qualitatively, we can develop the foundation for an interdisciplinary program of research that can lead to the emergence of new theories and research methods.

From a cross-cultural perspective, it will be interesting to learn how authentic leadership and followership develop and manifest themselves in different cultures. For example, to what extent are the cognitive, affective, conative, and spiritual facets of authentic leadership culturally contingent or to what extent are some of them universal? For example, Bass (1997) raised this question in relation to transformational leadership and reported that there is evidence that a preference for transformational leadership exists in most, if not all cultures. However, as the findings by Den Hartog and Verburg (1997) suggest, the *enactment* of transformational leadership is likely to be culture specific. This raises the question of what dimensions of cultural variation and theoretical frameworks may be most useful to understand cultural contingencies in authentic leadership and followership development.

For practicing leaders, the model suggests new roles that entail promises as well as perils. For example, as architects of authentic cultures, leaders create healing environments in which body, mind and spirit can be nurtured. In this role, the authentic leader facilitates renewal in the aftermath of traumatic organizational events, elicits authentic responses and can be instrumental in the organization's revitalization. Likewise, authentic leaders build hope, possibility, and commitment by creating processes that help followers experience success, model how to build hope, encouraging relationships and create shared contexts. On the other hand, authentic leadership does not come without a price: selflessness and self-sacrifice, personal loss and harm, willingness to live on the edge of chaos can be idolized or lead to loss of individual identity, personality fragmentation, and social ostracism.

In sum, authentic leadership and the development of authentic leaders, followers, and organizations is a promising emergent research domain and substantive research arena. As such, a multidisciplinary discourse is needed to foster applied theory building, hypothesis testing, applications of a wide range of research methodologies, and the continued search for linkages between the extant leadership research and this emergent body of theory. As we begin to develop good theory and accumulate validating data, helpful predictions become possible which potentially can affect extraordinary positive change for people, organizations or society.

ACKNOWLEDGMENTS

I sincerely thank Drs. Avolio, Gardner, Luthans and Walumbwa for their generous, critical and constructive feedback which was instrumental in the revisions of this chapter. I also thank the anonymous reviewer for the helpful comments.

REFERENCES

Armstrong, K. (2005). Compassion's fruit. *AARPMagazine, May-June*, 53–58.
Ashkanasy, N. M., & Tse, B. (2000). Transformational leadership as management of emotions: A conceptual review. In: N. Ashkanasy & C. Härtel (Eds), *Emotions in the workplace: Research, theory and practice* (pp. 221–235). Westport, CT: Quorum Books/Greenwood Publishing Group.

Ashmos, D., & Duchon, D. (2000). Spirituality at work: A conceptualization and measure. *Journal of Management Inquiry, 9*, 134–145.

Avolio, B. J., & Gardner, W. L. (2005). Authentic leadership development: Getting to the root of positive forms of leadership. *The Leadership Quarterly, 16*(3), 315–338.

Avolio, B. J., Gardner, W. L., Walumbwa, F. O., Luthans, F., & May, D. R. (2004). Unlocking the mask: A look at a process by which authentic leaders impact follower attitudes and behaviors. *The Leadership Quarterly, 15*, 801–823.

Avolio, B. J., & Locke, E. A. (2002). Contrasting different philosophies of leader motivation: Altruism versus egoism. *The Leadership Quarterly, 13*, 169–191.

Badaracco, J. (1997). *Defining moments: When managers must choose between right and wrong.* Cambridge, MA: Harvard University Press.

Bandura, A. (1982). Self-efficacy mechanisms in human agency. *American Psychologist, 37*, 122–147.

Bandura, A. (1986). *Social foundations of thought and action.* Englewood Cliff, NJ: Prentice-Hall.

Bandura, A. (1997). *Self-efficacy: The exercise of control.* New York: Freeman.

Barbuto, J., & Burbach, M. (2004). The emotional intelligence of transformational leaders. Paper presented at the Inaugural Gallup Leadership Summit, Omaha, NB, June.

Bass, B. M. (1985). *Performance beyond expectations.* New York: The Free Press.

Bass, B. M. (1988). The ethics of transformational leadership. In: J. Ciulla (Ed.), *Ethics: The heart of leadership* (pp. 169–192). Westport, CT: Praeger.

Bass, B. M. (1997). Does the transactional-transformational leadership paradigm transcend organizational and national boundaries? *American Psychologist, 52*, 130–139.

Bass, B. M. (2002). Cognitive, social, and emotional intelligence of transformational leaders. In: R. Riggio, S. Murphy & F. Pirozollo (Eds), *Multiple intelligences in leadership* (pp. 105–118). Mahwah, NJ: Lawrence Erlbaum Associates.

Bass, B. M., & Avolio, B. (1994). *Improving organizational effectiveness through transformational leadership.* Thousand Oaks, CA: Sage.

Bass, B. M., & Steidlmeier, P. (1999). Ethics, character, and transformational leadership behavior. *The Leadership Quarterly, 10*, 81–217.

Bateman, S., & Porath, C. (2003). Transcendent behavior. In: K. Cameron, J. Dutton & R. Quinn (Eds), *Positive organizational scholarship: Foundations of a new discipline.* San Francisco: Berrett-Koehler.

Burns, J. M. (1978). *Leadership.* New York: Harper.

Burns, J. M. (2003). *Transforming leadership.* New York: Atlantic Monthly Press.

Cameron, K., Dutton, J. E., & Quinn, R. (2003). *Positive organizational scholarship.* San Francisco: Berrett-Koehler.

Carey, M. (1992). Transformational leadership and the fundamental option for self-transcendence. *The Leadership Quarterly, 3*, 217–236.

Carver, C. S., & Scheier, M. F. (2002). Optimism. In: C. R. Snyder & S. J. Lopez (Eds), *Handbook of positive psychology* (pp. 231–243). Oxford: Oxford University Press.

Carver, C. S., & Scheier, M. F. (2003). Optimism. In: S. Lopez & C. Snyder (Eds), *Positive psychological assessment: A handbook of models and measures* (pp. 75–89). Washington: American Psychological Association.

Cash, K., & Gray, G. (2000). A framework for accommodating religion and spirituality in the workplace. *Academy of Management Executive, 14*, 124–133.

Cassell, E. (2001). Compassion. In: C. Snyder & S. Lopez (Eds), *Handbook of positive psychology* (pp. 434–445). Oxford: Oxford University Press.

Chan, K., & Drasgow, F. (2001). Toward a theory of individual differences and leadership: Understanding the motivation to lead. *Journal of Applied Psychology, 86*, 481–498.

Chemers, M. M., Watson, C. B., & May, S. T. (2000). Dispositional affect and leadership effectiveness. *Personality and Social Psychology Bulletin, 26*, 267–277.

Chen, G., & Bliese, P. D. (2002). The role of different levels of leadership in predicting self- and collective efficacy: Evidence for discontinuity. *Journal of Applied Psychology, 87*, 549–556.

Choi, Y., & Mai-Dalton, R. (1998). On the leadership function of self-sacrifice. *The Leadership Quarterly, 9*, 475–501.

Choi, Y., & Mai-Dalton, R. (1999). The model of followers' responses to self-sacrificial leadership: An empirical test. *The Leadership Quarterly, 10*, 397–421.

Cialdini, R., Brown, S., Lewis, B., Luce, C., & Neuberg, S. (1997). Reinterpreting the empathy-altruism relationship: When one into one equals oneness. *Journal of Personality and Social Psychology, 73*, 481–494.

Ciarocchi, J., Chan, A. Y. L., & Caputi, P. (2000). A critical evaluation of the emotional intelligence construct. *Personality and Individual Differences, 28*, 539–561.

Cloninger, C. R., Przybeck, T. R., Svarkic, D. M., & Wetzel, R. D. (1994). *The temperament and character inventory (TCI): A guide to its development and use*. St. Louis, MO: Center for Psychobiology of Personality, Washington University.

Conye, R. (1998). Personal experience and meaning in work group leadership: The views of experts. *Journal for Specialists in Work Groups, 23*, 245–256.

Csikentmihalyi, M. (1975). *Beyond boredom and anxiety*. San Francisco: Jossey-Bass.

Csikentmihalyi, M. (1990). *Flow*. New York: Harper & Row.

Csikentmihalyi, M. (1997). *Finding flow: The psychology of engagement with everyday life*. New York: Basic Books.

Davies, M., Stankov, L., & Roberts, R. (1998). Emotional intelligence: In: search of an elusive construct. *Journal of Personality and Individual Differences, 75*, 989–1015.

Deci, E. L., & Ryan, R. M. (2000). The 'what' and 'why' of goal pursuits: Human needs and the self-determination of behavior. *Psychological Inquiry, 11*, 227–268.

Den Hartog, D., & Verburg, R. (1997). Charisma and rhetoric: Communicative techniques of international business leaders. *The Leadership Quarterly, 8*, 355–391.

Druskat, V. U., & Wolff, S. (2001). Building the emotional intelligence of groups. *Harvard Business Review, 79*(3), 80–91.

Dutton, J. E., Frost, P. J., Worline, M. C., Lilius, J. M., & Kanov, J. (2002). Leading in times of trauma. *Harvard Business Review, 80*(1), 54–61.

Fairholm, G. (1998). *Perspectives on leadership: From the science of management to its spiritual heart*. Westport, CT: Quorum Books.

Frankl, V. (1963). *Man's search for meaning*. New York: Washington Square.

Frederickson, B. (2003). Positive emotions and upward spirals in organizational settings: Perspectives from the broaden-and-build theory. In: K. Cameron, J. Dutton & R. Quinn (Eds), *Positive organizational scholarship* (pp. 163–175). San Francisco: Berrett-Koehler.

Fry, J. (2003). Toward a theory of spiritual leadership. *The Leadership Quarterly, 14*, 693–727.

Gardner, J. (1993). *On leadership*. New York: The Free Press.

Gardner, W. L., Avolio, B. J., Luthans, F., May, D. R., & Walumbwa, F. O. (2005). "Can you see the real me?" A self-based model of authentic leaders and follower development. *The Leadership Quarterly, 16*(3), 343–372.

George, J. M. (2000). Emotions and leadership: The role of emotional intelligence. *Human Relations, 53*, 1027–1055.

Glaser, B. G., & Strauss, A. (1967). *The discovery of grounded theory.* Chicago: Aldine.

Goleman, D. (1995). *Emotional intelligence.* New York: Bantam Books.

Goleman, D., McKee, A., & Boyatzis, R. E. (2002). *Primal leadership: Realizing the power of emotional intelligence.* Boston: Harvard Business School Press.

Gunther, M. (2001). God and business. *Fortune, 144*, 59–80.

Guzzo, R. A., Yost, P., Campbell, R., & Shea, G. (1993). Potency in groups: Articulating a construct. *British Journal of Social Psychology, 32*, 87–106.

Halverson, S., Holladay, C., Kazama, S., & Quiñones, M. (2004). Self-sacrificial behavior in crisis situations: The competing roles of behavioral and situational factors. *The Leadership Quarterly, 15*, 263–275.

Hartsfield, M. (2003). The internal dynamics of transformational leaders: Effects of emotional intelligence, self-efficacy, and spirituality on transformational leadership. *Proceedings of the 21st annual conference of the Association of Management/International Association of Management* (Vol. 1, pp. 79–86).

Heidegger, M. (2002). *Vom Wesen der menschlichen Freiheit.* (English: The essence of human freedom: An introduction to philosophy. (Translation Ted Sadler). New York: Continuum.

Helminiak, D. (1987). *Spiritual development: An interdisciplinary study.* Chicago: Loyola University Press.

Himmelfarb, G. (2001). The idea of compassion: The British vs. *French enlightenment. Public Interest,, 145*, 3–24.

House, R., & Shamir, B. (1993). Toward the integration of transformational, charismatic, and visionary theories. In: M. Chemers & R. Ayman (Eds), *Leadership theory and research: Perspectives and directions* (pp. 81–107). San Diego, CA: Academic Press.

Humphrey, R. H. (2000). The many faces of emotional leadership. *The Leadership Quarterly, 13*, 493–504.

Husserl, E. (1970). *Logical investigation.* New York: Humanities Press.

Ilies, R., Morgeson, F. P., & Nahrgang, J. D. (2005). Authentic leadership and eudaimonic well-being: Understanding follower outcomes. *The Leadership Quarterly, 16*(3), 373–394.

Irving, J., & Klenke, K. (2004). Telos, chronos and hermeneia: The role of metanarrative in leadership effectiveness through the production of meaning. *International Journal of Qualitative Methods, 3*, 14–28.

James, W. (1994). *The varieties of religious experience.* New York: The Modern Library, (Original work published in 1902).

Jung, D. I., & Sosik, J. (2003). Group potency and collective efficacy: Examining their predictive validity, level and analysis, and effects of performance feedback on future group performance. *Group & Organization Management, 28*, 366–380.

Kanungo, R. A., & Mendonca, M. (1996). *Ethical dimensions in leadership.* Beverly Hills, CA: Sage.

Kegan, R. (1982). *The evolving self: Problem and process in human development.* Cambridge, MA: Harvard University Press.

Klenke, K. (1996). *Women and leadership: A contextual perspective.* New York: Springer.

Klenke, K. (2003). The leader's new work: Living with paradox. Paper presented at the 5th annual conference of the International Leadership Association, Guadalajara, Mexico, November 6–8.

Kohlberg, L. (1976). *Collected papers on moral development and moral education.* Cambridge: Harvard University Press.

Larson, C., & LaFasto, F. (1989). *Teamwork.* Newbury Park, CA: Sage.

Latham, G. P., & Locke, E. A. (1991). Self-regulation through goal setting. *Organizational Behavior and Human Decision Processes, 50,* 212–247.

Locke, K. (2001). *Grounded theory research in management.* Thousand Oaks, CA: Sage.

London, M., & Maurer, T. (2004). Leadership development. In: J. Antonakis, A. Cianciolo & R. Sternberg (Eds), *The nature of leadership.* Thousand Oaks, CA: Sage.

Lord, R. G., & Emrich, C. G. (2000). Thinking outside the box by looking inside the box: Extending the cognitive revolution in leadership research. *The Leadership Quarterly, 11,* 551–579.

Ludema, J., Wilmot, T., & Srivastra, S. (1997). Organizational hope: Reaffirming the constructive task of social and organizational inquiry. *Human Relations, 50,* 1015–1051.

Luthans, F. (2002). The need for and meaning of positive organizational behavior. *Journal of Organizational Behavior, 23,* 695–706.

Luthans, F., & Avolio, B. J. (2003). Authentic leadership: A positive developmental approach. In: K. Cameron, J. Dutton & R. Quinn (Eds), *Positive organizational scholarship* (pp. 241–258). San Francisco: Berrett-Koehler.

Luthans, F., Luthans, K., Hodgetts, R. M., & Luthans, B. (2001). Positive approach to leadership (PAL): Implications for today's organizations. *Journal of Leadership Studies, 8,* 3–20.

Marion, R., & Uhl-Bien, M. (2001). Leadership in complex organization. *The Leadership Quarterly, 12,* 389–418.

Maslow, A. (1954). *Motivation and personality.* New York: Harper.

Maslow, A. (1971). *The farther reaches of human nature.* New York: Penguin.

May, D. R., Chan, A. Y. L., Hodges, T. D., & Avolio, B. J. (2003). Developing the moral component of authentic leadership. *Organizational Dynamics, 32,* 247–260.

Mayer, J. D., Caruso, D., & Salovey, P. (2000). Emotional intelligence meets traditional standards of intelligence. *Intelligence, 27,* 267–298.

Mayer, J. D., Salovey, P., Caruso, D. R., & Sitarenios, G. (2001). Emotional intelligence as a standard intelligence. *Emotion, 1,* 232–242.

Mayer, J. D., Salovey, P., Caruso, D., & Sitarenios, G. (2003). Measuring emotional intelligence with the MSCEIT V2.0. *Emotion, 3,* 97–105.

McColl-Kennedy, J., & Anderson, R. E. (2002). Impact of leadership style and emotions on subordinate performance. *The Leadership Quarterly, 13,* 545–559.

McCormick, M. (2001). Self-efficacy and leadership effectiveness: Applying social cognitive theory to leadership. *Journal of Leadership Studies, 8,* 22–33.

Meindl, J. R., Ehrlich, S., & Dukerich, J. (1985). The romance of leadership. *Administrative Science Quarterly, 30,* 78–102.

Michie, S., & Gooty, J. (2005). Values, emotions, and authenticity: Will the real leader please stand up? *The Leadership Quarterly, 16*(3), 441–457.

Milliman, J., Czaplewski, A., & Ferguson, J. (2003). Workplace spirituality and employee work attitudes: An exploratory empirical assessment. *Journal of Organizational Change Management, 16,* 426–447.

Mitroff, I., & Denton, E. (1999). *A spiritual audit of corporate America.* San Francisco: Jossey-Bass.

Neal, J., & Banner, D. (1999). Spiritual perspectives on individuals, organizations, and societal transformation. *Journal of Organizational Change Management, 12,* 24–36.

Osborn, R. N., Hunt, J. G., & Jauch, L. (2002). Toward a contextual theory of leadership. *The Leadership Quarterly, 13*, 797–837.

Paglis, L., & Green, S. G. (2002). Leadership self-efficacy and managers' motivation to change. *Journal of Organizational Behavior, 23*, 215–235.

Peterson, C. (2000). The future of optimism. *American Psychologist, 54*, 44–55.

Piaget, J. (1965). *The moral judgment of the child*. New York: Free Press.

Piedmont, R. (1999). Does spirituality represent the sixth factor of personality? Spiritual transcendence and the factor-five model. *Journal of Personality, 67*, 985–1013.

Pinder, C. (1998). *Work motivation in organizational behavior*. Upper Saddle River, NJ: Prentice-Hall.

Price, T. (2003). The ethics of transformational leadership. *The Leadership Quarterly, 14*, 67–81.

Prussia, G., & Kinicki, A. (1996). A motivational investigation of group effectiveness using social-cognitive theory. *Journal of Applied Psychology, 81*, 187–198.

Regine, B., & Lewin, R. (2001). Leading at the edge: How leaders influence complex systems. *Emergence, 2*(2), 5–23.

Rest, J. R. (1999). *Postconventional moral thinking: A Neo-Kohlbergian approach*. Mahwah, NJ: Lawrence Erlbaum Associates.

Rousseau, D. M. (1985). Issues of level in organizational research. In: L. Cummings & B. Staw (Eds), *Research in organizational behavior*, (Vol. 7, pp. 1–37). Greenwich, CT: JAI Press.

Sangharakshita, J. (1990). *Vision and transformation: A guide to Buddha's noble eightfold path*. Glasgow: Windhorse.

Sashkin, M., & Sashkin, M. (2003). *Leadership that matters*. San Francisco: Berrett-Koehler.

Schein, E. J. (1985). *Organizational culture and leadership*. San Francisco: Jossey-Bass.

Schulman, M. (2002). How we become moral. In: C. R. Snyder & S. J. Lopez (Eds), *Handbook of positive psychology* (pp. 499–512). Oxford: Oxford University Press.

Schulman, M., & Mekler, E. (1994). *Bringing up a moral child: A new approach for teaching your child to be kind, just, and responsible*. New York: Doubleday.

Seligman, M. E. P. (1998). Positive social science. *APA Monitor, 29*, 5.

Seligman, M. E. P. (1999). The President's address. *American Psychologist, 54*, 559–562.

Seligman, M. E. P., & Csikentmihalyi, M. (2000). Positive psychology. *American Psychologist, 54*, 5–14.

Shamir, B., & Eilam, G. (2005). "What's your story?": A life-stories approach to authentic leadership development. *Leadership Quarterly, 16*(3), 395–417.

Shamir, B., House, R. J., & Arthur, M. B. (1993). The motivational effects of charismatic leadership: A self-concept based theory. *Organization Science, 4*, 577–594.

Shamir, B., & Howell, J. M. (2000). The role of followers in the charismatic leadership process: Susceptibility, social construction, and leader empowerment. Paper presented at the Academy of Management annual meeting, Toronto.

Shorey, H., Rand, K. L., & Snyder, R. (2005). The ethics of hope: A guide for social responsibility in contemporary business. In: R. Giacalone, C. Dunn & C. Jurkiewics (Eds), *Positive psychology in business ethics and corporate social responsibility*. Greenwich, CT: Information Age.

Sison, A. (2003). *The moral capital of leaders*. Northampton, MA: Edward Elgar.

Snyder, C. R. (1994). *The psychology of hope*. New York: The Free Press.

Snyder, C. R. (2000). *Handbook of hope*. San Diego: Academic Press.

Snyder, C. R. (2002). Hope theory: Rainbows of the mind. *Psychological Inquiry, 13*, 249–275.

Snyder C. R., & Shorey, H. (2005). The role of hope in effective leadership. In: K. Christensen (Ed.), *Encyclopedia of leadership*. New York: Berkshire Publishers.

Sosik, J. J. (2000). Possible selves and personal meaning of charismatic and non-charismatic leaders. *Journal of Leadership Studies, 7*, 3–13.

Sosik, J. J., & Megarian, L. (1999). Understanding leader emotional intelligence and performance: The role of self-other agreement on transformational leadership perceptions. *Group & Organization Management, 24*, 367–390.

Spreitzer, G., & Quinn, R. (1996). Empowering middle managers to be transformational leaders. *Journal of Applied Behavioral Science, 32*(3), 237–261.

Tepper, B. (2003). Organizational citizenship behavior and the spiritual employee. In: R. Giacalone & C. Jurkiewics (Eds), *Handbook of workplace spirituality and organizational performance* (pp. 181–192). New York: M.E. Sharpe.

Thompson, D. (2000). *Can you train people to be spiritual? Training and Development, 54*, 18–19.

Tosi, H. (1991). The organization as context for leadership theory: A multilevel approach. *The Leadership Quarterly, 2*, 205–228.

van Knippenberg, B., & van Knippenberg, D. (2005). Leader self-sacrifice and leadership effectiveness: The moderating role of leader prototypicality. *Journal of Applied Psychology, 90*, 25–37.

Wheatley, M. (1992). *Leadership and the new science: Learning about organizations from an orderly universe*. San Francisco: Berrett-Koehler.

Wilber, K. (1991). *Grace and grit*. Cambridge, MA: Yale University Press.

Wofford, J. C., & Goodwin, V. L. (1994). A cognitive interpretation of transactional and transformational leadership theories. *The Leadership Quarterly, 5*, 161–186.

Wolff, S. B., Pescosolido, A. T., & Druskat, V. U. (2002). Emotional intelligence as the basis of leadership emergence in self-managing team. *The Leadership Quarterly, 12*, 505–522.

Wong, P. (1998). Meaning-centered counseling. In: P. Wong & P. Fry (Eds), *The quest for human quest for meaning: A handbook of psychological and clinical application* (pp. 395–435). Mahwah, NJ: Erlbaum.

IN SEARCH OF AUTHENTICITY: SPIRITUAL LEADERSHIP THEORY AS A SOURCE FOR FUTURE THEORY, RESEARCH, AND PRACTICE ON AUTHENTIC LEADERSHIP

Louis W. (Jody) Fry and J. Lee Whittington

ABSTRACT

In this chapter, the emerging theory of authentic leadership is examined and extended using spiritual leadership theory and legacy leadership theory. Expanding the borders on authentic leadership requires a focus on three key issues: (1) achieving consensus on universal or consensus values that are necessary, though not sufficient, for authentic leadership; (2) the role of authentic leadership in achieving congruent and consistent values, attitudes, and behavior across the individual, group, and organizational levels; and (3) the personal outcomes or rewards of authentic leadership. Together, spiritual and legacy leadership theories address these issues and provide insights for authentic leadership theory, research, and practice.

Authentic Leadership Theory and Practice: Origins, Effects and Development
Monographs in Leadership and Management, Volume 3, 183–200

INTRODUCTION

The latest rash of corporate scandals has awakened our collective consciousness to the fact that self-interest unchecked by moral reasoning and obligation results in a destructive greed. This greed not only destroys the lives of the executives that are driven by it to ethical compromise, but ultimately impacts thousands of innocent individuals as the outcomes trickle down corporate hierarchies, spilling over into communities, and crashing through families.

The tragedies of Enron, WorldCom, Tyco, and Arthur Anderson raised awareness that perhaps the most powerful group in modern society is corporate executives. This realization led May (2001) to include corporate executives among his "beleaguered rulers," the various professionals that wield enormous power in contemporary society. Because they wield such power, he believes that it is imperative that we "examine directly the moral underpinnings of the market place and the moral status of corporate leaders within it" (May, 2001, p. 131). Yet, the call for new standards of integrity and accountability extends beyond those who hold formal positions of leadership. May (2001) extends this call to all modern professionals including medical doctors, lawyers, engineers, politicians, media professionals, ministers, and professors.

The recent headlines have sharpened the outcry for a new standard of integrity and public accountability. Authentic leadership (Luthans & Avolio, 2003) is emerging as one response to this call for higher standards of character and integrity. Authentic leadership is based on the tenets of positive psychology and seeks to find an avenue to move organizations, communities, and societies forward by focusing on what is right with people and building on their strengths. Thus, positive psychology contrasts with individual and organizational interventions that focus on what is wrong with people and their weaknesses (Luthans & Avolio, 2003).

In this chapter, the linkages between the emerging theory of authentic leadership and spiritual leadership theory (SLT) are examined. The central premise or argument is that expanding the borders on authentic leadership perspectives requires a focus on three key issues (Bass & Steidlmeier, 1999; Price, 2003; Singh & Krishnan, 2002) : (1) achieving consensus on universal or consensus values that are necessary (but not sufficient) for authentic leadership; (2) the role of authentic leadership in achieving value congruence and consistency of values, attitudes, and behavior across the individual, group, and organizational levels; and (3) the personal outcomes or rewards of authentic leadership. Finally, to enhance our understanding of authentic leadership and address the limitations of existing models, legacy leadership is offered as a more specific model within the spiritual leadership paradigm (Fry, 2003, 2005a, b; Malone & Fry, 2003; Fry, Vitucci, & Cedillo, 2005). Both spiritual leadership and legacy theory (1) speak to the key issues listed above and (2) have the potential for guiding future theory development, research, and practice of authentic leadership.

AUTHENTIC LEADERS DEFINED

Authentic leaders are characterized as hopeful, optimistic, resilient, and transparent. These leaders are described as moral/ethical, future-oriented individuals who make the development of others a priority. By being true to their own values and acting in ways that are consistent with those values, authentic leaders develop their associates into leaders themselves. Luthans and Avolio (2003) have identified several "proactive positive characteristics" that further define authentic leadership. According to Luthans and Avolio (2003), authentic leaders operate from a set of end values that focuses their behavior on doing what they perceive to be right for those they lead.

Because they are value centered, these leaders seek to reduce any existing gaps between their espoused values and their enacted values. This attempt to reduce any existing credibility gaps (Kouzes & Posner, 2003) requires authentic leaders to be aware of potential vulnerabilities and transparent enough to allow discussion of these areas with their followers. Authentic leaders also are willing to be the first mover, taking the lead even when there is great personal risk in doing so. By doing so, these leaders model a hopeful confidence in the future. Finally, authentic leaders have developed the capacity to examine moral dilemmas from several perspectives and make moral judgment calls when confronted with issues that do not have a clear solution.

In contrast to these qualities, many leaders who are driven to achieve, often skip or short cut the hard work of character development and the cultivation of self-awareness that characterizes authentic leaders. By doing so, these leaders can be very destructive (George, 2004). While they may manifest similar external behaviors, these leaders are not operating from the same value-centered foundation that authentic leaders operate from. These leaders are inauthentic or pseudo-authentic leaders. They attempt to mask their inadequacies, concentrate on cultivating an image or persona and close themselves off from, rather than opening up to others (Bass & Steidlmeier, 1999; Price, 2003). In the long run, this serves to foster mistrust and a sense of disconnection with followers and, ultimately, has a negative impact on personal, team, and organizational outcomes. Contrastingly, authentic leadership requires one to constantly reduce the gap between intended and perceived communication as the leader communicates his or her values as well as the organization's values every day in personal interaction with customers, employees and other key stakeholders. This requires that you know yourself authentically, listen authentically, express yourself authentically, appreciate authentically, and serve authentically (Cashman, 1998).

To date, it appears that there are still differing perspectives around the conception of authentic leadership. This is to be expected during the early phases of construct definition and theory development (Hunt, 1999). If authentic leadership is to provide an explicitly moral model for leaders, it must transcend the self and be anchored in a set of universal values. In order to do this, the borders of existing authentic leadership perspectives may need to be revised.

SPIRITUAL LEADERSHIP THEORY

Authentic leadership requires leaders to act from a set of internal values that are consistent with their attitudes and behavior (Fry, 2005a). Although recent formulations of authentic leadership theory certainly articulate that such leaders are centered on moral values, a deeper examination of the values underlying authentic leadership is worthwhile at this early stage in the theory development. To be truly authentic, leaders must act from a normative set of values and attitudes that are anchored in a set of universally accepted principles. The emerging spiritual leadership paradigm offers an alternative for the development of authentic leadership theory and practice (Fry, 2005b).

Fry (2003) developed a causal theory of spiritual leadership based on vision, altruistic love and hope/faith that is grounded in an intrinsic motivation theory. Spiritual leadership taps into the fundamental needs of both leader and follower for spiritual survival through calling – a sense that one's life has meaning and makes a difference – and membership – a sense that one is understood, appreciated, and accepted unconditionally (Fleischman, 1994; Maddock & Fulton, 1998). The purpose of spiritual leadership is to create vision and value congruence across the individual, empowered team, and organization levels and, ultimately, foster higher levels of both organizational commitment and productivity. This entails:

1. Creating a vision where organization members experience a sense of calling in that their life has meaning and makes a difference;
2. Establishing a social/organizational culture based on altruistic love whereby leaders and followers have genuine care, concern, and appreciation for *both* self and others, have a sense of membership, and feel understood and appreciated.

To summarize the posited relationships among the variables of the causal model of spiritual leadership (see Figs. 1 and 2), "doing what it takes" through faith in a clear, compelling vision produces a sense of calling – that part of spiritual survival that gives one a sense of making a difference and, therefore, that one's life has meaning. Hope/faith adds belief, conviction, trust, and action for performance of the work to achieve the vision. SLT proposes that hope/faith in the organization's vision keeps followers looking forward to the future and provides the desire and positive expectation that fuels effort through intrinsic motivation.

Altruistic love is given unconditionally upon entry into the organization and is received in turn from followers in pursuit of a common vision that drives out and removes fears associated with worry, anger, jealousy, selfishness, failure, and guilt and gives one a sense of membership – that part of spiritual survival that results in an awareness of being understood and appreciated. Thus, spiritual leadership is an intrinsic motivation cycle based on vision (performance), altruistic love (reward), and hope/faith (effort) that

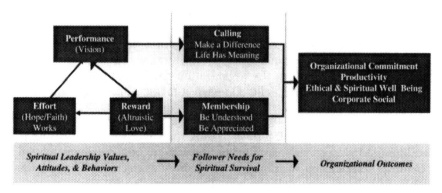

Fig. 1. Causal Model of Spiritual Leadership Theory (Fry, 2003, 2005a).

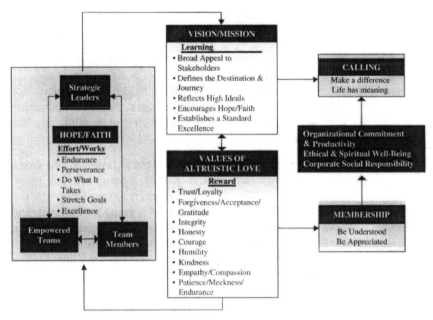

Fig. 2. Expanded Causal Model of Spiritual Leadership Theory as a Source of Ethical and Spiritual Well-Being Corporate Social Responsibility (Fry, 2005a).

results in an increase in one's sense of spiritual survival (e.g., calling and membership). Ultimately, positive organizational outcomes are posited to arise from spiritual leadership, such as increased:

(1) Organizational commitment – People with a sense of calling and membership will become attached, loyal to, and want to stay in organizations that have cultures based on the values of altruistic love, and

(2) Productivity and continuous improvement (Fairholm, 1998) – People who have hope/faith in the organization's vision and who experience calling and membership will "Do what it takes" in pursuit of the vision to continuously improve and be more productive.

Fry (2005a) extended SLT by exploring the concept of positive human health and psychological well-being through recent developments and scientific research on workplace spirituality, character ethics, positive psychology, and spiritual leadership. These areas provide a consensus on the values, attitudes, and behaviors necessary for positive human health and psychological well-being (Fry, 2005a). Ethical well-being is defined as authentically living one's values, attitudes, and behavior from the inside-out in creating a principled center congruent with the universal, consensus values inherent in SLT (Cashman, 1998; Covey, 1991; Fry, 2003). Because SLT anchors the leader's individual values to a set of universal values around which there is an emerging scientific consensus, SLT, through the concept of ethical well-being, addresses the congruence deficiency seen in the existing discussions of authentic leadership.

We therefore propose that (1) ethical well-being forms the essence of authentic leadership and (2) authentic leadership is a necessary component of spiritual leadership. Furthermore, ethical well-being and authentic leadership are viewed as necessary but not sufficient for spiritual well-being. To achieve spiritual well-being, in addition to ethical well-being, requires transcendence of self as one pursues a vision/purpose/mission in service to key stakeholders that satisfies one's need for spiritual survival.

Fry (2005a) proposed that individuals practicing spiritual leadership at the personal level will experience spiritual well-being and score high on both life satisfaction in terms of joy, peace, and serenity and the Ryff and Singer (2001) dimensions of well-being. In other words, they will experience greater psychological well-being and have fewer problems related to physical health in terms of allostatic load (cardiovascular disease, cognitive impairment, declines in physical functioning, and mortality). In addition, authentic leaders will have a high regard for one's self and one's past life, good-quality relationships with others, a sense that life is purposeful and meaningful, the capacity to effectively manage their surrounding world, the ability to follow inner convictions, and a sense of continuing growth and self-realization.

Spiritual Leadership and Vision and Value Congruence Across Levels

As described earlier, the spiritual leadership process is initiated by developing a vision/mission whereby strategic leaders and/or followers can meet or exceed the expectations of key stakeholders. This vision must vividly portray a journey which, when undertaken, will give one a sense of calling – of one's life having meaning and making a difference. The vision then forms the basis for the social construction of the organization's culture as a learning organization and the ethical system and values underlying it. In spiritual leadership, these values are prescribed and form the basis for altruistic love (see Fig. 2). Strategic leaders then embody and abide by these values through their everyday attitudes and behavior. In doing so, they create empowered teams where participants are challenged to persevere, be tenacious, do what it takes, and pursue excellence and challenging goals through hope and faith in the vision, their leaders and themselves. Supporting activities that foster the congruence process include: (1) behavior consistent with values; (2) creating a climate where morality and ethics are truly important; (3) legitimizing different viewpoints, values, and beliefs; (4) developing imagination, inspiration, and mindfulness; (5) letting go of expectations that are unrealistic; (6) acknowledgement of the efforts and accomplishments of others; (7) creating organizational processes that develop the whole person – not just exploiting current talents and strengths (Kriger & Hanson, 1999).

Empowerment is power sharing in the delegation of both power and authority and all but symbolic responsibility to organizational followers (Spreitzer, 1996). Empowered employees commit more of themselves to do the job through trust in the strategic leaders and the hope and faith that ensues from this trust. By providing employees with the knowledge to contribute to the organization, the power to make consequential decisions, and the necessary resources to do their jobs, strategic leaders provide the context for all organizational participants to receive altruistic love. This, in turn, forms the basis for intrinsic motivation through hope/faith in pursuit and implementation of the organization's vision and values in socially responsible service to internal and external stakeholders. By participating in these teams, followers gain recognition and celebration, experience a sense of membership, and feel understood and appreciated.

Additionally, strategic leaders must provide followers with the knowledge of how their jobs are relevant to the organization's performance and vision/mission. This understanding is necessary to create the cross level connection between team and individual jobs and the organization's vision/mission. Through this experience, followers, too, can begin to develop, refine and practice their own personal spiritual leadership that fosters value congruence in social interaction with internal and external stakeholders and, ultimately, ethical and spiritual well-being.

Personal Spiritual Leadership and Authentic Leadership

At a personal level for both leaders and followers, it is especially important to adhere to and practice five key spiritual practices in a continual quest for ethical and spiritual well-being, and professional development and effectiveness: (1) know one's self; (2) respect and honor the beliefs of others; (3) be as trusting as you can be; and (4) maintain a spiritual practice (e.g., spending time in nature, prayer, mediation, reading inspirational literature, yoga, shamanistic practices, writing in a journal) (Kurth, 2003). These spiritual practices are also necessary for development of personal spiritual leadership and, we propose, authentic leadership.

Personal spiritual leadership, by tapping into the fundamental spiritual survival dimensions of calling and membership, creates an intrinsic motivating force that elicits spontaneous, cooperative effort from people. Such leadership also makes it more likely for employees to learn, develop and use their skills and knowledge to benefit both themselves and their organizations. Through participation in self-directed, empowered teams, both leaders and followers begin to develop, refine, and practice their own personal leadership. Most importantly, it is necessary for the source of personal leadership to spring from the values underlying altruistic love that reflect a genuine care and concern for both self and others. Through visualization and positive affirmation of the values of hope/faith and altruistic love, leaders and followers at all levels in empowered teams practice personal spiritual leadership. By authentically pursuing a personal vision for their own lives through a self-motivated intrinsic process that creates a sense of calling and membership, both leaders and followers can achieve ethical and spiritual well-being and high levels of organizational commitment and productivity (see Fig. 2).

Thus, SLT specifically addresses the three critical issues raised earlier for authentic leadership in that it: (1) explicitly identifies and incorporates universal consensus values of altruistic love that are necessary for authentic leadership; (2) provides a process for achieving value congruence across the personal, empowered team, and organizational levels (see Fig. 2); and (3) predicts that authentic leaders will experience ethical well-being and, when coupled with a transcendent vision, spiritual well-being manifested as joy, peace, serenity, positive human health, and psychological well-being.

LEGACY LEADERSHIP: A MODEL OF SPIRITUAL LEADERSHIP

Recently, Whittington and his associates (Whittington, Kageler, & Pitts, 2002; Whittington, Pitts, Kageler, & Goodwin, 2005) developed a model of spiritual leadership referred to as legacy leadership. We believe this model has useful implications for authentic leadership, and we consider these implications below. These qualities are integrated into a causal model presented in Fig. 3.

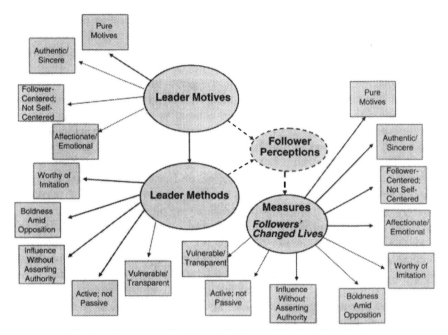

Fig. 3. Legacy Leadership: A Spiritual Model of Leadership.

Motives and Methods

Four basic motives are posited to drive legacy leadership: (1) a pure motive to achieve personal integrity and high standards of moral excellence; (2) a desire to be authentic and sincere; (3) a follower – as opposed to self-centered orientation; and (4) affectionate/emotional motives that reflect caring and altruistic love for others. These motives underlie five methods used by a legacy leader to influence his/her followers: (1) being worthy of imitation; (2) demonstrating boldness amidst opposition; (3) exerting influence without asserting authority; (4) staying active as opposed to passive; and (5) demonstrating vulnerability and transparency. Whittington et al. (2005) see the methods (leadership behaviors) of a legacy leader as a reflection of the leader's motives. That is, the leader's methods are rooted in his/her motives. Furthermore, the motives of the legacy leader are anchored to an external standard of universally accepted values. This point provides the most basic premise of our approach to authentic leadership: the behavior of a legacy leader is consistent with his/her internal motivation – and these motives are in turn anchored to an external standard. Thus, legacy leaders are seen as operating from an altruistic orientation that is self-transcendent (Michie & Gooty, 2005).

Follower Perceptions of the Legacy Leader's Motives and Methods

The true measure of the impact a leader has on others is represented by the degree to which the followers have incorporated the leader's qualities into their own lives (Avolio, 1999; Lord & Brown, 2004). In order for a leader to leave his or her legacy with a follower, however, the follower must perceive the leader as one with pure motives who is worthy of imitation. Only under these circumstances, will legacy leadership be perpetuated in the follower through his or her changed life. Thus, the legacy leader's motives and methods and the follower outcomes are mediated by followers' perceptions of the leader (see Fig. 3). The mediating mechanism of follower perceptions has been emphasized by Lord and his associates (Lord & Brown, 2004; Lord & Maher, 1993).

According to this perspective, leadership is not located solely in the leader or the follower, rather it involves the interpretation of behaviors, traits, and outcomes produced as interpreted by the followers (Lord & Maher, 1993). In fact, Lord and Maher (1993) define leadership as the process of being perceived as a leader. Yammarino and Dubinsky (1994) and Avolio and Yammarino (1990) also have examined the role of perceptions within the context of transformational leadership, suggesting it is "in the eyes of the beholder" (p. 193).

The interpretation of leader motives and behaviors by followers is crucial to the process of both spiritual and legacy leadership. Dasborough and Ashkanasy (2002) suggest that followers' perceptions of a leader's behavior will be influenced by: (1) characteristics of previous interactions between the leader and follower; (2) follower attributions regarding the leader's intentions; and (3) follower characteristics such as mood, experience, and role in the interaction (as a target or as a bystander). While acknowledging these situational influences on information processing, the focus of legacy leadership is on the importance of the role the leader plays in eliciting accurate perceptions of his/her motives and methods.

When followers accurately perceive congruence between the motives and methods of the leader, they are more likely to act in a way that emulates the leader, or in a way that reflects their internalization of the leader's motives and methods. Furthermore, followers must perceive that the leader's motives are congruent with universally accepted values. When the leader's values are seen as being consistent with universally accepted values, the leader is perceived to be authentic. Only when there is congruence between a leader's behaviors and perceived motives that are anchored in a universal set of values will followers be willing to internalize the leader's espoused values and seek to emulate that leader. This process is consistent with the personal and social identification processes used by followers who come to identify with authentic leaders and their values (Avolio, Gardner, Walumbwa, Luthans, & May, 2004; Gardner, Avolio, Luthans, May, & Walumbwa, 2005; Avolio & Gardner, 2005).

Changed Lives: The Real Measure of Leader Effectiveness

How is the effectiveness of leadership to be measured? Contemporary leadership scholars often measure the impact of leadership on individual dimensions such as in-role (i.e., job requirements) and extra-role (i.e., organizational citizenship behaviors) performance, satisfaction, and commitment, or organizational level performance (e.g., market share or profitability). Avolio (1999) has challenged these approaches to the measurement of leader effectiveness. Specifically, he argues that transformational leadership only has an indirect effect on these outcomes. The impact of a leader comes through building trust, identification, and a willingness to support the leader and the organization. More recently, the traditional approach to understanding leader effectiveness has also been challenged by Lord and Brown (2004). They content that "ultimately, leadership is a process of influence ... and the effectiveness of a leader depends on his or her ability to *change subordinates*" [italics added] (p. 7).

In the legacy leadership framework, "changed lives" provides a measure of the leader's influence on the lives of their followers (see Fig. 3). The lives of the followers change because they are able to see the authenticity of the legacy leader who walks the talk. This makes the legacy leader's message legitimate, personal, and attainable. Thus, they are willing to believe the leader and live their lives as evidence of that belief. From the perspective of legacy leadership, the changes in followers' lives will be internal first. Followers of legacy leaders internalize the motives and values they perceive in the leader. This internalization may result in a shift along the proposed continuum of egotistical to altruistic motives, or a strengthening of already existing altruistic motives.

Values also may shift such that leaders are not viewed as providing only instrumental value to followers' lives, but also as having intrinsic value

(Covey, 1991; Goodwin, Whittington, & Bowler, 2004). These internal changes in motives and values will result in changed attitudes toward the organization (e.g., job satisfaction, commitment), and in outward behaviors such as increased performance, organizational citizenship behaviors, and other pro-social behaviors. Koestenbaum (2002) advocates the position that leadership is not about what one does, but who one is. Thus, a leader's behavior should provide evidence for his/her motives and values regardless of the setting, and the leader's influence should likewise be demonstrated in the followers' lives as they assume the leader's motives and values as their own.

The legacy leadership model incorporates and extends the characteristics of authentic leadership as identified by Luthans and Avolio (2003) and is consistent with the principles of SLT (Fry, 2003). Legacy leadership is rooted in an altruistic motive pattern that is consistent with the follower concerns advocated by Luthans and Avolio (2003). Legacy leaders demonstrate boldness amid opposition that is consistent with the risk-taking and first-mover characteristics of authentic leadership. Legacy leaders also demonstrate congruence between their espoused and enacted values. Yet, legacy leadership transcends the current definitions of authentic leadership because the values espoused by legacy leaders are anchored to universal or consensus values.

The motives of a legacy leader influence the leader's choice of influence tactics and leadership methods. By observing these methods, the followers of a legacy leader infer the motives of the legacy leader. When followers perceive this connection, they internalize the legacy leader's motives and seek to emulate his or her behavior. Through this process legacy leaders also develop the next generation of leaders. The followers of legacy leaders become legacy leaders themselves who manifest the motives and methods of a legacy leader. Thus, legacy leadership is a process of not only leading authentically, but of developing authentic leaders (Luthans & Avolio, 2003).

DISCUSSION AND CONCLUSION

Spiritual leadership, legacy leadership, and authentic leadership can be viewed as theories that are in the initial concept/elaboration stage of development (Reichers & Schneider, 1990; Hunt, 1999). At this stage it is important that initial theories meet the four components that provide the necessary and sufficient conditions for the development of any theoretical model. They must identify: (1) the units or variables of interest;

(2) congruence as defined by the laws of relationship among units of the model that specify how these units are associated; (3) boundaries within which the laws of relationship are expected to operate; and (4) contingency effects that specify system states within which the units of the theory take on characteristic values that are deterministic and have a persistence through time (Dubin, 1978; Fry & Smith, 1987).

SLT was initially developed as a universal theory. Relative to Dubin's model of theory building, SLT satisfies these four conditions. It identifies units or variables in a causal model whose linkages are hypothesized to be positively related. Subject to further testing, it is currently proposed to be a universal (e.g., no contingency effects) theory that holds across the individual, team, and organizational levels. SLT prescribes a set of consensus values and motives that, when combined with hope/faith in a compelling vision, produces intrinsic motivation to satisfy needs for spiritual survival and, ultimately, positively influence human health and psychological well-being. In addition, SLT proposes that: (1) certain qualities must be inherent in the organization's vision; and (2) a specific leadership process is also necessary to achieve authenticity and value congruence across the individual, team, and organizational levels. This congruence across levels will positively impact organizational commitment and productivity and employee well-being. Furthermore, SLT theory proposes that this is true regardless of the characteristics of the organization's environment, its employees or jobs.

Science is beginning to do what philosophical inquiry and debate could not accomplish for three thousand years – establish a prescriptive domain of consensus values derived from research on religion, workplace spirituality, positive psychology, character education, and the new spiritual leadership paradigm. Given emerging scientific research (much of it from positive psychology) values are not relative. There is an emerging consensus that authentically living these values will lead to positive human health and psychological well-being (Fry, 2004). This is the essence of ethical well-being.

We have also proposed that: (1) ethical well-being is essential for authentic leadership; (2) authentic leadership is a necessary component of spiritual leadership; and (3) SLT addresses three key issues that must be resolved if theory and research on authentic leadership is to advance. Furthermore, legacy leadership has been discussed, within the context of SLT, as a model of authentic leadership that integrates the leader's motives and behaviors into the leadership process.

Because our approach to authentic leadership explicitly identifies leader motives, there is a need to investigate the motives – particularly the power orientation – of leaders. Moreover, future research should examine the degree to which a leader's espoused values are consistent with the universal consensus values of altruistic love that are critical for authentic leadership. The assessment of leader motives is an important dimension for future research. Of particular interest would be the relationship between the leader's motives and followers' perceptions of the leader's motives. Do followers make accurate attributions of the leader's motives? This approach to authentic leadership would be strengthened by integrating research on impression management (Rosenfeld, Giacalone, & Riordan, 1995) and self-monitoring (Snyder, 1987).

Nichols (2004) suggests that self-monitoring may help explain differences between authentic and inauthentic leaders. Authentic leaders would be expected to be low self-monitors because their methods (behaviors) are consistent with their internal motives, beliefs, and values. Authentic leaders would be less likely to be high self-monitors who change their behaviors to match the situation. Followers should be able to ascertain whether their leaders are low or high self-monitors, and with this information, improve upon the accuracy of their perceptions about the correspondence between the leader's motives and methods. Authenticity may lead to lower use of impression management techniques (Nichols, 2004).

The real measure of authentic leadership, according to Fry (2005a) and Whittington et al. (2005), is "changed lives," in terms of a transformation to the universal values and the subsequent attitudes and behavior that reflect them. Hence, research on these values and their relationship to attitudes and behavior is crucial for identifying the influence of a legacy leader on followers. Because change is advocated as the dependent variable, longitudinal research is the best approach.

This type of research will require a baseline measure of followers on a variety of constructs that might be influenced by the leader, such as ethical values, stage of moral development (Kohlberg, 1976), emotional intelligence, and motive pattern. These measures would need to be obtained prior to followers' exposure to a new leader. Then, attributes of the leader could be assessed to determine to what degree they exhibited the qualities associated with legacy leadership. Over time, the influence of legacy leaders on followers' behavior and attitudes could be determined. Moreover, cross-sectional research could be conducted to determine if followers actually begin to emulate the behaviors and attitudes of their leaders as advocated by legacy leadership (Whittington et al., 2005). This emulation, or self-perpetuation, is a key to the tenets of the legacy leadership model.

Research on several fronts is necessary to establish the validity of SLT and any theory of authentic leadership before they are widely applied as models of organizational/professional development to foster personal and systemic change and transformation. Empirical research is just beginning on the relationship between the qualities of spiritual leadership and organizational outcomes (see Fry, Vitucci, & Cedillo, 2005; Giacalone, Jurkiewicz, & Fry, 2005; Malone & Fry, 2003; Townsend, 1984). Other individual outcomes (e.g., joy, peace, and serenity) hypothesized to be affected by spiritual leadership need to be validated for SLT. Finally, the conceptual distinction between SLT constructs and other leadership theories and constructs needs to be refined. In particular, this chapter, as Fry (2003) demonstrated for motivation leadership theories – argues for the inclusiveness of authentic leadership within the spiritual leadership paradigm.

REFERENCES

Avolio, B.J. (1999). *Full leadership development*. Thousand Oaks, CA: Sage.

Avolio, B. J., & Gardner, W. L. (2005). Authentic leadership development: Getting to the root of positive forms of leadership. *The Leadership Quarterly, 16*, 315–338.

Avolio, B. J., Gardner, W. L., Walumbwa, F. O., Luthans, F., & May, D. R. (2004). Unlocking the mask: A look at the process by which authentic leaders impact follower attitudes and behaviors. *The Leadership Quarterly, 15*, 801–823.

Avolio, B. J., & Yammarino, F. (1990). Operationalizing charismatic leadership using a level of analysis framework. *The Leadership Quarterly, 1*, 193–208.

Bass, B. M., & Steidlmeier, P. (1999). Ethics, character, and authentic transformational leadership. *The Leadership Quarterly, 10*, 181–217.

Cashman, K. (1998). *Leadership from the inside out*. Provo, Ut: Executive Excellence Publishing.

Covey, S. R. (1991). *Principle-centered leadership*. New York: Simon & Schuster.

Dasborough, M. T., & Ashkanasy, N. M. (2002). Emotion and attribution of intentionality in leader- member relationships. *The Leadership Quarterly, 13*, 615–634.

Dubin, R. (1978). *Theory building*. New York: Free Press.

Fairholm, G. W. (1998). *Perspectives on leadership: From the science of management to its spiritual heart*. Westport, CT: Preager.

Fleischman, P. R. (1994). *The healing spirit: Explorations in religion & psychotherapy*. Cleveland: Bonne Chance Press.

Fry, L. W. (2003). Toward a theory of spiritual leadership. *The Leadership Quarterly, 14*, 693–727.

Fry, L. W. (2005a). Toward a theory of ethical and spiritual well-being and corporate social responsibility through spiritual leadership. In: R. A. Giacalone, C. L. Jurkiewicz (Eds), *Positive psychology in business ethics and corporate responsibility*. Greenwich, CT: Information Age Publishing, in press.

Fry, L.W. (2005b). Introduction to the special issue: Toward a paradigm of spiritual leadership. *The Leadership Quarterly, 16*(4), in press.

Fry, L.W., & Smith, D.A. (1987). Congruence, contingency, and theory building. *Academy of Management Review, 12*, 117–132.

Fry, L.W., Vitucci, S., & Cedillo, M. (2005). Transforming the army through spiritual leadership: Measurement and establishing a baseline. *The Leadership Quarterly, 16*(4), in press.

Gardner, W. L., Avolio, B. J., Luthans, F., May, D. R., & Walumbwa, F. O. (2005). Can you see the real me? A self-based model of authentic leader and follower development. *The Leadership Quarterly, 16*, 373–394.

George, W. (2004). Find your voice. *Harvard Business Review, 82*(1), 35.

Giacalone, R. A., Jurkiewicz, C. L., & Fry, L. W. (2005). From advocacy to science: The next steps in workplace spirituality research. In: R. Paloutzian (Ed.), *Handbook of psychology and religion*. Newbury Park, CA: Sage.

Goodwin, V. L., Whittington, J. L., & Bowler, M. (2004). LMX and social capital. Paper presented at the meeting of the academy of management, New Orleans, Louisiana.

Hunt, J. G. (1999). Transformational/charismatic leadership's transformation of the field: A historical essay. *The Leadership Quarterly, 10*, 129–144.

Koestenbaum, P. (2002). *Leadership: The inner side of greatness*. San Francisco: Jossey-Bass.

Kohlberg, L. (1976). Moral stages and moralization: The cognitive developmental approach. In: T. Likona (Ed.), *Moral development and behavior: Theory, research, and social issues*. Austin, TX: Holt, Rinehart and Winston.

Kouzes, J., & Posner, B. (2003). *The leadership challenge* (3rd ed.). San Francisco: Jossey-Bass.

Kriger, M. P., & Hanson, B. J. (1999). A value-based paradigm for creating truly healthy organizations. *Journal of Change Management, 12*, 302–317.

Kurth, K. (2003). Spiritually renewing ourselves at work. In: R. A. Giacalone, & C. L. Jurkiewicz (Eds), *Handbook of workplace spirituality and organizational performance* (pp. 447–460). New York: M. E. Sharp.

Lord, R. G., & Brown, D. A. (2004). *Leadership processes and follower self-identity*. Mahwah, NJ: Lawrence Erlbaum.

Lord, R. G., & Maher, K. J. (1993). *Leadership and information processing: Linking perceptions and performance*. Boston: Routledge.

Luthans, F., & Avolio, B. J. (2003). Authentic leadership development. In: K. Cameron, J. Dutton & R. Quinn (Eds), *Positive organizational scholarship: Foundations of a new discipline*. San Francisco: Berrett-Koehler Publishers.

Maddock, R. C., & Fulton, R. L. (1998). *Motivation, emotions, and leadership: The silent side of management*. Westport, CT: Quorum Books.

Malone, P. F., & Fry, L. W. (2003). Transforming schools through spiritual leadership: A field experiment. Paper presented at the meeting of the academy of management, Seattle, Washington.

May, W. (2001). *The public obligation of the professional*. Louisville, KY:Westminster John Knox Press.

Michie, S., & Gooty, J. (2005). Values, emotions, and authenticity: Will the real leader please stand up? *The Leadership Quarterly, 16*(3), in press.

Nichols, T. (2004). Identifying false leaders-Unmasking the masked. *University of North Texas, Department of Management*, Working Paper Series. Denton, TX.

Price, T. (2003). The ethics of authentic transformational leadership. *The Leadership Quarterly, 14*, 67–81.

Reichers, A. E., & Schneider, B. (1990). Climate and culture: An evolution of constructs. In: B. Schneider (Ed.), *Organizational climate and culture* (pp. 5–39). San Francisco: Jossey-Bass.

Rosenfeld, P., Giacalone, R.A., & Riordan, C. A. (1995). *Impression management in organizational life*. London: Routledge.

Ryff, C. D., & Singer, B. (2001). From social structure to biology: Integrative science in pursuit of human health and well-being. In: C. R. Snyder, & S. J. Lopez (Eds), *Handbook of positive psychology*. Oxford, UK: Oxford University Press.

Singh, R., & Krishnan, K. (2002). Impact of impression management and value congruence on attributed charisma. *NMIMS Management Review, 14*(1), 86–94.

Snyder, M. (1987). *Private appearance/public realities: The psychology of self-monitoring*. New York: Freeman.

Spreitzer, G. (1996). Social structural characteristics of psychological empowerment. *Academy of Management Journal, 39*, 483–504.

Townsend, J. S. (1984). The development of the spiritual leadership qualities inventory. *Journal of Psychology and Religion, 12*, 305–313.

Whittington, J.L., Kageler, W., Pitts, T., & Goodwin, V. L. (2005). Legacy leadership: The leadership wisdom of the apostle Paul. *The Leadership Quarterly: Special Edition on Spirituality in Leadership, 16*(4), in press.

Whittington, J.L., Kageler, W., & Pitts, T. (2002). Legacy leadership: The leadership wisdom of the apostle Paul. Paper presented at the academy of management annual meeting, Denver, CO.

Yammarino, F. J., & Dubinsky, A. J. (1994). Transformational leadership theory: Using levels of analysis to determine boundary conditions. *Personnel Psychology, 47*, 787–811.

PART II:
LEADERSHIP INTERVENTION
RESEARCH

WHERE ARE WE? THE STATUS OF LEADERSHIP INTERVENTION RESEARCH: A META-ANALYTIC SUMMARY

Rebecca J. Reichard and Bruce J. Avolio

ABSTRACT

Do leadership interventions make a difference? To determine where we are and what we know about leadership intervention research, the Gallup Leadership Institute (GLI) accumulated a large database of information on leadership intervention studies conducted over the last 100 years. Based on a well-established quantitative technique – meta-analysis – this chapter describes the key characteristics as well as the overall impact of leadership interventions including both laboratory and field studies. Recommendations for leadership development research and practice are provided.

While discussing authentic leadership development (ALD) in the forthcoming special issue of *The Leadership Quarterly*, Avolio and Gardner (2005) stated, "Indeed, almost any proposed causal link in theories of leadership could and should be tested by 'bringing them to life' via some form of

Authentic Leadership Theory and Practice: Origins, Effects and Development
Monographs in Leadership and Management, Volume 3, 203–223

experimental intervention..." The premise of ALD is a true and lasting change in leaders and followers to increase their capabilities and effectiveness. Investigating such processes require robust research designs to assess not only the development but also the impact of leaders. Scholars and practitioners in the field of leadership development have the responsibility to rigorously test their theories. Only through careful experimentation, revision, and retesting can leadership theories be sharpened. This chapter provides an overview of the key components of past leadership intervention studies conducted over the last 100 years, and synthesizes research findings into a framework that can guide future leadership intervention research.

The overarching purpose of this project was threefold. First, we reviewed the existing literature on leadership interventions. Our primary goal was to provide a snapshot of where the field currently is in terms of research on determining the impact of leadership interventions very broadly defined. As part of this snapshot, the types of interventions conducted, the different settings in which they were conducted, the use of high-quality characteristics of research design, and the various theoretical approaches taken are described. For a richer description, specific examples of studies are provided along the way.

With this base of knowledge established, the second goal was to determine if leadership interventions have had a positive impact on important outcomes. Meta-analytic techniques were implemented to assess the effects of the leadership intervention studies that have been conducted over the last 100 years. Meta-analysis is a quantitative procedure used to combine results of prior research studies and assess the strength of the findings produced by a body of research (Hunter & Schmidt, 1990).

Meta-analysis is especially useful in situations where the number of studies to review becomes large, and evaluating trends based on summary judgments may be unreliable. For example, an author qualitatively reviewing 200 studies may arrive at the conclusion that the results are mixed. Meta-analysis provides a tool to quantitatively aggregate such studies. Using meta-analysis, the author may find that these mixed effects are, in fact, positive. Not only that, the author can determine through meta-analysis under what research conditions these effects are strongest and weakest. Such detailed analyses are impossible by qualitatively *eyeballing* a large body of research.

Finally, to better understand when leadership interventions make a positive difference, the impact of interventions based on different leadership theories was examined. Based on the findings from these points, our ultimate goal was to make recommendations to leadership scholars.

Understanding both the trends and areas of strength and weakness in leadership intervention research enables future leadership development researchers to advance the field of leadership by building on strengths and addressing the weaknesses of previous research.

PROJECT BACKGROUND

This review is based on a 2-year effort and flagship project of a team of researchers at the Gallup Leadership Institute (GLI). The inclusion criteria set for this meta-analysis spanned all leadership intervention studies conducted over the last 100 years including both laboratory and field studies. Studies were included in these analyses if the following criteria were met: (1) the phenomenon under investigation was leadership, (2) the researcher manipulated this phenomenon, and (3) the effects of the leadership intervention were quantitatively measured and reported.

While there have been several reviews of the leadership field (e.g., Bass, 1990; Yukl & Van Fleet, 1992; Lowe & Gardner, 2001), the GLI effort focused specifically on those primary studies that included some type of leadership intervention designed to produce a positive change in outcomes. That is, the primary study manipulated leadership in some way (i.e., training, role play, assignment, etc.). Another distinguishing aspect of this review was its broad theoretical focus. While other leadership meta-analyses have focused on one major theoretical framework (e.g., transformational leadership; Dumdum, Lowe, & Avolio, 2002; Bono & Judge, 2004; Judge & Piccolo, 2004), the GLI review was inclusive by spanning the gamut of major theories investigated over a 100-year period. However, this review did not include correlational or survey research or research conducted by private organizations (e.g., The Gallup Organization, Linkage, etc.).

After specifying both the inclusion and exclusion criteria as discussed above, the GLI team undertook an extensive search process to identify extant leadership intervention research. To initiate the search, the research team conducted a comprehensive literature review of the leadership field. Based on this review, a list of 18 leadership research streams, each representing a different theoretical framework (e.g., transformational leadership theory, contingency theory), was developed. With search terms generated from the research streams, the team searched 17 electronic databases (e.g., Academic Search Elite, PsychInfo) and reviewed thousands of abstracts for relevant studies. In addition to electronic searches, the reference lists of all identified studies and over 30 related meta-analyses were reviewed for additional studies meeting the inclusion criteria.

Because the goal was to identify the entire population of leadership intervention studies, the search spanned all sources of studies, whether they were journal articles, book chapters, conference papers, dissertations, or unpublished studies. To overcome the file drawer problem (e.g., Rosenthal, 1979) associated with unpublished studies, over 600 leadership researchers were asked via e-mail to add to the list of identified leadership intervention studies. Finally, associates performed a manual search of the table of contents of all journals that traditionally publish leadership research (e.g., *The Leadership Quarterly, Journal of Applied Psychology, Academy of Management Journal,* etc.) and leadership handbooks to identify studies that may have been missed through the electronic search. The comprehensive search strategy netted 200 studies (169 published, 31 unpublished) meeting the inclusion criteria. Table 1 shows the distribution of leadership intervention studies over time.

As shown in Table 1, a growing number of leadership intervention studies have been conducted in the last 100 years. One of the earliest studies identified, investigated the aggressive behavior of children under democratic, authoritarian, or laissez-faire adult leadership (Lewin, Lippitt, & White, 1939). With just 12 studies identified before 1970 and 52 studies already conducted in the current decade, it is safe to conclude that after a slow start, intervention research has been escalating. For example, during the 1980s and 1990s, the number of leadership intervention studies carried out has increased by 62%. Based on projections, the current decade will close with over 133 leadership intervention studies completed. The GLI is interested in improving the quality of future studies by understanding what has been

Table 1.   Frequency of Leadership Intervention Studies by Decade.

Years	Frequency	Percent	Cumulative Percent
1900 – 1949	1	0.5	0.5
1950 – 1959	3	1.5	2.0
1960 – 1969	8	4.0	6.0
1970 – 1979	39	19.5	25.5
1980 – 1989	37	18.5	44.0
1990 – 1999	60	30.0	74.0
2000 – 2004	52	26.0	100.0
Total	200	100.0	

done and thinking creatively about what can and should be done to advance leadership theory and practice.

SNAPSHOT OF LEADERSHIP INTERVENTION RESEARCH

As stated, one of the goals of this chapter was to review various descriptive statistics of previous leadership intervention research. A more comprehensive analysis of specific intervention effects appears in Avolio, Reichard, Hannah, Walumbwa, and Chan (2005). To accomplish this goal, a project-specific database was developed to capture 86 study characteristics from each of the 200 studies. Study characteristics included both qualitative information such as a description of the experimental setting and methods of assignment of experimental participants, and also quantitative data such as sample sizes and mean scores. This provided a potential database of 17,200 data points, limited only by information not reported by the authors and otherwise not able to be calculated.

A coding team of 12 trained associates conducted data extraction and coding of study characteristics. Because coding of data in meta-analyses has been criticized as a subjective process (Wanous, Sullivan, & Malinak, 1989) and to overcome questionable judgment calls, both a primary and secondary coder reviewed all 86 characteristics coded for each study. Any and all discrepancies in coding between the pair were investigated and consensus reached by team members or referred to a third coder, ultimately resulting in 100% agreement.

This section reviews the types of interventions conducted over the years, the settings in which the interventions took place, and the research design quality of the interventions. Specific examples of studies are also provided. As will be described, the majority of studies: (1) implemented training interventions, (2) were conducted in laboratory settings, (3) had a U.S. sample base, (4) took place in educational organizations, and (5) used a moderate to low-quality research design.

Type of Intervention

The breakdown of studies by the type of leadership intervention implemented appears in Fig. 1. As shown, the types of interventions were divided into six exclusive categories: training, actor/role play, scenario/vignette, assignment,

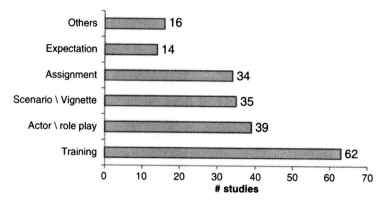

Fig. 1. Types of Leadership Interventions.

expectation, and others. Training interventions ($n = 62$) were the most frequent type of intervention performed.

An example of a training intervention was Towler's (2003) study. Towler's research examined whether charismatic leadership could be taught. Three groups of students were trained for two and a half hours in the following conditions: charismatic influence, presentation style, and control. Participants in the charismatic influence condition received training on visionary content, which included articulating a vision, appealing to followers' values, use of autobiography, use of metaphors, analogies, and stories, and selfefficacy language. After the training, participants in each condition made a videotaped presentation on the mock organization's strategy for selecting new employees. Results indicated that trainees in the charismatic influence training condition used more body gestures and told more stories than those in other conditions.

Together, interventions using actors/role playing ($n = 39$) and scenarios/ vignettes ($n = 35$) comprised 37% of studies. For example, in phase two of the Towler (2003) study, groups of two to three students viewed one of the videotaped speeches and then completed a performance task (evaluating resumes for a fictional organization). Results indicated that students who viewed the charismatic influence speech were more satisfied with the task, wrote a higher quality offer letter to the applicant, and were more accurate in their selection of high-quality applicants.

Another example of a study using an actor was a laboratory experiment where a graduate student played the role of the supervisor of temporary student employees (Gilmore, Beehr, & Richter, 1979). In the four experimental conditions, the actor changed his behavioral interactions with the workers to reflect high/low consideration and high/low structure. While the workers did not perceive the different leader behavior manipulations, results indicated differences in the quality and quantity of work. High-quality work was a result of high leader structure and low leader consideration.

Leadership can also be manipulated via assignment based on pre-existing individual differences. Seventeen percent of studies in the sample manipulated leadership via assignment ($n = 34$). One such individual difference variable that has been recently discussed with respect to ALD and relational authenticity is leader gender (Eagly, 2005). For example, Rice, Bender, and Vitters (1980) investigated the effects of leader gender on group task performance on a sample of cadets at the U.S. Military Academy. In this study, 72 groups with three male followers and half with female leaders completed two 30-min tasks varying in structure. Results indicated that group performance was significantly greater in groups with male leaders. Of the 200 studies in the current study, less than half ($n = 95$) reported the gender of the leader. Of those, nine reported all female leaders, 50 reported all male leaders, and 36 reported a mix of female and male leaders.

Finally, 14 of the studies manipulated leadership expectations (i.e., Pygmalion, discussed in detail below). The remainder of the studies manipulated leadership in some other way ($n = 16$).

Settings

Studies varied in terms of the setting in which they were conducted. Each study was coded based on its experimental setting, national setting, and organizational setting. As discussed below, the majority of studies were conducted in laboratory settings, which overlapped significantly with educational settings and the use of students as study participants. The prevalence of laboratory studies leaves room for caution about how well lab studies extend to applied work settings. Conversely, the paucity of field research highlights the apparent need to conduct research outside college and university laboratories with a broader range of experienced employees.

Experimental Setting

Sixty-four percent of the studies were conducted in laboratory settings ($n = 127$; see Table 2). A total of 33% of studies were conducted in field settings ($n = 66$). The remaining 3% of studies were either a mix of lab and field settings ($n = 2$) or did not clearly specify experimental setting ($n = 5$).

Table 2. Frequency of Leadership Intervention Studies by Setting.

Experimental setting			
Lab	Field	Mixed	Not Reported
127	66	2	5
Organizational setting			
Education	Military	Industrial	Other
129	30	18	23
National setting			
U.S.	Non-U.S.		
144	56		

National Setting

Seventy-two percent of identified studies were conducted within the United States ($n = 144$) and 28% of studies occurred in other countries ($n = 56$; see Table 2). Less than 10% of studies reported the nationality of focal leaders, and less than 11% reported follower nationality. There has been an apparent lack of cross-cultural intervention research available, which is further discussed below.

Organizational Setting

Studies were also sorted according to the organizational setting in which they were conducted. The resulting four categories were the military, educational institutions, industrial organizations, and an "other" category. The "other" category included a variety of organization types including medical organizations, the arts, and agriculture. As shown in Table 2, the majority of studies were conducted in educational settings ($n = 129$), with the majority (88%; $n = 114$) of these studies conducted in laboratory settings and most using students as study participants. Another 15% of studies were in the military ($n = 30$), 9% in industrial organizations ($n = 18$), and 12% in other types of organizations ($n = 23$).

Quality of Intervention

Not only did the sample of studies differ with regard to the types of intervention implemented and the setting within which they were conducted, but they also varied in the *quality* of the intervention in terms of study design, assignment of participants to groups, and use of manipulation checks (see Table 3). An important component inherent in leadership development studies is change over time. In terms of study design, the majority of leadership intervention studies used a cross-sectional design ($n = 112$) and one-third implemented a longitudinal design ($n = 68$). This can be contrasted with studies published between 1990 and 1999 in *The Leadership Quarterly* (Lowe & Gardner, 2001). Of those studies (including nonintervention studies), 82% were cross-sectional and 18% were longitudinal.

An example of a longitudinal experiment is a study by Dvir, Eden, Avolio, and Shamir (2002) with officers in the Israel Defense Forces. At the onset of the study, platoon leaders were randomly assigned to participate in a 3-day workshop focusing on either transformational leadership training or eclectic management training. The transformational leadership group received an additional booster session a month and a half after the initial training. Over a subsequent 4-month period, the leaders' performance was tracked. The study found that leaders trained in transformational leadership had a larger positive impact on their direct followers' development and indirect followers' performance as compared to leaders in the eclectic training group.

Of the 200 interventions conducted, just 9% exceeded 7 days (see Fig. 2). In fact, several of the interventions lasted only minutes. For example, in a laboratory study by Dobbins and Russell (1986), groups of college students were given either positive or negative random feedback following 20 min of group performance on a simulated manufacturing task. The study found that both leaders and followers made self-serving attributions for the group's performance. The entire study lasted less than one hour and the feedback intervention only minutes. Only 11 of the 200 intervention studies in the sample lasted longer than 1 month. Given the temporal component inherent in development, researchers are encouraged to incorporate time into theoretical frameworks and to implement longitudinal leadership interventions.

How participants are assigned to the experimental conditions is important for determining the causality of the intervention effects. The strongest control in an intervention study is random assignment, which statistically distributes individual differences equally across experimental conditions (Campbell & Stanley, 1966). A clear strength of the intervention studies reviewed is reflected in the widespread use of random assignment (see Table 3). Seventy-five percent of intervention studies analyzed used random assignment ($n = 150$), while the remaining 25% of studies either did not

Table 3. Crosstab of Quality Aspects of Leadership Intervention Studies.

	Longitudinal (n = 68)			Cross-sectional (n = 112)			Mixed (n = 20)		
	Random	Not random	Not reported	Random	Not random	Not reported	Random	Not random	Not reported
Manipulation check (n = 105)	21	2	4	52	6	12	7	0	1
No manipulation Check (n = 53)	15	6	0	17	5	3	6	0	1
Not reported (n = 42)	15	4	1	14	0	3	3	1	1

Note: Sample size for type of assignment was random (n = 150), not random (n = 24), not reported (n = 26).

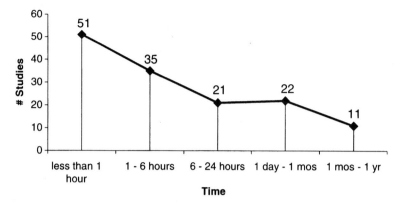

Fig. 2. Frequency of Leadership Intervention Studies by Length of Intervention.

report assignment methods ($n = 26$) or assigned participants using methods other than random ($n = 24$).

While the use of random assignment is promising, leadership researchers are encouraged to go one step further and to use random *selection* where possible. While random assignment distributes individual differences equally across groups within the study, it does not account for differences between the sample and the larger population. In order for the experimental sample to accurately reflect and generalize to the larger population, the use of random selection is required (Campbell & Stanley, 1966).

The final indicator of study quality as discussed here was the use of manipulation checks. A manipulation check ensures that the intended intervention treatment (the manipulation) actually was affected by the methods used by researchers (Cook & Campbell, 1979).

The use of manipulation checks is exemplified in a laboratory experiment where undergraduate students in three-member tank platoon teams participated in a low-fidelity tank simulation (Marks, Zaccaro, & Mathieu, 2000). Marks et al. created multiple intervention conditions by manipulating team-interaction training, leader briefings, and novelty of the performance context. Manipulations were checked using statistical procedures, such that the effect of each manipulation could be tested. For example, the team-interaction manipulation check consisted of a three-item composite on the team's knowledge of teamwork strategies and cooperative tank movement. The authors found that participants in each condition were influenced by interventions in the way that was intended by the researchers.

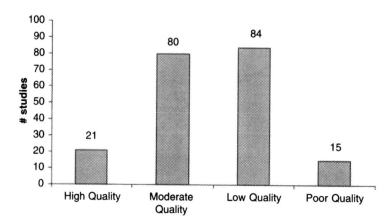

Note. High quality = Longitudinal design, random assignment, and manipulation check.

Fig. 3.   Frequency of Quality Leadership Intervention Studies.

In the current sample, 52% of leadership intervention studies conducted manipulation checks and the remaining 48% did not. For researchers to have confidence that experimental manipulations are having the intended effects, they must make certain that those manipulations are adequately tested.

Overall quality of each study was computed based on the utilization of the above mentioned criteria: longitudinal design, random assignment, and manipulation check. As shown in Fig. 3, 21 of the intervention studies in the sample reported use of all three high-quality criteria. Moderate quality was defined as studies having a combination of two of the three criteria. Eighty of the studies in the sample were rated as moderate in quality. Finally, low quality ($n = 84$) and poor quality ($n = 15$) reflect studies with one or zero of the three quality criteria, respectively.

IMPACT OF LEADERSHIP INTERVENTION RESEARCH

The effects of all 200 studies were quantitatively combined using meta-analysis techniques (Hunter & Schmidt, 1990) to produce one overall effect of leadership intervention. Based on a total sample of 13,656 participants and 140 independent effect sizes, findings indicated that leadership interventions had a positive and moderate impact on outcomes. This means that evidence supports that interventions designed to change the impact of leadership worked at least to some degree. If the effects were random, then there would be a 50/50 chance of a positive effect being observed. On average, a 66% chance of a positive effect of leadership was found in the current sample. In addition, leadership intervention studies conducted in laboratory/educational settings had a larger impact than those conducted in field settings. No clear differences were observed for interventions conducted in different national (U.S. versus non-U.S.) settings.

Next, the impact of leadership interventions based on different theoretical frameworks was examined. As stated earlier, 18 theoretical research streams were targeted in the initial search. However, after the identified studies were collected, they were divided into eight overarching theoretical categories. As shown in Table 4, traditional leadership theories were tested most frequently ($n = 69$).

Traditional theories included studies on leader behavior (e.g., initiating structure and consideration; Stogdill & Coons, 1957) and contingency theories (e.g., Fiedler, 1967; House, 1971). For example, as a test of the contingency model of leadership, Fiedler and Mahar (1979) conducted a field study to test the impact of leader match training on ROTC (Reserve Officers' Training Corps) cadet performance. The leadership intervention consisted of providing the cadets with a copy of the leader match IV manual for 2 weeks of self-study. Results indicated that trained cadets had higher overall performance as rated by platoon advisers and peer ratings than untrained cadets.

As stated, research on traditional theories dominated leadership research from the 1950s through the 1990s. In fact, of the 51 leadership intervention studies found before 1980, three-fourths tested a traditional leadership theory ($n = 38$). While other theories, such as attribution theory, appeared on the scene in the 1980s, traditional theories were still the most popular making up nearly half of the intervention studies conducted in that decade.

It was not until the 1990s that studies testing the new genre of leadership theories emerged and eventually dominated leadership intervention efforts. Two such theories were charismatic and transformational leadership theories. For instance, Barling, Weber, and Kelloway (1996) conducted a field experiment to test the effects of transformational leadership training for managers. Findings indicated that followers of trained managers had higher levels of commitment and financial outcomes.

Other examples of the new genre of leadership interventions are two studies testing the contagion of nonverbal behaviors of charismatic leaders

Table 4. Frequency of Leadership Intervention Studies by Theory and Decade.

Years	Leadership Theory								
	Attribution	Eclectic	Individual differences	LMX	New Genre[a]	Pygmalion	Team	Traditional[a]	Total
1900–1949	0	0	0	0	0	0	0	1	1
1950–1959	0	0	0	0	0	0	0	3	3
1960–1969	0	1	0	0	1	0	1	5	8
1970–1979	0	2	2	2	2	2	0	29	39
1980–1989	7	2	1	2	3	4	1	17	37
1990–1999	4	8	3	1	21	7	6	10	60
2000–2004	3	1	5	0	22	13	4	4	52
Total	14	14	11	5	49	26	12	69	200

Note: [a]New genre includes charismatic and transformational leadership theories. Traditional includes directive and participative research, contingency theory, Path goal theory, goal-setting, justice, and initiation and consideration research.

(Cherulnik, Donley, Wiewel, & Miller, 2001). In study one, participants watched simulated campaign speeches from charismatic college students, which included nonverbal behavior such as more smiles and visual attention to the audience. In study two, participants watched video clips of the 1992 Presidential debate, which were chosen to contrast charismatic and non-charismatic nonverbal behavior. In both studies, participants performed more charismatic behaviors after viewing a charismatic leader (Cherulnik et al., 2001). In sum, new genre of leadership interventions made up 38% of studies conducted in the last 15 years. In terms of the impact of leadership interventions based on traditional versus new genre of leadership theories, no difference in their effects was found. Overall, leadership interventions testing both theoretical frameworks had moderate, positive effects.

However, interventions testing Pygmalion leadership found particularly high effect sizes. In one such study, platoons in the Israel Defense Forces were randomly assigned to one of two conditions (Eden, 1990). In the high Pygmalion condition, the platoon leaders were informed that their platoon was full of high command potential soldiers. Conversely, the control condition platoon leaders received no information on the command potential of the soldiers. The findings indicated that Pygmalion platoons did, in fact, outperform the control platoons. While other Pygmalion research (Eden et al., 2000) found much smaller effects; overall, Pygmalion leadership interventions had significantly larger effects than interventions based on any of the other theories. In fact, participants receiving a Pygmalion intervention had up to a 79% chance of having a positive outcome, as compared to 50% chance at random.

Some of the major leadership theories have a surprisingly few number of intervention studies. One such theory that has received theoretical attention but has rarely been tested using intervention research is leader–member exchange (LMX) theory (see Schriesheim, Castro, & Cogliser, 1999, for review). First introduced by Dansereau, Graen, and Haga in 1975 as vertical dyad linkage (VDL) theory, both VDL and LMX emphasize the exchange relationship between leaders and followers. The impact of this theory is reflected conceptually in the ALD model, which focuses on the relational aspects of leader and follower development (Gardner, Avolio, Luthans, May, & Walumbwa, 2005).

Only five intervention studies were found testing VDL/LMX theory. One of these studies examined the effectiveness of an LMX intervention while controlling for the initial LMX quality in a sample of female employees and managers (Scandura & Graen, 1984). The study found that employees having initially low LMX quality with their managers had the largest gains in productivity and satisfaction after the implementation of leadership training designed to encourage the managers to improve their dyadic exchange relationships. However, because of inadequate data reported in this and most of the other LMX studies, only a single useable effect size was extracted to represent an LMX leadership effect.

Leadership scholars not only need to continue the trend and conduct more leadership intervention studies, but they also must conduct more research on those neglected theoretical frameworks. While the most popular theories have generated some research, theories such as LMX and team leadership have gone virtually untested. While only six effects were extracted from team leadership interventions, the findings still indicate moderately positive outcomes comparable to the traditional and new genre of leadership findings.

To further investigate the effects of traditional theories and new genre of leadership theories, the relative impact of each theory on different types of outcomes was investigated. To do so, outcome variables were coded into one of three mutually exclusive categories: affective, behavioral, and cognitive. Enjoyment of work, number of problems solved, and self-efficacy are examples of affective, behavioral, and cognitive outcomes, respectively. Leadership interventions designed to test new genre of leadership theories had larger effects than those based on traditional theories for both affective and cognitive outcomes. In addition, interventions anchored in traditional theories had a larger effect on behavioral outcomes than did new genre of leadership interventions.

These findings imply that to obtain the largest effects researchers should accurately match theoretical frameworks with chosen outcomes. Even when the design of the leadership intervention is rigorous, oftentimes leadership researchers neglect to focus on the nature and quality of the performance criterion chosen for inclusion in their research programs. This is probably even more problematic in field intervention research in that leadership researchers oftentimes have to settle for whatever performance measures are available and used by the field site organization. Very likely, the impact of leadership interventions may be underestimated given the potential problems frequently encountered in using performance data collected in applied settings.

Moreover, for theories of leadership such as transformational leadership, predicting typical business performance is not a central component of the theory, which suggests that transformational leadership predicts *performance beyond expectations*. Very few studies in the literature have actually included performance measures that tap into performance beyond expectations or comparing typical versus exemplary performance. Paying closer attention to the nature of one's performance criterion would seem to be a future area on which future researchers may benefit to focus.

SUMMARY AND RECOMMENDATIONS

Researchers at the Gallup Leadership Institute (GLI) sought to answer the simple question: Do leadership interventions make a difference? To determine just where we are and what we know within the field of leadership, the GLI accumulated a large database of information on leadership intervention studies conducted over the last 100 years. Based on the GLI database and the quantitative technique of meta-analysis, this chapter described both the key characteristics of leadership research, and also the overall impact of leadership interventions with the goal of pointing to new directions for an aggressive campaign to ramp up field intervention research studies on leadership and its development.

Specifically, dominant characteristics of previous leadership intervention research included the use of training manipulations, a preponderance of laboratory studies conducted in educational settings, interventions lasting less than one hour, moderate to low quality research designs, and a shift from traditional theories (e.g., leader behavior, contingency) to a focus on a new genre of leadership (e.g., transformational, charismatic). Furthermore, quantitative findings of the meta-analysis indicated that overall leadership interventions did make a positive difference on a broad range of criterion measures at multiple levels of analysis. While the impact was about the same for new genre of leadership studies and traditional models of leadership, studies testing Pygmalion leadership had the largest impact, which is ironic because these studies are based on lying to the target leaders. Furthermore, the size of effects for new genre and traditional theories varied based on the focus of the outcome of interest.

Thus far, the important characteristics of 200 leadership intervention studies conducted over the last 100 years have been reviewed. While there has been an exponential increase in intervention studies in the last few decades, readers are urged to bridge the researcher–practitioner divide and conduct a greater number of high-quality experimental labs and field intervention studies. It is important to emphasize the need for intervention research in order to adequately test theoretical propositions. While correlational research is often easier to conduct and can test predicted relationships among important variables (Campbell & Stanley, 1966), only experimental and quasi-experimental research designs provide a rigorous test of leadership theory. By doing so, leadership scholars take responsibility for fully testing leadership theory, advancing what is known about leadership, and providing a superior service in support of applied leadership development.

Furthermore, we would like to stress the importance of conducting rigorous leadership intervention research to make sure that theories are being adequately tested. For future leadership intervention studies to be of high quality, researchers should include longitudinal designs, random assignment/selection, and manipulation checks as part of the study design. While the use of these methods is much easier to accomplish in the laboratory, it is perhaps even more imperative in field settings.

Going forward, leadership researchers and practitioners must work together to secure top management support for high-quality intervention studies. This can be accomplished by conducting an organizational-specific needs analysis and by linking the proposed leadership intervention to the organization's goals and performance criteria. Leadership researchers should emphasize to top management that it is essential to determine the impact of leadership interventions and push for the use of sound research designs that can actually test whether training costs are used efficiently and what the Return on Development (R.O.D.) turns out to be.

Researchers should translate findings into dollar amounts through utility analysis to provide management with the bottom line impact of leadership interventions. Over time top management will view high-quality leadership interventions as a business advantage and all stakeholders, including the field of leadership, will benefit. The use of information technology as a tool to improve research design quality is also encouraged. By implementing these high-quality criteria in future interventions, scholars can become more certain regarding the conclusions of our research.

Not only should future intervention research be of high quality, but equally important, it should also be theory-based. Cooper, Scandura, and Schriesheim (2005) recently described important theoretical issues related to the authentic leadership development. These include definition and measurement of constructs, convergent and discriminant validity of constructs, and the framing of constructs within a nomological network. In fact, those intervention studies based on eclectic/no theories had the smallest positive effect on outcomes as contrasted to interventions based on a developed theoretical framework, thus supporting the suggestions of Cooper et al.

In addition, other research streams (e.g., cross-cultural/global, ethical/moral, strategic) included in the initial search resulted in few to no intervention studies. One study somewhat related to cross-cultural leadership investigated the differing effects of transformational and transactional leadership in individualistic versus collectivistic cultures on group brainstorming (Jung & Avolio, 1999). However, this study was considered a more direct test of the new genre of leadership than cross-cultural leadership. While great progress has been made in investigating cross-cultural aspects of leadership through the GLOBE studies (House, Hanges, Javidan, Dorfman, & Gupta, 2004), intervention research is also needed to determine whether positive leadership intervention results reported in North America generalize to other regions of the world. As stated only 28% of studies were set outside of the United States. Not only is more intervention research needed, but especially non-U.S. based research.

In sum, recommendations for future leadership development studies include the following: (1) continuing the increase of conducting more leadership intervention studies, (2) implementing high-quality research designs by leveraging top management support and technology, (3) basing interventions on sound theory that takes into account the temporal component of development, and (4) filling gaps where tests of other leadership theories have fallen short. With knowledge of the characteristics of previous leadership intervention research, leadership development researchers have the opportunity to strengthen future research and to expand the impact such interventions have on the growth and development of both public and private sector organizations.

REFERENCES

Avolio, B. J., & Gardner, W. L. (2005). Authentic leadership development: Getting to the root of positive forms of leadership. *The Leadership Quarterly, 16*(3), 315–338.

Avolio, B. J., Reichard, R. J., Hannah, S., Walumbwa, F. O., & Chan, A. (2005). 100 years of leadership intervention research: A meta analysis. (Tech. Rep.). University of Nebraska-Lincoln, Gallup Leadership Institute.

Barling, J., Weber, T., & Kelloway, E. K. (1996). Effects of transformational leadership training on attitudinal and financial outcomes: A field experiment. *Journal of Applied Psychology, 81*, 827–832.

Bass, B. M. (1990). *Bass and Stogdill's handbook of leadership: Theory, research, and managerial applications* (3rd ed.). New York: Free Press.

Bono, J. E., & Judge, T. A. (2004). Personality and transformational and transactional leadership: A meta-analysis. *Journal of Applied Psychology, 89*, 901–910.

Campbell, D. T., & Stanley, J. C. (1966). *Experimental and quasi-experimental designs for research*. Boston: Houghton Mifflin.

Cherulnik, P. D., Donley, K. A., Wiewel, T. S. R., & Miller, S. R. (2001). Charisma is contagious: The effect of leaders' charisma on observers' affect. *Journal of Applied Social Psychology, 31,* 2149–2159.

Cook, T. D., & Campbell, D. T. (1979). *Quasi-experimentation: Design and analysis issues for field settings*. Boston: Houghton Mifflin.

Cooper, C. D., Scandura, T. A., & Schriesheim, C. A. (2005). Looking forward but learning from our past: Potential challenges to developing authentic leadership theory and authentic leaders. *The Leadership Quarterly, 16*(3), 475–494.

Dansereau, F., Graen, G. B., & Haga, W. J. (1975). A vertical dyad linkage approach to leadership within formal organizations: A longitudinal investigation of the role making process. *Organizational Behavior and Human Performance, 13,* 46–78.

Dobbins, G. H., & Russell, J. M. (1986). Self-serving biases in leadership: A laboratory experiment. *Journal of Management, 12,* 475–483.

Dumdum, U. R., Lowe, K. B., & Avolio, B. J. (2002). A meta-analysis of transformational and transactional leadership correlates of effectiveness and satisfaction: An update and extention. In: B. J. Avolio & F. J. Yammarino (Eds), *Transformational and charismatic leadership: The road ahead* (pp. 35–66). Oxford, UK: Elsevier Science.

Dvir, T., Eden, D., Avolio, B. J., & Shamir, B. (2002). Impact of transformational leadership on follower development and performance: A field experiment. *Academy of Management Journal, 45,* 735–744.

Eagly, A. H. (2005). Achieving relational authenticity in leadership: Does gender matter? *The Leadership Quarterly, 16*(3), 459–474.

Eden, D. (1990). Pygmalion without interpersonal contrast effects: Whole groups gain from raising manager expectations. *Journal of Applied Psychology, 75,* 394–398.

Eden, D., Geller, D., Gerwirtz, A., Gordon-Terner, R., Inbar, I., Liberman, M., Pass, Y., Salomon-Segev, I., & Shalit, M. (2000). Implanting Pygmalion leadership style through workshop training: Seven field experiments. *The Leadership Quarterly, 11,* 171–210.

Fiedler, F. E. (1967). *A theory of leadership effectiveness*. New York: McGraw-Hill.

Fiedler, F. E., & Mahar, L. (1979). A field experiment validating contingency model leadership training. *Journal of Applied Psychology, 64,* 247–254.

Gardner, W. L., Avolio, B. J., Luthans, F., May, D. R., & Walumbwa, F. O. (2005). Can you see the real me? A self-based model of authentic leader and follower development. *The Leadership Quarterly, 16*(3), 343–372.

Gilmore, D. C., Beehr, T. A., & Richter, D. J. (1979). Effects of leader behaviors on subordinate performance and satisfaction: A laboratory experiment with student employees. *Journal of Applied Psychology, 64,* 166–172.

House, R. J. (1971). A path-goal theory of leader effectiveness. *Administrative Science Quarterly, 16,* 321–338.

House, R. J., Hanges, P. J., Javidan, M., Dorfman, P. W., & Gupta, V. (Eds) (2004). *Culture, leadership, and organizations: The GLOBE study of 62 cultures*. Thousand Oaks, CA: Sage.

Hunter, J. E., & Schmidt, F. L. (1990). *Methods of meta-analysis: Correcting error and bias in research findings*. Newbury Park, CA: Sage.

Judge, T. A., & Piccolo, R. F. (2004). Transformational and transactional leadership: A meta-analytic test of their relative validity. *Journal of Applied Psychology, 89,* 755–768.

Jung, D. I., & Avolio, B. J. (1999). Effects of leadership style and followers' cultural orientation on performance in group and individual task conditions. *Academy of Management Journal, 42*, 208–218.

Lewin, K., Lippitt, R., & White, R. K. (1939). Patterns of aggressive behavior in experimentally created "social climates". *The Journal of Social Psychology, 10*, 271–299.

Lowe, K. B., & Gardner, W. L. (2001). Ten years of the leadership quarterly: Contributions and challenges for the future. *The Leadership Quarterly, 11*, 459–514.

Marks, M. A., Zaccaro, S. J., & Mathieu, J. E. (2000). Performance implications of leader briefings and team-interaction training for team adaptation to novel environments. *Journal of Applied Psychology, 85*, 971–986.

Rice, R. W., Bender, L. R., & Vitters, A. G. (1980). Leader sex, follower attitudes toward women, and leadership effectiveness: A laboratory experiment. *Organizational Behavior and Human Performance, 25*, 46–78.

Rosenthal, R. (1979). The "file drawer problem" and tolerance for null results. *Psychological Bulletin, 86*, 638–641.

Scandura, T. A., & Graen, G. B. (1984). Moderating effects of initial leader–member exchange status on the effects of a leadership intervention. *Journal of Applied Psychology, 69*, 428–436.

Schriesheim, C. A., Castro, S. L., & Cogliser, C. C. (1999). Leader–member exchange (LMX) research: A comprehensive review of theory, measurement, and data-analytic practices. *The Leadership Quarterly, 10*, 63–114.

Stogdill, R. M., & Coons, A. E. (1957). *Leader behavior: Its description and measurement.* Columbus: Ohio State University, Bureau of Business Research, Monograph No. 88.

Towler, A. J. (2003). Effects of charismatic influence training on attitudes, behavior, and performance. *Personnel Psychology, 56*, 363–381.

Wanous, J. P., Sullivan, S. E., & Malinak, J. (1989). The role of judgment calls in meta-analysis. *Journal of Applied Psychology, 74*, 259–264.

Yukl, G., & Van Fleet, D. D. (1992). Theory and research on leadership in organizations. In: M. D. Dunnette & L. M. Houghs (Eds), *Handbook of industrial and organizational psychology*, (Vol. 3, 2nd ed., pp. 147–198). Palo Alto, CA: Consulting Psychologists Press.

PART III:
MEASURING AUTHENTIC
LEADERSHIP

AUTHENTIC LEADERSHIP MEASUREMENT AND DEVELOPMENT: CHALLENGES AND SUGGESTIONS

Adrian Chan

ABSTRACT

How does one measure and develop authentic leadership? Such a question presumes a general consensus on what authentic leadership is and what aspects of authentic leadership should be developed. It would be premature to recommend specific ways of measuring authentic leadership without first making a contribution to helping the field achieve consensus on the preceding two issues at hand. This chapter identifies four theoretical lenses adopted by various authentic leadership scholars and their implications for measurement. Next, four working assumptions concerning the development of authentic leadership are made. Finally, suggestions are made in four areas for future authentic leadership measurement.

INTRODUCTION

This chapter is a collection of ideas arising from conversations within the Gallup Leadership Institute (GLI), as well as between GLI and leadership

Authentic Leadership Theory and Practice: Origins, Effects and Development
Monographs in Leadership and Management, Volume 3, 227–250
Copyright © 2005 by Elsevier Ltd.

227

scholars interested in advancing authentic leadership theory. This chapter does not aim to replicate efforts elsewhere in describing the ontology and epistemology of authentic leadership. Rather, it outlines several implications for measurement arising from the different theoretical lenses adopted by various authentic leadership scholars. Next, several working assumptions regarding the nature of authentic leadership development interventions are advanced. Finally, this chapter concludes with several suggestions for future efforts in measuring authentic leadership.

To begin, it is pragmatic to first ask oneself exactly which aspect of authentic leadership is amenable to development. This is because ontologically, authentic leadership theory has a strong emphasis on development (Avolio, Gardner, Walumbwa, Luthans, & May, 2004; Luthans & Avolio, 2003). Also, from a practical standpoint, measures that focus on aspects of authentic leadership that cannot be developed offer little benefit for the utility of the measures in evaluating the efficacy of authentic leadership interventions.

Part of the answer to identifying which aspects of authentic leadership are developable lies in understanding the theoretical lenses that authentic leadership scholars have adopted. This is because depending on the type of lenses adopted, different aspects of authentic leadership have been identified for development. Also, the different theoretical lenses may lead to variation in the ontological descriptions of authentic leadership.

Instead of reiterating the nuances in such variations already described by various authentic leadership scholars (Avolio & Gardner, 2005; Eagly, 2005; Gardner, Avolio, Luthans, May, & Walumbwa, 2005; Ilies, Morgeson, & Nahrgang, 2005; Michie & Gooty, 2005; Shamir & Eilam, 2005; Sparrowe, 2005), or repeating suggestions made by these scholars for operationalizing authentic leadership, I will instead examine the implications of these various theoretical lenses for authentic leadership measurement.

FOUR THEORETICAL LENSES TO AUTHENTIC LEADERSHIP

There are at least four theoretical lenses adopted by scholars engaged in the ongoing ontological conversations regarding authentic leadership, ranging from the intrapersonal, developmental, interpersonal to the pragmatic. The *intrapersonal lens* is adopted by scholars who focus on any form of within-person processes (e.g., meta-cognitive, self-regulatory and self-concept developmental processes) that are key to the functioning, emergence and behavioral manifestation of the authentic leader (Chan, Hannah, &

Gardner, 2005; Shamir & Eilam, 2005). This lens also encompasses affective and self-reflective components of authentic leadership, such as the role played by positive emotions and self-transcendent values, as well as life-story narratives on authentic leadership emergence and development (Michie & Gooty, 2005; Shamir & Eilam, 2005).

The emergence of authentic leadership, particularly over long spans of time, is a key focus of scholars who adopt a *developmental lens* (e.g., Michie & Gooty, 2005; Shamir & Eilam, 2005; Sparrowe, 2005). These scholars view the acquisition of positive values, the development of one's authenticity, and the narration of life stories as central to authentic leadership emergence. Both the intrapersonal and developmental lenses share the burden of explaining how authentic leadership emerges, but the differences between them lie in the level of analysis and the metric of time used (Klein & Koslowski, 2000; Singer & Willett, 2003). Both of these issues will be elaborated upon in the chapter.

Leadership is about influencing and influences in relationships (Brower, Schoorman, & Tan, 2000). This necessitates an *interpersonal lens*, which includes all conceptualizations of authentic leadership as a dyadic, group or collective phenomena (e.g., Eagly, 2005; Gardner et al., 2005; Ilies et al., 2005; Luthans & Avolio, 2003). For example, Eagly's (2005) theory of relational authenticity focused purely on the interpersonal aspects of authentic leadership as she examines the impact of gender and members of outsider groups on their accessibility to leadership roles and legitimacy. Ilies et al. (2005) explored how within-person factors of self-awareness and unbiased processing arising out of authenticity is related to eudaemonic and hedonistic well-being.

The last lens is the *pragmatic* worldview. The best explanation of a pragmatic worldview, and the one adopted by this chapter, is provided by William James, who is considered by many as the father of American Pragmatism. According to James, the pragmatist first allows for the concession that a given idea or belief is true. However, the real issue for the pragmatist is the impact that this concession makes in the lives of those who believe, as opposed to those who do not (James, 1906).

In other words, the truthfulness of a concept lies in its truth-value in real, experiential terms. For the pragmatist deciding on the value of a theory such as authentic leadership theory, its truth-value impact probably occupies a higher priority than its existential reality. Good theories are proven by their usefulness (Lewin, 1945); bad theories, on the other hand, are those that corrupt good practices, regardless of how 'good' they are in their conceptualizations (Ghoshal, 2005). Such a lens can be seen in Bill George's promotion of his brand of authentic leadership as the panacea for the ills of today's corporate woes (George, 2003).

Table 1 summarizes the various lenses discussed so far, and their impact. Collectively, these lenses lend richness and depth to the present discussion of authentic leadership. However, the different worldviews inherent in these lenses also present measurement challenges due to potential differences in metrics, methodologies and recommended measurement tools. The next section will elaborate on four measurement issues in particular.

ISSUES IN AUTHENTIC LEADERSHIP CONCEPTUALIZATION AND MEASUREMENT

Issue 1: Variation in Level of Analysis

The level at which a leadership theory should be analyzed is dependent on the level at which it is conceptualized and operationalized (Dansereau, Yammarino, & Markham, 1995; Klein, Dansereau, & Hall, 1994; Klein, Tosi, & Cannella, 1999). Most leadership research have been conducted at either the individual, dyadic or group level of analysis (Yukl, 2002). In the last decade, efforts to capture leadership across multiple levels have become increasingly prevalent (Avolio & Bass, 1995; Hall & Lord, 1995; Sosik, Godshalk, & Yammarino, 2004; Waldman & Yammarino, 1999; Yammarino & Bass, 1990). Authentic leadership and authentic leadership development theories can be conceptualized and operationalized at different levels. Nonetheless, similar difficulties face the researcher of both authentic leadership and authentic leadership development.

First, conceptualizing and operationalizing leadership and leadership development at multiple levels can still be difficult to achieve. Improper matching of theory to measures or analyses across these levels can result in a host of errors, biases and ecological artifacts that are collectively known as "level of analysis" problems (Freeman, 1980; Robinson, 1950; Thorndike, 1939). On the other hand, the cost of not conceptualizing leadership or leadership development from a multilevel perspective is to over-simplify leadership by downplaying both the *embedded* nature of leadership and its development within the organizational hierarchy it is part of, as well as the *emergent* effects of leader and follower cognitions on the leadership and its development process (for a more in-depth discussion of construct emergence and embeddedness, please see Klein & Koslowski, 2000). Leadership and

Table 1. Types of Theoretical Perspectives and its Impact.

Perspective	Key Elements	Examples of Articles	Focal Constructs for Development	Level of Analysis	Metric of Time	Nature of Measure	Nature of Sample
Intrapersonal	Authentic leadership as a system of internal processes	Chan, Hannah, and Gardner (2005); Michie and Gooty (2005)	Self-awareness, self-regulation, meta-cognition, values	Individual	Typically very short	Both normative and ipsative	Broad range
Interpersonal	Authentic leadership as a positive relational force	Eagly (2005); Ilies, Morgeson and Nahrgang (2005)[a]	Relational transparency, behavioral consistency, relational orientation	Dyad and above	Varies	Typically normative	Broad range
Developmental	Authentic leadership as a personal journey of growth	Sparrowe (2005); Shamir and Eilam (2005)[a]	Narratives, life-stories, insight, themes, self-reflection	Individual	Typically very long	Typically ipsative	Small, selected sample
Pragmatic	Authentic leadership as a means for veritable outcomes	Luthans and Avolio (2003)[a]; Gardner, Avolio, Luthans, May and Walumbwa (2005)[a]	Performance beyond expectations, veritable growth	Dyad and above	Varies	Typically normative	Broad range

[a]*Note:* Some articles have a mix of perspectives and may fit into more than one category. In such instances, their membership into a particular category is determined on which perspective is more predominant.

leadership development is, after all, a multiple level, multi-dimensional phenomenon (Yammarino, Dansereau Jr., & Kennedy, 2001).

Authentic leadership scholars have subscribed to this more complete view of leadership by conceptualizing the theory as a multilevel construct from the onset (Avolio & Gardner, 2005; Avolio et al., 2004; Luthans & Avolio, 2003). Specifically, Avolio and colleagues maintain that authentic leadership is by nature a complex phenomenon, and therefore should be explored as a multilevel phenomenon across multiple levels of analysis. This inherent complexity has raised calls for a clearer construct definition with well-specified (and simpler) levels of analysis (e.g., Cooper, Scandura, & Schriesheim, 2005). In addition, multilevel research requires a change in research mindset, especially for "organizational scholars trained, for the most part, to 'think micro' or 'think macro' but not to 'think micro and macro' "(Klein & Koslowski, 2000, p. 11). A multilevel theory of authentic leadership has the potential to contribute to the growing impetus in the leadership field to move toward a multilevel conceptualization and operationalization, which one may argue is more true (authentic) to the real nature of leadership.

Issue 2: Variation in Metrics of Time

Another area where authentic leadership scholars claim the theory can be distinguished from other theories is through an emphasis on development. A direct consequence of this claim is that it creates temporal variance (Allmendinger, 2002). This manifests itself in greater variation with regard to the length of the actual leadership interventions needed, as well as the time needed for effects to emerge. Contributing to this temporal variance is another claim that authentic leadership is multi-dimensional. Multi-dimensionality could produce a consequence of different dimensions of authentic leadership being grounded in different time metrics.

For example, the highly developed self-concept and rich life narratives that characterize authentic leadership takes time to emerge (Shamir & Eilam, 2005). Conversely, acts of relational authenticity may occur within a much shorter time span (Eagly, 2005). Also, perceptions of authenticity may be instantaneous, while the development and execution of actual authentic leadership behaviors may be painstakingly long, especially for higher-order aspects of authentic leadership dealing with ethical standards, moral conduct and transparency.

Framing leadership as a multi-dimensional phenomenon lends complexity to its measurement (Yammarino et al., 2001). Its existence is more likely indicated when there is evidence in at least more than one dimension. In the same way, a multi-dimensional framework of authentic leadership requires measurement efforts to similarly demonstrate evidence in more than one dimension. Therefore, triangulation, not only across methods but across time may be required to attain some degree of confidence that authentic leadership manipulations have been successfully achieved (Berson, 1999). By measuring the effect of the manipulation using different methods and at different times, focusing on different aspects of authentic leadership being manipulated, consistent confirmation across these methods gives the researcher a high degree of confidence that the manipulation was success-ful – this confirmation across different sources is known as triangulation.

Issue 3: Variation in Nature of Measurement and Design

If the development of authentic leaders entails a focus on the development of their self-concepts as proposed by Shamir and Eilam (2005), one would need to take a closer look at the individual developmental profiles of these leaders over time. An implication arising from this is that authentic lead-ership researchers will need to add more *ipsative* approaches to the more traditional normative approaches for measuring authentic leadership.

Ipsative approaches adopt the view that it is more meaningful to compare within-person change using the person as the yardstick, rather than pit the change against a set of established norms (Saville & Wilson, 1991). In mathematical terms, these individuals will have different starting points and different growth rates, or growth factors, as they are typically termed in latent growth modeling literature (Muthen, 1991). In addition, as they de-velop over time, the variance in the growth factors between individuals increases as well, resulting in a *fan spread* (Kline, 1998). The wider the fan spread, the greater is the variation between individuals in terms of their development. With greater variation, ipsative comparisons become more meaningful than normative comparisons.

The types of growth profiles described above can be handled by a whole host of longitudinal data analysis techniques (Hanges & Day, 2002). Some of these techniques (e.g., Latent Growth Modeling) are able to not only explore *alpha* change or quantitative change in the level of a construct, but also explore proposed *gamma* change or qualitative change in the concep-tualization of the construct of interest, independent of the unit of theory specified (Chan, 2003). Exploring gamma change is particularly of interest to authentic leadership researchers who adopt a developmental lens.

According to the typology of change offered by Golembiewski and colleagues (e.g., Golembiewski, Billingsley, & Yeager, 1976), gamma change refers to change in the meaning or conceptualization of a construct. Statistically, this translates into changes in the number of factors, factor pattern, or factor inter-correlations over time or across groups (Chan, 1998).

Implied in the developmental lens adopted by researchers is the notion that authentic leadership and some of its key components will undergo gamma change over time. For example, the level of moral development, a key construct in the nomological network of authentic leadership, is theorized to undergo change in stages, and is therefore qualitatively different in children versus those of emerging adults and mature adults (Kohlberg, 1969, 1976, 1984). Similarly, the level of cognitive complexity and meta-cognitive ability, another construct central to authentic leadership, is also hypothesized to develop in stages (Flavell, 1987; Kegan, 1994). Likewise, some leadership scholars who adapt the ideas of Kohlberg and Kegan to transformational and transactional leadership development also envision leadership to be conceptually different across different leadership levels (Kuhnert & Lewis, 1987).

Hence, given the manner in which some of the constructs central to authentic leadership mentioned above develop, it is logical to infer that over time, authentic leadership may be qualitatively different in its conceptualization and consequently its measurement. As such, longitudinal approaches to measuring authentic leadership may be useful to capture the hypothesized quantitative and qualitative changes that authentic leaders go through, as well as the changes authentic leadership have on its associated outcomes. Longitudinal data analysis methods can cast light on individual variation in growth as they are still dependent on normative constraints. For example, many of longitudinal data analysis techniques specify that the measures used should display invariance across groups and across time (Chan, 2002). Also, individual growth factors are compared against some group means (Ployhart, Holtz, & Bliese, 2002).

Shamir and Eilam (2005) suggested that authentic leadership development research needs to move away from measuring normative behaviors to measuring unique identities and their development. Ipsative measures and research designs with strong ideographic emphasis (e.g., single case studies, repeated measures design) can make comparison between samples difficult (Popper, 1997). However, they are useful for providing respondents with a frame of reference that is uniquely their own, thereby making feedback for development extremely personalized. This makes the research true to the original intent of putting development in the foreground. Research with strong idiographic emphasis can contribute to the understanding and fine-tuning of nomothetic principles, especially when such principles are not clear in the first place, or when the requisite samples are difficult to obtain. In sum, it would appear that validating authentic leadership theory will require a substantial use of ipsative measures, longitudinal approaches to data analysis, and research designs that are more idiographic in nature.

Issue 4: Variation in Nature of Sample

The multi-dimensional and developmental nature of authentic leadership, together with the gamma change it demonstrates over time, necessitates that special consideration needs to be given with regards to the proper use of research sample. For example, the intrapersonal approach to authentic leadership outlined above proposes that a key process found in authentic leaders is the development of one's self-concept through life narratives (Sparrowe, 2005). One implication of this recognition is that students are less likely than mature adults to have higher developed self-concepts, as they have less elaborated life-narratives simply by virtue of having lived less time. This implies further that using student samples will result in a lower chance of detecting the presence of authentic leadership if the richness of life-narratives were used as a primary measure of the level of development of one's authentic leadership.

In a meta-analysis conducted by the GLI (see Reichard & Avolio, 2005 in this volume), 64.5% of the leadership intervention studies were conducted in educational settings, using predominantly student samples. If this trend of preponderance for student samples is carried over into authentic leadership research, this could result in only a narrow spectrum of research focus on what constitutes authentic leadership.

On the other hand, it is important to distinguish between antecedents to authentic leadership versus the actual construct itself. For example, the self-reinforcing mechanisms to be elaborated on in the next section contribute to the development of authentic leadership, but are not part of the actual construct. Hence, the use of student samples may still be appropriate for the manipulation and measurement of some of these antecedents to authentic leadership. As is often the case when conducting research, the type of sample chosen is an important consideration. In the case of authentic leadership research, this consideration takes on greater significance, given the potential for gamma change in the construct.

WORKING ASSUMPTIONS REGARDING AUTHENTIC LEADERSHIP INTERVENTIONS

Having identified these four measurement implications, the second part of this chapter will propose four working assumptions regarding the nature of authentic leadership interventions based on the varied theoretical lenses previously described. At this early stage in the development of authentic leadership theory, Cooper et al. (2005) have offered a preliminary critique of the theory in which they caution against putting the development cart before the ontological horse. Researchers in this area would be wise to heed their advice. Similarly, Avolio and Gardner (in press) also argue against simple training and development strategies for authentic leadership development. Yet, because authentic leadership theory has a strong developmental focus, identifying working assumptions to help clarify the nature of authentic leadership interventions is important. Speculating about the nature of the development cart will help reinforce what is needed for the ontological horse, the nature of authentic leadership.

Assumption 1: Targeted, Customized Interventions

Because of the complexity of the authentic leadership construct, interventions that target the entire spectrum of developable dimensions in short, one-shot training sessions are unlikely to be effective. Given these constraints, targeted training focusing on those aspects of authentic leadership that are most essential to the leadership system and most amenable to development with available resources, are likely to gain favor. In other words, there is no default one-size-fits-all authentic leadership training system that will work well with a similar one-size-fits-all measurement regime.

Rather, approaches to developing authentic leadership will most probably need to be modeled after transformational leadership development regimes to provide individualized consideration of persons, groups and all levels of context (Avolio & Bass, 1995; Bass & Avolio, 1990; Bass, Avolio, Bebb, & Waldman, 1987). Such individually considerate approaches are targeted to the specific needs of individuals and requirements of the organizational contexts/cultures in which those individuals are embedded (Gnyawali & Madhavan, 2001; Granovetter, 1985; Osborn & Ashforth, 1990; Yukl & Howell, 1999).

These types of interventions should experience the greatest buy-in (reactions), learning, transfer and also generate the greatest improvement in real results (Kirkpatrick, 1994). These two factors will in turn determine whether real change occurs at the personal and organizational level, thereby validating the authentic leadership training to be truly authentic. Making the development real is important, because the authenticity of developmental interventions is a key overriding factor in moving the field of leadership development forward in examining and validating 'genuine' interventions that actually do develop leadership.

Assumption 2: High Frequency, Micro Interventions

From a developmental perspective, one way to model what authentic leaders go through in real life is to simulate their learning episodes with high frequency, micro interventions. Such interventions may shorten the time needed to develop authentic leadership. This is an important consideration if one is to achieve success in causing authentic leadership to emerge quickly enough to be useful.

Another reason for such interventions lies in the need to achieve automatization for selected controlled processes (Schneider, 2003). One can reconceptualize the interplay between the cognitive and social processes that goes on in authentic leadership and its development as a dynamic mix of controlled and automatic processes (Shriffrin & Schneider, 1977). Authentic leaders have acquired expertise in their leadership skill set. This expertise can be viewed as a form of automated mental scripts customized to expend the most economical cognitive resources on complex tasks (Hersey, Walsh, Read, & Chulef, 1990; Murphy, Blyth, & Fiedler, 1992).

For the novice trainee, what appears automatic to the expert leader is exceedingly difficult to master given limited cognitive processing capabilities and requires constant controlled processing, leaving no room for attending to higher level processes (Schneider & Chein, 2003). Hence, one would assume that a major goal of authentic leadership development interventions would be to selectively automatize some cognitive processes, while consciously controlling others.

As an illustrative example, authentic leadership development may entail the reduction of errors introduced by the correspondence bias in an effort to achieve balanced processing. The correspondence bias is the tendency for one to over-attribute to dispositional factors while underestimating the effect of situational factors in explaining social behavior (Gilbert & Malone, 1995). The correspondence bias can be an impediment to balanced processing of person perception (Fiske & Taylor, 1991). Biased processing of person

perception can lead to a host of leader-member related issues such as improper activation of stereotypes, misjudgment of behavior and triggering
of wrong behavior as a response (Devine, 1989; Kawakami, Young, &
Dovidio, 2002; Kunda & Spencer, 2003).

The correspondence bias can be reduced. Once considered to be a universal bias, there is increasing evidence that the correspondence bias is more
prevalent in individualist than collectivist cultures (Miller, 1984; Triandis,
1995). One body of evidence suggests that this could be due to the cultural
preference for collectivist cultures to engage in holistic thinking, whereby
such cultures take situational factors and context into greater account
(Chiu, 1972; Choi, Nisbett, & Norenzayan, 1999; Lloyd, 1990). Other evidence suggests that this preference for holistic thinking is a socialized process (Choi et al., 1999; Miller, 1987), and correction of correspondence bias
can be made automatic so that more cognitive resources can be made
available for higher order tasks (Knowles, Morris, Chiu, & Hong, 2001).

Hence, a goal of authentic leadership development may entail selectively
automatizing the effects of the correspondence bias to create more cognitive
resources to attend to the complexity of leadership across different contexts.
It allows the novice leader to consciously attend to the cognitive processes
designated for conscious control, such as those pertaining to meta-cognition
(Flavell, 1979, 1987), self-development and the near and far transfer of the
learning (Cormier & Hagman, 1987). Automatization has been shown to
clearly distinguish between novice and expert leaders. In one study, working memory for higher tasks was shown to increase by as much as 90%
(Schneider, 2003).

Automatization of cognitive processes entails over-learning and habit
formation, which can be hastened with high frequency of practice. To
achieve mastery of complex controlled processing, these processes will need
to be broken down into simpler steps. Cooper et al. (2005) suggested the use
of chaining from reinforcement theory (Skinner, 1969). Chaining entails
reinforcing simpler behaviors that collectively make up the overall complex
repertoire. Hence, it is plausible that similarly chaining micro-interventions
together will achieve the overall desired impact of authentic leadership
development interventions.

Assumption 3: Self-Reinforcing Interventions (Over Time)

The developmental lens adopted by researchers mentioned previously implies that authentic leadership interventions ought to be self-reinforcing in

some way so as to sustain development over time. Several self-reinforcing mechanisms are relevant to authentic leadership that is amenable to intervention. One pathway is through the efficacy derived from enactive mastery (Bandura, 1997), which leads to more engagement in the particular leadership development activity, thereby creating a continuing cycle of self-development.

Another pathway is through self-verification (Swann, 1983, 1990). This mechanism has been outlined in another chapter in this book and will not be elaborated here (see Chan et al., 2005, this volume). Essentially, the authentic leader receives positive input from followers regarding his/her authenticity, thereby bolstering his/her self-concept as a leader, and motivating the leader to further engage in more acts of authenticity. Through this process of self-verification, the authentic leaders are motivated to continue to engage in future acts of authenticity, and to develop themselves to become more authentic.

A third pathway for development entails raising the motivation for leader self-reflection regarding past leadership episodes. Self-reflection raises self-awareness and reinforces the leader's implicit leadership theory held in long term memory (Eden & Leviatan, 1975; Offerman, Kennedy, & Wirtz, 1994). This enriched implicit leadership theory offers higher concept accessibility of one's idea of authentic leadership (Higgins, King, & Mavin, 1982). An enriched implicit leadership theory in turn makes more information available for priming and activation in the leader's working self-concept (Lord & Brown, 2004; Lord & Emrich, 2001). With a primed working self-concept that is self-schematic on authentic leadership, the leader will display a higher frequency of authentic leadership behaviors, thereby enriching his/her leadership episodes for future self-reflection.

Self-reinforcing mechanisms such as those outlined above require time to emerge. Yet, of 200 leadership interventions evaluated in a recent meta-analysis, only 9% exceeded 7 days or more (see Reichard & Avolio, 2005, this volume). To achieve a better understanding of how these self-reinforcing mechanisms can improve authentic leadership interventions, there is a need to engage in more longitudinal studies, a call not dissimilar to those made for leadership research in general (Day, 2000). Rich databases from existing longitudinal studies such as the LSAY (Longitudinal Study of American Youths) are readily available for exploratory analysis. Such data sets are important for explanation and prediction. In addition, they can potentially reveal what types of constructs are important for inclusion into the nomological network of authentic leadership over time, as well as provide baselines for predicting the emergence of authentic leaders.

Assumption 4: Multilevel, Nested Interventions

The final assumption has been alluded to in the discussion so far. Authentic leadership development interventions, like other leadership interventions in general, will need to incorporate the context and take levels of analysis issues into account (London, 2002). Exactly how this can be achieved will vary. However, there are common measurement issues to be considered, and these will be elaborated on in the next section.

SUGGESTIONS FOR MEASURING AUTHENTIC LEADERSHIP

Suggestion 1: Clarifying the Role of Context

Although authentic leaders are embedded and operate within their context, they are also agentic (Bandura, 1997; Chan et al., 2005). This means that authentic leaders are not completely at the mercy of situational forces, or blind to the power of the situation (Ichheiser, 1943). At the same time, leaders who are authentic do not practice self-deception in their perception of the situation, so that they neither intentionally underestimate its power (Gilbert & Malone, 1995), nor overestimate its importance (Trope, 1986). The agentic view of authentic leadership does call into question the precise nature of the impact that context has on authentic leadership behavior and processes. Hence, there needs to be a better understanding of the interplay between authentic leadership and its context.

One approach to addressing this issue is to conceptualize leadership as being embedded in its context. The central idea behind embeddedness is the issue of social ties and obligations (Mitchell, Holtom, Lee, Sablynski, & Erez, 2001). The premise is that human beings are social creatures, and human behavior is influenced by social realities (Granovetter, 1985). Given that leadership is a social construction, it makes sense for leadership to be examined in terms of its associated social ties.

The idea of leadership embeddedness is implicit in the measurement of social relationships, or sociometry and social network analysis (Brass, 1985; Granovetter, 1973). Leadership embeddedness is a key rationale underlying the use of social network analysis to examine leader–member exchange (Sparrowe & Liden, 1997), transformational leadership (Bono & Anderson, in press) and charismatic leadership (Pastor, Meindl, & Mayo, 2002). Hence, sociometric approaches likewise possess great potential for measuring authentic leadership.

In terms of interventions, the idea of embeddedness is also relevant to understanding how learning can occur in authentic leadership development. For example, situated learning theories (McLellan, 1995) rely on the fact that knowledge and learning need to occur in their authentic context to provide the necessary affordances (Gibson, 1977). The closer the learning context is to the actual performance environment, the more salient are the social and cognitive cues available to facilitate learning. Motivationally, authentic collaborators and fellow learners are necessary to provide the socialization impetus and interaction for social learning (Bandura, 1977; Vygotsky, 1978).

Suggestion 2: Clarifying the Role that Behaviors Play

Shamir and Eilam's (2005) suggestion to move away from developing and measuring skills and leadership styles that display authentic leadership in favor of measuring leader self-development and the development of leader self-concept need not be seen as a call to abandon the use of behavioral indicators altogether. Rather, what is needed is a re-tuning of existing methods to identify and measure behaviors not as a terminal objective, but as an intermediate objective with the ultimate aim of interpreting the extent that these behaviors reflect changes in one's self-concept and identity. Part of the solution may entail developing separate authentic leadership measures for learning versus performance in recognition of the fact that authentic leaders are able to fulfill performance goals and still pursue their own development (Locke, Frederick, Lee, & Bobko, 1984; Locke & Latham, 1990). In support of this approach, authentic leadership scholars may also need to identify when and how authentic leaders balance between learning and performance goal-setting processes, especially given the often conflicting nature of short versus long-term goals (Koestner, Lekes, Powers, & Chicoine, 2002).

Suggestion 3: Clarifying the Roles of Controlled and Automatic Processes

Recent conceptualizations of authentic leadership assert that balanced processing is a key component of authentic self-regulation (Avolio & Gardner, 2005; Gardner et al., 2005; Ilies et al., 2005). This assertion opens up a broad area for research to flesh out the mechanisms by which balanced processing occurs. One possibility may be that it arises from the appropriate use of anchors in the decision making of authentic leaders (Tversky & Kahneman, 1974). Another possible reason could lie in the possibility that authentic leaders are less affected by biases in person perception, such as the correspondence effect (Gilbert & Malone, 1995).

Yet another possible reason why authentic leaders achieve balanced processing may be revealed by their social networks. Leaders who are authentic may surround themselves with followers who are, or develop followers to become equally consistent in their behavior. Such networks manifest themselves as higher levels of meta-accuracy in meta-perceptions – i.e., one's social perceptions of oneself and of others are consistent with others' perceptions of themselves and the relationship (Kenny, 1994).

For the mechanisms described above, the underlying automatic and controlled processes need to be identified. The perceptual, cognitive and social processes involved in causing authentic leaders to employ anchoring appropriately may significantly distinguish authentic leadership. Measuring the anchors used by authentic leaders in initial impression formation, and their overall social perceptions may provide a way to qualitatively distinguish the balanced processing achieved by authentic leaders from biased information processing by less authentic leaders.

An alternative avenue to explore is to examine the implicit theories that authentic leaders and followers hold. Implicit theories initially were applied by Dweck and colleagues (e.g., Dweck, 1996; Dweck, Chiu, & Hong, 1995; Dweck, Hong, & Chiu, 1993) to describe perceptions of traits such as personality and morality. For example, implicit personality theories are the beliefs that people hold about the relationship between the traits of people (Grant & Holmes, 1981). These beliefs may be formed spontaneously, for example, as is the case for spontaneous trait inferences (Moscowitz & Uleman, 1987). It may be informative to examine the role that self-regulation plays in the formation of these implicit theories within the context of authentic leader–follower relationships.

Suggestion 4: Clarifying the Role that Leadership Events Plays

How does one interpret the role of leadership events or episodes? Like the discussion concerning the role of context, leadership episodes are both the end product of authentic leadership as well as the "raw material" for further authentic leadership development. Yet, at the same time, the episodes themselves are non-indicative of development. Authentic leadership development entails more than encountering a multitude of leadership episodes; rather, it is the meaning attributed to these episodes by those involved in the authentic leadership process that make these episodes real "moments that matter" (Avolio et al., 2004). The occurrence of such leadership episodes may be unintentional, but the responses to these episodes can be indicative of authentic leadership in action. Jolts, shocks or crises are important learning episodes for the development of authentic leadership (Fiol & Lyles, 1985). Hence, breaking down these critical events and analyzing the meanings leaders associate with them may be another way to measure authentic leadership and its development.

CONCLUDING REMARKS: THE ROLE OF CULTURE

This chapter began with four observations regarding the four theoretical lenses that have emerged from ongoing conversations about authentic leadership. From these lenses, four issues pertaining to measurement were raised. Next, four working assumptions were made concerning the nature of authentic leadership interventions. Finally, suggestions were made in four areas that may help advance authentic leadership measurement methods.

In concluding, I would like to highlight another issue that may present a huge challenge towards the scholarship of authentic leadership – the influence of culture. The discussion on the gamma change in authentic leadership across time and groups, and the illustrative example provided on selective automatization of person perception processes as part of authentic leadership development highlights the influence that culture can have on how authentic leadership is defined and developed.

At its core, authentic leadership is the relational extension of the authentic person embedded in a network of social relationships (Avolio & Gardner, 2005). While relationships are universally important, the meanings attached to relationships are different across different cultures (Rothbaum, Pott, Azuma, Miyake, & Weisz, 2000). In *independent* cultures, the emphasis is on the unique individual who is complete on his own, free to enter and leave relationships, and who is even required to be on the guard to protect one's identity from influence by others (Markus & Kitayama, 1994). The authentic leader then, is one who first achieves authenticity as a person, and is able to remain true to oneself over and above, or in spite of, the leadership roles he or she is called to perform. In doing so, he/she distinguishes himself or herself with desirable individual attributes that define authentic leadership, such as transparency and moral worthiness. The authentic leadership relationship is therefore one of transparency, openness, trust and emphasis on mutual development between the leader and his/her associates (Gardner et al., 2005).

On the other hand, in interdependent cultures, the emphasis is on the individual who understands his/her place within the collective, and accepts that being embedded within relationships bring roles and responsibilities that he/she must fulfill (Lebra, 1976; Tu, 1994). To be authentic as a person is to be first and foremost true to these roles and responsibilities. To be valued in society, one must be able to subordinate individual needs and goals for the good of interpersonal harmony (Zahn-Wexler, Friedman, Cole, Mizuta, & Hiruma, 1996). In other words, the relationships that a person is embedded within sets the stage for how he/she can develop authentically as a person. Authenticity in interdependent cultures is not meaningful unless one also considers the social networks of individuals.

This cultural difference presents issues of gamma change across groups on at least four fronts: (1) the level of conceptualization of what constitutes authenticity is different; (2) the interdependent authentic leader is more greatly influenced by the relational context; (3) the interdependent authentic leader is not going to possess as much of the *inviolable* or *core* self, and is going to possess more of the *relational* self, than his/her counterparts from independent cultures; and (4) the conceptualization of authentic leadership is less dispositional, and more situational in interdependent cultures. Ultimately, to better understand the exact nature of these gamma changes, it may be necessary for authentic leadership scholars to embark on a worldwide project along the lines of the Global Leadership and Organizational Behavior Effectiveness (GLOBE) Research Project, a multi-phase, multi-method endeavor involving investigators from all over the world examining the inter-relationships between societal culture, organizational culture, and organizational leadership (House, Hanges, Javidan, Dorfman, & Gupta, 2004).

In concluding, it is important to note that authentic leadership is, to adopt the pragmatic lens, possessive of truth-value far too great to ignore. The measurement challenges posed in this chapter should not be seen as stumbling blocks to our understanding of authentic leadership and its development. Rather, it is my hope that they serve as guiding posts in our quest to develop authentic leaders across all cultures.

REFERENCES

Allmendinger, P. (2002). Towards a post-positivist typology of planning theory. *Planning Theory*, *1*, 77–100.

Avolio, B. J., & Gardner, W. L. (2005). Authentic leadership development: Getting to the root of positive forms of leadership. *The Leadership Quarterly, 16,* 315–338.

Avolio, B. J., & Bass, B. M. (1995). Individual consideration viewed at multiple levels of analysis: A multi-level framework for examining the diffusion of transformational leadership. *The Leadership Quarterly, 6,* 199–218.

Avolio, B. J., Gardner, W. L., Walumbwa, F. O., Luthans, F., & May, D. R. (2004). Unlocking the mask: A look at the process by which authentic leaders impact follower attitudes and behaviors. *The Leadership Quarterly, 15,* 801–823.

Bandura, A. (1977). *Social learning theory.* Englewood Cliffs, NJ: Prentice-Hall.

Bandura, A. (1997). *Self-efficacy: The exercise of control.* New York: Freeman.

Bass, B. M., & Avolio, B. J. (1990). The implications of transactional leadership for individual, team, and organizational development. *Research in Organizational Change and Development, 4,* 231–272.

Bass, B. M., Avolio, B. J., Bebb, M., & Waldman, D. A. (1987). Transformational leadership and the falling dominoes effect. *Group and Organizational Studies, 12,* 73–87.

Berson, Y. (1999). *A comprehensive assessment of leadership using triangulation of qualitative and quantitative methods.* Dissertation Abstracts International.

Bono, J. E., & Anderson, M. H. (in press). The advice and influence networks of transformational leaders. *Journal of Applied Psychology.*

Brass, D. J. (1985). Men's and women's networks: A study of interaction patterns and influence in an organization. *Academy of Management Journal, 28,* 327–343.

Brower, H. H., Schoorman, F. D., & Tan, H. H. (2000). A model of relational leadership: The integration of trust and leader-member exchange. *The Leadership Quarterly, 11,* 227–251.

Chan, D. (1998). Functional relations among constructs in the same content domain at different levels of analysis: A typology of composition models. *Journal of Applied Psychology, 83,* 234–246.

Chan, D. (2002). Latent growth modeling. In: F. Drasgow & N. Schmitt (Eds), *Measuring and analyzing behavior in organizations* (pp. 302–349). San Francisco, CA: Jossey-Bass.

Chan, D. (2003). Data analysis and modeling longitudinal processes. *Group & Organization Management, 28,* 341–365.

Chan, A. Y. L., Hannah, S. T., & Gardner, W. L. (2005). Veritable authentic leadership: Emergence, functioning, and impacts. In: W. B. Gardner, B. J. Avolio & F. O. Walumbwa (Eds), *Authentic leadership theory and practice. Origins, effects, and development.* Amsterdam: Elsevier.

Chiu, L. H. (1972). A cross-cultural comparison of cognitive styles in Chinese and American children. *International Journal of Psychology, 8,* 235–242.

Choi, I., Nisbett, R. E., & Norenzayan, A. (1999). Causal attribution across cultures: Variation and universality. *Psychological Bulletin, 125,* 47–63.

Cooper, C. D., Scandura, T. A., & Schriesheim, C. A. (2005). Looking forward but learning from our past: Potential challenges to developing authentic leadership theory and authentic leaders. *The Leadership Quarterly, 16,* 475–494.

Cormier, S. M., & Hagman, J. D. (1987). *Transfer of learning: Contemporary research and application.* San Diego, CA: Academic Press.

Dansereau, F., Yammarino, F. J., & Markham, S. E. (1995). Leadership: The multiple-level approaches. *The Leadership Quarterly, 6,* 97–109.

Day, D. V. (2000). Leadership Development: A review in context. *The Leadership Quarterly, 11,* 581–614.

Devine, P. G. (1989). Stereotypes and prejudice: Their automatic and controlled components. *Journal of Personality and Social Psychology*, *56*, 5–18.

Dweck, C. S. (1996). Implicit theories as organizers of goals and behavior. In: P. M. Gollwitzer & J. A. Bargh (Eds), *The psychology of action: Linking cognition and motivation to behavior*. New York: Guildford.

Dweck, C. S., Chiu, C. Y., & Hong, Y. Y. (1995). Implicit theories and their role in judgments and reactions: A world from two perspectives. *Psychological Inquiry*, *6*, 267–285.

Dweck, C. S., Hong, Y. Y., & Chiu, C. Y. (1993). Implicit theories: Individual differences in the likelihood and meaning of dispositional inference. *Personality & Social Psychology Bulletin*, *19*, 644–656.

Eagly, A. H. (2005). Achieving relational authenticity in leadership: Does gender matter? *The Leadership Quarterly*, *16*, 459–474.

Eden, D., & Leviatan, U. (1975). Implicit leadership theories as a determinant of the factor structure underlying supervisory behavior scales. *Journal of Applied Psychology*, *60*, 736–741.

Fiol, C. M., & Lyles, M. A. (1985). Organizational learning. *Academy of Management Review*, *10*, 803–813.

Fiske, S. T., & Taylor, S. E. (1991). *Social cognition*. New York: McGraw-Hill.

Flavell, J. H. (1979). Metacognition and cognitive monitoring: A new era of cognitive development inquiry. *American Psychologist*, *34*, 906–911.

Flavell, J. H. (1987). Speculations about the nature and development of metacognition. In: F. E. Weinert & R. H. Kluwe (Eds), *Metacognition, motivation and understanding* (pp. 21–29). Hillside, NJ: Lawrence Erlbaum Associates.

Freeman, J. (1980). The unit problem in organizational research. In: W. M. Evan (Ed.), *Frontiers in organization and management* (pp. 59–68). New York: Praeger.

Gardner, W. L., Avolio, B. J., Luthans, F., May, D. R., & Walumbwa, F. O. (2005). "Can you see the real me?" A self-based model of authentic leader and follower development. *The Leadership Quarterly*, *16*, 343–372.

George, W. (2003). *Authentic leadership: Rediscovering the secrets to creating lasting value*. San Francisco: Jossey-Bass.

Ghoshal, S. (2005). Bad management theories are destroying good management practices. *Academy of Management Learning and Education*, *4*, 75–91.

Gibson, J. J. (1977). The theory of affordances. In: R. Shaw & J. Bransford (Eds), *Perceiving, acting and knowing*. Hillsdale, NJ: Erlbaum.

Gilbert, D. T., & Malone, P. S. (1995). The correspondence bias. *Psychological Bulletin*, *117*, 21–38.

Gnyawali, D. R., & Madhavan, R. (2001). Cooperative networks and competitive dynamics: A structural embeddedness perspective. *Academy of Management Review*, *26*, 431–446.

Golembiewski, R. T., Billingsley, K., & Yeager, S. (1976). Measuring change and persistence in human affairs: Types of change generated by OD designs. *Journal of Applied Behavioral Science*, *12*, 133–157.

Granovetter, M. S. (1985). Economic action and social structure: The problem of embeddedness. *American Journal of Sociology*, *91*, 481–510.

Granovetter, M. S. (1973). The strength of weak ties. *American Journal of Sociology*, *6*, 1360–1380.

Grant, P. R., & Holmes, J. G. (1981). The integration of implicit personality theory schemas and stereotype images. *Social Psychology Quarterly*, *44*, 107–115.

Hall, R. J., & Lord, R. G. (1995). Multi-level information-processing explanations of followers' leadership perceptions. *The Leadership Quarterly, 6,* 265–287.

Hanges, P. J., & Day, D. V. (2002). Quantitative methods special series: Statistical methodology for longitudinal leadership research. *The Leadership Quarterly, 14,* 453.

Hersey, D. A., Walsh, D. A., Read, S. J., & Chulef, A. S. (1990). The effects of expertise on financial problem solving: Evidence for goal-directed problem solving scripts. *Organizational Behavior and Human Decision Processes, 46,* 77–101.

Higgins, E. T., King, G. A., & Mavin, G. H. (1982). Individual construct accessibility and subjective impressions and recall. *Journal of Personality & Social Psychology, 43,* 35–47.

House, R. J., Hanges, P. J., Javidan, M., Dorfman, P. W., & Gupta, V. (2004). *Culture, leadership, and organizations: The GLOBE study of 62 cultures.* Thousand Oaks, CA: Sage.

Ichheiser, G. (1943). Misinterpretations of personality in everyday life. *Character and Personality, 11,* 145–160.

Ilies, R., Morgeson, F. P., & Nahrgang, J. D. (2005). Authentic leadership and eudaemonic well-being: Understanding leader-follower outcomes. *The Leadership Quarterly, 16,* 373–394.

James, W. (1906). What pragmatism means. Retrieved 2/27, 2005, from http://www.marxists.org/reference/subject/philosophy/works/us/james.htm.

Kawakami, K., Young, H., & Dovidio, J. F. (2002). Automatic stereotyping: Category, trait and behavioral activations. *Personality & Social Psychology Bulletin, 28,* 3–15.

Kegan, R. (1994). *In over our heads: The mental demands of modern life.* Cambridge, MA: Harvard University Press.

Kenny, D. A. (1994). *Interpersonal perception: A social relations analysis.* New York: Guilford Press.

Kirkpatrick, D. L. (1994). *Evaluating training programs: The four levels.* San Francisco, CA: Berrett-Koehler.

Klein, K. J., Dansereau, F., & Hall, R. J. (1994). Levels issues in theory development, data collection and analysis. *Academy of Management Review, 19,* 195–229.

Klein, K. J., & Koslowski, S. W. J. (2000). *Multilevel theory, research, and methods in organizations: Foundations, extensions, and new directions.* San Francisco, CA: Jossey-Bass.

Klein, K. J., Tosi, H., & Cannella, A. A. (1999). Multilevel theory building: Benefits, barriers and new developments. *Academy of Management Review, 24,* 243–248.

Kline, R. (1998). *Principles and practice of structural equation modeling.* New York: Guildford Press.

Knowles, E. D., Morris, M. W., Chiu, C. Y., & Hong, Y. Y. (2001). Culture and the process of person perception: Evidence for automaticity among East Asians in correcting for situational influences on behavior. *Personality & Social Psychology Bulletin, 27,* 1344–1356.

Koestner, R., Lekes, N., Powers, T. A., & Chicoine, E. (2002). Attaining personal goals: Self-concordance plus implementation intentions equals success. *Journal of Personality and Social Psychology, 83,* 231–244.

Kohlberg, L. (1969). Stage and sequence: The cognitive-developmental approach to socialization. In: D. A. Goslin (Ed.), *Handbook of socialization theory and research* (pp. 347–480). Chicago: Rand McNally.

Kohlberg, L. (1976). Moral stages and moralization. In: T. Lickona (Ed.), *Moral development and behavior* (pp. 31–53). New York: Holt, Rinehart and Winston.

Kohlberg, L. (1984). *The psychology of moral development.* New York: Harper and Row.

Kuhnert, K. W., & Lewis, P. (1987). Transactional and transformational leadership: A constructive/developmental analysis. *Academy of Management Review*, *12*, 648–657.

Kunda, Z., & Spencer, S. J. (2003). When do stereotypes come to mind and when do they color judgment? A goal-based theoretical framework for stereotype activation and application. *Psychological Bulletin*, *129*, 522–544.

Lebra, T. S. (1976). *Japanese patterns of behavior*. Honolulu: University of Hawaii Press.

Lewin, K. (1945). The research center for group dynamics at Massachusetts Institute of Technology. *Sociometry*, *8*, 126–135.

Lloyd, G. E. R. (1990). *Demystifying mentalities*. New York: Cambridge University Press.

Locke, E. A., Frederick, E., Lee, C., & Bobko, P. (1984). The effects of self-efficacy, goals and task strategy on task performance. *Journal of Applied Psychology*, *69*, 241–251.

Locke, E. A., & Latham, G. P. (1990). *A theory of goal setting and task performance*. Englewood Cliffs, NJ: Prentice-Hall.

London, M. (2002). *Leadership development: Paths to self-insight and professional growth*. Mahwah, NJ: Erlbaum.

Lord, R. G., & Brown, D. J. (2004). *Leadership processes and follower self-identity*. Mahwah, NJ: Erlbaum.

Lord, R. G., & Emrich, C. G. (2001). Thinking outside the box by looking inside the box: Extending the cognitive revolution in leadership research. *The Leadership Quarterly*, *11*, 551–579.

Luthans, F., & Avolio, B. J. (2003). Authentic leadership: A positive developmental approach. In: K. S. Cameron, J. E. Dutton & R. E. Quinn (Eds), *Positive organizational scholarship* (pp. 241–261). San Francisco: Barrett-Koehler.

Markus, H. R., & Kitayama, S. (1994). A collective fear of the collective: Implications for selves and theories of selves. *Personality & Social Psychology Bulletin*, *20*, 568–579.

McLellan, H. (1995). *Situated learning perspectives*. Englewood Cliffs, NJ: Educational Technology Publications.

Michie, S., & Gooty, J. (2005). Values, emotions and authenticity: Will the real leader please stand up? *The Leadership Quarterly*, *16*, 441–458.

Miller, J. G. (1984). Culture and the development of everyday explanation. *Journal of Personality and Social Psychology*, *46*, 961–978.

Miller, J. G. (1987). Cultural influences on the development of conceptual differentiation in person description. *British Journal of Developmental Psychology*, *5*, 309–319.

Mitchell, T. R., Holtom, B. C., Lee, T. W., Sablynski, C. J., & Erez, M. (2001). Why people stay: Using job embeddedness to predict voluntary turnover. *Academy of Management Journal*, *44*, 1102–1121.

Moscowitz, G. B., & Uleman, J. S. (1987). The facilitation and inhibition of spontaneous trait inferences at encoding. Paper presented at the 95th Annual Convention of the American Psychological Association, New York.

Murphy, S. E., Blyth, D., & Fiedler, F. E. (1992). Cognitive resource theory and the utilization of the leader's and group members' technical competence. *The Leadership Quarterly*, *3*, 237–255.

Muthen, B. O. (1991). Analysis of longitudinal data using latent variable models with varying parameters. In: L. M. Collins & J. L. Horn (Eds), *Best methods for the analysis of change* (pp. 1–17). Washington, DC: American Psychological Association.

Offerman, L. R., Kennedy, J. K., Jr., & Wirtz, P. W. (1994). Implicit leadership theories: Content, structure, and generalizability. *The Leadership Quarterly*, *5*, 43–58.

Osborn, R. N., & Ashforth, B. E. (1990). Investigating the challenges to senior leadership in complex, high-risk technologies. *The Leadership Quarterly, 1,* 147–163.

Pastor, J. C., Meindl, J. R., & Mayo, M. C. (2002). A network effects model of charisma attributions. *Academy of Management Journal, 45,* 410–420.

Ployhart, R. E., Holtz, B. C., & Bliese, P. D. (2002). Longitudinal data analysis: Applications of random coefficient modeling to leadership research. *The Leadership Quarterly, 13,* 455–487.

Popper, S. E. (1997). Validity of using non-pilot subjects to represent pilots in a sustained acceleration environment. *Aviation Space and Environmental Medicine, 68,* 1081–1087.

Reichard, B., & Avolio, B. J. (2005). Where are we? The status of leadership intervention research: A meta-analytic summary. In: W. B. Gardner, B. J. Avolio & F. O. Walumbwa (Eds), *Authentic leadership theory and practice. Origins, effects, and development.* Amsterdam: Elsevier.

Robinson, W. S. (1950). Ecological correlations and the behavior of individuals. *American Sociological Review, 15,* 351–357.

Rothbaum, R., Pott, M., Azuma, H., Miyake, K., & Weisz, J. (2000). The development of close relationships in Japan and the United States: Paths of symbiotic harmony and generative tension. *Child Development, 71,* 1121–1142.

Saville, P., & Wilson, E. (1991). The reliability and validity of normative and ipsative approaches to the measurement of personality. *Journal of Occupational Psychology, 64,* 219–238.

Schneider, W. (2003). Automaticity in complex cognition. Retrieved December 1, 2003, from http://coglab.psy.cmu.edu/index_main.html.

Schneider, W., & Chein, J. M. (2003). Controlled and automatic processing: Behavior, theory and biological mechanisms. *Cognitive Science, 27,* 525–559.

Shamir, B., & Eilam, G. (2005). "What's your story?" A life-stories approach to authentic leadership development. *The Leadership Quarterly, 16,* 395–418.

Shriffrin, R. M., & Schneider, W. (1977). Controlled and automatic human information processing. Perceptual learning, automatic attending and a general theory. *Psychological Review, 84,* 127–190.

Singer, J. D., & Willett, J. B. (2003). *Applied longitudinal data analysis. Modeling change and event occurrence.* New York, NY: Oxford University Press.

Skinner, B. F. (1969). *Schedules of reinforcement.* New York: Appleton-Century-Crofts.

Sosik, J. J., Godshalk, V. M., & Yammarino, F. J. (2004). Transformational leadership, learning goal orientation and expectation for career success in mentor-protege relationships: A multiple levels of analysis perspective. *The Leadership Quarterly, 15,* 241–262.

Sparrowe, R. T. (2005). Authentic leadership and the narrative self. *The Leadership Quarterly, 16,* 419–440.

Sparrowe, R. T., & Liden, R. C. (1997). Process and structure in leader-member exchange. *Academy of Management Review, 22,* 522–552.

Swann, W. B., Jr. (1983). Self-verification: Bringing social reality into harmony with the self. In: J. R. Suls & A. G. Greenwald (Eds), *Psychological perspectives on the self,* (Vol. 2, pp. 33–66). Hillsdale, NJ: Erlbaum.

Swann, W. B., Jr. (1990). To be adored or to be known: The interplay of self-enhancement and self-verification. In: R. M. Sorrentino & E. T. Higgins (Eds), *Motivation and cognition,* (Vol. 2, pp. 408–448). New York: Guilford.

Thorndike, E. L. (1939). On the fallacy of imputing the correlations found for groups to the individuals or smaller groups composing them. *American Journal of Psychology*, *52*, 122–124.

Triandis, H. C. (1995). *Individualism and collectivism*. Boulder, CO: Westview Press.

Trope, Y. (1986). Identification and inferential processes in dispositional attribution. *Psychological Review*, *93*, 239–257.

Tu, W. (1994). Embodying the universe: A note on Confucian self-realization. In: R. T. Ames, W. Dissanayake & T. P. Kasulis (Eds), *Self as person in Asian theory and practice* (pp. 177–186). Albany, NY: State University of New York Press.

Tversky, A., & Kahneman, D. (1974). Judgment under uncertainty: Heuristics and biases. *Science*, *185*, 1124–1131.

Vygotsky, L. S. (1978). *Mind in society*. Cambridge, MA: Harvard University Press.

Waldman, D. A., & Yammarino, F. J. (1999). CEO charismatic leadership: Levels of management and levels of analysis. *Academy of Management Review*, *24*, 266–285.

Yammarino, F. J., Dansereau, F., Jr., & Kennedy, C. J. (2001). A multiple-level, multidimensional approach to leadership: Viewing leadership through an elephant's eye. *Organizational Dynamics*, *29*, 149–164.

Yammarino, F. J., & Bass, B. M. (1990). Transformational leadership and multiple levels of analysis. Human Relations, *43*, 975–995.

Yukl, G. (2002). *Leadership in Organizations* (5th ed.). Upper Saddle Creek, NJ: Prentice-Hall.

Yukl, G., & Howell, J. M. (1999). Organizational and contextual influences on the emergence and effectiveness of charismatic leadership. *The Leadership Quarterly*, *10*, 257–283.

Zahn-Wexler, C., Friedman, R. J., Cole, P. M., Mizuta, I., & Hiruma, N. (1996). Japanese and United States preschool children's responses to conflict and distress. *Child Development*, *67*, 2462–2477.

PART IV:
PERCEPTIONS OF AUTHENTIC LEADERSHIP: EXPLORATORY STUDIES

LEADER AUTHENTICITY MARKERS: FINDINGS FROM A STUDY OF PERCEPTIONS OF AFRICAN AMERICAN POLITICAL LEADERS

Todd L. Pittinsky and Christopher J. Tyson

ABSTRACT

In this study we focus on perceptions of the authenticity of leaders, specifically African American political leaders. This approach provides an important direction for understanding authenticity dynamics between leaders and followers. We introduce and apply the concept of leader authenticity markers, which are the features and actions people use to determine the degree of authenticity of the leader. We present findings from an exploratory study, which identifies seven authenticity markers and five themes about authenticity markers. The implications of these findings for leadership studies and practice are discussed, as are directions for future research.

Authentic Leadership Theory and Practice: Origins, Effects and Development
Monographs in Leadership and Management, Volume 3, 253–279

INTRODUCTION

Leadership models are increasingly focusing on the concept of authenticity, but the discussion is often one-sided. Normative models of leadership increasingly advise leaders to "be authentic" and there is related discussion of how to do so. Yet, leaders only exist in relation to followers. As a practical matter, followers' perceptions of the authenticity of a leader are as important to consider as are the actual thoughts and actions of a leader being perceived.

Numerous definitions of "authenticity" have been suggested in the literature (Erickson, 1995; Harter, 2002); to date, none has yet proven definitive. If there is no certainty amongst researchers about what exactly "leader authenticity" is (Avolio & Gardner, 2005; Shamir & Eilam, 2005), neither is there certainty amongst ordinary people – voters, for example. Hence, authenticity is not something with which leaders alone must grapple. Followers, too, grapple with authenticity questions. Specifically, followers judge the authenticity, or inauthenticity, of their leaders. For each individual leader struggling to be authentic, many more followers are looking on and evaluating, by a mix of commonly accepted and idiosyncratic criteria, the degree to which he or she appears to them to be authentic or inauthentic.

These evaluations are themselves problematic. It is well established by research, and well known through everyday experience, that interior states are not always readily apparent to observers. For example, certain cues are commonly employed in perception to infer if another is being deceptive (e.g., Kraut & Poe, 1980), yet, people are notoriously inaccurate in those perceptions (Kraut & Poe, 1980; Kohnken, 1987). In fact, evidence suggests that the more confident one is in his or her judgment of another's deception, the more likely one is to be wrong (Kohnken, 1987).

Because the authenticity literature often relies on normative arguments, we know little from empirical perspectives about the perceptions of leader authenticity among followers. This study focuses on perceptions of the authenticity of leaders – in this case, African American political leaders – rather than the actual authenticity of these leaders. This approach provides an important direction for understanding authenticity dynamics between leaders and followers. In particular, we address the question of what cues or markers affect whether followers perceive a leader as authentic?

In this study, we examine authenticity and leadership by studying the authenticity markers of African American political leaders. We advance the scholarship on leadership, authenticity, and minority communities by (a) contributing an empirical perspective on authenticity, (b) studying leader authenticity from the perspective of the followers rather than the leaders, (c) focusing on perceptions of the authenticity of leaders rather than the actual authenticity of these leaders, and (d) expanding what is known about political leadership in the African American community by studying authenticity in political leadership in that community.

We do not advance our own definition of authenticity. Nor is the use of authenticity markers an alternative approach to determine which leaders are or are not authentic. Rather, we take an empirical approach, observing and recording how a variety of individuals determine the presence or absence, and evaluate the quality, of whatever it is each of them means by "authenticity."

Authenticity and Leadership

Authenticity is commonly addressed in normative discussions of "good leadership" (e.g., Jaworski, 1996). Indeed, some have gone so far as to argue that authenticity is the central organizing principle of leadership (Terry, 1993). The notion of the authentic leader is surfacing in discussions of leadership in diverse settings, including leadership in business (Argyris, 1982; George, 2003), religious institutions (Pembroke, 2002), rebellions (Nadeau, 2002), the nursing profession (Swanson, 2000; Marcus & Liberto, 2003), and the military (Gayvert, 1999).

Education, in particular, is a domain in which the authenticity of leaders and authentic leadership is commonly discussed (e.g., Begley, 2001; Evans, 1996; Thompson, 2003; Fernandez & Hogan, 2002; Sweetland, 2001; Villani, 1999; Yerkes & Guaglianone, 1998). Authentic leadership is even being used as a lens to understand historical events and historical transitions (e.g., Ramsey, 1999; Young, 2001), current events (Borger, 2001), and current political leaders (Kramer, 1995; Hays, 1999; Ezrahi, 1988; Luckowski & Lopach, 2000). Leadership development programs are similarly focusing in on the "authentic leader" (A fresh new look, 2004; Anderson & Terry, 1996).

Although important work has been done on authenticity, the construct of the authentic leader has yet to be rationalized.[1] The types of leadership described as "authentic" are as varied as the settings in which this descriptor is used. What is meant by authentic leadership is not clear, and the constructs are not always clearly articulated. This may be, in part, because some internal inconsistencies in arguments about authenticity in social settings in general, and leadership in particular, have not yet been reconciled.

Important work is being done to explicate authentic leadership. Gardner, Avolio, Luthans, May, and Walumbwa (2005) argue that an authentic leader must first and foremost achieve individual authenticity, yet, must also have authentic relations with followers and associates. Individual authenticity, their work illustrates, includes self-awareness, self-acceptance, and authentic actions. Authentic leader-follower relationships are characterized by (a) transparency, openness, and trust; (b) guidance toward an objective; and (c) an emphasis on follower development (Gardner et al., 2005). Thus, authentic leadership involves an authentic leader achieving authenticity and further encompasses authentic leader relations with followers. Authentic leaders, then, are persons who have achieved high levels of authenticity in that they know who they are and what they believe and value, and act upon those values and beliefs while transparently interacting with others (Avolio, Gardner, Walumbwa, Luthans, & May, 2004). Luthans and Avolio (2003) approach authentic leadership as a process, which results in greater self-awareness and self-regulated positive behaviors on the part of leaders and associates, fostering positive self-development.

The authenticity markers' approach is important for understanding authentic leadership in general, and the development of authentic leadership in particular, because it allows us to understand how followers perceive authenticity as leaders develop it.

Leader Authenticity Markers

Authenticity is not only something individuals, including individual leaders, must achieve. It is something about which others must make assessments. By focusing only on the leader's need to be authentic and his or her attempts to be authentic, we lose sight of the follower's need to assess the authenticity (or inauthenticity) of various leaders and his or her methods of doing so. Interestingly, Burns (1978), in an early use of the currently popular phrase, "authentic leadership," recognized the need to locate authenticity in leadership processes rather than in leaders. He identified authentic leadership as a collective process, emerging from both the clash and the convergence of the motives, and goals of leaders and followers.

In this study, we coin the term *leader authenticity markers* to refer to those features and actions of an individual leader which lead others to conclude that she or he is authentic.[2]

African American Political Leadership

Judgments of authenticity are particularly interesting and important in the context of ethnic groups. There is much debate about what is an authentic African American, an authentic Latino/Latina, or an authentic Asian American (e.g., Cohen, 1999). Scientific study of the social self has demonstrated that every individual has multiple identities, including private identities and those shared identities commonly referred to as social identities (Schlenker, 1985; Tajfel & Turner, 1986). Understanding an individual as authentic requires understanding authenticity not only along private identities, but also along social identities. Ethnic identity is one of the most important social identities. In this study, we consider ethnic authenticity markers used by the generation of African Americans born between 1965 and 1980, often referred to as the Hip-Hop Generation (Kitwana, 2002; Marable, 2002). We focus on the Hip-Hop Generation, instead of going across all ages, for five reasons.

First, the Hip-Hop Generation is the first generation of Blacks to grow up in the post-segregation era. Their worldview is shaped by the unique contradictions and complexities of race in the immediate aftermath of the country's racial apartheid system.

Second, this cohort's worldview is shaped by the growing complexity of Black life, most dramatically felt in increasing economic stratification within the Black community. The growth of the Black middle class (Patillo-McCoy, 1999) and the growth of racialized mass imprisonment (Garland, 2001; Mauer & Chesney-Lind, 2002; Parenti, 1999) are at the poles of the modern day Black experience. Dramatic progress has been made, but evidence continues to show that traditionally racist policies and practices persist in socially accepted modern manifestations (Marable, 2002). While the formal Jim Crow apparatus has been defeated, race continues to characterize substantial gaps in access and opportunity. Navigating this deceptive reality requires African Americans to operate in many environments, some more accommodating than others. For this generation of African Americans, the quest for authenticity reflects the struggle of juggling competing demands on identity.

Third, the post-segregation period has witnessed a heightened focus on cleavages in African American society in general and African American politics in particular (Cohen, 1999; Dawson, 2001). This makes questions of authenticity particularly salient for this community. Far from being merely an academic distinction, therefore, questions of the authenticity of current and aspiring African American political leaders are vital concerns for African American politics.

Fourth, this cohort is a growing voting block whose political values are less known than those of African Americans raised in the civil rights era (Dawson, 2001; Kitwana, 2002). Finally, the Hip-Hop Generation has had greater access to and participation in mainstream society than any previous generation of African Americans, but too little is known about how this has impacted their political consciousness.

Like its mainstream counterpart, Generation X, the Hip-Hop Generation is often defined and discussed in terms of popular culture trends. In fact, it has been shaped by a variety of important social, economic, cultural, and political reorganizations affecting inner city life and the African American community more generally in the post-segregation era (Kitwana, 2002; Wilson, 1996).[3] Key experiences of this generation of African Americans include school integration, inner city isolation spurred by deindustrialization and global corporate reorganization (Kitwana, 2002; Wilson, 1996), the expansion and increasing complexity of the African American middle class (Patillo-McCoy, 1999), and the "Blackening" of poverty and crime, most notably through the "underclass" debate of the 1980s and 1990s (O'Connor, 2001; Wilson, 1987).

The challenge of authenticity in the Hip-Hop Generation can be summarized in the popular slogan, "keep it real." More than a mere refrain of Hip-Hop music and dialogue, "keep it real" captures the challenges of African American identity formation in the post-segregation era. For example, while the state of African American health and wealth remains disturbingly below that of white Americans, the post-segregation era African American community participates in the American mainstream more fully and in more different capacities than any previous generation of African Americans. It is amidst these new, uncharted spaces that new questions of authenticity come to the forefront.

The question of what constitutes African American authenticity has long been a contested issue in the African American community. Toni Morrison ignited a firestorm of controversy and confusion when she dubbed William Jefferson Clinton "our first Black president. Blacker than any actual Black person who could ever be elected in our children's lifetime" (Morrison & Malcolm, 1998). "Clinton displays almost every trope of Blackness," she continued, "single-parent household, born poor, working-class, saxophone-playing, McDonald's-and-junk-food-loving boy from Arkansas." Morrison's comments commanded such attention and controversy, not only because she identified a white man – the President, no less – as African American, but also because of the deeply problematic and stereotypical characteristics upon which she based Clinton's "Blackness." These were her markers for African American authenticity.

Recent scholarship adds to the confusion, albeit in a much more responsible and productive fashion, by challenging the homogeneity of African American society, not only in contemporary times but throughout its history (Kelley, 1994; Cohen, 1999; Dawson, 2001). Undoubtedly, there are common experiences that are felt strongly among a majority of African Americans (Dawson, 1995), such as the second-class citizenship which America's racialized capitalist democracy has historically imposed on them (Dawson, 1995). Interestingly, the very process of debate and disagreement concerning such issues is part of a unique and shared African American experience.

If the nature of African American authenticity is controversial, even more controversial may be what constitutes an authentic African American political leader. But the political process does not wait for communities to resolve such deep-rooted questions. Every day, political leaders seek advancement, communities seek representation, and individuals make judgments about which leaders are authentic. Thus, there is a need for the study of authenticity markers, the features and actions those individuals will use to make those judgments.

Indeed, several recent elections appear to have hinged on shifting and conflicting conceptions of who is and who is not authentically African American. In the 2001 Newark, New Jersey mayoral race, a civil rights generation incumbent, Sharpe James, deliberately challenged his young, middle-class, Ivy League-educated opponent, Cory Booker, by publicly saying: "You have to learn to be an African American, and we don't have time to train you all night" (Hubbard, 2002). In the 2001 Birmingham, Alabama Congressional race between incumbent Earl Hilliard and a younger challenger, Artur Davis, the Reverend Al Sharpton, in support of Hilliard, warned a crowd at a rally: "Everybody your color ain't your kind" (Boyer, 2002). Like James, Hilliard represented what might be termed the "civil rights old guard": African American leaders trained in the crucible of the civil rights movement. Both Booker and Davis, in contrast, were Ivy League-educated, middle-class, conservative democrats who attracted considerable white support. At the heart of the African American community's decision-making process, in both elections, was the issue of which candidate better represented the community's perception of its historical experience.

Conflicts about African American authenticity are not limited to the electoral arena. In September 2002, Harry Belafonte labeled Secretary of State, Colin Powell a "house Negro" (Powell acts, 2002), challenging his legitimacy and authenticity as an African American man and an appropriate African American public leader.

These challenges all rest on contested authenticity. Who constitutes an authentically African American political leader? Interestingly, the discussion does not concern how authentic or inauthentic these leaders personally perceive themselves to be, or how authentic they are vis-à-vis a normative standard, but rather how authentic or inauthentic they are perceived to be by others. They may feel authentic while being perceived as inauthentic; they may even feel inauthentic while being perceived as authentic.

Of course, any notion of authentic African American leadership hinges on notions of what is authentically African American, perhaps an indefinable quality except in its normative form. Yet, the debate over who is or is not an authentic African American political leader will take place whether or not there is such a thing as an authentic African American leader. Furthermore, any lack of consensus on what constitutes African American authenticity will only increase the debate over who is an authentic leader.

The Present Study

This research study answers two questions: (1) What markers do African Americans of the Hip-Hop Generation use to evaluate an African American leader's authenticity?; and (2) What themes emerge, from the data collected, concerning what markers are used, how, and by whom?

This is the first study to address authenticity markers of political leaders in general, and authenticity markers in an ethnic minority community in particular. As such, the appropriate methodology was an exploratory one. The study was designed to surface the contours of the phenomenon by unearthing the range of markers considered, rather than to attempt the detailed analysis of particular markers or the precise determination of their relative emphasis.

METHODS

Sample

A gender-balanced, socioeconomically and geographically diverse cohort of African Americans of the Hip-Hop Generation ($n = 28$) were run in a set of focus groups ($n = 6$) during April and May of 2003. To ensure geographical diversity, two focus groups were held in each of three major cities with large and active African American communities: Atlanta, Georgia;

Boston, Massachusetts; and New York, New York. All participants fit the generational criterion, ranging in age from 23 to 38, the mean being 29. Forty-three percent were male; 57% were female.

Participants were recruited using a snowball sampling strategy (Miles & Huberman, 1984). The researchers identified a small number of individuals who had the ethnic and economic characteristics required. These people were then used as informants to identify others who qualified for inclusion and these, in turn, identified yet others. To insure diversity of sample, several institutions served as sources of research participants, including a social service center (in Boston) and a community arts organization (in New York). A snowball sampling technique was selected because we wished to study a population not easily accessible through more traditional methods; we wished to move outside college-aged populations, to study a particular ethnic group, and to investigate qualitative issues not included in large-scale nationally representative survey programs. This methodology fit the study's exploratory goal of surfacing the contours of the phenomenon.

Participants were recruited to include three levels of socioeconomic status (SES), defined by occupation and education: lower SES (occupations included clerical, janitorial, and low-level retail; educational achievement included high school), middle SES (occupations included graduate student, teacher, managerial, medium and high-level retail and service professions, and trained professional in service industries; educational achievement included Associates or 4-year college degree), and high SES (occupations included consultant, lawyer, and banker; educational achievement included one or more graduate degrees).

The sample was selected to meet the goals of the research: to identify the range of markers of authenticity rather than to test the relative prevalence of any one marker.

Procedure

The focus groups were presented to participants as being about African American politics and preferences, sponsored by a university professor. The groups were separated by SES (two low-SES groups, two middle-SES groups, and two upper-SES groups) to enable exploratory comparisons across SES groups. Focus group participants were not explicitly made aware of the SES groupings; debriefing of participants revealed that the intentional SES groupings for research purposes was not surmised.

Participants were offered a hot lunch or dinner, both as compensation and to serve as an icebreaker. The focus groups lasted between one and a half and two hours.

The focus groups were conducted by a 28-year-old African American male. All group sessions were audio-taped and the responses were later transcribed, coded, and analyzed. Data are reported using pseudonyms.

Instrument

Each focus group was asked the same set of questions, organized into (a) a section asking participants their thoughts and feelings about authenticity of African American political leaders in general terms and (b) a section inviting participants to discuss authenticity in the context of particular African American leaders. This mix provided us with both general insights and grounded insights.

In the first set of questions, five primary questions were asked: "What are African American interests?", "What makes an African American leader authentic?", "What makes an African American leader inauthentic?", "Is there an issue that would turn you against an African American political candidate?", and "Which leaders are real, and what makes them that way?"

The second set of questions invited participants to discuss the authenticity of five African American political leaders: Colin Powell, Jesse Jackson, Reverend Al Sharpton, Condoleezza Rice, and Louis Farrakhan. Participants were asked to comment on the authenticity of each leader, and to specify why they judged each one the way they did. The set of individuals was selected by the researchers to provide participants with an array of high-profile, nationally recognized African American leaders. Nationally recognized leaders were selected to ensure that regional differences, varying levels of exposure to media, and other individual variables would not prevent an individual from participating fully.

In several groups, participants chose to discuss other examples as well. Supreme Court Justice Clarence Thomas was the most frequent addition.

Data Analysis

The study data were analyzed according to a categorization and theme analysis methodology derived from Miles and Huberman (1984) by one of the study investigators. This methodology involves a progression from the initial reading of the transcripts, in which the researchers identified the first-order (informant) terms and concepts, to subsequent stages of cyclical comparisons, in which the researchers discerned shared concepts. This occurred through the triangulation on shared concepts from comparative data, gathered from different informants at different times. In this chapter, we report on the first stages of a larger grounded theory research program on the perception of leader authenticity.

Data points – sections of each transcript – were initially identified and coded as referring to a particular type of authenticity marker or to a more general theme. The themes served as the beginning codes for subsequent, more refined categorizing and sorting of the qualitative data. In several cases, a data point was coded as informing multiple concepts. The data was then organized in a spreadsheet. A row was used for each data point identified and analyzed. Columns were used to code the data points. As themes were refined over the course of the research, more detailed sets of codes were developed. For each new code developed, a new column was added and the pertinent data points were recoded to reflect the increasing refinement of the study's themes and findings. As the codes became more refined, the data could be reviewed at different levels of abstraction. The use of a spreadsheet enabled the researchers to sort and examine the data along several key dimensions.

In addition to the analysis described above, a second investigator conducted a "gestalt" or impressionist analysis to gain a general sense of the patterns in the data (see, for example, Van Maanen, 1988). The degree of convergence between the results produced through the two techniques was then assessed to establish confidence in the findings.

In this approach, the theoretical perspective is grounded in the data and emerges from it (Glaser & Strauss, 1967; Miles & Huberman, 1984). This is a particularly good methodological fit with the research questions, since empirical and theoretical work on leader authenticity markers has not previously been done.

RESULTS AND DISCUSSION

This study was designed to unearth a range of authenticity markers used rather than to rank order their importance. Seven leader authenticity markers are presented and discussed: experience of racism, policy positions, liberal party affiliation, speech patterns and mannerisms, experience of struggle, participation in the Black Church, and connection to historical

African American events and to other African Americans. In addition to the markers, five themes about the authenticity markers emerged. They are discussed after the markers.

Markers

Experience of Racism

Participants in all the focus groups recognized the centrality of experiences with racism to the African American identity. It was commonly felt that African American political leaders should be able to relate to the experience of resisting racism in order to be perceived as authentic. In the rare instance that an African American political leader might lack personal experience of racism, a consciousness of the collective experience with racism, both in historic and present-day terms, was taken for granted as necessary. The comment of a young female law student illustrates the common reference to experience of racism, recognized or unrecognized, as a marker of what makes an authentic leader. She observed that "Black people have only been free for a small number of years – the history and legacy of slavery is still with us [and our leaders]."

Policy Positions

In all focus groups, participants frequently referenced a set of policy issues and topics that have been traditionally related to African American politics, casting them as authentic issues for an African American political leader. These issues were: racial equality, affirmative action, poverty and educational progress, economic development, and community building. Family-related issues (such as teen pregnancy and divorce) and health care were also cited. When pressed for the single most important policy issue for an authentic African American leader to champion, participants across socioeconomic groups cited economic issues. Economic development and political advancement were consistently seen as closely connected, the latter inherently leading to the former.

One participant, Jamal, discussed the intertwined nature of economic and political development, and the need for political leaders who understand the intersection, a view expressed by many in the groups:

> I think now we are at a point where we cannot rely on the legal system to move us forward as a people and we need to start thinking about how we move ourselves forward ... one of the keys to that is through economic empowerment and freedom and gaining

access to the political structure through becoming more involved in the economic structure of this country.

It is worth noting that, despite the diversity of SES groups, only one participant, in a middle-SES group, offered what might be termed a radical
policy option: large-scale wealth redistribution. Her comments were mild
compared to traditional strands of African American radical thought and to
other contemporary theorists (Marable, 2000; Robinson, 2000), and while
economic development can be thought to imply some sort of radical redis-
tributive political project, it often embraces rather than challenges the
legitimacy of the existing workings of capitalism. Kiesha differentiated her
point of view and explained:

> I really believe that there needs to be more redistribution of funds in our country and
> I have a serious problem with the disparities in our country and how much the haves are
> able to have. That's a deal breaker for me ... I'm for constraining capitalism ....

Stacy, a member of the same focus group, quickly responded to Kiesha's
remarks with a view that, while not commonly voiced, was not rejected or
denounced:

> I have worked hard for the things I have and if I can afford a BMW.... I'm going to buy
> one and if I can afford to go skiing every weekend because that's what I want to do then
> I am going to do it ... there are people who do have that opportunity [to go to school]
> and do not take advantage of it and it is not my responsibility to give them what I have if
> they made a choice to not take advantage of that opportunity.

In all the groups, one facet of economic development policy, affirmative
action, emerged as a litmus test of sorts for authenticity in African American
leaders. One participant remarked:

> I think that affirmative action is a big part of my evaluation of authenticity ... anytime
> you don't recognize that African American people still struggle and that there is a fight
> to win in 2003 and that affirmative action is one way to win something then I can't vote
> for you. You are not recognizing who you are and you are downgrading what's going on
> around you.

There was also convergence around health care as an authentic African
American issue, and poverty more generally. Poverty, however, was only
sporadically raised, and policy remedies for it were inconsistently cited.

It is interesting, and perhaps problematic, that the questions of which
issues are authentic and which positions on those issues are authentic became difficult, if not impossible, to differentiate. It was certainly impossible
to parse them out in the responses. It appeared in our study that authentic
African American political leaders must have more than just an idea or
critique of a particular issue; they must have a plan of action.

In fact, it is not so much that certain issues are considered authentic issues, but that certain policy positions in response to certain issues signal authenticity, while the failure to take those positions on those issues signals inauthenticity. A political leader championing an "authentic" issue may nevertheless be perceived as inauthentic if his or her policy recommendations do not reflect the perspective of the African American mainstream.

Liberal Party Affiliation

Liberal party affiliation appears to operate as an authenticity marker for a significant subset of African Americans. For example, Arnold speaks of liberal political affiliation as more authentically African American:

> When we hear the term conservatism, what are they conserving? They are conserving wealth. That's what conservative means, which is why when I hear 'Black conservative' it's an oxymoron because we don't have anything to conserve. We don't maintain any wealth on a community level. When I hear 'Black conservative,' off the top of my head I am thinking 'self-serving' – he's rich so he's trying to conserve himself.

No participant acknowledged conservatism as a marker of African American authenticity, even though Black conservatism is recognized as a marginal yet constant strand in African American political thought (Dawson, 2001) and despite the fact that some accomplished African American political leaders have been political conservatives.

Speech Patterns and Mannerisms

Participants considered mannerisms and speech to be markers of the authenticity or inauthenticity of African American political leaders. For example, when asked, "How do African American political leaders demonstrate a connection [to the African American community]," Rodney quickly replied:

> One of the things we haven't talked about is charisma. That is one of the biggest things we look for. If someone is awkward when they talk we write them off. When you look at older African American leaders they are very charismatic – they are like preachers.

The discussion continued to focus on the ways that specific speech patterns, mannerisms, and grooming can mark an authentic African American leader. It was interesting that most participants referred to these characteristics as markers, which other people read as markers of authenticity, rather than claiming to use them as markers themselves. One might ask whether participants felt they knew what others were thinking, or said so as a substitute for acknowledging what they themselves were thinking.

Markers could signal authenticity to some participants while signaling inauthenticity to others. For example, some participants saw a "traditionally Black" speech pattern as signaling authenticity, while others saw it as a marker of inauthenticity:

> For me, I am turned off by Black politicians who rhyme and dime – to me that's saying that if I don't rhyme it, you can't understand it or that I have to make it sing-songy to have Black people understand it ... that turns me off immediately. To me it sends a message to the general politician. I feel like we're already stereotyped in that manner – you know, shucking and jiving – and that that's all we know how to do ... I feel like that feeds the stereotype.

For this participant, the public use of Black English conjures up insecurities and self-conscious feelings rooted in the traditional stereotypes of African American culture. Black English (as opposed to Black street slang) has long been recognized as a legitimate and linguistically specific vernacular (Rickford & Rickford, 2000). But in the aftermath of the Ebonics controversy of the mid-1990s, it seems that Black English continues to be of questionable legitimacy among the Hip-Hop Generation, arguably the generation most responsible for the vernacular's widespread exposure. Despite such misgivings about Black English, many members in each of the focus groups used it, not only in their casual discussions before and after the sessions, but in their formal responses to questions.[4]

Hip-Hop culture, in particular, has exploded the boundaries between public and private African American speech, using mass media to expose the fractional character of African American society. Therefore it is remarkable that African Americans of the Hip-Hop Generation are still very conscious of the public/private nature of African American culture and speech. Juxtaposing the use of Black English in the focus groups with the participants' concern that the public use of Black English reinforces historic stereotypes of African American cultural inferiority reveals a nuance of African American political authenticity. The authenticity of Black English was validated through its casual use, yet, recognized as a negative and potentially inauthentic trait for African Americans in mainstream or white space.

Experience of Struggle

It was clear from the focus group discussions that identification with struggle – loosely defined yet almost synonymous with racism – is an authenticity marker. Even participants who did not explicitly discuss experiences of struggle as an authenticity marker sometimes referenced it implicitly in the scenarios they described. Yet, this was also seen as problematic by an upper-middle-class participant:

> I think we recognize what the stereotypes are [of being authentically Black] but then recognize that that is not always what's authentically African American or of the African American experience. To define it we think that African American people struggle. If you have a politician from a single parent home and who struggled we immediately say, "that's real." As opposed to someone who grew up in a privileged background – we immediately separate that from the African American experience.

This comment reveals that the post-segregation generation, like their parents, still feel a sense of linked fate within African American society based on the foundational realities of living in a racialized society (Dawson, 1995).

Participation in the Black Church

Many participants viewed participation in what is known as the "Black Church" as a marker of authenticity of African American leaders. As Eric remarked: "I think [authenticity is]... going into the Black churches and sitting with the Black congregation." In fact, African American religious participation is spread across different religions and not at all restricted to the traditional "Black Church" (Taylor, Chatters, Jayakody, & Levin, 1996).[5] Yet, participation in any religious group other than the traditional Black Church does not seem to signal an authentic African American politician, particularly among young people.

Connection to Historical African-American Events and to other African Americans

It was clear that African American political leaders must not only be connected to events or periods of great importance, but must openly embrace them, in order to be perceived as authentic. The importance of claiming a stake in the African American historical experience could be seen clearly in the way participants felt about National Security Advisor Condoleezza Rice's somewhat surprising failure to do so. Rice grew up in Birmingham, Alabama during the civil rights era, amidst a struggle that became a globally recognized benchmark for all social movements and a defining point in African American history. Yet, to many she appears to have been unaffected by it at the time.

One respondent remarked:

> I have to give her credit for the position that she holds, but to look at where she comes from I don't think she is a very good role model. She grew up in the heart of the civil rights movement in Birmingham; I think two or three blocks away from where the church bombing took place. To hear her story about her mother teaching her [the] classics instead of having her out there marching and being able to identify ... I'm not

saying you have to be front and center, but I wouldn't report that ... I am not proud to know that she lived in the heart of the civil rights movement where a very significant act took place and what is highlighted about her is that she was in the house learning the piano, the classics, and learning to speak Russian.

Another in the same group remarked:

She [Condoleezza Rice] comes from Birmingham during the civil rights movement. I know she was sheltered, but she never talks about it. That had to affect her. It's some things that happen to all Black people growing up in this country. I don't get that from her.

It was generally felt that Rice was isolated – either by her own doing or by that of her family – and her perceived distance from these events made her seem inauthentic.

Connectedness to other African Americans also operates as an authenticity marker. Condoleezza Rice was again mentioned by several participants as an illustrative example, because she did not attach herself to traditional political networks and paths to power used by other African American leaders.

This desire for connection is considered important not only at the macro level of which networks one joins or where one's power is derived, but also at the micro level of everyday interactions. Alan offered an example:

If you walk past Black people and you are with a group of white people, you acknowledge them. I know if I am in a room full of white people and there are a few Black people in the room I guarantee that we will speak.

The other members of Alan's group agreed.

Interestingly, connectedness is read not only in past experience and present behaviors, but also in visions for the future. As one participant explained: "A person has to be one who knows where they have truly come from, what they want to do, and where they want to go with the people, not without the people."

Themes

In the analyses, the data were examined for the leader authenticity markers described above and for themes in how perceived authenticity is constructed. Five themes emerged:

Shared Traits are Sometimes Perceived as Distinctly African American
There is a curious paradox of group identity in general, and group identity as perceived authenticity in particular, which we call perceived distinctiveness.

Some of the traits and features which members of a group perceive to be distinct to their group, are actually perceived by other groups to be distinct to themselves. For example, most ethnic groups in the United States will report family ties as a particular emphasis of their group. The apparent commonness of this so-called distinctive trait suggests that its distinctiveness is one of perception, rather than fact.

In this study, health care was often acknowledged to be an "authentic" African American issue, very important to the African American community. Yet, health care is very much a mainstream issue, seen by many American voters as the most important issue political leaders should be addressing. It is therefore, quite possible that other markers signaling the authenticity of African American leaders may not, in fact, differentiate African Americans and their leaders from other groups, but may be perceived by many groups as distinct to themselves.

Inauthenticity is Detected More Clearly Than Authenticity

Interestingly, although the participants began with the question of what makes someone authentic, they were far more comfortable discussing inauthenticity. One participant, when asked "What makes an authentic African American political leader?" noted the tendency, in himself and the others in the group, to default to the other end of the continuum: "I keep thinking in the negative ... the first thing inauthentic that comes to my mind is Jesse Jackson." It appears that followers are more certain; what constitutes a breach of authenticity than what constitutes positive expression of authenticity. Perhaps this finding reflects an openness to various forms of identity and expression within African American society, but within certain bounds. For example, claiming and owning African American identity, being aware of and resisting negative stereotypes of African American identity, and recognizing the protracted struggle of African American life may be non-negotiable authenticity traits, beyond which considerable departures are allowed.

Perceived Authenticity is Problematic for Political Figures

The American public holds many cynical views of political leaders' power motives, making it difficult for followers to view political leaders as truly authentic. This general cynicism appears to extend to African Americans. One respondent's feelings about Jesse Jackson revealed this problem well:

> I still respect Jesse for things he's done – I don't really know what he's done or specific proposals he has, but he always seems to show his face anytime there is a camera around, and that bugs me. It shows his cause is not steadfast; it's wavering with the times. He's

not steadfast as to what he thinks African American people need. He keeps injecting himself into situations and I don't like that.[6]

Another participant in another group voiced similar sentiments and critiqued Jackson as a political careerist:

It's a good and bad thing because of how he exploits us sometimes, but there's just not many people left who will do that. He just seems to show up sometimes when people don't recognize.

Leaders can Signal too much Authenticity

Being perceived as authentic appears, in general, to be a desirable trait in leaders. However, the markers through which followers read authenticity in this study were not linearly related to authenticity, but curvilinearly related. So, while there were risks to showing too few authenticity markers, there also seemed to be counterproductive effects of showing too many markers and being perceived as forced, artificial, or contrived. Ultimately, it brought participants right back to a place of perceived inauthenticity.

For example, while acknowledging a connection to African American people and the African American experience was a significant authenticity marker for many of the respondents, many also perceived trying too hard to connect with African American people as suspicious and even inauthentic. In the course of a conversation, in which the many ways Reverend Al Sharpton connects with the African American community were being discussed, one respondent remarked:

Al Sharpton is trying to go for the presidency ... I think it is a matter of image. I don't see trueness with Al Sharpton. I don't see a Martin Luther King type of [spirituality] ... not saying that everybody has to be the same, but I don't feel that. I don't feel a Malcolm X image coming from the brother. I feel I am going to go out here and try to be the first Black candidate.

Here, in contrast to the perceptions expressed about Condoleezza Rice, overidentification rather than underidentification seemed to be a marker of inauthenticity. African American leaders have a balance to strike, identifying strongly enough to be perceived as authentic, but not overidentifying at the risk of being perceived as opportunistic and exploitative of the mass-mobilizing power of African American politics.

Authenticity Markers versus Divisions in African American Society

There is agreement on leader authenticity markers despite commonly referenced divisions in African American society. One of the most striking themes in the data was, the consensus across the different socioeconomic status groups on what is perceived as authenticity in political leaders, despite presentations in the media and recent trends in African American scholarship focusing on cleavages in African American life. The consensus observable in this study raises the question of whether the cleavages in contemporary African American life have been overestimated or leader authenticity markers happen to be a subject of agreement across these chasms. It appears that whatever barriers might arise in response to economic class differences in the African American community are not as prominent, or as potent, as the feelings of linked fate due to race. Indeed, there was the commonly shared view across SES groups that race is still a significant determinant of opportunity in America.[7]

CONCLUSION

Leadership studies have discovered authenticity. Being authentic is a particularly difficult task for an African American leader in the post-segregation generation, as the boundaries of African American experience are expanding (Cohen, 1999). It is also a challenge – overlooked in the research – for followers, who must evaluate the authenticity of their leaders. In this study, we examined what markers followers use to decide the authenticity, or inauthenticity, of their leaders. Thus, instead of authenticity, we focused on perception of authenticity. We then examined several themes in the application of these authenticity markers.

Most fundamentally, the work illustrates that perceptions of authenticity operate alongside authentic leadership and that the two have tensions. What one does to be an authentic leader may not always translate into being perceived as authentic. The finding on policy positions as an authenticity marker clearly illustrates the tensions. Our data suggest that, in order to be seen as an authentic African American leader, one must hold certain political positions – that is, one must be aligned to some extent with public opinion. However, the definition of an authentic leader is someone whose values and beliefs drive behavior that is consistent regardless of public opinion. Here is the crux of perception of authenticity versus the action of authenticity.

As our research was deliberately qualitative, seeking to uncover important markers rather than to rank, quantify, or compare them analytically, a logical next step would be a quantitative approach to the same phenomena. And as the snowball technique helped us answer the question of what markers people are using, answering subsequent questions on the incidence and prevalence of those markers will require alternative research methods.

Our work also suggests a fruitful line of research exploring which leader authenticity markers are used by majority group members, and by other minority group members, such as Latinos/Latinas and Asian Americans, in their perceptions of African American political leaders. More generally, how do members of one group perceive the authenticity of leaders of another group? Such research should extend beyond the study of ethnic groups to ask who will be perceived by the general public as an authentic labor leader or an authentic proponent of women's rights? The present research, which treats authenticity as an important variable in understanding the relationship between leaders and followers, rather than as something that unfolds within the leader, can be coupled with the viewpoint of intergroup relations to give us a provocative new lens for understanding politics and leadership in pluralistic settings.

Another arena for future work is the role of authenticity in driving political behavior, such as voting. Research has already uncovered a set of psychological assessments which, along with policy positions, influence voting behavior. As authenticity is increasingly discussed as something normatively desirable for leaders, empirical research should examine the importance of authenticity to voting. Data collected in this study suggests that perceptions of a candidate's authenticity play an important role in espoused voting behavior.

The finding that participants were more comfortable discussing inauthenticity than authenticity, suggested the possibility that African American society is open to various forms of identity, but within certain bounds, with the result that inauthenticity is more clearly defined and easier to detect than authenticity. Future research might try to determine whether this is really the case and, if so, the range and bounds of that openness.

Researchers into leader authenticity markers will naturally wonder whether their work, should it reach a state of sufficient richness and rigor, might be absorbed into the market research methodology that seems to guide so many efforts in contemporary society. And beyond the possibility of potential exploitation of those authenticity markers which are already in use, it is possible for leaders to deliberately introduce new authenticity markers into society. For example, Croats and Serbs speak a common language known as Serbo-Croatian. With the breakup of Yugoslavia, nationalist leaders in the two independent and deeply hostile nations, Serbia and Croatia, each now claim to have their own languages, Serbian and Croatian. Thus, two languages that, for all practical purposes, do not even exist, have now been crafted as symbols of national authenticity.

This chapter has focused principally on introducing the perception of authenticity into the literature on authentic leadership by presenting a first set of data. The task remains to integrate it with theories of leadership, including work on implicit theories of leadership (e.g., Lord, 1977, 1985; Lord & Alliger, 1985; Lord & Maher, 1993; Phillips & Lord, 1981) and theories of attributional processes and leadership (e.g., Martinko & Gardner, 1987).

Researchers should eventually be able to combine the results of authenticity studies in a much wider range of contexts to seek more general patterns of authenticity perception. Are there general categories of authenticity markers which would obtain whether people are judging the authenticity of political leaders or musicians, business managers or poets?

Within leadership studies, the applications of these advances in the study of authenticity will be great. People will always be searching for authentic leaders. As we learn more about how authenticity operates, we will learn more about who can bridge gaps and be seen as credible and trustworthy political representatives of groups and communities, particularly ethnic minority communities. Furthermore, the study of leader authenticity markers enhances our understanding of important feelings and behaviors, which political leaders seek to inspire, and which authenticity helps foster. Perceived authenticity, for example, is a critical factor in generating and sustaining trust in leaders (Bennis, 1999).

This study, by taking an empirical rather than a normative approach, and focusing on perceptions of authenticity, offers the first steps toward an understanding of leader authenticity as a process of perception.

NOTES

1. Chris Argyris's work on authenticity may offer the most systematic approach to date. Argyris has reported on over four decades of research on business organizations, examining how they systematically foster modes of communication that defeat authenticity. In Argyris' terminology, the difference between "what I say" and "what I mean" is the measure of authenticity (e.g., Argyris, 1982).

2. Markers differ from stereotypes – beliefs about the personal attributes of a group of people, typically overgeneralized and often inaccurate – in three important ways. First, stereotypes describe the way a perceiver thinks the world is, while authenticity markers describe the way a perceiver thinks the world should be. Second, a leader could be perceived as stereotypical but not authentic. Indeed, our research finds that, on the whole, people do not believe that leaders are authentic, suggesting that stereotypes and authenticity markers are by no means interchangeable. Third, there are widely diverging opinions about which features and actions qualify as

authenticity markers, while stereotypes are, by definition, generalizations about which there is social consensus.

3. Influential Hip-Hop Generation thinkers and activists include Bakari Kitwana (2002), Kevin Powell (1997), and Joan Morgan (1999).

4. For a more in-depth discussion of the linguistic and cultural foundations of Black English, see *Spoken Soul: The Roots of Black English* (Rickford & Rickford, 2000).

5. The Black Church in the African American experience usually refers to seven major historic Black denominations: the African Methodist Episcopal (AME) Church; the African Methodist Episcopal Zion (AMEZ) Church; the Christian Methodist Episcopal (CME) Church; the National Baptist Convention, U.S.A., Incorporated (NBC); the National Baptist Convention of America, Unincorporated (NBCA); the Progressive National Baptist Convention (PNBC); and the Church of God in Christ (COGIC) (Lincoln & Mamiya, 1990). More recently developed denominations include the National Missionary Baptist Convention (NMBC) and the Full Gospel Baptist Church Fellowship (FGBCF), although the FGBCF does not refer to itself as a denomination.

However, significant numbers of African Americans were and are members of predominantly white denominations such as the Episcopal, Presbyterian, Congregational, United Methodist, and Roman Catholic churches. Outside Christianity, there are African American Muslims (Turner, 2003). Statistics on ethnicity and religion are hard to find; the United States government does not collect them as individual religious groups and denominations vary in their ability and willingness to keep track of this information. It does appear, however, that African American spiritual life is far more diverse than the relatively narrow set of religious cues used to assess the authenticity of African American political leaders, particularly among young people.

For example, there are cohort differences in religious participation among African Americans (Sherkat, 2001). Cohort-specific shifts in religious participation across denominations demonstrate the secularization of African American mainline Methodist and Baptist groups and the early-stage growth of newer "nondenominational" churches alongside the traditional sectarian denominations (Sherkat, 2001). If one looks at it by ethnicity of co-congregants, rather than denomination, a similar picture emerges. Roper polling data found that 22% of African American respondents reported that, at the church or other place of worship they attend, the people were "All White," "Mostly White", or "Half [White] and half [Black]" (Gallup, 1997). And these figures are restricted to those African Americans who report regularly attending a church or other place of worship.

Thus, while participation in a historical and generalized "Black Church" is viewed by many as a marker of authenticity of African American leaders, this authenticity cue operates within the great religious pluralism of the African American community. And many African American voters are neither religiously affiliated nor regular attendees of religious organizations.

6. It is interesting to note the use of first names in discussing these figures. For example, Jackson was referred to as "Jesse" in a manner that would suggest that everyone at the table knew him personally. His authenticity was challenged and defended in emotional terms, validating that he was part of a larger community that,

for better or worse, identified him as a member, an extension of their collective identity, and accountable to them whether they liked him or not.

7. This is not to overlook the diversity within the African American community or to promote the myth of an African American monolith, but the data collected in this study surfaced compelling evidence of commonalities rather than of cleavages. One possible explanation for why more pronounced class differences were not observed is the transitory nature of African American class identities. Individuals and families can travel across socioeconomic lines between and even within generations (Tyson, 2003). Additionally, the African American middle and upper classes remain linked to the working class and the poor through shared community institutions such as churches, schools, and extended families (Patillo-McCoy, 1999). While class realities can color one's experience in a racialized society, they do not diminish the impact of that racialization.

Outside the realm of the data discussed here, the persistence of block voting, cultural practices, racialized residential patterns, and the day-to-day experiences with white supremacy (in the workplace, in schools, etc.) validate that there is much tying the African American community together. Some poll data reveal that the perceived class and generational gap in African American society on political issues is marginal.

Recent trends in African American scholarship have focused on divisions within African American society, not only as a means of demystifying notions of a monolithic and homogeneous African American identity, but as a way of problematizing Black identity formation (Dawson, 1995, 2001; Gregory, 1999; Patillo-McCoy, 1999; Kelley, 1994). In the political realm, however, African Americans continue to recognize the same sets of issues as important and vote mostly as a block.

The perceived schisms in the Hip-Hop Generation in particular, likely result from romanticized and oversimplified understandings of the civil rights era. Intra-racial tensions and conflict in that period have long been ignored, making the community today look more divided by comparison than it likely is. When our focus groups discussed ideological cleavages in contemporary African American society, the values of the Hip-Hop Generation, and the present strength of African American politics, countless contrasts were made to the 1960s. One respondent, for example, remarks: "Maybe during the civil rights movement there was more of a solidarity and you could pigeonhole all interests in one box. Now with the Black community being so diverse in terms of economics, social class, it's hard to say what are Black interests and what aren't."

ACKNOWLEDGMENTS

We thank Barbara Kellerman, John Elder, and three anonymous reviewers for helpful comments on an early draft of this manuscript.

REFERENCES

Anderson, S. R., & Terry, R. W. (1996). *Transforming public education through authentic leadership*. Minneapolis, MN: Humphrey Institute.

Argyris, C. (1982). *Reason, learning and action*. San Francisco: Jossey Bass.

Avolio, B. J., & Gardner, W. L. (2005). Authentic leadership development: Getting to the root of positive forms of leadership. *The Leadership Quarterly, 16*, 315–338.

Avolio, B. J., Gardner, W. L., Walumbwa, F. O., Luthans, F., & May, D. (2004). Unlocking the mask: A look at the process by which authentic leaders impact follower attitudes and behaviors. *The Leadership Quarterly, 15*, 801–823.

Begley, P. T. (2001). In pursuit of authentic school leadership practices. *International Journal of Leadership in Education, 4*(4), 353–366.

Bennis, W. (1999). The leadership advantage. *Leader to Leader, 12*, 18–23.

Borger, G. (2001). Naive no more. *U.S. News & World Report,, 131*(13), 34.

Boyer, D. (2002). Mideast fires up Alabama run-off. *The Washington Times*, June 25 p. A01.

Burns, J. M. (1978). *Leadership*. New York: Harper & Row.

Cohen, C. J. (1999). *The boundaries of Blackness: AIDS and the breakdown of Black politics*. Chicago: University of Chicago Press.

Dawson, M. C. (1995). *Behind the mule: Race and class in African American politics*. Princeton: Princeton University Press.

Dawson, M. C. (2001). *Black visions: The roots of contemporary African-American political ideologies*. Chicago: University of Chicago Press.

Erickson, R. J. (1995). The importance of authenticity for self and society. *Symbolic Interaction, 18*(2), 121–144.

Evans, R. (1996). *The human side of school change: Reform, resistance, and the real-life problems of innovation*. San Francisco: Jossey-Bass.

Ezrahi, Y. (1988, February 21). Breaking the deadlock: An Israeli view. *New York Times Magazine, 137*(4711), 27–30.

Fernandez, J. E., & Hogan, R. T. (2002). Value-based leadership. *Journal for Quality & Participation, 25*(4), 25–28.

Gardner, W. L., III, Avolio, B. J., Luthans, F., May, D. R., & Walumbwa, F. O. (2005). "Can you see the real me?" A self-based model of authentic leaders and follower development. *The Leadership Quarterly, 16*, 373–394.

Garland, D. (2001). *Mass imprisonment: Social causes and consequences*. London: Sage.

Gayvert, D. R. (1999). Leadership and doctrinal reform. *Military Review, 79*(3), 18–22.

George, B. (2003). *Authentic leadership: Rediscovering the secrets to creating lasting value*. San Francisco: Jossey-Bass.

Glaser, B. G., & Strauss, A. (1967). *The discovery of grounded theory: Strategies for qualitative research*. Chicago: Aldine.

Gregory, S. (1999). *Black corona: Race and the politics of place in an urban community*. Princeton, NJ: Princeton University Press.

Harter, S. (2002). Authenticity. In: C. R. Snyder & S. Lopez (Eds), *Handbook of positive psychology* (pp. 382–394). Oxford, U.K.: Oxford University Press.

Hays, S. (1999). Leadership from the inside out. *Workforce, 78*(11), 27–30.

Hubbard, L. (2002, May 5). Hip-Hop vs. civil rights. Retrieved April 10, 2003 from www.daveyd.com.

Jaworski, J. (1996). *Synchronicity: The inner path of leadership*. San Francisco: Berrett-Koehler.

Kelley, R. D. G. (1994). *Race rebels: Culture, politics, and the Black working class*. New York: Free Press.

Kitwana, B. (2002). *The Hip-Hop Generation: Young Blacks and the crisis in African-American culture*. New York: Basic Civitas.

Kohnken, G. (1987). *Training police officers to detect deceptive eyewitness statements: Does it work? Social Behavior, 2,* 1–17.

Kramer, M. (1995). *Will the real Bob Dole please stand up? Time, 146*(21), 58–66.

Kraut, R. E., & Poe, D. (1980). Behavioral roots of person perception: The deception judgments of customs inspectors and laymen. *Journal of Personality and Social Psychology, 39,* 784–798.

Lincoln, E. C., & Mamiya, L. H. (1990). *The Black church in the African American experience.* Durham, NC: Duke University Press.

Lord, R. G. (1977). Functional leadership behavior: Measurement and relation to social power and leadership perceptions. *Administrative Science Quarterly, 22,* 114–133.

Lord, R. G. (1985). An information processing approach to social perceptions, leadership perceptions, and behavioral measurement in organizational settings. In: B. M. Straw & L. L. Cummings (Eds), *Research in organizational behavior,* (Vol. 7, pp. 87–128). Greenwich, CT: JAI Press.

Lord, R. G., & Alliger, G. M. (1985). A comparison of four information processing models of leadership and social perceptions. *Human Relations, 38,* 47–65.

Lord, R. G., & Maher, K. J. (1993). *Leadership and information processing. Linking perceptions and performance.* London: Routledge.

Luckowski, J. A., & Lopach, J. J. (2000). Critical thinking about political commentary. *Journal of Adolescent & Adult Literacy, 44*(3), 254–259.

Luthans, F., & Avolio, B. J. (2003). Authentic leadership development. In: K. S. Cameron, J. E. Dutton & R. E. Quinn (Eds), *Positive organizational scholarship: Foundations of a new discipline* (pp. 241–258). San Francisco: Berrett-Koehler.

Marable, M. (2000). *How capitalism underdeveloped Black America: Problems in race, political economy, and society.* Cambridge, MA: South End Press.

Marable, M. (2002). *The great wells of democracy: The meaning of race in American life.* New York: Basic Civitas.

Marcus, J., & Liberto, L. (2003). Create accountable, balanced work environments. *Nursing Management, 34*(10), 25–27.

Martinko, M. J., & Gardner, W. L. (1987). The leader/member attribution process. *Academy of Management Review, 12,* 235–249.

Mauer, M., & Chesney-Lind, M. (2002). *Invisible punishment: The collateral consequences of mass imprisonment.* New York: The New Press.

Miles, M. B., & Huberman, A. M. (1984). *Qualitative data analysis: A sourcebook of new methods.* Newbury Park, CA: Sage.

Morgan, J. (1999). *When chickenheads come home to roost: My life as a Hip-Hop feminist.* New York: Simon & Schuster.

Morrison, T., & Malcolm, J. (1998). The talk of the town. *New Yorker, 74*(30), 31–35.

Nadeau, K. (2002). Peasant resistance and religious protests in early Philippine society: Turning friars against the grain. *Journal for the Scientific Study of Religion, 41*(1), 75–86.

O'Connor, A. (2001). *Poverty knowledge: Social science, social policy, and the poor in twentieth century U.S. history.* Princeton, NJ: Princeton University Press.

Parenti, C. (1999). *Lockdown America: Police and prisons in the age of crisis.* London: Verso.

Patillo-McCoy, M. (1999). *Black picket fences: Privilege and peril among the Black middle class.* Chicago: University of Chicago Press.

Pembroke, N. (2002). Rising leaders need authentic leadership. *Clergy Journal, 78*(8), 17–19.

Phillips, J. S., & Lord, R. G. (1981). Causal attributions and perceptions of leadership. *Organizational Behavior and Human Performance, 28,* 143–163.

Powell, K. (1997). *Keepin' it real.* New York: One World/Ballantine.

Powell acts like a house slave, Belafonte says. (2002, October 10). *The Houston Chronicle,* p. A2.

Ramsey, R,W. (1999). Latin America: A booming strategic region in need of an honest introductory textbook. *Parameters: US Army War College, 29*(1), 168–172.

Rickford, J. R., & Rickford, R. (2000). *Spoken soul: The roots of Black English.* New York: Wiley.

Robinson, R. (2000). *The debt: What America owes to Blacks.* New York: Penguin.

Schlenker, B. R. (1985). Identity and self-identification. In: B. R. Schlenker (Ed.), *The self and social life* (pp. 65–99). New York: McGraw-Hill.

Shamir, B., & Eilam, G. (2005). "What's your story?": A life-stories approach to authentic leadership development. *The Leadership Quarterly, 16*(3), 395–417.

Sherkat, D. E. (2001). Investigating the sect-church-sect cycle: Cohort-specific attendance differences across African-American denominations. *Journal for the Scientific Study of Religion, 40*(2), 221–233.

Swanson, J. W. (2000). Zen leadership: Balancing energy for mind, body, and spirit harmony. *Nursing Administration Quarterly, 24*(2), 29–34.

Sweetland, S. R. (2001). Authenticity and sense of power in enabling school structures: An empirical analysis. *Education, 121*(3), 581–588.

Tajfel, H., & Turner, J. C. (1986). The social identity theory of intergroup behavior. In: S. Worchel & W. G. Austin (Eds), *Psychology of intergroup relations,* (2nd ed.) (pp. 7–24). Chicago: Nelson-Hall Publishers.

Taylor, R. J., Chatters, L. M., Jayakody, R., & Levin, J. S. (1996). Black and white differences in religious participation: A multisample comparison. *Journal for the Scientific Study of Religion, 35*(4), 403–410.

Terry, R. W. (1993). *Authentic leadership: Courage in action.* San Francisco: Jossey-Bass.

Thompson, S. (2003). Creating a high-performance school system. *Phi Delta Kappan, 84*(7), 488–496.

Turner, R. B. (2003). *Islam in the African-American experience* (2nd ed.). Bloomington, IN: Indiana University Press.

Tyson, C. J. (2003). Black middle class poverty consciousness: Class and leadership within 20th century Black America. *Harvard Journal of African American Public Policy, 9,* 13–31.

Van Maanen, J. (1988). *Tales of the field: On writing ethnography.* Chicago: University of Chicago Press.

Villani, S. (1999). *Are you sure you're the principal? On being an authentic leader.* Thousand Oaks, CA: Corwin Press.

Wilson, W. J. (1987). *The truly disadvantaged: The inner city, the underclass, and public policy.* Chicago: University of Chicago Press.

Wilson, W. J. (1996). *When work disappears: The world of the new urban poor.* New York: Vintage Books.

Yerkes, D. M., & Guaglianone, C. L. (1998). *Where have all the high school administrators gone? Thrust for Educational Leadership, 28*(2), 10–14.

Young, A. (2001). The United States and Africa: Victory for diplomacy. *Foreign Affairs, 59*(3), 651–652.

FOLLOWER EMOTIONAL REACTIONS TO AUTHENTIC AND INAUTHENTIC LEADERSHIP INFLUENCE

Marie T. Dasborough and Neal M. Ashkanasy

ABSTRACT

We propose a model of authentic leadership based on follower attributions and emotional reactions, where authentic leadership is manifest in perception that the leader's influence is grounded in moral behavior and intentions. Our model is defined in terms of followers' positive and negative emotional reactions following attributions of the leader's intentions. The resulting 2 × 2 model has four cells. The "Unpleasantness" condition (high negative affect, low positive affect), or "Refusal" in the leadership context, is associated with inauthentic leadership; while the "Pleasantness" condition (high positive affect, low negative affect) or "Zealous" in the leadership context, is associated with authentic leadership.

INTRODUCTION

In this chapter, we present a new model of authentic leadership based on the basic proposition that leadership is a process of social interaction (Yukl,

Authentic Leadership Theory and Practice: Origins, Effects and Development
Monographs in Leadership and Management, Volume 3, 281–300
Copyright © 2005 by Elsevier Ltd.

2002). In this instance, the success or otherwise of a leader's attempts to influence followers is determined to a large extent by the cognitive and emotional reactions of the followers to the influence attempt. Humphrey (2002) has argued more specifically that followers' emotional reactions to leadership influence attempts to play a critical role but, to date, this idea has received little attention in the leadership literature. In this respect, Dasborough and Ashkanasy (2002) posited that critical mechanisms of follower responses constitute the followers' attributions of sincere or manipulative intent to the leader, and the resulting emotional reactions the followers' experience. In this chapter, we briefly describe some findings from recent qualitative and quantitative research, and propose a new theory of authentic leadership, based on the nature of followers' emotional reactions to a leader's influence attempt.

We focus in particular on the processes that differentiate authentic from inauthentic leadership influence. Authentic leadership is an emerging theory of leadership, which has been initiated partly due to recent cases of inauthentic leadership highlighted in the press (e.g. Enron). Authentic leaders are those who "are deeply aware of how they think and behave and are perceived by others as being aware of their own and others' values/moral perspectives, knowledge, and strengths; (and are) aware of the context in which they operate" (Avolio, Luthans, & Walumbwa, 2003, p. 4; see also Avolio, Gardner, Walumbwa, Luthans, & May, 2004). This broad definition suggests that authentic leadership can appropriately be examined from the perspective of leader behaviors, as well as follower attributions of these behaviors. These attributions are determined by follower perceptions of leader transparency, leader openness, and trust; leader guidance toward worthy objectives; and leader emphasis on follower development (Gardner, Avolio, Luthans, May, & Walumbwa, 2005).

Authentic Leader Motives: Ethical and Moral

In view of the ethical corporate meltdowns of recent years, the spotlight has shifted to leader authenticity, ethicality, morality, and integrity (Gardner & Schermerhorn, 2004; Lorenzi, 2004; May, Chan, Hodges, & Avolio, 2003; Gardner et al., 2005). As a result, the neocharismatic (House & Aditya, 1997) and new leadership (Bryman, 1992) paradigms have teamed with the positive psychology movement (see Gardner & Schermerhorn, 2004), shifting the focus to ethical and moral leadership. Transformational leadership in particular, has been criticized by some who think it is unethical, because "the rhetoric may appeal to emotions rather than reason" (Bass & Steidlmeier,

1999, p. 211). Further, charismatic leadership also has a dark side – the potential for personalized charismatic types (Gardner et al., 2005).

It appears moreover that the major factor determining if a leader is authentic or moral is the locus of the leader's motivation. Lubit (2002) presents two case studies of destructively narcissistic managers. Narcissism can aid a manager's rise to the top of the organization, owing to the leader's self-confidence and drive for power, but can be destructive when the leader does not respect others' rights and becomes arrogant, devaluing, and exploitative in interactions with others. Clearly, this sort of behavior has consequences for followers, who observe the leader's behavior and draw conclusions about the nature of the leadership they see. This is the focus of the theory we develop in the following paragraphs.

We argue that a follower's attribution of a leader's intentions constitute the most critical determinant of authenticity perceptions. As Cooper, Scandura, and Schriesheim (2005) explain, if followers do not perceive that the leader is trying to enact positive psychological states, then they will not perceive the leader as being authentic (regardless of the leader's true intentions). To be perceived by followers as being authentic, leaders must display exemplary behaviors, resulting in attributions that she/he is trustworthy, morally worthy or responsible, and possesses a high degree of integrity (Gardner & Avolio, 1998).

In this respect, Bass and Steidlmeier (1999) argue that authentic leadership must be grounded in moral behavior and intentions. This is in contrast to inauthentic leadership, where the leader sets out to manipulate followers for the leader's own self-serving purposes, which may or may not be ethical. Inauthentic leaders fail to recognize moral dilemmas, do not have transparent evaluations of alternatives, and do not intend to act authentically in the first place (May et al., 2003). In particular, inauthentic leadership is characterized by the leader's self-centered motivation in place of a focus on the needs of the organization and its stakeholders (see Conger, 1990). From a follower's perspective, therefore, it is important that they can recognize when their leader is manifesting inauthentic behaviors. As Weierter (1997) noted, followers track the behaviors and expressions of their leaders in order to decide what type of leader they are following and whether they should be following the leader in the first instance.

Attribution and Emotion

The theoretical basis of our model can be found in attribution theory (Green & Mitchell, 1979; Mitchell, Green, & Wood, 1981; Weiner, 1985; Martinko,

1995, 2004) and affective events theory (Weiss & Cropanzano, 1996). Both of these theories have been proposed as having potential to explain leadership processes (e.g., see Ashforth & Humphrey, 1995; Ashkanasy, 2003a; Ashkanasy & Tse, 2000; Dasborough & Ashkanasy, 2002), in that they attempt to model the cognitive and affective elements of leadership as seen from the perspective of followers.

Attribution Theory
Attribution theory is based on Heider's (1958) concept of the "naïve scientist," where people unconsciously form and test hypotheses as a means to understand the causes of their own and others' behavior. Ferris, Bhawuk, Fedor, and Judge (1995) have noted in particular that people search for the intentions or motives underlying behavior. Ferris and his colleagues presented their model in a general organizational context, where organizational members play the role of observers who perceive an actor's behavior, and then attribute motives that in turn determine the member's behavior. Applying this model to leadership, Dasborough and Ashkanasy (2002) argued that followers' attributions of a leader's intention are a critical determinant of the follower's subsequent attitudes toward the leader. Dasborough and Ashkanasy's model was positioned in the transformational leadership domain, and distinguished between true transformational leaders and pseudo-transformational leaders.

In this respect, transformational leaders are those who transform followers and organizations, through intellectual stimulation, inspirational motivation, individualized consideration, and idealized influence (Bass, 1998). On the one hand, "true" transformational leaders exhibit behaviors that are moral and ethical, and demonstrate sincere intentions (thus, true transformational leaders are authentic leaders). On the other hand, as Dasborough and Ashkanasy (2002) explain, "pseudo" transformational leaders manifest insincere, unethical, and immoral intentions. These leaders are not authentic; they are using their transformational skills for self-serving purposes. May et al. (2003) explain further that, while authentic leaders may not necessarily display transformational, visionary, or charismatic behaviors, such leadership is still fundamental to all positive forms of leadership. We therefore argue that, to be a true transformational leader, a leader must first be seen to be authentic. Thus, only after a moral foundation for the leader's behavior is established in the eyes of followers can the leader be labeled as a "true" transformational leader.

It follows that attributions of intention are important determinants of followers' perceptions and cognitive/affective reactions to their leader's behaviors, especially when the leader is attempting to influence followers to behave according to the leader's wishes (Dasborough & Ashkanasy, 2002). In this sense, transformational leaders entice followers to join them in achieving their visionary goals and motivate followers to behave in a way that contributes to the leader's overall organizational plan (Ashkanasy & Tse, 2000). A follower's commitment to the leader's vision depends on a leader's capacity for building trust with the followers (Yukl, 2002). Trust is therefore also an important variable to consider when evaluating the impact of charismatic/transformational leadership (Bass, 1998). If a leader is seen to be authentic, followers are likely to perceive their leader to be trustworthy, genuine, and reliable (May et al., 2003).

Affective Events Theory
The second theoretical foundation of our model is Affective Events Theory (Weiss & Cropanzano, 1996). In this theory, "affective events" constitute the everyday hassles and uplifts that employees experience at work. Leaders are thus seen to be a major source of these hassles and uplifts (Dasborough & Ashkanasy, 2003; Gaddis, Connelly, & Mumford, 2004). In essence, employees experience emotional reactions to these hassles and uplifts that then determine their direct behaviors as well as their attitudes. For example, an employee subject to an ongoing series of hassles at work, especially from superiors, is likely to act spontaneously in an antisocial way (Ashkanasy & Daus, 2002), and to form a negative opinion of the organization and its management. Conversely, an employee experiencing positive feedback from a leader is likely to experience an affective uplift, and therefore is going to be more likely to help other employees, and to harbor favorable attitudes toward the organization (Dasborough & Ashkanasy, 2003). These arguments fit in with Ashkanasy's (2003a) multilevel theory of emotion. In this model, emotion is present across all levels of the organization, for example, from individual affective events, through individual differences and to relationships between leaders and followers.

Authentic leadership has also been associated with various positive psychological states. Avolio et al. (2004) and Gardner et al. (2005) argue that authentic leaders are confident, hopeful, and optimistic. If authentic leaders do feel and display such positive psychological states, they are likely to foster positive follower emotions, which can be transferred to other followers through emotional contagion (see Barsade, 2002; Gaddis et al., 2004). Gardner and Schermerhorn (2004) explain how authentic leaders build follower confidence through increasing their followers' self-efficacy. They build follower hope through establishing follower feelings of competency, and setting achievable goals. Authentic leaders also transform pessimistic followers into optimistic followers through training and development (Gardner & Schermerhorn, 2004). Clearly, authentic leaders are associated with arousing positive follower emotions and avoiding negative emotions.

The ability to arouse emotions in others is linked to the concept of emotional intelligence. It has been argued that emotional intelligence contributes to organizational leadership (Cherniss & Adler, 2001; Goleman, 1998; Mayer, Salovey, & Caruso, 2000). Emotional intelligence is defined as "the ability to perceive and express emotions, assimilate emotion in thought, understand and reason with emotion, and regulate emotions in the self and others" (Mayer et al., 2000, p. 396). Given that these abilities influence social interactions, it is clear that emotional intelligence has implications for organizational relationships, and leader – follower relationships in particular (see Goleman, 1998; Cooper & Sawaf, 1997).

Emotions are considered to be reactions to interpersonal evaluations (Weiner, Graham, & Chandler, 1982). Although attributions are cognitive in nature, they are linked to affective outcomes (Weiner, 1977). Weiner was the first to argue that locus of causality influences the affective or emotional consequences of achievement outcomes. Smith, Haynes, Lazarus, and Pope (1993) note further that attributions of intentionality lead even more directly than locus of causality to emotional reactions. This has been demonstrated empirically in studies by Leon and Hernandez (1998) and Betancourt and Blair (1992). Thus, our model of authentic leadership is cognitive and emotional in nature, utilizing both attribution theory and affective events theory as a base.

EMPIRICAL STUDIES

In the following section of this chapter, we briefly describe two studies that have recently been undertaken as a means to understand better the processes of follower cognitive and emotional reactions to authentic and inauthentic leadership influence. First, we explore how leader behavior evokes emotional reactions in followers (Study 1). Then, to determine the cause of the emotional reactions, Study 2 explores the attributions made about leader behaviors.

Study 1: A Qualitative Investigation of Follower Emotional Reactions to Leadership Influence

The aim of this exploratory study, described in detail in Dasborough and Ashkanasy (2003), was to investigate research questions relating to the nature of affective employee reactions to leadership influence attempts. In line with Affective Events Theory, we anticipated that leader behavior would bring about emotional responses in followers. The specific purpose of this study was to determine what kinds of leader behaviors prompted negative emotions in their followers, and was based on the notion that negative emotions have more serious consequences on organizations.

In the study, focus groups were conducted with 24 employees from three organizations. Half the participants were females. The organizations were selected at random and participants from these organizations were invited to participate. Participants ranged from 19 to 50 years of age, and held various positions in the organizational hierarchy (e.g., job titles are: junior secretary, marketing coordinator, accounts officer, etc.).

The interviewer asked the participants to describe in as much detail as possible an "emotional interaction" they have had with their leader at work. Participants could report positive or negative interactions. Content analysis was utilized to identify critical patterns in the responses (Larsson, 1993), with particular attention paid to leader behaviors that prompted negative emotional responses. The sentences in the interview transcripts were coded for the leader behavior, the follower's emotional response, and the outcome of the interaction. The content analysis was conducted using NUD*IST (Qualitative Solutions and Research, Non-numerical Unstructured Data Indexing Searching and Theorizing) software.

Findings indicated that, when leaders displayed inappropriate behaviors as perceived by the followers, followers experienced negative emotions such as anger and frustration. Inappropriate behaviors were those behaviors that followers did not expect of an "ideal leader," or behaviors that surprised them given their own leaders' behavior in the past. Examples of leader behavior that was perceived by followers as inappropriate included the leader giving instructions, but failing to provide sufficient information for successful execution of the task. Some employees reported feeling that they were "out of the loop" on daily issues; others reported that their leader "does not let us know what is happening with the unit as a whole." These employees reported feeling frustrated and, especially in cases where they were not given specific information required for the job, they reported feeling agitated and angry with their leader.

Another leader behavior that initiated negative responses was a lack of confidence in employees. Employees reported "she wants to do it all herself and doesn't feel comfortable with others doing it, she does not trust us." Further, leaders who failed to act as role models, or "do as they said," were also associated with negative emotional responses such as disappointment.

Some employees reported that they did not think their manager had the "hands-on skills" required for work in their departmental area. Finally, perceptions of the leader's intentions were also considered important. For example, one employee commented that "there is no motivation other than client fees – you know, the dollar sign." When employees perceived their leaders to be focused only on financial gain, they felt disappointed and in some cases disgusted with their leader's intentions.

The above summary of findings highlights some of the leader behaviors that bring about negative emotional responses in employees. These behaviors are consistent with the behaviors we would expect from a leader who is not authentic. Authentic leaders are transparent (May et al., 2003), and they do not withhold information from employees. Authentic leaders build employee confidence and self-efficacy; they create hope and optimism, and they strengthen resilience (Gardner & Schermerhorn, 2004). When authentic leaders show trust in employees, these employees reciprocate with trust in their leader. Leading by example, or exemplification, is highly important for successful leadership (House & Aditya, 1997). In this sense, only those leaders who are perceived as authentic as well as capable will be considered worthy of imitation by followers. Thus, and as Dasborough and Ashkanasy (2002) note, attributions of leader intentionality are critical. Consistent with May et al. (2003), authentic leaders come to be perceived by their followers as acting morally and ethically, and with sincere intentions.

In summary of Study 1, the leaders who prompted negative emotional responses in employees did not show these authentic qualities. It was thus their lack of authentic behaviors that bought about the negative emotional responses in their followers.

Study 2: A Laboratory Investigation of Follower Cognitive and Emotional Reactions to Leadership Influence

Study 1 shed light on the emotional impact of inauthentic leadership behaviors within workplace settings. Study 2 was designed to build upon the findings in Study 1, by enabling us to learn more about the cognitive basis for these emotional reactions through an experimental design. In Study 2, reported in detail in Dasborough and Ashkanasy (2004), 137 undergraduate students first viewed a video of a leader making an appeal for extra effort to organizational members; ostensibly behaving in a charismatic, transformational manner, and appealing to organizationally focused goals. The video was based on a video developed by Awamleh and Gardner (1999), designed to depict a highly charismatic leader (high vision/strong delivery).

Following, the video, participants received an e-mail, purportedly from the same leader, asking them to invest extra effort in the company (this email was printed out and handed to participants individually). There were two versions of the email; one worded in terms of self ("I"), and the other in terms of organizational goals ("we"). In effect, the content of the email manipulated authentic leadership. The leader in the video displayed organizationally focused behaviors, so the participants would be likely to expect the same behavior to be reflected in the email. In cases of the "we" email, the video and email both focused on the organization, so that the leader would be perceived to be acting authentically (May et al., 2003). In the inauthentic "I" email, however, there was a mismatch between the messages in the email and the video. While the leader in the video spoke of "our organization" that "we" can work hard for, the email from the inauthentic leader contradicted these views. Based on the arguments of Gardner et al. (2005), we expected therefore that this inconsistency between word and deed would result in follower perceptions of leader inauthenticity.

Immediately following the video and email, participants responded to measures of attribution of intent, labeling of the leader as transformational, positive and negative affective reactions, trust in the leader, intention to comply with the leader's request, and future behavioral intentions (see Dasborough & Ashkanasy, 2004 for details of the measures). We anticipated that the results would conform to the model proposed by Dasborough and Ashkanasy (2002), where follower perceptions of leader behavior result in (1) attributions of the leader's intentions (sincere vs. manipulative), (2) an emotional reaction to the leader's influence attempt, (3) labeling of the leader as transformational, and (4) trust (or otherwise) in the leader. These reactions, in turn, were anticipated to predict the follower's intention to comply with the leader's request, and the follower's future behavioral intentions to work for the advancement of the organization.

Following an exploratory factor analysis, a confirmatory factor analysis was conducted as a more rigorous simultaneous assessment of convergent and discriminant validity (Bradfield & Aquino, 1999) of measures. The analysis examined the fit of a model in which measures of all the items (i.e., attributions, positive emotions, negative emotions, labeling, trust, and future behavioral intentions) loaded on their respective factors. Dasborough and Ashkanasy (2004) analyzed the model using structural equation modeling, and found good fit for the model illustrated schematically in Fig. 1. Chi-square and fit statistics (GFI, CFI, AGFI, RMSR, and RMSEA) all within the normally accepted tolerances (see Dasborough & Ashkanasy, 2004, for further details).

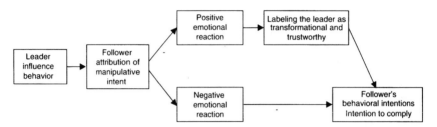

Fig. 1.   Results of Study 2 (schematic outline).

In a nutshell, results showed that the followers' perceptions of the leader's authentic or inauthentic influence attempts led to attributions that the leader was being manipulative or sincere. This attribution of intent resulted in turn in positive and negative affective reactions to the leader. Importantly, the study found that positive affective reactions were associated with attitudes to the leader, including viewing the leader as transformational and trustworthy. Thus, positive affective reactions had an *indirect* effect on follower willingness to comply with the leader's request and the followers' future behavioral intentions. In effect, the effects of positive emotions on the dependent variables were mediated by labeling of the leader as transformational and trustworthy. By contrast, negative affective reactions were found to have a *direct* effect on the dependent variables.

These findings can be explained by Fredrickson's broaden-and-build model (2001, p. 218), which posits that experiences of positive emotions broaden people's momentary thought–action repertoires, which then builds their personal resources (e.g. intellectual resources, social resources, etc.). Fredrickson (2001) argues that, while positive emotions broaden and build, negative emotions actually narrow the thought–action repertoire. Here, in contrast to the effects of positive emotion, negative emotion results in a more direct focus on action outcomes.

In summary, Study 2 explored the process of follower attribution formation and emotional reactions to authentic and inauthentic leader behaviors. In the case of authentic leadership, where the leader was sending congruent, organizationally focused messages, followers attributed sincere intentions resulting in positive affect; they consequently reported increased trust in the leader and labeled the leader as transformational, and were thus more likely to comply with requests made by the authentic leader. When the leader was seen to be inauthentic, manifesting mixed messages, followers attributed manipulative intentions resulting in negative affect; and were less likely to comply with requests made by the inauthentic leader.

A NEW THEORY OF AUTHENTIC LEADERSHIP BASED ON FOLLOWER AFFECTIVE REACTIONS

Overall, the two studies provide evidence in support of the model of leader intentionality and emotions proposed earlier by Dasborough and Ashkanasy (2002), and shed new light on the notion of authentic leadership. The leader's influence attempts in these studies appear to have generated an affective event for followers, and consistent with affective events theory, the affective events lead to attitudinal and behavioral consequences for followers. In particular, and consistent with attribution theory (Green & Mitchell, 1979; Weiner, 1985), results of both studies sustain the notion that affective reactions to a leader's influence attempts are associated with the followers' attributions of sincere versus manipulative leader motives. Importantly, the consequences of positive and negative emotional reactions were shown to act through different channels, as argued by Fredrickson's (2001) broaden-and-build theory. Positive affect appears to work through cognitive processes of labeling and trust (as suggested by Dasborough & Ashkanasy, 2002, and consistent with Isen & Baron, 1991), while negative affective reactions appear to have a more direct effect on behavioral intentions.

In interpreting these results, it is important to understand that positive and negative affect do not constitute poles of a unidimensional continuum. Watson and Tellegan (1985), for example, proposed a taxonomy of affect based on the "Affect Circumplex," which they defined in terms of orthogonal dimensions of positive and negative affect. This idea is consistent with the results of Study 2, where positive and negative emotional responses to the leader's influence were significantly and negatively correlated. Based on the idea of orthogonal dimensions of positive and negative affect, therefore, we propose a new model of follower reaction to leadership influence, illustrated in Fig. 2.

The model we propose is defined in terms of four quadrants, which we have labeled according to the Watson and Tellegan (1985) circumplex. Also shown in the figure are the number of participants who were categorized in each quadrant based on a median split of positive and negative affect scores, together with corresponding mean scores and standard deviations for labeling (as a transformational leader) and intention to comply with the leader's request. Most of the participants in our study were in the upper right (authentic leadership) and lower left (inauthentic leadership) quadrants of the figure, reflecting the negative correlation between positive and negative affect we noted above. Note, however, that a significant minority were in the other quadrants.

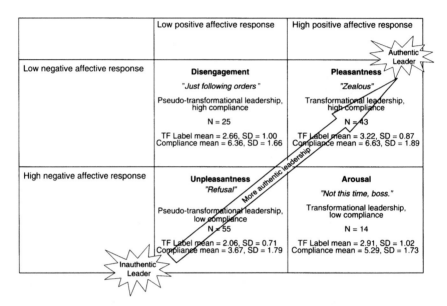

Fig. 2. A New Model of Leadership Based on Follower Positive and Negative Affective Reactions to Authentic and Inauthentic Leadership Influence.

To test the prediction that the quadrants in Fig. 2 will predict followers' labeling of the leader and intention to comply, we employed a two-way ANOVA with high and low positive and negative affect groups defined by a median split. Separate ANOVAs were conducted for labeling and intention to comply. We expected to find that labeling would be higher for higher levels of positive affect, and compliance would be lower for higher levels of negative affect.

Results were a main effect of positive affect for both label, $F(1, 133) = 17.77$, $p < 0.01$, eta-squared $= 0.12$; and for compliance, $F(1, 133) = 7.21$, $p < 0.01$, eta-squared $= 0.05$. Similarly, a main effect was evident on negative affect for both label, $F(1, 133) = 7.33$, $p < 0.01$, eta-squared $= 0.05$; and for compliance, $F(1, 133) = 33.10$, $p < 0.01$, eta-squared $= 0.20$. The respective interactions were not significant, $F(1, 133) = 0.77$ and 3.67. The strong eta-squared values for the main effects of positive affect on labeling and negative affect on compliance suggest that it would be appropriate to categorize the groupings in each quadrant according to the Watson and Tellegan (1985) circumplex, as we discuss in the following paragraphs.

Beginning with the upper-right quadrant in the figure, we see that this corresponds to Watson and Tellegan's "Pleasantness" condition, where followers act "zealously." In this instance, followers experience high positive affect and low negative affect. They view the leader as transformational (high positive affect) and are motivated to do what the leader asks (low negative affect). We associate this condition with *authentic* leadership behavior because it embodies transformational leadership that is accepted by followers as legitimate and positive. In this instance, and consistent with theory (e.g., May et al., 2003) leaders who display authentic behavior evoke high positive emotion and low negative emotion in their followers.

Moving to the upper-left quadrant, we find that this matches Watson and Tellegan's (1985) "Disengagement" condition. Here, positive and negative affective reactions to the leader's request are both low. The follower, in this situation, experiences low positive affect, and therefore does not see the leader to be transformational. At the same time, negative affect is low, and the follower is inclined to comply with the leader's request. In effect, the follower is "just following orders." In this condition, we cannot predict if the leader is perceived by followers as being an authentic or inauthentic leader. Although followers will most likely perceive the leader to be either authentic or inauthentic, in this condition we cannot make a prediction due to the low emotional response of the follower to the leader.

In the lower-left quadrant, we find that the follower here experiences low positive affect and with high negative affect, matching Watson and Tellegan's (1985) "Unpleasantness" condition. The leader in this instance is seen as pseudo-transformational (low positive affect) and the follower refuses to comply with the leader's request (high negative affect). We have therefore represented this situation as the follower's "refusal to comply." This condition is associated with *inauthentic* leadership because the leader displays the characteristics of a pseudo-transformational leader, and followers question the legitimacy of the leader's requests. We argue that leaders who are inauthentic will evoke strong negative emotional reactions, and low positive emotional reactions. This is the worst case scenario for organizations, as inauthentic leaders will be unable to achieve organizational goals because of a lack of trust and support from followers.

Finally, in the lower-right quadrant, we find high negative affect and high positive affect occur simultaneously. This matches the "Arousal" condition in the Watson and Tellegan's (1985) circumplex. Clearly, this would be unusual, but not impossible (see Larsen, McGraw, & Cacioppo, 2001). One interpretation of this finding is that the followers may see the leader as transformational (high positive affect), but experience at the same time high negative affect, resulting in our characterization of this situation as, "Not this time, boss." Under this scenario, the follower is in a quandary; in some ways the leader appears authentic, but in other ways (i.e., the nature of the request) appears inauthentic. Larsen et al. (2001) describe such equivocation as rare and at best unstable. In this case, a repetition of this behavior on the behalf of the leader would be likely to lead followers to the conclusion that the leader is, in fact, inauthentic.

LIMITATIONS

Although the findings from Study 1 are limited because of the small sample size, Study 2 suffers from greater concerns over external validity. Laboratory studies have long been criticized due to the potential for participants to not attribute the same meaning to variables of interest as participants would in field settings (Ilgen, 1986). Nevertheless, Locke (1986) and Mook (1983) maintain that results of laboratory studies generalize surprisingly well from the laboratory to the field, especially in psychological research. Further, as argued by Murphy, Herr, Lockhart, and Maguire (1986), the use of an artificial leader displaying behavior through a written scenario allows for more powerful manipulations of experimental variables (stronger signals) and less ambiguity in the task of responding to the leader (less noise). Validity is also threatened through the use of a student sample (Robson, 1994). In the instance of attributions and emotional reactions, however, which represent basic brain processes, there is no reason to believe that similar reactions would not occur in the workplace. Further, Judd, Smith, and Kidder (1991) have argued that, for most psychological research, student samples are not functionally different from other samples.

With regards to leader authenticity, we acknowledge that we have not measured perceived leader authenticity in this study. Although we have drawn inferences about leader authenticity, these inferences are based on follower attributions of leader intentions. Although we acknowledge this as a limitation, we believe nonetheless that, by measuring follower attributions of leader intentions and their emotional responses to their attributions, we have effectively tapped into the concept of leader authenticity. Future research, however, would do well to measure perceived authenticity of leaders for a more direct assessment of this phenomenon.

Finally, we note that our study was based on subjective, self-report measures of all but one of our variables. This leaves open the possibility that our results could be subject to common methods bias (Podsakoff, MacKenzie, Lee, & Podsakoff, 2003). We utilized different scale formats, for example a faces scale, likert scales, and semantic differential scales, to minimize these effects. In addition, a confirmatory factor analysis indicated that our measures were tapping distinct constructs. Nonetheless, we acknowledge that use of objective measures (e.g., third-person ratings) would provide a stronger hedge against this bias.

To shed more light on the issue of attributions and emotional reactions to authentic leadership influence, future research should be conducted in field settings. The examination of actual responses to real organizational leaders would be valuable, particularly if follower performance could be assessed also.

IMPLICATIONS FOR LEADERSHIP RESEARCH AND AUTHENTIC LEADERSHIP DEVELOPMENT

Although preliminary, the model we propose has implications for leadership theory and practice, and also for authentic leadership development. First and foremost, we believe that the results of both studies outlined in this chapter further confirm the emerging view that emotion plays a central role in leadership processes, especially from the follower's perspective. In this instance, our research provides additional substance in support of Ashforth and Humphrey's (1995) position that leadership research needs to include affect dimensions. Moreover, this conclusion underlines the need for authentic leaders to take direct account of emotions in making decisions that impact their subordinates' well-being.

Our studies also lend support to Ashkanasy's (2003a) multilevel theory of emotion. In this model, emotion is viewed as an integrating mechanism that links attitudes and behaviors across levels of organization from individual affective events, through individual differences and relationships between leaders and followers, to the group level, and even the organization as a whole (see also Ashkanasy, 2003b). The research that we describe here includes elements at each of these levels.

Our findings demonstrate that leaders evoke follower emotions. A corollary of this is that it must also be important to consider the emotional intelligence of the leader. In this respect, leader emotional intelligence has been associated with elements of essential leadership (see George, 2000), increased performance (Goleman, 1998), leadership emergence in self-managing teams, follower attitude and performance (Wong & Law, 2002), and creativity (Zhou & George, 2003). Emotional intelligence has also been studied in the team context; for example, Wolff, Pescosolido, and Druskat (2002) argued that emotional intelligence influences the emergence of informal leaders in groups. Similar to Gardner et al. (2005), we argue therefore that leader emotional intelligence may enable authentic leaders to promote positive employee responses and minimize negative responses. Thus, authentic leadership development may be enhanced through emotional intelligence training. Future research should consider the association between leader emotional intelligence, leader authenticity, and follower outcomes.

In summary, the findings of this research have clear implications for the emerging theory of authentic leadership. In particular, our results make it clear that scholars should at least consider very carefully whether an affective dimension needs to be included in theoretical and empirical work. We argue that authentic leadership will always bring about strong positive emotional responses in followers, insofar as this kind of leadership is at the base of all positive, socially constructive forms of leadership (May et al., 2003; Avolio et al., 2004; Gardner et al., 2005). We hope that our initial attempts to explore emotional responses to authentic leadership will motivate future studies along the same path. Further, with respect to positive psychology, our findings support the broaden-and-build theory of positive emotion (Fredrickson, 2001), and provide a preliminary empirical link between positive psychology and authentic leadership.

Turning now to the practice of leadership, we argue that the studies we describe in this chapter demonstrate clearly the importance of attributional processes as determinants of follower attitudes and behavior in response to authentic and inauthentic leadership influence. After all, it is the attributions of the leader intentions that evoke the emotional responses in followers. The implication here is that authentic leaders need to understand the impact of their influence attempts on their followers, and the cognitive and affective consequences of their demands. Authentic leaders need to be sensitive especially to the way that their followers perceive their behavior and, if necessary, to be prepared to take positive action to correct inaccurate employee perceptions of their intentions (see also Gardner et al., 2005). As May et al. (2003) suggest, because leadership is a socially constructed process, the critical issue is not necessarily the substance of the leader's actions. Instead, it is clear from our research that the way an authentic leader's followers perceive the leader's behavior can be at least as important, if not more so. In this instance, it seems sensible for authentic leaders to take a little time to explain to their followers just why they are requesting certain behaviors.

Finally, and consistent with Ashkanasy's (2003a) multilevel model, follower attributions of leader intentionality may also have considerable impact on the organization as a whole. Perceptions of leaders, especially senior leaders, by their followers are a vital tenet of organizational culture (Schein, 2004). In this instance, perceptions of followers that a leader lacks authenticity can be expected to reflect on the organization as a whole, leading to lowered morale and finished performance. Conversely, when leaders are seen by followers to be authentic, the organization as a whole will benefit.

In conclusion, our findings reinforce the central role that emotions and attributions play in defining the nature of authentic leadership. In the case of authentic leadership, our results suggest that that positive emotions associated with attributions of sincere intentions bring about increased trust in the leader, follower perceptions that the leader is transformational, and increased compliance with leader requests. This highlights the practical benefits of authentic leader behavior, supporting the assertions of Gardner and Schermerhorn (2004), who suggest that performance gains will be made if leaders are authentic. Given that enhancing organizational performance is an ideal, surely, all leaders should strive to find their authentic selves, and organizations should ensure those promoted to higher-level positions are capable of embodying authentic leadership.

ACKNOWLEDGMENT

We would like to express our appreciation to Bill Gardner, Bruce Avolio, and Fred Walumbwa and the anonymous reviewers for their assistance and insightful comments on the earlier drafts of this chapter.

REFERENCES

Ashforth, R. E., & Humphrey, R. H. (1995). Emotion in the workplace: A reappraisal. *Human Relations, 48,* 97–125.

Ashkanasy, N. M. (2003a). Emotions in organizations: A multilevel perspective. In: F. Dansereau & F. J. Yammarino (Eds), *Research in multi-level issues, Vol. 2: Multi-level issues in organizational behavior and strategy* (pp. 9–54). Oxford, UK: Elsevier Science.

Ashkanasy, N. M. (2003b). Emotions at multiple levels: An integration. In: F. Dansereau & F. J. Yammarino (Eds), *Research in multi-level issues, Vol. 2: Multi-level issues in organizational behavior and strategy* (pp. 71–81). Oxford, UK: Elsevier Science.

Ashkanasy, N. M., & Daus, S. D. (2002). Emotion in the workplace: The new challenge for managers. *Academy of Management Executive, 16,* 76–86.

Ashkanasy, N. M., & Tse, B. (2000). Transformational leadership as management of emotion: A conceptual review. In: N. M. Ashkanasy, C. E. J. Härtel & W. J. Zerbe (Eds), *Emotions in working life: Theory, research and practice* (pp. 221–235). Westport, CT: Quorum Books.

Avolio, B. J., Gardner, W. L., Walumbwa, F. O., Luthans, F., & May, D. R. (2004). Unlocking the mask: A look at the process by which authentic leaders impact follower attitudes and behaviors. *The Leadership Quarterly, 15,* 801–823.

Avolio, B. J., Luthans, F., & Walumbwa, F. O. (2003). *Authentic leadership: Theory-building for verifiable sustained performance.* Working Paper, University of Nebraska.

Awamleh, R., & Gardner, W. L. (1999). Perceptions of leader charisma and effectiveness: The effects of vision, content, delivery and organizational performance. *The Leadership Quarterly, 10,* 345–373.

Barsade, S. G. (2002). The ripple effect: Emotional contagion and its influence on work groups. *Administrative Science Quarterly, 47,* 644–675.

Bass, B. M. (1998). *Transformational leadership: Industrial, military, and educational impact.* Mahwah, NJ: Lawrence Erlbaum Associates.

Bass, B. M., & Steidlmeier, P. (1999). Ethics, character, and authentic transformational leadership behavior. *The Leadership Quarterly, 10,* 181–217.

Betancourt, H., & Blair, I. (1992). A cognition(attribution)-emotion model of violence in conflict situations. *Personality and Social Psychology Bulletin, 18,* 343–350.

Bradfield, M., & Aquino, K. (1999). The effects of blame attributions and offender likeableness on forgiveness and revenge in the workplace. *Journal of Management, 25,* 607–631.

Bryman, A. (1992). The new leadership and charisma. *Charisma and leadership in organizations* (pp. 91–114). London: Sage Publications.

Cherniss, C., & Adler, M. (2001). *Promoting emotional intelligence in organizations.* Alexandria, VA: American Society for Training & Development (ASTD).

Conger, J. A. (1990). The dark side of leadership. *Organizational Dynamics, 19,* 44–55.

Cooper, C. D., Scandura, T. A., & Schriesheim, C. A. (2005). Looking forward but learning from our past: Potential challenges to developing authentic leadership theory and authentic leaders. *The Leadership Quarterly, 16,* 475–493.

Cooper, R. K., & Sawaf, A. (1997). *Executive EQ: Emotional intelligence in leadership & organizations.* New York: Grosser/Putnam.

Dasborough, M. T., & Ashkanasy, N. M. (2002). Emotion and attribution of intentionality in leader–member relationships. *The Leadership Quarterly, 13,* 615–634.

Dasborough, M. T., & Ashkanasy, N. M. (2003). Leadership and affective events: How uplifts can ameliorate employee hassles. In: C. Cherrey, J. J. Gardner & N. Huber (Eds), *Building leadership bridges,* (Vol. 3, pp. 58–72). College Park, MD: James MacGregor Burns Academy of Leadership.

Dasborough, M. T., & Ashkanasy, N. M. (2004). Responses to leadership behavior: The role of follower attributions of intentionality and affective reactions. Paper presented at the Annual Meetings of the Academy of Management, New Orleans, U.S.A.

Ferris, G. R., Bhawuk, D. P. S., Fedor, D. B., & Judge, T. A. (1995). Organizational politics and citizenship: Attributions of intentionality and construct definition. In: M. J. Martinko (Ed.), *Advances in attribution theory: An organizational perspective* (pp. 231–252). Delray Beach, FL: St. Lucie Press.

Fredrickson, B. L. (2001). The role of positive emotions in positive psychology: The broaden-and-build theory of positive emotions. *American Psychologist, 56,* 218–226.

Gaddis, B., Connelly, S., & Mumford, M. D. (2004). Failure feedback as an affective event: Influences of leader affect on subordinate attitudes and performance. *The Leadership Quarterly, 15,* 663–686.

Gardner, W. L., & Avolio, B. J. (1998). The charismatic relationship: A dramaturgical perspective. *Academy of Management Review, 23,* 32–58.

Gardner, W. L., Avolio, B. J., Luthans, F., May, D. R., & Walumbwa, F. O. (2005). "Can you see the real me?" A self-based model of authentic leader and follower development. *The Leadership Quarterly, 16,* 373–394.

Gardner, W. L., & Schermerhorn, J. R. (2004). Unleashing individual potential: Performance gains through positive organizational behavior and authentic leadership. *Organization Dynamics, 33,* 270–281.

George, J. M. (2000). Emotions and leadership: The role of emotional intelligence. *Human Relations, 53,* 1027–1055.

Goleman, D. (1998). *Working with emotional intelligence.* New York: Bantam.

Green, S. G., & Mitchell, T. R. (1979). Attributional processes in leader-member interactions. *Organizational Behavior and Human Performance, 23,* 429–458.

Heider, F. (1958). *The psychology of interpersonal relations.* New York: Wiley.

House, R. J., & Aditya, R. N. (1997). *The social scientific study of leadership: Quo vadis? Journal of Management, 23,* 409–473.

Humphrey, R. H. (2002). The many faces of emotional leadership. *The Leadership Quarterly, 13,* 493–504.

Ilgen, D. R. (1986). Laboratory Research: A question of when, not if. In: E. Locke (Ed.), *Generalizing from laboratory to field settings.* Toronto, ON: Health.

Isen, A. M., & Baron, R. A. (1991). Positive affect as a factor in organizational behavior. *Research in Organizational Behavior, 13,* 1–53.

Judd, C. M., Smith, E. R., & Kidder, L. H. (1991). *Research methods in social relations.* Fort Worth, TX: Holt, Rinehart, & Winston.

Larsen, J. T., McGraw, A. P., & Cacioppo, J. T. (2001). *Can people feel happy and sad at the same time? Journal of Personality and Social Psychology, 81,* 684–696.

Larsson, R. (1993). Case survey methodology: Quantitative analysis of patterns across case studies. *Academy of Management Journal, 36,* 1515–1546.

Leon, I., & Hernandez, J. A. (1998). Testing the role of attribution and appraisal in predicting own and other's emotions. *Cognition and Emotion, 12,* 27–43.

Locke, E. A. (1986). *Generalizing from laboratory to field settings.* Lexington, MA: Lexington Books.

Lorenzi, P. (2004). Managing for the common good: Pro-social leadership. *Organizational Dynamics Special: New leadership for a new time, 33,* 282–291.

Lubit, R. (2002). The long-term organizational impact of destructively narcissistic managers. *Academy of Management Executive, 16*(4), 127–138.

Martinko, M. J. (Ed.) (1995). *Attribution theory: An organizational perspective.* Delray Beach, FL: St. Lucie Press.

Martinko, M. J. (Ed.) (2004). *Attribution theory in the organizational sciences: Theoretical and empirical contributions.* Greenwich, CT: Information Age Publishing.

May, D. R., Chan, A. Y. L., Hodges, T. D., & Avolio, B. J. (2003). Developing the moral component of authentic leadership. *Organizational Dynamics, 32*(3), 247–260.

Mayer, J. D., Salovey, P., & Caruso, D. R. (2000). Competing models of emotional intelligence. In: R. J. Sternberg (Ed.), *Handbook of intelligence,* (2nd ed.). Cambridge, UK: Cambridge University Press.

Mitchell, T. R., Green, S. G., & Wood, R. E. (1981). *An attributional model of leadership and the poor-performing subordinate: Development and validation, Research in Organizational Behavior, 3,* 197–234.

Mook, D. M. (1983). In defense of external validity. *American Psychologist, 38,* 379–387.

Murphy, K. R., Herr, B. M., Lockhart, M. C., & Maguire, E. (1986). Evaluating the performance of paper people. *Journal of Applied Psychology, 71,* 654–661.

Podsakoff, P. M., MacKenzie, S. B., Lee, J. Y., & Podsakoff, N. P. (2003). Common method biases in behavioral research: A critical review of the literature and recommended remedies. *Journal of Applied Psychology, 88,* 879–903.

Robson, C. (1994). *Experiment, design and statistics in psychology.* Harmondsworth, UK: Penguin Education.

Schein, E. J. (2004). *Organizational culture and leadership* (3rd ed.). San Francisco: Jossey-Bass.

Smith, C. A., Haynes, K. N., Lazarus, R. S., & Pope, L. K. (1993). In search of 'hot' cognitions: Attributions, appraisals, and their relation to emotion. *Journal of Personality and Social Psychology, 65,* 916–929.

Watson, D., & Tellegan, A. (1985). Towards a consensual structure of mood. *Psychological Bulletin, 98,* 219–235.

Weierter, S. J. M. (1997). Who wants to play "follow the leader?" A theory of charismatic relationships based on routinized charisma and follower characteristics. *The Leadership Quarterly, 8,* 171–193.

Weiner, B. (1977). Attribution and affect: Comments on Sohn's critique. *Journal of Educational Psychology, 69,* 506–511.

Weiner, B. (1985). An attributional theory of achievement motivation and emotion. *Psychological Review, 92,* 548–573.

Weiner, B., Graham, S., & Chandler, C. (1982). Pity, anger, and guilt: An attributional analysis. *Personality and Social Psychology Bulletin, 8,* 226–232.

Weiss, H., & Cropanzano, R. (1996). Affective events theory: A theoretical discussion of the structure, causes and consequences of affective experiences at work. *Research in Organizational Behavior, 18,* 1–79.

Wolff, S. B., Pescosolido, A. T., & Druskat, V. U. (2002). Emotional intelligence as the basis of leadership emergence in self-managing teams. *The Leadership Quarterly, 13,* 505–522.

Wong, C., & Law, K. (2002). The effects of leader and follower emotional intelligence on performance and attitude: An exploratory study. *The Leadership Quarterly, 13,* 243–274.

Yukl, G. (2002). *Leadership in organizations* (5th ed.). Englewood Cliffs, NJ: Prentice-Hall.

Zhou, J., & George, J. M. (2003). Awakening employee creativity: The role of leader emotional intelligence. *The Leadership Quarterly, 14,* 545–568.

PART V:
MOVING FORWARD

RESILIENCY DEVELOPMENT OF ORGANIZATIONS, LEADERS AND EMPLOYEES: MULTI-LEVEL THEORY BUILDING FOR SUSTAINED PERFORMANCE

Carolyn M. Youssef and Fred Luthans

ABSTRACT

The need for understanding the development of resilient organizations, leaders, and employees – those able to adapt, bounce back, and flourish despite adversity – has never been greater. Although receiving attention in clinical psychology, to date little attention has been given to resiliency in the workplace in general and the field of leadership in particular. After first identifying resiliency as a positive psychological state that is open to development, propositions for testing our proposed model's antecedents, mediating factors, and relationships with work attitudes and performance are presented.

Conceptualizing and understanding the significant contribution of resilient organizations, leaders, and employees – those able to survive, adapt, swiftly

Authentic Leadership Theory and Practice: Origins, Effects and Development
Monographs in Leadership and Management, Volume 3, 303–343

bounce back, and flourish despite uncertainty, change, adversity, or even failure – has recently had a surge of interest among management scholars and practitioners (Coutu, 2002; Horne & Orr, 1998; Klarreich, 1998; Luthans, 2002a; Luthans & Avolio, 2003; Mallak, 1998; Reivich & Shatte, 2002; Sutcliffe & Vogus, 2003; Worline, Dutton, Frost, Kanov, Lilius, & Maitlis, 2002). Dealing effectively with the turbulence and uncertainty so far in the 21st century geopolitical, economic, social, and ethical environment may be helped by shifting to an emphasis on proactive endurance and a positive outlook. Highly visible resilient organizations (e.g., Microsoft, Harley-Davidson, United Airlines, or even the Catholic Church) and resilient leaders (e.g., Bill Gates or Jeff Bezos) would be examples.

The positive psychology movement (Keyes & Haidt, 2003; Seligman & Csikentmihalyi, 2000; Sheldon & King, 2001; Snyder & Lopez, 2002), and applications to the workplace such as positive organizational scholarship (POS) (Cameron, Dutton, & Quinn, 2003) and positive organizational behavior (POB) (Luthans, 2002a,b), signify the power of a positive orientation and approach. However, with the exception of these recent positive initiatives, to date, the literature that expands the boundaries of positive psychological capacities to workplace contexts and the field of leadership is still emerging. In particular, resiliency has been given considerable surface recognition, but has not yet been systematically understood, researched, or applied at the organizational level or to authentic leadership development.

In the initial conception of authentic leadership development, resiliency is specifically included as an important antecedent positive psychological capacity ("who I am") of self-awareness (Luthans & Avolio, 2003). Luthans and Avolio (2003, p. 243) note that "the authentic leader is confident, hopeful, optimistic, resilient, transparent, moral/ethical, future-oriented, and gives priority to developing associates to be leaders." In today's unprecedented, turbulent times, this positive psychological capacity of resilience, i.e., the ability to adapt, bounce back, and flourish despite adversity, we would argue is crucial to authentic leadership development.

In this chapter, building on the book's theme on authentic leadership development, we attempt to begin to fill the gap between surface recognition of resiliency and deeper theoretical understanding and direction for future research. In particular, we will propose and support that in "contemporary times, where the environment is dramatically changing, where the rules that have guided how we operate no longer work, and where the best leaders will be transparent with their intentions, having a seamless link between their espoused values, actions, and behaviors" (Luthans & Avolio, 2003, p. 242), resiliency development plays an important role in authentic leadership development. Our purpose is to contribute to theory-building and provide propositions for testing a new, multi-level model, in which organizational, leader, and employee resiliency can be developed, and in turn contribute to authentic leadership development and impact attitudinal and performance outcomes.

DEFINING RESILIENCY AS STATE-LIKE AND OPEN TO DEVELOPMENT

Although resiliency has a long history in child psychotherapy and numerous definitions in that literature (e.g., see Block & Block, 1980), as a dimension of the recently emerging positive psychology movement, Masten and Reed (2002, p. 75) define resiliency as "a class of phenomena characterized by patterns of positive adaptation in the context of significant adversity or risk." At the organizational level, Hamel and Välikangas (2003) define resiliency as the ability to dynamically reinvent business models and strategies as circumstances change.

Recent work from POS, such as Worline et al. (2002) or Klarreich (1998), can be drawn from to define organizational resiliency as "the structural and processual dynamics that allow an organization or a unit to absorb strain and retain coherence and the capacity to bounce back, thus enabling the ongoing engagement of risk." At the individual level, we draw from POB (Luthans, 2002a) to define resiliency as "the developable capacity to rebound or bounce back from adversity, conflict, and failure or even positive events, progress, and increased responsibility." This "bouncing back" capacity involves flexibility, adjustment, adaptability, and continuous responsiveness to change and uncertainty that can otherwise represent a source of psychological strain and challenge one's well-being over the long term.

In line with the above definitions, we support viewing both organizational and individual resiliency as being dynamic and open to change and development, i.e., being state-like. Our definitions do not support resiliency being a deterministic characteristic or what Sutcliffe and Vogus (2003) call "super material" that distinguishes survivors from failures, or an individual difference that is solely determined through genetics or dispositional, trait-like factors (Masten, 2001; Masten & Reed, 2002). As examples of resiliency being open to development, Coutu (2002) recognizes Salvatore R. Maddi, the Director of the Hardiness Institute, on his use of resiliency training and George Vaillant, the Director of the Study of Adult Development at

Harvard Medical School, on how some people become markedly more resilient over their lifetimes. Also, Wolin and Wolin's (2003) Project Resilience, which offers a resiliency assessment and training program, has been
recognized in educational, treatment, and, most importantly, preventative
contexts.

Of particular relevance to our definition and model is the work of Masten
and Reed (2002), who identify three sets of strategies for promoting resiliency development. The first set includes risk-focused strategies, which emphasize the prevention and reduction of risks and stressors that can increase
the probability of undesired outcomes. The second includes asset-focused
strategies, which focus on enhancing resources that increase the probability
of positive outcomes, in terms of effective adaptive processes. The third set
of resiliency development strategies are process-focused and involve the
mobilization of the power of human adaptational systems.

Within the context of application to the workplace, Reivich and Shatte's
(2002) resiliency development program has over 15 years of experience with
corporate interventions. Conner (1993, 2003) also offers training interventions and solutions in developing resiliency in the contexts of leadership
development and change management in organizations such as Sun Microsystems. In other words, there is considerable practical experience with resiliency training and application. However, to date there is no published
direct empirical research regarding the effectiveness of resiliency development interventions in the workplace. This dearth of research can be attributed in part to the complexity and interactional nature of resiliency as a
construct, leading Sutcliffe and Vogus (2003) to describe resiliency as "in-
adequately theorized" and its research to date at best "fragmented."

The need for theory development and research propositions of resiliency
in today's workplace we propose calls for an integrative, multi-level approach that takes into consideration environmental, organizational, leader,
and employee factors. There seems to be a need for an integrative, cross-
disciplinary perspective that draws from well-researched relevant areas such
as clinical, developmental, and positive psychology, and the newly emerging
POB approach to resiliency (Luthans, 2002a; Luthans, Avolio, Walumbwa,
& Li, 2005). The purpose of this chapter is to begin to build such a multi-
level resiliency development theory, in which antecedents and mediating
factors of organizational, leader, and employee resiliency are identified and
relationships with work-related attitudes and performance are proposed.
Fig. 1 summarizes our proposed multi-level theoretical model of resiliency
development for today's workplace in general and authentic leadership
development in particular and serves to organize the discussion.

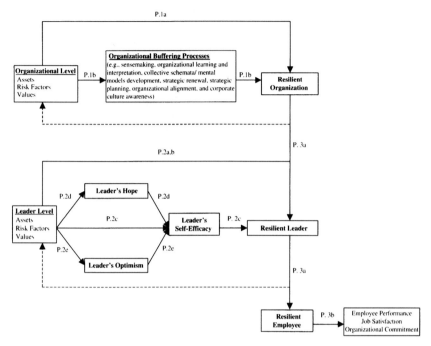

Fig. 1. A Multi-Level Resiliency Development Model for the Workplace.

ORGANIZATIONAL RESILIENCY DEVELOPMENT

In a deductive process, drawing from Masten (Masten, 2001; Masten & Reed, 2002), the top portion of Fig. 1 first identifies organizational level assets, risk factors, and values as proposed antecedents and then suggests buffering processes that mediate the development of resilient organizations.

The Role of Organizational Assets and Risk Factors

In relation to resiliency, Masten and Reed (2002, p. 76) define an asset as "a measurable characteristic in a group of individuals or their situation that predicts a positive outcome in the future on a specific outcome criterion." At the organizational level, Worline et al. (2002, p. 36) refer to assets contributing to resiliency as "resources that contribute to a unit's capacity to absorb strain (such as) knowledge and skill, trust and heedfulness, positive emotion, felt community and commitment. The structure and practices of a unit create, transform, and redirect these resources in ways that build different kinds of capabilities for developing resiliency." Examples of such assets possessed by an organization include structural capital, knowledge management systems resulting in shared information, clear communication channels, and career development opportunities for personal and professional growth. Each of these examples of assets, if positioned correctly, can provide a foundation for organizational resiliency. These assets can minimize the dysfunctional reactive downside of adversity and help reduce the negative effect of the encountered risks.

Masten and Reed (2002, p. 76) define risk in relation to resiliency as an "elevated probability of an undesirable outcome." Such risks expose the organizational participants to specific negative or undesirable outcomes (Cowan, Cowan, & Schulz, 1996). Despite the traditional research emphasis, as well as the face validity of the necessity for reducing or avoiding risks (e.g., Masten, 2001), in the proposed model, risk is viewed as inevitable. Thus, risk is not necessarily to be avoided, but rather controlled and managed as a part of the process toward nurturing the resiliency process. Cowan et al. (1996, p. 9) support this view when they assert that, "the active ingredients of a risk do not lie in the variable itself, but in the set of processes that flow from the variable, linking risk conditions with specific dysfunctional outcomes."

Given the current turbulent environment with downsizing, re-engineering, restructuring, and outsourcing (e.g., Vickers & Kouzmin, 2001), work-life balance problems, emotional labor/burnout, poor leadership, inadequate resources (e.g., Hills, 2000), declining profitability or competitiveness, scarcity of competently trained human resources, and deficient or misdirected research and development efforts (e.g., Nohara & Verdier, 2001), there are numerous examples that fit within the category of risk. Each of these pose a threat and a chance for an undesirable outcome, but each also offers an opportunity for resiliency development and sustained success.

Moreover, some organizational level assets can change into risk factors over time and negatively impact organizational resiliency. For example, in Rudolph and Repenning's (2002) model of disaster dynamics, trouble-free organizational systems are eroded through the accumulation of frequent, routine, but threshold-inducing interruptions, and/or novel disasters. In their view, a presently resilient entity can be on the verge of an unexpected, quantity-induced collapse. Thus, smoothly-functioning, self-regulating organizational systems can be a deception that masks future trauma. In fact, approaches that are usually recommended for qualitatively different situations, such as assumption-challenging, can result in reaching a "tipping threshold" in situations where crises arise from gradually precipitating, non-novel interruptions.

Hamel and Välikangas (2003) also support the view that business-as-usual does not necessarily imply organizational resiliency. In the past, organizations were able to maintain their survival and profitability through the momentum of their regulatory environment, loyal customers, stable demand, first-mover advantages, and high entry barriers. In such an environment, traumas could be dealt with on a case-by-case basis through one-time turnaround strategies, and incremental change was enough to adapt to other, less substantial changes. However, in an environment of frequent revolutionary change, resiliency necessitates continuous anticipation, adjustment, and proactive adaptation before organizational viability becomes permanently eroded. Thus, today's and tomorrow's organizations can only develop and maintain their resiliency, and consequently their success, through the creative destruction of strategies and business models that continuously get out of synch as opportunities and discontinuities emerge, or what Hamel and Välikangas (2003) refer to as "zero trauma."

The Role of Organizational Values

Besides the importance of assets and risk factors, Coutu (2002) emphasizes the importance of values in developing organizational resiliency. She asserts that, "strong values infuse an environment with meaning because they offer ways to interpret and shape events" (Coutu, 2002, p. 52). Values take on the role of a compass for the organization. They provide unwavering direction so that when the ambiguity and speed of the current environment facing organizations are heightened, clarity is provided to the decisions necessary to navigate the challenges presented.

Weick (1993) suggests that organizational rules and regulations that seemingly introduce rigidity and hinder creativity are often necessary and can be effective structuring tools that foster an organization's resiliency in times of turbulence. He notes that, "when people are put under pressure, they regress to their most habituated ways of responding" (Weick, 1993, pp. 638–639). Thus, properly established and reinforced organizational values are necessary antecedents for organizational resiliency. An organization's values can create stability and allow for positive and effective habituated responses to turmoil. These values allow the organization to adapt, accumulate knowledge, broaden perspective, build resources, and restore collective efficacy toward developing its resiliency, rather than panicking and down-spiraling into cognitive narrowing and threat-rigidity cycles (Sutcliffe & Vogus, 2003).

In order to ensure thorough adoption, organizational values contributing to resiliency must be communicated and demonstrated consistently from multiple sources. As Coutu points out, "if resilient employees are all interpreting reality in different ways, their decisions and actions may well conflict, calling into doubt the survival of their organization" (2002, p. 52). Since resiliency involves the ability to withstand and produce successful, sustainable results in the midst of turbulence and change, the elevation of stable, meaning-providing values by the organization's leadership may actually be more important for organizational resiliency than simply selecting and developing resilient individuals (Coutu, 2002). In their model of organizational resiliency, Horne and Orr (1998, p. 31) highlight the importance of a "whole-system response," and provide empirical evidence that "a collection of resilient individuals within a company does not add up to a resilient organization as a whole. Indeed, in some cases, it may be counterproductive because strong resilient individuals may dominate and override the shared vision of others."

Two types of organizations that thoroughly adopt resiliency-enhancing values are Gallup's notion of strength-based organizations (Buckingham & Coffman, 1999) and Pfeffer's (1998) world-class organizations. Strength-based organizations emphasize the importance of selection and placement of individuals in positions that provide them with daily opportunities to work within their areas of strength, and focus growth and development around objectively assessed talents (Buckingham & Coffman, 1999). Strength-based organizations are expected to be more resilient, since they instill a culture of positivity and engagement (Harter, Schmidt, & Hayes, 2002), where weaknesses are not focused upon, and where the discovery of talents is viewed as an opportunity to capitalize on potential areas of excellence.

Pfeffer (1998) explains that only about one-eighth of organizations believe in the importance of human resources as a major source of competitive advantage, and act upon that conviction consistently over time, as evidenced by their adoption and maintenance of high performance work practices (HPWPs). These HPWPs include pay for performance, 360 degree feedback, behavioral management, and self-managed teams. Interestingly, such organizations are documented to be world-class, compared to those that only believe and buy into the idea (about one-half), and those that both believe and take action to implement (about one-quarter), but do not "stick to it" (only one-eighth) (Pfeffer, 1998). Examples of such "one-eighth" world-class organizations include Microsoft, General Electric, Southwest Airlines, and others. They are generally recognized to be among the most resilient organizations, as evidenced by their growth and sustained effectiveness, even within the increasingly uncertain and turbulent business environment in which they have operated in the last several years. We would expect that organizations characterized by the highest levels of organic growth over extended periods of time would be those organizations that display greater resiliency.

Ethical organizational values are not included in most definitions of resiliency. Only the inclusion of a stable, meaning-providing set of values is specified in depicting resiliency (Coutu, 2002). So, it will be necessary for the organization to utilize the appropriate leadership style to demonstrate positive values. Both transformational and authentic leadership demonstrate values that define the process and decisions necessary for the organization to attain beneficial results for all stakeholders. Bass and Avolio (1994) suggest that not only leaders, but also organizations, could exhibit characteristics of transformational leadership. A key component for organizational resiliency development offered by transformational leadership is the development of leadership within followers.

Moreover, in the positive organizational context that Luthans and Avolio (2003) offer as an antecedent for authentic leadership, the cultural values associated with resiliency would be expected to become normative, replacing negative values, such as cynicism and political maneuvering. This focus on transformational leadership development combined with a definition of authentic leadership that contains resiliency as a part of its core (Luthans & Avolio, 2003), makes such leadership optimal for the development of a resilient organization. Based on the above conceptual support, the following proposition is offered:

Proposition 1a. The more an organization enhances its assets and values and manages its risk factors, the more resilient the organization will be.

The Mediating Role of Buffering Processes for Organizational Resiliency Development

According to Cowan et al. (1996), a buffer for resiliency is a protective mechanism that acts like an immunization process allowing for exposure to a small dose of the disease, but at the same time reduces the probability of the negative or undesirable outcomes. In other words, the organization's buffering processes can help shape the perceptions and consequences of assets, risk factors, and values. These buffering processes, along with an organization's structures and practices, combine in dynamic ways to allow for the emergent effective utilization and management of assets, risk factors, and values.

Drawing from the organizational cognition literature, we propose mediating buffering processes such as sensemaking (e.g., Weick, 1995), organizational learning and interpretation (e.g., Argyris & Schon, 1996; Crossan, Lane, & White, 1999; Daft & Weick, 1984; Huber, 1991), collective schemata/mental models development (e.g., Fiske & Taylor, 1991; Weick & Roberts, 1993), and strategic renewal (e.g., Crossan & Berdrow, 2003; Hamel & Välikangas, 2003; Huff, Huff, & Thomas, 1992). These are representative buffering processes that can mediate assets, risk factors, and values in developing organizational resiliency.

To illustrate, an organization that possesses desirable resources and information (i.e., assets) is unlikely to maintain its sustainable success and competitive advantage without effectively developing and implementing these assets. Organizations develop their unique, differentiated "competitive repertoires" (Miller & Chen, 1996) through the continuous interpretation of data and events. This interpretation process is influenced by the social, cultural, and competitive context within which it takes place (i.e., risk factors), as well as the organization's values, beliefs, goals, and politics (Daft & Weick, 1984). The resultant learning process is a continuous interaction of intuition, interpretation, integration, and institutionalization (Crossan et al., 1999). Through this process, an organization can achieve the delicate balance between "exploration" (development of new competencies) and "exploitation" (utilization of existing competencies). This balance results in an effective level of strategic renewal and alignment between the organization's strategy and environment (Crossan & Berdrow, 2003; Huff, Huff, & Thomas, 1992). Such a dynamic equilibrium equips the organization with the resilient capacity to accept, welcome, and bounce back from adversity, change, and uncertainty.

Drawing from the limited research in this area, Horne and Orr (1998) also propose buffer-like processes such as strategic planning, organizational alignment, organizational learning, and corporate culture awareness to significantly contribute to building organizational resiliency. Strategic planning allows resiliency to be built-in as a priority and an integral part of the organization's purpose. It can facilitate the construction and development of response mechanisms that permit sustainable growth and the effective achievement of further goals. Aligning organizational units encourages the support and mentorship by exemplary units for low-resiliency units.

Organizational learning not only facilitates this alignment and knowledge sharing process, but also allows for the combinatory nature of knowledge to operate and facilitate the generation of new knowledge that enhances adaptability and flexibility. Finally, corporate culture awareness permits the uncovering of priorities and competencies (i.e., assets and values), as well as rigidities and areas of vulnerability (i.e., risk factors) (Horne & Orr, 1998). Organizational culture is a powerful double-edged sword. If not carefully analyzed, frequently challenged, and consciously refined, organizational culture not only can be a force for achievement and growth (e.g., Southwest Airlines), but also can build momentum and limit the trajectories for proactive exploration and innovation (e.g., General Motors), hindering the resiliency development process (Reivich & Shatte, 2002).

Worline et al. (2002) also propose that organizational resiliency can be enhanced through the dynamic interaction of three other buffering types of processes: strengthening, replenishing, and limbering. We view these as buffering processes in building organizational resiliency in an analogous way to how various physical resistance exercises such as weight lifting are applied to create muscle mass in the body. Weights (risk factors) are gradually and specifically increased in combination with nutrition (strengthening), proper rest (replenishing), and stretching (limbering). Over time, more muscle mass (resiliency) is created. In the proper combination, strength and balance are increased. Adversities and setbacks are less likely to cause permanent damage for an organization that consistently applies such buffering processes as it becomes more capable of recovering more swiftly. In other words, as Rutter (1987) notes, resiliency is the final product of buffering processes, which do not eliminate risk, but rather encourage the effective engagement of risk taking.

The interaction between assets, risk factors, and values, as well as buffering mechanisms, is dynamic and ongoing. Layers of buffering are continuously created for the organization. These buffers affect the organization in a positive trajectory toward situations involving uncertainty and risk-taking. Unknown outcomes and lack of precedent are anticipated and engaged to turn threats into opportunities. Risk-taking is anticipated to eventually lead to success, and setbacks are viewed as learning experiences.

The buffering process as a mediator for organizational resiliency should not be viewed as a "magic bullet" or one-time pursuit. It is not a simple approach that eliminates risk factors or steers effort away from engagement with risk. Rather, the buffering process is a way to incorporate risk factors as an input for discovery, innovation, and, especially, sustainability. Buffering helps organizations soften the distraction caused by the often negative and reactive nature of risk. Buffering processes can be viewed as "values in action," operationalizing the synergy between assets, risk factors, and values in a practical fashion. Unless buffering processes bring assets and values to life, they can be reduced to ink on paper. Based on this conceptual support, the following proposition is offered:

Proposition 1b. The organization's buffering processes partially mediate the relationship between organizational level assets, risk factors, and values, and organizational resiliency.

A Snapshot of the Resilient Organization

Although organizational resiliency is a dynamic, continuously evolving process, a specific description of what constitutes a resilient organization would be helpful. To date, however, the notion of organizational resiliency is still very vague in the resiliency literature (Sutcliffe & Vogus, 2003). Observable characteristics of resilient organizations would facilitate effective benchmarks, as well as assist organizational diagnosis preceding planned change and subsequent intervention assessment.

Examples of the most widely recognized characteristics of resilient organizations include community, competence, connections, commitment, communication, coordination, and consideration (Horne & Orr, 1998). Clearly, some of these characteristics are based on the organization's assets as defined in our model. For example, the pool of knowledge and skills available for an organization enhances competence, while relationships and networks contribute to connections. Open channels and effective structure and design are necessary for communication and coordination. On the other hand, some of these characteristics are more related to what we define as organizational values contributing to resiliency. For example, a sense of community and resulting resiliency is generated when organizational members collectively internalize the organization's vision, mission, strategies, and goals.

Recently in the professional literature Hamel and Välikangas (2003) describe resilient organizations as those that are able to deal with four primary challenges. The first is the "cognitive challenge," in which organizations breed cultures of denial and arrogantly assume that they are immune from the changes occurring outside their walls. The second is the "strategic challenge," where satisficing needs to be replaced with the ability to generate a wider variety of strategic possibilities and alternatives. Third is the "political challenge," in which risks and potentially promising organizational experiments are to be endowed with the appropriate resources despite organizational politics and power games that tend to control resource allocation. Fourth is the "ideological challenge" of substituting the current mentality of optimization with a more creative, innovative, and renewal-oriented approach to change. Meeting such challenges can provide an example for operationalizing the resilient organization.

Concluding the Organizational Level

A final organizational level linkage that should be noted is the feedback loop shown in Fig. 1. This recognizes that organizational resiliency development is in turn likely to enhance organizational assets, enrich risk management strategies, and nurture more mature organizational values and culture. This feedback loop allows for a broader perspective that equips the organization to take on its next phase of resiliency development.

With this proposed theoretical model for organizational level resiliency serving as a foundation and point of departure, a shift to leader resiliency development is presented next. This deductive conceptual framework for multi-level resiliency development is based on the fact that leaders always operate and function in a social context, or they are not leading. Especially relevant to the development of organizational leaders is the organizational context (Avolio, 2002; Day, 2000; Luthans & Avolio, 2003) and it therefore follows that the proposed resilient organization is critical to the development of resilient leaders.

RESILIENT LEADER DEVELOPMENT

Resiliency is not just a favorable final product; it also enriches people's lives and increases chances of success, fulfillment, and their authentic leadership. Similar to authentic leadership development, resiliency is a life-long journey, an elaborate process that develops competence, over time, in the face of adversity, and in the context of interactions between the person and his/her environment (Egeland, Carlson, & Sroufe, 1993). As identified in our proposed resilient organizational development model, the antecedents are assets, risk factors, and values. As shown in Fig. 1, the same types of antecedents are proposed for the next level of authentic leader resiliency development.

The simplest way to present assets, risk factors, and values is that they are externally determined by contextual factors, as established in the child psychotherapy literature (e.g., Masten, 2001; Masten & Reed, 2002), and, in the context of organizational resiliency, by organizational level strategic, structural and processual variables (Klarreich, 1998; Worline et al., 2002). However, we propose that individual leader level assets, risk factors, and values are also salient antecedents. These serve to enhance both the development and maintenance of authentic leader resiliency, and as input for the proposed mediators (hope, optimism, and self-efficacy) of authentic leader resiliency development.

Leader Level Assets and Risk Factors

Leaders bring into their organizations various positive and negative aspects of themselves, such as their personal characteristics, backgrounds, strengths, vulnerabilities, insights, and perceptual biases. Trait theories of leadership give emphasis to these individual differences and view them as antecedent assets and risk factors for leadership success and effectiveness (e.g., Fleishman, Zaccaro, & Mumford, 1991; Judge, Ilies, Bono, & Gerhardt, 2002). Both the positive psychology (Snyder & Lopez, 2002) and positive organizational scholarship (Cameron et al., 2003) literatures are rich with descriptions of dispositional character virtues and traits that can enhance people's success and satisfaction, and, if absent or deficient, can hinder them from achieving their full potential. These traits or assets include general efficacy (e.g., Judge & Bono, 2001), dispositional hope (Snyder et al., 1991), trait optimism (Peterson, 2000; Scheier & Carver, 1992), positive/negative affectivity (e.g., Chemers, Watson, & May, 2000; Staw & Barsade, 1993), and others.

The human and social capital streams of research also emphasize the uniqueness and strategic importance of the educational background and experience that individuals bring as assets into an organization, and their relationships and networks that lead to value-creation and action facilitation, respectively (e.g., Adler & Kwon, 2002; Coleman, 1988; Hitt & Ireland, 2002). Research on managerial activities has also found that networking is related to managerial success (e.g., Luthans, 1988).

In the clinical psychology literature, Masten (2001) presents various personal assets that act as antecedents for resiliency. These include cognitive abilities, temperament, positive self-perceptions (self-efficacy), faith, a positive outlook on life, emotional stability and self-regulation, a sense of humor, and general appeal or attractiveness. She also discusses several relationship-based assets applicable to children and youth such as care-giving adults, effective parenting, pro-social and rule-abiding peers, and collective efficacy in the community. In line with these personal and relationship types of assets, Gorman (2005) also supports the notion that those who discover and hone their talents and find effective role models who can act as champions are more likely to enhance their resiliency and chances of success.

A direct connection can be made between the presence (or lack) of these personal and relationship-based assets in the child and adolescent psychotherapy context and individual differences, dispositional positive psychology traits, and human and social capital in the leadership context. In the same way that the presence of assets and/or the absence of risk factors can foster a child's resiliency, leaders who possess assets such as traits, knowledge, experience, skills, and relationships that predict success are likely to be resilient.

By the same token, several individual-level risk factors, often referred to as "vulnerability factors" (Kirby & Fraser, 1997), have also been recognized in the resiliency literature. These risk factors include alcoholism and drug use (e.g., Johnson, Bryant, Collins, Noe, Strader, & Berbaum, 1998; Sandau-Beckler, Devall, & de la Rosa, 2002), stress (e.g., Baron, Eisman, Scuello, Veyzer, & Lieberman, 1996; Smith & Carlson, 1997), poor health, under-education, unemployment (e.g., Collins, 2001), and exposure to traumatic experiences such as political violence (Qouta, El-Sarraj, & Punamaki, 2001).

Although primarily discussed in relation to children and youth, leaders are also exposed to similar risk factors. Stress and burnout are becoming commonplace in today's fast-paced work environment (e.g., Edwards, 1992; Maslach, Schaufeli, & Leiter, 2001; Nelson & Sutton, 1990; Zunz, 1998). Workaholism is on the rise as Americans and others extend their working hours, at the expense of personal and family time (e.g., Greenhouse, 2001; Koretz, 2001). Alcohol and drug abuse remain a big problem in the workplace (e.g., Feinauer, 1990; Harris & Heft, 1992; Schweitzer, 2000; Sell & Newman, 1992). In this post 9–11 era, organizational and personal traumatic experiences have been accumulating at an ever faster pace, making organizational leaders increasingly vulnerable (e.g., Brown, 1997). Thus, the following is proposed:

Proposition 2a. The higher the leader's assets and/or the lower the leader's risk factors, the more resilient the leader will be.

However, an important caveat to this proposition is to recognize the non-linear nature of assets and risk factors. Assets are not simply the sum of resources and capabilities available to an individual, although the larger that sum, the more likely it is that the person will be resilient. Moreover, resiliency is not entirely predicted by the number and strength of the above-mentioned assets an individual has been endowed with, less the number and amount of risk factors present in his/her life. Assets and risk factors are both cumulative and interactive in nature, and the particular "sequence" in a "risk chain" is an integral factor in determining a person's resiliency level (Sandau-Beckler et al., 2002).

Leader Level Values

Values and beliefs provide a source of meaning. They make sometimes overwhelmingly difficult present more manageable, and link it to a more fulfilling future. Resiliency develops in the face of adversity when leaders can elevate themselves over their difficult present, and values play a salient role in presenting different approaches for interpreting and shaping events. Most importantly, the role of values in enhancing a leader's resiliency is largely based on the stability of those values as a source of meaning. In other words, for values to serve a resiliency function, they must be strong enough to warrant a stable source of meaning (Coutu, 2002; Kobsa, 1982). Research shows the role of meaning-providing values and beliefs in enhancing resiliency through extreme physical (e.g., Holaday & McPhearson, 1997) or psychological (Wong & Mason, 2001) challenges. Substantial freedom, energy, and resiliency are also evident in those who operate within their innate moral frameworks (Richardson, 2002).

In an analogous way that stable organizational values can enhance organizational resiliency, the presence of stable leader values and beliefs can contribute to a leader's resiliency. That is, such values and beliefs can provide a steady framework for dealing with the levels of stress, change, and uncertainty that leaders face in a crisis or just every day on the job. The stability of values and beliefs can help the leader build consistent experiences and heuristics for problem handling, decision-making, and crisis management. Without at least a threshold level of consistency, the leader is likely to resort to a reactionary, fire-fighting approach. Besides overwhelming the leader with constantly bombarding new situations, an inconsistent leader can also be overwhelming for followers, who look up to the leader for balance, meaning, stability, and direction. Therefore, the following proposition is offered:

Proposition 2b. The more stable and consistent the leader's values and beliefs, the more resilient the leader will be.

The Mediating Role of the Leader's Self-Efficacy

Drawing from the extensive theory and research of Bandura (1997, 2001), self-efficacy can be defined as "one's belief about his or her ability to mobilize the motivation, cognitive resources, and courses of action necessary to execute a specific action within a given context" (Stajkovic & Luthans, 1998b, p. 66). People who are self-efficacious are likely to select and welcome challenging endeavors, invest the effort and motivation necessary to successfully accomplish them, and persevere in the face of obstacles throughout the process. A meta-analysis of 114 studies found a strong positive correlation between self-efficacy and work-related performance (Stajkovic & Luthans, 1998a). Self-efficacy can be developed through mastery experiences (performance attainments), vicarious learning (modeling), social persuasion, and psychological and physiological arousal (Bandura, 1997, 2000).

We propose self-efficacy is a mediator between leader's assets, risk factors, and values and their resiliency. First, other things being equal, the higher the leader's success-predicting personal characteristics, traits, knowledge, skills, and abilities, the more likely the leader will experience success and performance attainments. Mastery experiences have been established in the self-efficacy literature as the most effective approach to building self-efficacy (Bandura, 1997). Second, the higher the leader's social capital, such as a sound network of relationships, the more likely the leader will be successful (e.g., Luthans, 1988), again enhancing the leader's self-efficacy. Moreover, leaders who have higher social capital are likely to have significantly more opportunities for finding relevant role models, increasing their opportunity for vicarious learning, another contributing factor in building self-efficacy. Social capital is also likely to increase the leader's sources of social persuasion, which contributes to the development of self-efficacy. Finally, assets such as physical and psychological health are salient contributors to physiological and psychological arousal, which in turn contributes to enhancing self-efficacy.

On the other hand, asset deficiencies and risk factors are predictors of failure, setbacks, and negative outcomes in general (Masten & Reed, 2002), which can reduce mastery experiences, the most salient factor in building self-efficacy. However, the idea of risk factors as opportunities and areas for development is of particular relevance here. Although risk factors increase the probability of failure, when viewed positively, they can become welcomed as challenges, which can contribute to the leader's efficacy. When balanced with appropriate assets, leaders are likely to persevere when faced with obstacles, and pursue success despite setbacks, which, in turn, plays a part in subsequently increasing self-efficacy. Moreover, stable values and a sense of meaning and purpose are likely to increase leaders' acceptance of challenges, effort to achieve goals, and persistence when faced with obstacles, i.e., their self efficacy.

Although the linkages between self-efficacy and resiliency are just emerging in the literature (e.g., Holaday & McPhearson, 1997; Masten & Reed, 2002), extensive empirical and meta-analytical support exists for the relationship between self-efficacy and psychosocial and health functioning (Holden, 1991; Holden, Moncher, Schinke, & Barker, 1990). Moreover, to counter recent research findings by Vancouver and colleagues (Vancouver, Thompson, & Williams, 2001; Vancouver, Thompson, Tischner, & Putka, 2002) that self-efficacy built on past performance may have a negative impact on subsequent performance, Bandura and Locke (2003) cite a substantial number of empirical studies utilizing interventions, pre-post measures, and multiple controls, which clearly establish the direction of causality between efficacy and performance. The studies that they cite, which span more than three decades of research, show that efficacy beliefs result in increased perceptions of personal control, which in turn significantly contributes to effective management of stressful factors, fear-inducing environments, and challenging situations (Bandura & Locke, 2003). In other words, self-efficacy equips people with better capacities to deal with adversity and setbacks, i.e., we propose it contributes to their resiliency.

The above evidence indicates the more efficacious leaders are, the more resilient they are likely to be. When faced with obstacles, they persist. When faced with challenges, they welcome them, because they are confident of their ability to "mobilize the motivation, cognitive resources, and courses of action necessary" (Stajkovic & Luthans, 1998b, p. 66) to overcome adversity and achieve their goals. When faced with negative outcomes, they fall back on their efficacy beliefs. Bandura and Locke (2003, p. 92) support this conclusion when they assert: "In the pursuit of difficult challenges, people have to override a lot of dissuading negative feedback if they are to realize what they seek. Resilient belief that one has what it takes to succeed provides the necessary staying power in the face of repeated failures, setbacks, and skeptical or even critical social reactions that are inherently discouraging. Those beset by self-doubts become early quitters rather than successful survivors."

Without self-efficacy, the mere possession of assets or lack of risk factors may not contribute to building resiliency. Leaders who lack self-efficacy will rarely employ all the resources in their possession, let alone welcome challenges and take risks. This is because those of high self-efficacy focus on the opportunities worth pursuing, whereas the less self-efficacious dwell on the risks to be avoided (Krueger & Dickson, 1993, 1994). Moreover, setbacks and uncertainty are given in any leadership role. Leaders who lack self-efficacy are less likely to persevere, motivate themselves, and get back on track. Based on the above support, the following proposition is made:

Proposition 2c. Leaders' self-efficacy partially mediates the relationships between their assets, risk factors, and values and their resiliency.

The Mediating Role of the Leader's Hope

Prior to the positive psychology movement, hope had been traditionally viewed as simply positive or wishful thinking. In everyday language, people tend to use hope as a loosely defined term for focusing on favorable expectations (e.g., let's hope for the best). Hope is sometimes even used to imply doubt or uncertainty (e.g., hopefully I will be able to do this). However, based on the theory-building and research of Snyder (2000), Snyder, Irving, and Anderson (1991) and Snyder et al. (1996), hope is operationally defined as "a positive motivational state that is based on an interactively derived sense of successful (1) agency (goal-directed energy) and (2) pathways (planning to meet goals)" (Snyder et al., 1991, p. 287). Thus, Snyder's hope theory posits that there are two essential factors for goal-directed humans to achieve their goals: agency (willpower) and pathways (waypower).

Agency is the internalized determination, investment, and energy exerted toward goal achievement. When one starts to view oneself as the "author of causal chains of events," agency thoughts are developed (Snyder, Rand, & Sigmon, 2002, p. 259). The term pathways refers to the capability to generate ways to achieve goals and to create alternative routes if the original ones are blocked. Pathways thinking develops through the systematic observation and refinement of "lessons of correlation/causality" (Snyder et al., 2002, p. 259). When one can predict and explain events that are related in time and logical sequence, pathway thoughts are developed.

Research shows that hope is positively related to success in various life domains (see Snyder, 2000 for comprehensive reviews) and recent research gives initial support for the positive relationship between organizational leaders' level of hope and the profitability of their units and the satisfaction and retention of their employees (Peterson & Luthans, 2003). There is also recent empirical evidence that workers' level of hope is related to their performance (Luthans et al., 2005). Moreover, Snyder's (2000) research shows that hope can be both a dispositional trait and a developmental state.

We propose that hope at least partially mediates the relationship between leaders' assets, risk factors, and values and their self-efficacy. Leaders who possess assets such as success-predicting personal characteristics, traits, experience, knowledge, skills, abilities, and relationships, are likely to have wider choices of alternative pathways toward the achievement of their goals. They have a richer variety of resources to allocate and combine. Leaders who possess stable values and beliefs, and who consequently find meaning in life despite adversity (Coutu, 2002), are also likely to be more determined to achieve future goals that can raise them above their less desired present situation. Rather than being viewed as problems that need to be eliminated, insufficient assets and values, along with personal risk factors and deficiencies, may be seen as opportunities that are open to development. In this alternative perspective and approach, risk factors may even enrich hope, since they provide continuous challenges and opportunities for the generation and testing of alternative pathways, and hence the enhancement of waypower.

Furthermore, as shown in Fig. 1, we propose that the more hopeful leaders are, the more self-efficacious they will be. The agency component of hope implies that leaders who are determined to achieve their goals will exert the necessary investment and energy to accomplish those goals. Bandura (1997) asserts that the "efficacy expectancies," implied in one's sense of agency and control (Snyder, 2000), are strong predictors of behavior. Social cognitive theory and self-efficacy are "rooted in an agentic perspective in which people function as anticipative, purposive, and self-evaluating proactive regulators of their motivation and actions" (Bandura & Locke, 2003, p. 87). Snyder's (2000) notion of agency incorporates the assertiveness to "stick to" one's goals, and not give up, i.e., persistence.

Since hopeful leaders know that they are able to generate alternative routes toward their goals, the pathways component of hope can be compared to the fuel that energizes persistence in the face of obstacles. The more pathways leaders are able to generate, the more motivated and persistent they are likely to be, since they know there are still uncharted routes that have yet to be drawn upon. In other words, the willpower and waypower from their hope can make leaders believe they are more capable of employing their assets and values and managing risk factors to facilitate goal accomplishment.

As stated earlier, among the established approaches of building self-efficacy are mastery experiences (repeated experiences of success over time) and vicarious learning (observing the successful experiences of relevant role models) (Bandura, 1997, 2000). Hopeful leaders, possessing the agency and pathways components, by definition have the determination and invest the energy necessary to achieve their goals. They determine new pathways when faced with obstacles. Such high hope leaders are more likely to experience success than those with low hope levels (who have less determination, energy, perseverance, and waypower). Then, over time, the more frequent success experiences are conducive to the development of higher levels of self-efficacy. In addition, since mastery and vicarious experiences are primarily perceptual (Maddux, 2002), without a sense of agency and waypower these experiences are less likely to be internalized, reducing the chances that they can contribute to self-efficacy. Based on this conceptualization, it follows that:

Proposition 2d. Leaders' level of hope partially mediates the relationship between their assets, risk factors, and values and their self-efficacy.

The Mediating Role of the Leader's Optimism

Similar to hope, early conceptualizations of optimism emphasized its emotional, and even illusional, nature (e.g., Taylor, 1989; Tiger, 1979). However, drawing from attribution theory, Seligman (1998) introduces optimism as a leading construct in the positive psychology movement, and differentiates optimists from pessimists based on their explanatory styles and causal attributions for favorable or negative outcomes. People who have an optimistic explanatory style attribute positive events to personal, permanent, and pervasive causes and negative events to external, temporary, and situation-specific causes. Pessimists do exactly the opposite. They attribute positive events to external, temporary, and situation-specific causes, and attribute negative events to personal, permanent, and pervasive ones.

Seligman (1998) emphasizes that an optimistic explanatory style is a teachable, developable capacity. He and others (e.g., Schneider, 2001) highlight the importance of "realistic optimism," which does not take an extreme position in externalizing and eliminating personal responsibility for poor choices. He and others (e.g., Peterson, 2000) also recommend "flexible optimism," which can adapt and use alternative explanatory styles depending on the situation at hand. Seligman's (1998) research shows that optimism is related to psychological health, success, satisfaction, and "authentic happiness" (Seligman, 2002) in various life domains, including work, education, sports, politics, and health.

As shown in Fig. 1, we propose that realistic, flexible optimism at least partially mediates the relationship between leaders' assets, risk factors, and values and their self-efficacy. Seligman (1998, p. 282) warns that two of the primary causes of depression and helplessness in the lives of multitudes of people today are "the waxing of the self and the waning of the commons." In the past, people drew meaning for their lives from values that provided the self with a context that is larger than itself (which Seligman calls "the commons"). When faced with adversity, people used to stop and reflect on their "spiritual furniture," including values and beliefs in their country, religion, family, or purposes that surpass their own selves and lives.

Today, Seligman (1998, 2002) maintains these fundamental sources of meaning are losing their significance. Divorce, mobility, the erosion of national and religious commitment, and other risk factors, that have caused the demise of many stable foundations of life, are obvious manifestations of the "waning of the commons." Moreover, individualism and the tremendously increased scope for choice and personal control (for example, as evidenced by the millions of products and brands in the consumer market), have resulted in a "maximal self." He argues that this results in considerable focus and energy being directed toward pleasing the exalted self. Consequently, the loss of values and beliefs that give meaning to life beyond the self has led to extensive personalization of pleasures and pains. There is an exponential increase in experiences of helplessness as the self strives for more fulfillment of whims and personal control in the search for meaning (Seligman, 1998).

Based on this argument, we propose that leaders who are armed with meaning-providing stable assets and values are likely to possess a more optimistic explanatory style. This is because, in Seligman's term, their "spiritual furniture" allows them to view causes for negative events that are beyond themselves. This, in turn, permits them to attribute failures to external, temporary, and situational reasons when necessary. In other words, such leaders will be able to view risk factors and their lack of full control as their "expected and accepted lot in life" that they should make the best of, rather than dealing with setbacks as "something to remedy" (Seligman, 1998, p. 282). In addition, other things being equal, leaders who possess success-predicting personal characteristics, experience, traits, knowledge, skills, abilities, and relationships, are likely to have a more optimistic explanatory style, at least with respect to positive events, since they possess more internal, permanent, and pervasive assets and values to which they can attribute success.

Finally, as shown in our model in Fig. 1, we propose that the more optimistic leaders are, the more self-efficacious they will be. An optimistic explanatory style is likely to act as a buffer against being depressed and learned helplessness (Seligman, 1998). Optimistic leaders have an attributional style that shields them from a sense of despair and enhances their persistence when faced with obstacles. Bandura (1997) believes that "efficacy expectancies," one's belief in his/her ability to successfully perform a certain task, are even stronger predictors of behavior than "outcome expectancies," one's confidence that performance of a specific task will lead to the desired outcome(s). Maddux (2002) views success as a subjective perceptual experience. Since people tend to discount information that conflicts with their pre-established self-view, success experiences (positive outcomes) may not be automatically translated into self-efficacy beliefs for those who are accustomed to failure.

In order for success to be interpreted as mastery experiences, and thus contribute to enhancing self-efficacy, it should be attributed to one's own effort and ability, rather than to external causes. In other words, an optimistic explanatory style that attributes positive events to personal, permanent, and pervasive causes is likely to enhance a leader's efficacy expectancies. This is because such optimism will allow the leader to (legitimately) take credit for achievements and success, and thus enhance the perceptions and impact of mastery experiences. However, even when negative outcomes occur, leaders with an optimistic explanatory style will attribute them to external, temporary, and situation-specific causes. It follows that the negative outcomes do not counterbalance previously built efficacy beliefs. This is also in line with Bandura's (1997) assertions about the superiority of efficacy expectancies over outcome expectancies. Even when outcomes are negative, internalized efficacy expectancies can offset the unfavorable impact of adversities and produce persistence. In other words, realistic, flexible optimism can boost the impact of the leader's assets and values and buffer the impact of risk factors on the leader's self-efficacy. Thus, based on this conceptual support we propose the following:

Proposition 2e. Leaders' optimism partially mediates the relationship between their assets, risk factors, and values and their self-efficacy.

Although arguments can be made for the direct relationships between hope and resiliency, and optimism and resiliency, in line with our view of resiliency development as a long-term reiterative process, we propose there is a gradual upward spiral in which the cognitive and affective dimensions of hope and optimism contribute to the development of self-efficacy. This input of hope and optimism into self-efficacy in turn gradually enhances and enriches leaders' resiliency. As leaders' resiliency develops, it is expected to positively impact their reservoir of experiences, successes, and adaptive mechanisms, further enhancing their assets and risk management strategies, and refining their values and beliefs. This is depicted in Fig. 1 through the feedback loop between resilient leaders and their assets, risk factors, and values.

THE CASCADING, CONTAGION EFFECT
OF RESILIENCY

In earlier discussion, we noted that an organization does not necessarily become resilient by just being staffed with resilient managers and employees. However, it can also be argued that although a collective of resilient employees does not necessarily create a resilient organization, organizational resiliency can cascade and have a contagion effect on participants from the top down. In other words, a resilient organization may enhance the resiliency of its leaders, and resilient leaders may in turn have a positive impact on their employees'/associates' resiliency. Revisiting an earlier example may be helpful to also illustrate this point.

Leaders who work for strength-based organizations are more likely to develop resiliency, since they are provided with opportunities to utilize and enhance their assets everyday (Buckingham & Coffman, 1999). Their risk factors (e.g., a lack of certain talents) may not hinder their growth. This is because they can manage around these risks by emphasizing and utilizing other areas of strength that they possess. The social support that they receive through strong interpersonal relationships can buffer against various dysfunctional beliefs about inadequacy and behaviors of disengagement. Strength-based organizations are likely to provide cultures that support community, connections, commitment, communication, and consideration (Horne & Orr, 1998). In turn, such strength-based, nurturing cultures can enhance leaders' resiliency directly, as well as indirectly by helping them to: (a) discover and refine their assets, (b) manage around their risk factors,

(c) buy into stable, meaning-providing values, and (d) build their hope, optimism, and self-efficacy.

The individual level of analysis utilized to describe the leader resiliency development process we propose is relevant at any level (top management, middle management, supervisors, or frontline operating employees). Resilient leaders, committed to such strong organizational values as caring appreciation of others' talents and strengths, are likely to be effective mentors for their associates through a similar journey of self-discovery. However, we propose that a direct cascading, contagion effect of resiliency also comes into play. As leaders exhibit increasing levels of resiliency, they can become models for followers. This resiliency modeling from leaders is especially important to those relatively new to the organization.

Newcomers have not yet been fully socialized into the organization's culture and values. They have not had the chance to enrich their assets, nor build their hope, optimism, and self-efficacy. Instead of just depending on their own resources which they may be unsure of, newer followers may initially draw their agency, pathways, optimism, and efficacy from what they believe the leader can do. This resiliency modeled from the leader will help them to bounce back from initial failures and setbacks. With time, these followers are likely to start their own resiliency development journey. Their resiliency development will be supported by the modeling and mentorship by resilient leaders and the values, resources and support of resilient organizations. Thus, the following proposition is offered:

Proposition 3a. The more resilient an organization, the more resiliency its leaders are likely to develop, and the more resilient their associates in turn will become.

PERFORMANCE IMPLICATIONS

To complete the model in Fig. 1 and keep the theory-building within the domain of workplace and authentic leadership development, the expected impact of resiliency on desirable outcomes such as employee attitudes (e.g., job satisfaction and organizational commitment) and performance needs to be examined. Over the years, under the psychotherapeutic model, resiliency has been mainly limited to a reactive capacity, allowing people to cope and survive in the face of trauma and adversity. Emphasis in the resiliency literature has traditionally been placed on bringing the deficiencies of those performing under adverse conditions up to average (Masten, 2001; Masten & Reed, 2002). However, today's organizations and authentic leaders cannot afford to have just average performing participants and followers. They are seeking "better than OK" (Sutcliffe & Vogus, 2003) performers that can not only survive, cope, and recover, but also thrive and flourish through difficult and uncertain times (Ryff & Singer, 2003). Moreover, in today's competitive environment, only leaders and employees who can achieve excellence and constantly excel under pressure are likely to be successful.

We have made the case that resiliency is not just reactive, but can also be a proactive capacity. Resilient people can "bounce back" not only to their performance level prior to the adversity, but also to sustainable higher levels. The scope of resiliency applied to authentic leadership development would be far too limited if it is only viewed as a maintenance mechanism with a zero net gain. We would argue that sustainable positive gains can be achieved. For example, Reivich and Shatte (2002) make the case that people's resiliency involves the capacity to overcome, steer through, bounce back, and, most importantly, reach out and commit themselves to the pursuit of new knowledge and experiences, deepen their relationships with others, and find meaning in life.

Research in the area of Posttraumatic Growth (PTG), as opposed to Posttraumatic Stress Disorder (e.g., Tedeschi, Park, & Calhoun, 1998), clearly reveals that resilient people can "springboard" out of adversities. For example, Ryff and Singer (2003, p. 24) note that resilient people experience: "increased self-reliance and self-efficacy; heightened awareness of one's own vulnerability and mortality; improvement in ties to others – greater self-disclosure and emotional expressiveness, more compassion and capacity to give to others; clearer philosophy of life – renewed sense of priorities and appreciation of life; and deeper sense of meaning and spirituality." Richardson (2002) refers to such positive outcomes as "resilient reintegration," in which a disruption of life's routine promotes the identification, access and nurture of one's resilient qualities, resulting in introspection, adaptation, growth, knowledge, self-understanding, strength, and wholeness. In other words, resiliency implies growth and increased toughness through trauma, adversities, and troubled times.

Bandura and Locke's (2003) recent discussion of the role of self-regulation in creating resilient self-efficacy provides useful insights regarding the proactive nature of resiliency. They assert that people are not only motivated by discrepancy reduction. In fact, people proactively create discrepancies through setting progressively more challenging goals and higher performance standards, and then extend their effort, resources and motivation in the anticipation of achieving them. Bandura and Locke (2003) pose the challenge of explaining why and how people pursue growth, rather than complacency. Drawing from these points and their supporting research, we offer resiliency, in its proactive manifestation, as having an impact on enhanced work-related attitudes and increased performance.

This positive, proactive view of resiliency, cascading down through an organization-wide system of resiliency to leaders and employees, is proposed to result in desired outcomes. For example, organizational values that place employees first, reflect assets such as high performance work practices, and utilize buffering mechanisms such as strategic and strength-based initiatives, are documented by a wealth of research through the years supporting a positive impact on performance (e.g., see Locke (2000) for research-based summary articles on these areas).

We argue that, besides contributing to organizational resiliency, such dimensions also enhance leader and employee resiliency, which in turn leads to attitudinal and performance enhancement. Once again, this is because a resilient organizational context provides opportunities for the development of leader and employee assets, risk management strategies, and values. The resilient organizational context facilitates authentic leadership development. Authentic leaders' higher internal self-set standards are based on strong foundations of clear awareness of personal strengths and areas of vulnerability. Most importantly, resilient organizational contexts nurture the capacity for leaders' forethought, and allow them and their followers to enhance the levels of self-efficacy, hope and optimism, even in times of adversity and uncertainty.

The development of assets, risk factors, values, and buffering processes that characterize resilient organizations does not only enhance sustainable performance by directly increasing the effectiveness of leaders and employees, but also has indirect positive effects. These positive effects occur through the cognitive components of self-evaluation and engagement, which are documented to contribute to job satisfaction (Judge & Bono, 2001), workplace happiness (Thottam, 2005), and business-unit productivity and profitability (Harter, Schmidt, & Hayes, 2002). Such attitudinal impacts are also likely to lead to both affective and cognitive types of commitment (Meyer & Allen, 1991). Affective commitment has been shown to be related to the relationship-based support and sense of community that resilient organizations tend to provide, while more cognitive types of commitment (e.g., calculative) are likely to be enhanced through forethought capacity and expectation of positive future outcomes (Allen & Meyer, 1996; Meyer & Allen, 1991). Based on this support, our final proposition is the following:

Proposition 3b. The greater the cascading, contagion effects of organizational resiliency on leaders and employees, the more positive impact there will be on work-related outcomes such as employee attitudes of job satisfaction and commitment and sustainable organizational performance.

PRACTICAL IMPLICATIONS

The theoretical model proposed in this chapter has a number of implications for the actual practice of not only developing resiliency, but also authentic leadership. These implications can be classified into at least two major developmental levels. The first emphasizes the salience of organizational-level resiliency as the context within which the resiliency of authentic leaders and their associates can be developed. The second is a proposed program for developing resiliency directly at the individual level, which emphasizes not only the leader resiliency development process, but also can be transferred to followers/associates at various levels of the organization.

The Salience of the Context: Organizational-level Resiliency

A point to again emphasize is that although resilient organizations are key to developing resilient leaders and employees, the opposite may not be true. The practical guideline here is that merely selecting resilient leaders and employees on the basis of their assets and values may not be sufficient to create and maintain resiliency at the organizational level. By the same token, organizational assets, risk factors, values, and buffering processes are all important antecedents for organizational resiliency, which in turn are contextual preconditions for leaders' and employees' resiliency. Many of the organizational assets discussed earlier, such as structural capital, knowledge management, communication, and various best practices, as well as buffering processes such as organizational learning, strategic renewal, and organizational alignment, can enhance individual level resiliency. Thus, the practical guideline is to use these organizational factors to help compensate for individual level deficiencies and risk factors in developing their resiliency.

A guideline to remember is that risk factors curtailing organizational resiliency can also hinder the development of its members' resiliency. For example, lack of effective placement and succession planning systems can result in poor matching between people and positions, which, particularly in leadership positions near the top of the organization, can both threaten organizational resiliency and effectiveness, and reduce individual level satisfaction, commitment, and performance. This in turn can reduce leaders' and associates' hope, optimism, and self-efficacy. For example, organizational contexts with a high, unmanaged emotional labor content can result in stress, emotional dissonance, and burnout (e.g., Morris & Feldman, 1996). These dysfunctional outcomes all exert negative influence on leaders' and associates' physiological and psychological health with resulting deterioration of their resiliency. However, sufficient buffering processes such as social support, sense of mission, and recognition, have been shown to enhance managers' resiliency, even in such high-pressure, stressful contexts (Zunz, 1998).

Organizational values are also of major importance in enhancing resiliency, not only at the organizational, but also at the individual level. Since values and beliefs draw their significance from their stability and the fact that they are larger than one's self (Seligman, 1998), it follows that organizational values may have a stronger impact on leaders' resiliency than their own, self-constructed values and beliefs. The visions, missions, and values of resilient organizations "change very little over the years and are used as scaffolding in times of trouble" (Coutu, 2002, p. 52). Organizational values tend to go beyond any one person or situation, offering ways for interpreting and shaping one's life course.

Developing and Managing Leaders' Assets, Risk Factors, and Values

One of the primary criteria of the positive organizational behavior approach is that psychological capacities such as resiliency must be developable states (Luthans, 2002a, b). Based on our proposed model, authentic leader resiliency can be developed by enhancing and managing its antecedents, both at the organizational and individual levels. The above discussion emphasizes resiliency development from the organizational perspective, but a practical guideline is to also focus on developing the individual-level antecedents and components of resiliency that we suggest would contribute to the authentic leadership development process.

The antecedents shown in Fig. 1 can serve as the foundation upon which authentic leaders' resiliency is built. These antecedents exert both direct and indirect effects on leader resiliency through their impact on hope, optimism, and self-efficacy. Many well-established approaches, such as training, coaching, and mentoring for the enhancement of knowledge, skills, and abilities (and the consequent reduction of risk factors and deficiencies) exist. However, some of the assets and risk factors discussed earlier (e.g., individual differences in personal characteristics and dispositional traits) are hard to change, implying the importance of careful selection and placement.

On the other hand, individual values are possible to alter and align to organizational values by changing perceptions of contextual factors such as the magnitude of consequences (Flannery & May, 2000), interests of group members, and role responsibilities (Trevino & Victor, 1992). In particular, the positive organizational behavior states of hope, optimism, and self-efficacy are proposed to be open to development, thereby promoting leaders' resiliency, and specific guidelines have been outlined for doing so (Luthans & Youssef, 2004; Masten, 2001; Masten & Reed, 2002).

Developing Authentic Leaders' Self-Efficacy

As proposed in our model (see Fig. 1), self-efficacy may have the biggest direct impact on the development of resiliency and in turn authentic leaders. Again drawing from Bandura's (1997) four approaches of mastery experiences (performance attainments), vicarious learning (modeling), social persuasion (positive feedback), and psychological and physiological arousal (wellness), Luthans and colleagues (Luthans et al., 2001, 2004; Luthans & Youssef, 2004; Stajkovic & Luthans, 1998a, b) present specific recommendations for developing leaders' self-efficacy. With respect to mastery experiences, they recommend that leadership training exercises and on-the-job training should focus on allowing leaders to experience success. Career planning should also be carefully designed to lead to mastery and success. However, they warn that success should be a challenging, rather than an easy accomplishment, so that it can accomplish its purpose of building efficacy. Maddux (2002) also emphasizes the importance of concrete, specific and proximal goals and strategies. He suggests the use of "guided mastery," as would be found in effective coaching of developing leaders.

Regarding modeling and vicarious learning from successful others, Luthans et al. (2001) recommend that the developing leader be assigned to shadow a successful mentor, and/or that they watch relevant models effectively handling and solving realistic leadership situations in the context of experiential training sessions. Bandura (1997) also emphasizes the importance of the perceived relevance of the model and the situation for the development of efficacy. In other words, the model should be viewed by the leader being developed as similar to himself/herself, and as dealing with situations that are similar to those likely to be encountered. Maddux (2002) also suggests that when actual models and vicarious learning opportunities are not available, "imaginal experience," in which the individual can imagine him/herself succeeding in effectively dealing with difficult situations and challenges, can be used. This can substitute for actual modeling, with the successful self acting as the relevant model.

Another way to build efficacy is through social persuasion and the use of contingent reinforcement (e.g., positive feedback). Again, coaches and mentors can provide such positive feedback and reinforce perseverance and progress. Finally, with respect to physiological and psychological arousal, Luthans and his colleagues (Luthans et al., 2001; Luthans & Youssef, 2004; Stajkovic & Luthans, 1998a, b) draw attention to the importance of the physical and psychological fitness of developing leaders, which can be achieved through comprehensive wellness programs, as well as stress management approaches.

Maddux (2002) extends the developmental approaches of self-efficacy to include two additional techniques, namely enhancing the impact of success and collective efficacy. In order for performance attainments to be interpreted as success, competence should be viewed as incremental and malleable, rather than fixed. Success should be attributed to one's own effort and ability, rather than to external causes. Finally, in cases of severe discouragement, encouragement of "minor distortions in the perception of control" may be necessary, since they can lead to self-confirming efficacy beliefs (Maddux, 2002).

Collective efficacy emphasizes the "social embeddedness of the individual" (Maddux, 2002, p. 284). This is a case where the resilient organization can be contextually important to building collective efficacy. For example, a resilient organization where goals are mostly shared and accomplished through collaborative thinking, decision making, and the efforts of groups and teams can result not only in increases in collective efficacy, but also contribute to organizational, authentic leader, and follower resiliency.

Developing Authentic Leaders' Hope

Defined earlier and discussed in relation to its mediation effects, Snyder, Rand, and Sigmon's (2002) recent "full hope model" provides many useful insights into the development of authentic leaders' hope. In particular, authentic leaders' hope can be developed by drawing from proven guidelines from clinical and developmental psychology. By rewarding appropriate performance outcomes, as well as the means utilized to achieve those outcomes, the correlation and causal relationship between individual and organizational goals become established. Rewarding the right means (pathways) and ends (agency) can help in consistently aligning individual goals to the organizational vision, mission, values, and objectives, thus resulting in increased hope and in turn work attitudinal and performance outcomes. Veninga's (2000) notion of an organizational "dream" that can capture everyone's enthusiasm and enlist support to build hope seems particularly relevant here. More pragmatically, however, reinforcement should be contingent upon such hope-related behavior (Stajkovic & Luthans, 1997).

Agency thoughts for hope development can be facilitated through delegation and empowerment. Such thoughts are also related to authentic leader self-awareness, since the individual is the "author" of his/her own decisions, goals, pathways, and outcomes. Finally, by selecting the rewards that are valuable to the leader whose hope is being developed, the valence of desired behaviors and outcomes can be increased and enhance the leader's motivation (Vroom, 1964). Consequently, the continuous iteration of agency and pathway thoughts is triggered and maintained, increasing hope levels over time (Snyder, 2000).

One of Snyder's (1995b) practical recommendations for increasing hope in the workplace is to do so through shared goals. For authentic leaders' hope to develop, they should be able to create and share their own groups' goals, rather than simply being tools for making the overall organization's goals happen. Sharing also implies that goals should be negotiated and compromises achieved in order for cooperation to be directed toward agreed upon objectives. Moreover, open lines of communication are vital for sharing both hope and fears. Goals that can help build hope should be clearly defined, realistic, measurable, and challenging (i.e., stretch goals). In addition, throughout the process of hope development, leaders should be provided with a fair opportunity to achieve their goals, and should be treated "as if they are going to succeed" (Snyder, 1995b, p. 7). Snyder et al. (2000b) also stress the importance of matching goals to talents and areas of strength.

Snyder et al. (2000a) recommend that even though goals should be slightly high to be challenging, "stepping," which they define as "breaking down complex long-term goals into several substeps," is a useful approach to focus attention on "temporally close" goals, and away from "maladaptive preoccupation with unattained long-term goals" (2000a, p. 138). When progress can be observed, reinforced, and celebrated, hope is incrementally, but effectively, built. Moreover, by more frequently experiencing success (and getting reinforced for it by self or others), self-efficacy is enhanced as well.

Another approach to building hope that is particularly relevant for authentic leader resiliency development is "mental rehearsals" (Snyder et al., 2000a). This involves the visualization of important expected events, forecasting of potential obstacles, and mentally picturing possible alternate pathways to overcome those obstacles. Leaders who learn to engage in mental rehearsals are likely to be more prepared to handle blockages, since this type of mental exercise enhances their pathways component of hope. Action planning and what-if analysis are other effective approaches to the development of the pathways component of hope (Luthans & Jensen, 2002; Luthans et al., 2001). Related to this idea is the importance of viewing obstacles as challenges and as a natural part of everyday life that should be anticipated and managed, rather than avoided (Snyder et al., 2000b). Recalling one's past successes, as well as the success stories of other role models, can be very helpful, particularly when faced with blockages (Snyder, 1995a).

Snyder also warns against several pitfalls in the hope development process. A major problem that can result in diminishing hope is overplanning (Snyder, 1995b). Another critical factor is the enjoyment of the journey of trying and learning, not just the outcomes (Snyder et al., 2000b). "Regoaling" when faced with "absolute goal blockage" is also necessary to avoid false hope (Snyder, 1995a).

Developing Authentic Leaders' Optimism

As previously discussed, optimistic leaders are likely to be more resilient due to their ability to hold onto "a context of meaning" (Seligman, 1998, p. 284) that is larger than themselves in times of adversity, and an attributional style that protects them from giving up (persistence) when faced with obstacles. As noted, flexible optimism in particular is likely to contribute to authentic leaders' resiliency by increasing their adaptability in facing and responding to adversity. Therefore, developing and managing optimism should increase resiliency for authentic leadership.

Schneider (2001) proposes three forms of realistic optimism that are applicable in the context of leadership development. The first form is "leniency for the past." Leaders should be able to reframe and accept their unchangeable failures and setbacks, giving themselves the benefit of the doubt, and resisting their perfectionist tendencies. The second form is "appreciation for the present," i.e., contentment and thankfulness about the positive aspects of the current situation, which is particularly relevant to the idea of enjoying the long development journey, a common theme throughout the resiliency development process. The third form is "opportunity-seeking for the future," which is particularly relevant to the idea of viewing risks as opportunities and challenges, rather than just threats and problems.

Similar to Seligman's (1998) view about the importance of meaning (i.e., providing stable values and beliefs), Peterson (2000, p. 49) highlights the importance of "big optimism," an optimistic explanatory style with respect to large, general, less well-defined expectations, at higher levels of abstraction, in producing "a general state of vigor and resilience." He asserts that big optimism can be "cultivated" by finding ways "to harness [it] to a concern with the commons" (Peterson, 2000, p. 51). For example, he proposes a return to the emphasis on religion, since religion provides more certainty and value stability. In fact, the relationship has even been established between religiosity and mental health (e.g., Bergin, 1983; Larson, Pattison, Blazer, Omran, & Kaplan, 1986; Ness & Wintrob, 1980), happiness (Paul, 2005), and coping with traumatic experiences (Baron et al., 1996; Gibbs, 1989; Tebbi, Mallon, Richards, & Bigler, 1987). Although these relationships with religiosity may be beyond the scope of organizational leadership development, recognizing that leaders with spiritual tendencies may have positive outcomes such as optimism has implications for future exploration and study (Watson, 2000; Pargament & Mahoney, 2002).

Another recommendation by Peterson (2000) for developing optimism is lifestyle change toward reduced stress, work-life balance, wellness programs, employee assistance programs, and other approaches that aim to reduce risk factors at the individual and the organizational level. Peterson (2000) also discusses the role of social learning and vicarious modeling in the acquisition of optimism. These approaches were previously given attention in the context of developing and managing self-efficacy.

CONCLUSION

Developing resilient organizations, leaders, and employees is a difficult but attainable journey that takes proactive effort and persistence on the part of the organization as a whole, as well as its leaders and operating-level employees. The organizational level of resiliency development focuses on assets, risk factors, and values and providing the buffering processes that are necessary preconditions for developing resiliency in authentic leaders and their followers.

However, without the active involvement and development of organizational members themselves, especially leaders, this development will be limited. They need to draw from the resilient organizational context, while proactively operating on their own assets, risk factors, and values. They also need to draw from the other positive psychological capacities of hope, optimism, and self-efficacy depicted in the initial model of authentic leadership development (Luthans & Avolio, 2003). Without these inputs, the resilient organization may not necessarily have resilient members. In other words, although resiliency is expected to cascade down organizational levels and have a contagion effect from top to bottom, blockages at any level may prevent individual level resiliency from being effectively developed. Self-serving biases, perceptual/attributional errors, self-defeating beliefs and false optimism, hope, and efficacy are potential sources of such blockages. Therefore, both organizational and individual level resiliency need to be, and can be, proactively developed in the authentic leadership process.

Although the way of operationalizing and research testing of the proposed multi-level model may be a challenging undertaking, we believe that the complexity of the resiliency construct necessitates the initiation of a theory-building approach as proposed in this chapter. For resiliency to be appropriately conceptualized, researched, developed, and applied, a multi-level, multivariate approach seems necessary. Obviously, the next step is to do research on the propositions in order to validate the model and continue to build a theory of resiliency development for authentic leadership development. Regardless of how this research and continued theory-building turns out, one thing is certain, resilient organizations, leaders, and employees are needed now and even more so in the foreseeable future.

REFERENCES

Adler, P. S., & Kwon, S. (2002). Social capital: Prospects for a new concept. *Academy of Management Review, 27,* 17–40.

Allen, N. J., & Meyer, J. P. (1996). Affective, continuance, and normative commitment to the organization: An examination of construct validity. *Journal of Vocational Behavior, 49,* 252–276.

Argyris, C., & Schon, D. (1996). *Organizational learning II: Theory, method, and practice.* Reading, MA: Addison-Wesley.

Avolio, B. J. (2002). Examining the full range model of leadership: Looking back to transform forward. In: D. Day & S. Zaccarro (Eds), *Leadership development for transforming organizations*. Mahwah, NJ: Erlbaum.

Bandura, A. (1997). *Self-efficacy: The exercise of control*. New York: Freeman.

Bandura, A. (2000). Cultivate self-efficacy for personal and organizational effectiveness. In: E. Locke (Ed.), *Handbook of principles of organizational behavior* (pp. 120–136). Oxford, UK: Blackwell.

Bandura, A. (2001). Social cognitive theory: An agentic perspective. *Annual Review of Psychology, 52*, 1–26.

Bandura, A., & Locke, E. A. (2003). Negative self-efficacy and goal effects revisited. *Journal of Applied Psychology, 88*, 87–99.

Baron, L., Eisman, H., Scuello, M., Veyzer, A., & Lieberman, M. (1996). Stress resilience, locus of control, and religion in children of Holocaust victims. *Journal of Psychology, 130*, 513–525.

Bass, B. M., & Avolio, B. J. (1994). *Improving organizational effectiveness through transformational leadership*. Thousand Oaks, CA: Sage.

Bergin, A. (1983). Religiosity and mental health: A critical re-evaluation and meta-analysis. *Professional Psychology Research and Practice, 14*, 170–184.

Block, J. H., & Block, J. (1980). The role of ego-control and ego-resiliency in the organization of behavior. In: W. A. Collins (Ed.), *Minnesota Symposium of Child Psychology* (pp. 39–101). Hillsdale, NJ: Erlbaum.

Brown, E. (1997). Improving organizational health by addressing organizational trauma. *Journal of Organizational Change, 10*, 175–178.

Buckingham, M., & Coffman, C. (1999). *First break all the rules: What the world's greatest managers do differently*. New York: Simon & Schuster.

Cameron, K., Dutton, J., & Quinn, R. (Eds) (2003). *Positive organizational scholarship*. San Francisco: Berrett-Koehler.

Chemers, M. M., Watson, C. B., & May, S. T. (2000). Dispositional affect and leadership effectiveness: A comparison of self-esteem, optimism, and efficacy. *Personality and Social Psychology Bulletin, 26*, 267–277.

Coleman, J. S. (1988). Social capital in the creation of human capital. *American Journal of Sociology, 94*, S95–S120.

Collins, M. E. (2001). Transition to adulthood for vulnerable youths: A review of research and implications for policy. *Social Service Review, 75*, 271–291.

Conner, D. (1993). *Managing at the speed of change: How resilient managers succeed and prosper where others fail*. New York: Villard Books.

Conner, D. (2003). Training & Development - Solutions at Sun Microsystems. www.odrinc.com. May 12.

Coutu, D. L. (2002). How resilience works. *Harvard Business Review, 80*(5), 46–55.

Cowan, P. A., Cowan, C. P., & Schulz, M. S. (1996). Thinking about risk and resilience in families. In: E. M. Hetherington & E. A. Blechman (Eds), *Stress, coping, and resiliency in children and families* (pp. 1–38). Mahwah, NJ: L. Erlbaum Associates.

Crossan, M., & Berdrow, I. (2003). Organizational learning and strategic renewal. *Strategic Management Journal, 24*, 1087–1105.

Crossan, M., Lane, H., & White, R. K. (1999). An organizational learning framework: From intuition to institution. *Academy of Management Review, 24*, 522–537.

Daft, R. L., & Weick, K. (1984). Toward a model of organizations as interpretative systems. *Academy of Management Review, 9,* 284–296.

Day, D. V. (2000). Leadership development: A review in context. *The Leadership Quarterly, 11,* 581–614.

Edwards, J. (1992). A cybernetic theory of stress, coping, and well-being in organizations. *Academy of Management Review, 17,* 238–274.

Egeland, B., Carlson, E., & Sroufe, L. A. (1993). Resilience as a process. *Development and Psychopathology, 5,* 517–528.

Feinauer, D. (1990). The relationship between workplace accident rates and drug and alcohol abuse: The unproven hypothesis. *Labor Studies Journal, 15*(4), 3–15.

Fiske, S. T., & Taylor, S. (1991). *Social cognition.* New York: McGraw-Hill.

Flannery, B. L., & May, D. R. (2000). Environmental ethical decision making in the U.S. metal finishing industry. *Academy of Management Journal, 43,* 642–662.

Fleishman, E. A., Zaccaro, S. J., & Mumford, M. D. (1991). Individual differences and leadership. *The Leadership Quarterly, 2,* 237–245.

Gibbs, M. (1989). Factors in the victim that mediate between disaster and psychotherapy: A review. *Journal of Traumatic Stress, 2*(4), 489–514.

Gorman, C. (2005). The importance of resilience. *Time, 165*(3), A52–A55.

Greenhouse, S. (2001). Report shows Americans have more labor days. *New York Times, 150*(51863), A6.

Hamel, G., & Välikangas, S. (2003). The quest for resilience. *Harvard Business Review, 81*(9), 52–63.

Harris, M., & Heft, L. (1992). Alcohol and drug use in the workplace: Issues, controversies, and directions for future research. *Journal of Management, 18,* 239–266.

Harter, J. K., Schmidt, F.L., & Hayes, T. L. (2002). Business-unit-level relationship between employee satisfaction, employee engagement, and business outcomes: A meta-analysis. *Journal of Applied Psychology, 87,* 268–279.

Hills, A. (2000). Revisiting institutional resilience as a tool in crisis management. *Journal of Contingencies and Crisis Management, 8,* 109–118.

Hitt, M. A., & Ireland, D. (2002). The essence of strategic management: Managing human and social capital. *Journal of Leadership & Organizational Studies, 9*(1), 3–14.

Holaday, M., & McPhearson, R. (1997). Resilience and severe burns. *Journal of Counseling and Development, 75,* 346–356.

Holden, G. (1991). The relationship of self-efficacy appraisals to subsequent health-related outcomes: A meta-analysis. *Social Work in Health Care, 16,* 53–93.

Holden, G., Moncher, M., Schinke, S., & Barker, K. (1990). Self-efficacy in children and adolescents. A meta-analysis. *Psychological Reports, 66,* 1044–1046.

Horne, J., III., & Orr, J. (1998). Assessing behaviors that create resilient organizations. *Employment Relations Today, 24*(4), 29–39.

Huber, G. (1991). Organizational learning: The contributing processes and the literatures. *Organization Science, 2,* 88–115.

Huff, J., Huff, A., & Thomas, H. (1992). Strategic renewal and the interaction of cumulative stress and inertia. *Strategic Management Journal, 13,* 55–75.

Johnson, K., Bryant, D., Collins, D., Noe, T., Strader, T., & Berbaum, M. (1998). Preventing and reducing alcohol and other drug use among high-risk youths by increasing family resilience. *Social Work, 43,* 297–308.

Judge, T., & Bono, J. (2001). Relationship of core self-evaluations traits – self-esteem generalized self-efficacy, locus of control, and emotional stability – with job satisfaction and job performance: A meta-analysis. *Journal of Applied Psychology, 86*, 80–92.

Judge, T. A., Ilies, R., Bono, J. E., & Gerhardt, M. (2002). Personality and leadership: A qualitative and quantitative review. *Journal of Applied Psychology, 87*, 765–780.

Keyes, C. L. M., & Haidt, J. (2003). *Flourishing: Positive psychology and the life well-lived.* Washington, DC: APA.

Kirby, L., & Fraser, M. (1997). Risk and resilience in childhood. In: M. Fraser (Ed.), *Risk and resilience in childhood* (pp. 10–33). Washington, DC: NASW Press.

Klarreich, S. (1998). Resiliency: The skills needed to move forward in a changing environment. In: S. Klarreich (Ed.), *Handbook of organizational health psychology: Programs to make the workplace healthier* (pp. 219–238). Madison, CT: Psychosocial Press.

Kobsa, S. C. (1982). The hardy personality. In: G. S. Sauders & J. Suls (Eds), *Social psychology of health and illness.* Hillsdale, NJ: Erlbaum.

Koretz, G. (2001). Why Americans work so hard. *Business Week, June 11*(3736), 34.

Krueger, N., & Dickson, P. (1993). Self-efficacy and perceptions of opportunities and threats. *Psychological Reports, 72*, 1235–1240.

Krueger, N., & Dickson, P. (1994). How believing in ourselves increases risk-taking: Perceived self-efficacy and opportunity recognition. *Decision Sciences, 25*, 385–400.

Larson, D., Pattison, E., Blazer, D., Omran, A., & Kaplan, B. (1986). Systematic analysis of research on religious variables in four major psychiatric journals, 1978–1982. *American Journal of Psychiatry, 143*, 329–334.

Locke, E. (Ed.) (2000). *Handbook of principles of organizational behavior.* Oxford, UK: Blackwell.

Luthans, F. (1988). Successful vs. effective real managers. *Academy of Management Executive, 2*, 127–132.

Luthans, F. (2002a). The need for and meaning of positive organizational behavior. *Journal of Organizational Behavior, 23*, 695–706.

Luthans, F. (2002b). Positive organizational behavior: Developing and managing psychological strengths. *Academy of Management Executive, 16*, 57–72.

Luthans, F., & Avolio, B. J. (2003). Authentic leadership: A positive development approach. In: K. S. Cameron, J. E. Dutton & R. E. Quinn (Eds), *Positive organizational scholarship* (pp. 241–258). San Francisco: Berrett-Koehler.

Luthans, F., Avolio, B. J., Walumbwa, F. O., & Li, W. (2005). The psychological capital of Chinese workers: Exploring the relationship with performance. *Management and Organization Review* (in press).

Luthans, F., & Jensen, S. M. (2002). Hope: A new positive strength for human resource development. *Human Resource Development Review, 1*, 304–322.

Luthans, F., Luthans, K., Hodgetts, R. M., & Luthans, B. (2001). Positive approach to leadership (PAL): Implications for today's organizations. *The Journal of Leadership Studies, 8*(2), 3–20.

Luthans, F., Luthans, K., & Luthans, B. (2004). Positive psychological capital: Going beyond human and social capital. *Business Horizons, 47*(1), 45–50.

Luthans, F., & Youssef, C. M. (2004). Human, social and now positive psychological capital management: Investing in people for competitive advantage. *Organizational Dynamics, 33*, 143–160.

Maddux, J. E. (2002). Self-efficacy: The power of believing you can. In: C. R. Snyder & S. Lopez (Eds), *Handbook of positive psychology* (pp. 257–276). Oxford, UK: Oxford University Press.

Mallak, L. (1998). Putting organizational resilience processes to work. *Industrial Management, 40*, 8–14.

Maslach, C., Schaufeli, W., & Leiter, M. (2001). Job burnout. *Annual Review of Psychology, 52*, 397–422.

Masten, A. S. (2001). Ordinary magic: Resilience process in development. *American Psychologist, 56*, 227–239.

Masten, A. S., & Reed, M. J. (2002). Resilience in development. In: C. R. Snyder & S. Lopez (Eds), *Handbook of positive psychology* (pp. 74–88). Oxford, UK: Oxford University Press.

Meyer, J. C., & Allen, N. J. (1991). A three-component conceptualization of organizational commitment. *Human Resource Management Review, 1*, 61–89.

Miller, D., & Chen, M. (1996). The simplicity of competitive repertoires: An empirical analysis. *Strategic Management Journal, 17*, 419–439.

Morris, J. A., & Feldman, D. C. (1996). The dimensions, antecedents, and consequences of emotional labor. *Academy of Management Review, 21*, 986–1010.

Nelson, D., & Sutton, C. (1990). Chronic work stress and coping: A longitudinal study and suggested new directions. *Academy of Management Journal, 33*, 859–869.

Ness, R., & Wintrob, R. (1980). The emotional impact of fundamentalist religious participation. *American Journal of Orthopsychiatry, 50*, 302–315.

Nohara, H., & Verdier, E. (2001). Sources of resilience in the computer and software industries in France. *Industry and Innovation, 2*, 201–220.

Pargament, K. L., & Mahoney, A. (2002). Spirituality. In: C. R. Snyder & S. Lopez (Eds), *Handbook of positive psychology* (pp. 646–659). Oxford, UK: Oxford University Press.

Paul, P. (2005). The power to uplift. *Time, 165*(3), A46–A48.

Peterson, C. (2000). The future of optimism. *American Psychologist, 55*, 44–55.

Peterson, S., & Luthans, F. (2003). The positive impact and development of hopeful leaders. *Leadership and Organization Development Journal, 24*, 26–31.

Pfeffer, J. (1998). *The human equation*. Boston: Harvard Business School Press.

Qouta, S., El-Sarraj, A., & Punamaki, R. (2001). Mental flexibility as resiliency factor among children exposed to political violence. *International Journal of Psychology, 36*(1), 1–7.

Reivich, K., & Shatte, A. (2002). *The resilience factor: 7 essential skills for overcoming life's inevitable obstacles*. New York: Random House.

Richardson, G. (2002). The metatheory of resilience and resiliency. *Journal of Clinical Psychology, 58*, 307–321.

Rudolph, J. W., & Repenning, N. P. (2002). Disaster dynamics: Understanding the role of quantity in organizational collapse. *Administrative Science Quarterly, 47*, 1–30.

Rutter, M. (1987). Psychosocial resilience and protective mechanisms. *American Journal of Orthopsychiatry, 57*, 316–331.

Ryff, C. D., & Singer, B. (2003). Flourishing under fire: Resilience as a prototype of challenged thriving. In: C. Keyes & J. Haidt (Eds), *Flourishing: Positive psychology and the life well-lived* (pp. 15–36). Washington, DC: APA.

Sandau-Beckler, P., Devall, E., & de la Rosa, I. (2002). Strengthening family resilience: Prevention and treatment for high-risk substance-affected families. *Journal of Individual Psychology, 58*, 305–327.

Scheier, M. F., & Carver, C. S. (1992). The effects of optimism of psychological and physical well-being. *Cognitive Theory and Research, 16*, 201–228.

Schneider, S. L. (2001). In search of realistic optimism. *American Psychologist, 56*, 250–263.

Schweitzer, M. (2000). Bargaining under the influence: The role of alcohol in negotiations. *Academy of Management Executive, 14*(2), 47–57.

Seligman, M. E. P. (1998). *Learned optimism*. New York: Pocket Books.

Seligman, M. E. P. (2002). *Authentic happiness*. New York: Free Press.

Seligman, M. E. P., & Csikentmihalyi, M. (2000). Positive psychology. *American Psychologist, 55*, 5–14.

Sell, A., & Newman, R. (1992). Alcohol abuse in the workplace: A managerial dilemma. *Business Horizons, 35*(6), 64–71.

Sheldon, K. M., & King, L. (2001). Why positive psychology is necessary. *American Psychologist, 56*, 216–217.

Smith, C. A., & Carlson, B. (1997). Stress, coping, and resilience in children and youth. *Social Service Review, 71*, 231–256.

Snyder, C. R. (1995a). Conceptualizing, measuring, and nurturing hope. *Journal of Counseling and Development, 73*, 355–360.

Snyder, C. R. (1995b). Managing for high hope. *R & D Innovator, 4*(6), 6–7.

Snyder, C. R. (2000). *Handbook of hope*. San Diego: Academic Press.

Snyder, C. R., Harris, C., Anderson, J. R., Holleran, S. A., Irving, L. M., Sigmon, S. T., Yoshinobu, L., Gibb, J., Langelle, C., & Harney, P. (1991). The will and the ways. Development and validation of an individual-differences measure of hope. *Journal of Personality and Social Psychology,, 60*, 570–585.

Snyder, C. R., Ilardi, S., Michael, S. T., & Cheavens, J. (2000a). Hope theory: Updating a common process for psychological change. In: C. R. Snyder & R. E. Ingram (Eds), *Handbook of psychological change: Psychotherapy processes and practices for the 21st century* (pp. 128–153). New York: Wiley.

Snyder, C. R., Irving, L. M., & Anderson, J. R. (1991). Hope and health: Measuring the will and the ways. In: C. R. Snyder & D. R. Forsyth (Eds), *Handbook of social and clinical psychology* (pp. 285–305). Elmsford, NY: Pergamon.

Snyder, C. R., & Lopez, S. (2002). *Handbook of positive psychology*. Oxford, UK: Oxford University Press.

Snyder, C. R., Rand, K. L., & Sigmon, D. R. (2002). Hope theory. In: C. R. Snyder & S. Lopez (Eds), *Handbook of positive psychology* (pp. 257–276). Oxford, UK: Oxford University Press.

Snyder, C. R., Sympson, S. C., Ybasco, F. C., Borders, T. F., Babyak, M. A., & Higgins, R. L. (1996). Development and validation of the state hope scale. *Journal of Personality and Social Psychology, 70*, 321–335.

Snyder, C. R., Tran, T., Schroeder, L. L., Pulvers, K. M., Adam III, V., & Laub, L. (2000b). Teaching the hope recipe: Setting goals, finding pathways to those goals, and getting motivated. *National Educational Service,* (Summer), 46–50.

Stajkovic, A. D., & Luthans, F. (1997). A meta-analysis of the effects of organizational behavior modification on task performance:1975–95. *Academy of Management Journal, 40*, 1122–1149.

Stajkovic, A. D., & Luthans, F. (1998a). Self-efficacy and work-related performance: A meta-analysis. *Psychological Bulletin, 124*, 240–261.

Stajkovic, A. D., & Luthans, F. (1998b). Social cognitive theory and self-efficacy: Going beyond traditional motivational and behavioral approaches. *Organizational Dynamics, 26,* 62–74.

Staw, B. M., & Barsade, S. G. (1993). Affect and managerial experience: A test of the sadder-but-wiser vs. *happier-and-smarter hypotheses. Administrative Science Quarterly., 38,* 304–331.

Sutcliffe, K. M., & Vogus, T. (2003). Organizing for resilience. In: K. S. Cameron, J. E. Dutton & R. E. Quinn (Eds), *Positive organizational scholarship* (pp. 94–110). San Francisco: Berrett-Koehler.

Taylor, S. E. (1989). *Positive illusions.* New York: Basic Books.

Tebbi, C., Mallon, J., Richards, M., & Bigler, L. (1987). Religiosity and locus of control of adolescent and cancer patients. *Psychological Reports, 61,* 683–696.

Tedeschi, R., Park, C., & Calhoun, L. (Eds) (1998). *Posttraumatic growth: Positive changes in the aftermath of crisis.* Mahwah, NJ: Erlbaum.

Thottam, J. (2005). Thank God it's Monday!. *Time, 165*(3), A58–A61.

Tiger, L. (1979). *Optimism: The biology of hope.* New York: Simon and Schuster.

Trevino, L. K., & Victor, B. (1992). Peer reporting of unethical behavior: A social context perspective. *Academy of Management Journal, 35,* 38–64.

Vancouver, J., Thompson, C., Tischner, E., & Putka, D. (2002). Two studies examining the negative effect of self-efficacy on performance. *Journal of Applied Psychology, 87,* 506–516.

Vancouver, J., Thompson, C., & Williams, A. (2001). The changing signs in the relationship between self-efficacy, personal goals, and performance. *Journal of Applied Psychology, 86,* 605–620.

Veninga, R. L. (2000). Managing hope in the workplace: Five simple strategies can help transform organizations. *Health Progress, 81,* 22–24.

Vickers, M. H., & Kouzmin, A. (2001). Resilience in organizational actors and rearticulating voice. *Public Management Review, 3*(1), 95–119.

Vroom, V. H. (1964). *Work and motivation.* New York: Wiley.

Watson, D. (2000). *Mood and temperament.* New York: Guilford.

Weick, K. E. (1995). *Sensemaking in organizations.* Thousand Oaks, CA: Sage.

Weick, K. E. (1993). The collapse of sensemaking in organizations: The Mann Gulch disaster. *Administrative Science Quarterly, 38,* 628–652.

Weick, K. E., & Roberts, K. (1993). Collective mind in organizations: Heedful interrelating on flight decks. *Administrative Science Quarterly, 38,* 357–381.

Wolin, S., & Wolin, S. (2003). Project resilience. www.projectresilience.com. May 12.

Wong, J., & Mason, G. (2001). Reviled, rejected, but resilient: Homeless people in recovery and life skills education. *Georgetown Journal on Poverty Law and Policy, 8,* 475–503.

Worline, M. C., Dutton, J. E., Frost, P. J., Kanov, J., Lilius, J. M., & Maitlis, S. (2002). Creating fertile soil: The organizing dynamics of resilience. Paper presented at the annual meeting of the Academy of Management, Denver.

Zunz, S. (1998). Resiliency and burnout: Protective factors for human service managers. *Administration in Social Work, 22*(3), 39–54.

AUTHENTIC LEADERSHIP IN *IN EXTREMIS* SETTINGS: A CONCEPT FOR EXTRAORDINARY LEADERS IN EXCEPTIONAL SITUATIONS [☆]

Thomas A. Kolditz and Donna M. Brazil

ABSTRACT

In this chapter we argue that, in dangerous settings, leader optimism, hope, and resilience are especially valued, and therefore authentic leaders will assert a particularly powerful influence in such settings. While researchers find such high-risk situations, to be challenging and inhospitable, they provide ideal settings for seeking and identifying authentic leaders, and for assessing authenticity in leader behavior. We describe ongoing work to study authentic leadership occurring in such in extremis settings, across a variety of circumstances where death must be actively avoided. Finally, we examine theories that inform the understanding of authentic leadership in dangerous settings, as well as the ability to develop authentic leadership skills in these settings.

[☆] The ideas expressed by the authors are theirs, and do not represent the U.S. Military Academy, the U.S. Army, or the Department of Defense.

Authentic Leadership Theory and Practice: Origins, Effects and Development
Monographs in Leadership and Management, Volume 3, 345–356

INTRODUCTION

One of the most severe criticisms that could be levied against a person leading an organization would be that they were merely posing as a leader, falsely currying the favor and trust of followers by superficially self-promoting, yet behaving in ways that betray insincerity or lack of character. When compared to an insincere person who acts out a leadership role, a transparent, genuine leader commands unparalleled respect and admiration. Consider the battalion commander who sensed that the soldiers in his command were shaken when they lost two comrades to an improvised explosive device on the streets of Afghanistan. He spoke with them before their next mission, but more importantly, he opted to accompany them on their next mission, not as a commander, but as a member of the squad, sharing their experience and showing them the way.

In another example, MG Eric Olson, commander of the elite 25th Infantry Division left the relative comfort of his headquarters in Bagram, Afghanistan on Christmas morning and flew to one of his remote bases. There he selected two junior soldiers who were scheduled for patrol and sent them back to Bagram in the chopper to relax, eat, and enjoy the holiday. MG Olson took their place on patrol that day, sitting in the back of a Humvee with the other soldiers instead of being escorted as he normally would have been as a general officer. The soldier's reaction was immediate and positive, "to sit in a cav truck in one of the worst seats and ride with us, to come and pull guard with us ... makes lower enlisted soldiers like myself feel good about him as our leader" (Rhen, 2005, p. 1). It is little wonder that both of these soldiers recently re-enlisted in the army.

In straightforward terms, these influential leaders and others like them are *authentic*. Authentic leadership theory (ALT) represents the formal development of the idea that followers are attentive to, and able to recognize, a lack of sincerity or clumsy impression management strategies displayed by someone in a leadership position or role (Luthans & Avolio, 2003). Authentic leaders are confident, optimistic leaders of high moral character who are aware of their own thoughts, behaviors, abilities, and values. Authentic leaders are also attentive to these characteristics in others and the situational context in which they operate (Avolio, Gardner, Walumbwa, Luthans, & May, 2004). In elaborating ALT, the states of optimism, hopefulness, and resiliency reflecting positive psychology (Seligman, 2002) provide the key to understanding why leaders who are authentic are also effective at commanding follower loyalty, obedience, admiration, and respect.

It follows, then, that in circumstances where leader optimism, hope, and resilience are especially valued, authentic leaders will assert a particularly powerful influence. Specifically, in situations where followers perceive their lives are threatened, feelings of optimism, hope, and resilience literally define the promise of future life, and are therefore desperately sought by those at risk. Such high-risk situations, though challenging and inhospitable for researchers, are ideal settings to seek and find authentic leaders, and to assess authenticity in leader behavior. In this chapter, we describe ongoing work to study authentic leadership occurring "at the point of death," or, more correctly, under circumstances where death must be actively avoided. It makes sense to refer to such leaders and situations with a unique term, *in extremis*, or, "at the point of death." In concept, this chapter proposes that men and women who lead other people in places and through situations that most of us would find intimidating, if not outright horrifying, will often behave in ways that are indicative of authentic leadership. The in-depth study of these *in extremis* leaders may also provide insights for the development of authentic leadership.

In Extremis Leadership

In extremis leadership is defined as giving purpose, motivation, and direction to people when there is eminent physical danger, and where followers believe that leader behavior will influence their physical well-being or survival (Kolditz, 2004). *In extremis* leadership is not a leadership theory. It simply is an approach that views leader and follower behaviors under a specific set of circumstances – circumstances where outcomes mean more than mere success or failure, but instead involve life or death.

The threat of death can have a powerful influence on human behavior. In their study of soldiers during World War II, Stouffer and his colleagues found that when inexperienced soldiers were most fearful of death, they became desperate for almost any type of leader – in short, they simply looked for someone to lead them through the difficult experience (Stouffer, Suchman, DeVinney, Star, & Williams, 1949). In purely psychological terms, an individual's enhanced awareness of death is called *mortality salience*. Mortality salience has been manipulated in experimental studies by asking subjects to imagine, in detail, the circumstances of their physical death (Rosenblatt, Greenberg, Solomon, Pyszczynski, & Lyon, 1989). This simple manipulation was successful at determining more closely the characteristics that followers desire in a leader during these stressful moments.

Participants demonstrated a preference for charismatic, followed by task-oriented, and relationship-oriented leader communications (Cohen, Solomon, Maxfield, Pyszczynski, & Greenberg, 2004). Specifically, participants were more influenced by charismatic leader messages when recently focused on their own mortality. When coupled with messages about specific events, mortality salience may directly influence political beliefs, as well as voting behavior (Landau et al., 2004). It follows, then, that circumstances that cause followers to fear death may encourage the development and exercise of specific patterns of leadership by leaders who routinely operate in such circumstances. The projects discussed in this chapter provide an opportunity to study leaders in *in extremis* situations in order to identify the unique leader behaviors required in these situations as well as an organization's ability to develop these behaviors in future leaders.

LINKING CONCEPTS TO PRACTICE IN DANGEROUS CIRCUMSTANCES

Many people, particularly public servants such as police, fire fighters, and members of the military, live and work in dangerous settings. For leaders in dangerous callings, organizational outcomes are not open to negotiation, but instead are governed by forces of absolute power: physics, aerodynamics, fire, and weather dominate the *in extremis* environment. Socially, *in extremis* leaders face hatred, criminality, and war. Their place in the world is earned through competence, determination, and courage. The best word to describe the character of leaders in such settings is *authentic,* as their success truly is measured in the units of authentic leadership: moral character, trust, hope, optimism, and positive emotionality. Thus, ALT can be advanced and understood very effectively by studying *in extremis* leaders and leadership.

The methodological challenges associated with the study of *in extremis* leadership are significant, but not insurmountable. Three research projects currently underway reveal various methods that may be used to study authentic leadership in *in extremis* settings (Kolditz, Ruth, & Banks, 2004). The guiding questions throughout these research projects are designed to determine the psychological constructs involved in leader–follower exchanges in *in extremis* settings. We seek to determine what effect the threat of death has on both leader actions and follower reactions. We examine how the risk involved in *in extremis* settings differs from other forms of risk, in perhaps less threatening settings. Finally, we examine the development of leaders in *in extremis* settings to determine how development of these constructs might best be accomplished. We describe these projects below.

Interviews with In Extremis versus Organizationally Effective Leaders

The first project examines and compares approaches to leadership by contrasting in-depth interviews with *in extremis* leaders (New York and San Francisco Federal Bureau of Investigation Special Weapons and Tactics (FBI SWAT) team chiefs, mountain climbing guides, outward bound leader, lead commander in attack on Baghdad, national parachute event leader, jungle video team chief, etc.) with interviews of organizationally effective business and academic leaders (high school principal, school superintendent, Fortune 500 executives) who face no physical risk. Leaders from both spheres were selected based on their accomplishments within their organizations.

The main difference between the two groups is the fact that the decisions of the organizationally effective leaders, while important and far reaching, do not involve life and death. All of these leaders are asked to define success and failure and to identify those qualities aside from technical competence that make them an effective leader. Leaders are also asked to describe themselves as they believe their direct reports would describe them.

Because interviewees are, in a sense, self selected, an instrument measuring the trait of hardiness (Maddi & Khoshaba, 2001) is also included to assess a potentially relevant individual difference variable to leadership in these extreme contexts (Maddi, 2002). We singled out the measure of hardiness due to the anticipated relationship of hardiness constructs such as resiliency and coping with the traits of authentic leadership. For example, it seems reasonable to assume that leaders who inspire confidence and optimism might also exhibit personal hardiness. The interviews draw comparisons and reveal differences in the areas of trust, shared risk, commonality of lifestyle, and loyalty. Content analysis will be used to identify all applicable leader behaviors and attributes and in particular to examine the authentic leadership constructs of hope, resiliency, and optimism, as well as the moral challenges faced by leaders who balance ambition and goals with the risk of human life.

Interviews with Followers of Combat Leaders

The second ongoing research project is directed at *follower* perspectives of leaders in extreme environments, such as combat. The project seeks to

determine the requisite conditions and leader qualities or attributes necessary for individuals to follow their leader into harm's way. It uses a content
analysis of in-depth interviews with more than 85 U.S. and Iraqi soldiers
performed by a team of military and civilian researchers in Baghdad,
Al Hillah, and Um Qasr, Iraq in April and May, 2003, prior to the formal
cessation of hostilities between U.S. coalition and Iraqi forces (Wong,
Kolditz, Millen, & Potter, 2003; Kolditz & Wong, 2003). U.S. soldiers who
participated in the initial attack on Baghdad under extremely dangerous
conditions and Iraqi soldiers captured by coalition forces were asked to
describe the interpersonal relationships in their units to include the dyadic
relationship between them and their leader. They were also asked to list the
reasons why they fought or failed to fight. The interviews are being analyzed
with a focus on task cohesion, social cohesion, and leadership.

Preliminary analysis of the data gathered from these soldiers draws comparisons and reveals differences in follower trust, motivation and loyalty,
and ties these outcomes to the perceived competence and morality of leaders
in combat. The will of the followers to continue to fight is also examined in
terms of the relationship developed with their leaders, and in particular the
level of identification established between leader and follower (Avolio et al.,
2004). Interview comments from both U.S. and Iraqi soldiers support the
premise that personal and social identification with the leader fosters higher
levels of trust, hope, and optimism in followers. The opposite was also
found to be true: a weak relationship with the leader resulted in a lack of
trust, hope, and optimism.

Case Study of the U.S. Military Academy's Elite Sport Parachute Team

The third research project is a detailed case study of how leaders develop
when required to operate in dangerous environments. It addresses the issue
of whether authentic leader behavior patterns can be best developed or
taught in *in extremis* settings. The project is focused on the U.S. Military
Academy's elite sport parachute team. This 30-member, co-educational
team operates as a 3 year, high risk, leader development laboratory and, in
the past 4 years, has produced not only nationally ranked sport parachutists
but also the Academy's upper tier student leaders, including three "Cadet
First Captains" (the highest ranking commander of the Corps of Cadets)
and two winners of prestigious Rhodes scholarships.

Several of the team members studied, including one of the Rhodes scholars, were interviewed by either online chat or satellite telephone because they

had deployed to a combat zone soon after graduation. Cadets traditionally join the sport parachute team when they are 19 years old. During the following 3 years they develop and grow as leaders in the Corps of Cadets and on the parachute team. The project seeks to identify differences in development experienced by these cadets as members of this team that competes in *in extremis* situations. Interviewees were asked to describe how their participation on the team impacted their leader development and how the nature if the *in extremis* sport contributed to their development of leadership skills and thus their ability to lead. Finally, they were asked how their ability to regulate their emotions impacted their overall effectiveness as a leader on the parachute team and in the Corps of Cadets. As with the leaders in study 1, leaders on the parachute team are self selected. Therefore each cadet is given an instrument to measure hardiness as an exploratory assessment of possible individual differences (Maddi & Khoshaba, 2001).

A unique aspect of West Point is that all cadets must participate on athletic teams, therefore the study examined the ability of dangerous versus safe sports to contribute to the development of authentic leadership. In addition to the members of the sport parachute team, cadets who participate in team sports (football, hockey, rugby) and cadets who participate in individual sports (track, swimming) were interviewed and asked the same questions. Our analyses drew comparisons and examined differences in the development of authentic leadership skills and techniques among these three groups of student athletes. Preliminary results from these comparisons support our hypothesis that *in extremis* team membership will result in increased development of these skills. Specifically, members of the sport parachute team demonstrated higher levels of competence, trust and loyalty than members of the safe sports teams. Moreover, they were not as concerned with motivating their subordinates as were members of other teams and were instead focused on learning, decision making, and executing – all key aspects of authentic leadership.

Clearly, the *in extremis* settings that foster authentic leadership are unusual and in most cases dangerous, but they do not preclude systematic study and research. Aside from war zones, most *in extremis* settings are publicly accessible – admittedly, with effort. In addition, *in extremis* settings are never "pure"; in most cases there are periods of relatively low perceived threat punctuated by grave moments. Therefore, findings derived from these field settings have considerable relevance and can be useful across both academic and numerous practical settings. Qualitative and quasi-experimental structured interviews (with subsequent content analysis) and systematic behavioral observation are the most practical research tools available for the study of authentic leadership in *in extremis* settings.

In addition to the relatively risk free telephonic interviews our researchers have conducted, our studies thus far have required deployment to a combat zone, active participation in special operations free fall school, and flying in an aircraft to observe the actions of cadet jumpmasters. Further research will continue to require "going to where the action is" to gather observational data on the reaction of subordinates to the actions of these in extremis leaders. Only by studying both the actions of these leaders and the impact on their followers will we be able to make the direct connection to ALT.

BENEFITS OF STUDYING AUTHENTIC LEADERSHIP IN *IN EXTREMIS* SETTINGS

There are important reasons to study authentic leadership in *in extremis* settings. Whether the goal of the leader under study is to photograph a wild tiger or to arrest a drug dealer, whether followers are inside an M1 tank moving 50 mph down a Baghdad freeway or preparing to enter a burning building, the study of authentic leadership in *in extremis* settings promises high risk, high payoff outcomes. This is a world where adrenaline courses through the veins of people who live extraordinary lives, and do extraordinary things. It's a world of extreme settings which most people neither experience nor fully understand. Likely in these unique performance domains we will see how authentic leadership performs by testing its upper boundaries, which typically is not done in leadership research. Indeed, oftentimes researchers have examined charismatic or inspiring leadership to see how it predicts the most mundane performance criterion. In doing so, they are very likely underestimating the predictive validity of such leadership styles. We should not make the same mistake again as we begin to study what constitutes the positive root to all forms of effective leadership, which would be authentic.

On a practical level, research *in extremis* settings has considerable value in the area of public service. The majority of *in extremis* leaders are public servants. W.R. Mead, a senior Fellow of the Council on Foreign Relations, recently acknowledged public appreciation for actions akin to *in extremis* leadership in the 2004 Presidential election, when he remarked, "People need to feel that the President is not going to be fazed by life and death decisions. And the only way you can demonstrate that is by showing that you've made some" (Toner, 2004, p. 2). For public service leaders, the value of being transparent and showing consistency among their values, ethical reasoning and actions can contribute immeasurably to the broader public good. Neither leaders nor followers who risk their lives in the public service are paid more than an average wage, and few appear to be motivated solely by transactional benefits (Kolditz et al., 2004). They are, instead, inspired by their role in society, and by leaders who have a strong mission and beliefs about the value of their activities, who are widely known and respected for their integrity – authentic leaders. Such a remarkable phenomenon is worthy of greater elaboration and understanding not only in the context of leadership theory and research, but as a public service.

The study of authentic leaders in *in extremis* settings could also have significant utility and value when applied to business practice. Authentic leadership – with its emphasis on the development of hope, resilience, and optimism – gets at the heart of what motivates a follower. Authentic leaders – whose behavior reveals a heightened moral and ethical perspective (Luthans & Avolio, 2003), earn the trust of followers who interpret their motivation in a positive way. In business, leadership is often treated as a skill, or style, to increase the effectiveness of the organization and consequently increase the bottom line. Such an approach is inherently transactional because the primary motivation is known to be profit-based. People in *in extremis* settings move beyond transactional concerns; coercive leaders are eventually ignored, and bonuses or promises of other tangible rewards are less relevant when it comes to putting one's life in the hands of a leader. The primary focus is on the preservation of life and success at the task or mission (Kolditz, 2003). Business leaders who find it difficult to make the transition from transactional to a more authentic perhaps transformational leadership approach may gain both understanding and inspiration from authentic leader role models. Learning how such leaders operated *in extremis* environments can provide lessons learned that can be applied to some of the stressful challenges facing leaders today even if the risks are not the same.

ONGOING APPLICATION: PRODUCING AUTHENTIC COMBAT LEADERS

The U.S. Military Academy offers a course titled *Leadership in Combat*. The course is required for those cadets who choose to major in either *Leadership* or *Military Art and Science* at West Point. As of this writing, no cadets with combat experience have enrolled in the course, although by 2006, there will be more than 20 combat veterans in their senior year at the Academy. For all others, however, coming to understand the dynamics of leading in combat is a significant challenge. The seminar involves coming to understand the psychology of extreme stress, group dynamics in extreme settings, and the application of those principles in combat case studies. In generic terms, it's a seminar of practice. In addition, cadets enrolled in the seminar are treated to visits by more than a dozen highly experienced combat veterans who provide living oral history about leading in combat. They vary in rank from four-star general to sergeant.

One quality that stands out among the combat leaders who have come to share their stories with cadets is that they continue to critique themselves and their actions. They understand themselves and the situation they were in and attempt to learn from those experiences and help others learn from those experiences. These men and women do more than share war stories; they share lessons learned. One critical component of authentic leadership is the idea that to begin to approach authenticity, you must first have an accurate self-assessment.

A universal comment from experienced combat veterans is that it is quite difficult, perhaps impossible, to describe the influence of combat to those who have not experienced it. War is very serious business, and those who have engaged in the grisly matter of killing, even killing for politically, socially, or morally justified reasons, are sometimes traumatized and often hesitant to be forthcoming and descriptive. The veterans advise the uninitiated, "You have to have been there to know what it was like." In the *Leadership in Combat* course, we give cadets permission to interpret such a statement as a challenge for understanding, rather than a dismissal from the responsibility to think about leading in combat.

The combat veteran's admonishment takes on new meaning, however, when compared with that of a 20-year-old college student bubbling with excitement over her first skydive, or a climber freshly returned from summit of a life threatening peak. People whose experiences are unique and dangerous also often say, "you have to have been there to know what it was like," but unlike the more silent and reserved combat veterans, these survivors enjoy telling stories, sometimes for hours, about the excitement and challenge that they overcame. Such stories are so common among climbers, skydivers, and other adventuresome athletes that, in catalogs catering to extreme sports, one can purchase t-shirts sporting the phrase, "No s—t, there I was ..." We would argue that the shirt should be changed to,

"No s—t, there WE were," because under grave circumstances, less experienced individuals were usually led by an instructor, an expert, or a professional guide who gave them confidence, optimism, hope, and resilience – in sum, they followed an authentic leader. Therein lies the value of the *in extremis* perspective – the perspective of a combat veteran, formerly impossible to share, can be approached conceptually as a case of authentic leadership in an *in extremis* setting. Subsequently these constructs can be studied, deconstructed, and discussed in constructive ways by looking across *in extremis* settings and comparing the actions and behaviors of these leaders with leaders in less risky situations.

LESSONS LEARNED AND FUTURE DIRECTIONS

From the on-going projects described above, we have learned some key lessons and raised more questions for the study of leaders in *in extremis* settings. The most important lesson we have learned is to be very stringent in the selection of the leaders to study. We focused only on leaders who are actively engaged in *in extremis* settings. This is critical when seeking to determine possible differences across settings.

With respect to future research, we offer the following questions as promising avenues for investigation. (1) What are *in extremis* leaders thinking before, during, and after they are in these *in extremis* situations, whether the situation is combat, a tiger shoot or a police raid? (2) How do *in extremis* leaders process these events, a day, a week, a month, and years later? (3) How do *in extremis* leaders perceive their relationships with followers prior to, during, and after the events? (4) What would an *in-extremis* have done to prepare differently, if given the opportunity, and what seemed to prepare them best? (5) What do the followers in *in extremis* settings need and desire from their leaders in order to become fully engaged in these activities? (6) What are the implications of adaptive leadership for *in extremis* leadership? (7) How can attributes associated with adaptability be developed in future leaders?

In sum, *in extremis* settings represent a superb opportunity for the study of authentic leadership. Additional work to define, measure, and elaborate on the *in extremis* paradigm promises to serve ALT in constructive ways. Those who risk their lives in the public service may reap practical benefits by reflecting on their circumstances, and developing insights into leadership, followership, and personal effectiveness. The characteristics displayed by authentic leaders hold value for organizations and individuals across contexts and circumstances. When exhibited by *in extremis* leaders in high-risk settings, the returns may be priceless.

REFERENCES

Avolio, B.J., Gardner, W.L., Walumbwa, F.O., Luthans, F., & May, D.R. (2004) Unlocking the mask: A look at the process by which authentic leaders impact follower attitudes and behaviors. *The Leadership Quarterly, 15*, 801–823.

Cohen, F., Solomon, S., Maxfield, M., Pyszczynski, T., & Greenberg, J. (2004). The effects of mortality salience on evaluations of charismatic, task-oriented, and relationship-oriented leaders. *Psychological Science, 15*, 846–851.

Kolditz, T.A. (2003). Leadership learnings from Iraq. *Opening Bell, 5*, 1–2.

Kolditz, T.A. (2004). *In extremis leadership and the assumption of risk: An academy deployed.* Keynote speech delivered to State Superintendent of Insurance executive staff, New York State Insurance Department.

Kolditz, T.A., & Wong, L. (2003). Why do they fight? Combat motivation in Operation Iraqi Freedom. Paper presented at the American political science association, international security and arms control conference, Carlisle, PA.

Kolditz, T.A., Ruth, S., & Banks, B.B. (2004, August). Defining in extremis leadership. Paper presented at the annual meeting of the academy of management, New Orleans, LA.

Landau, M.J., Solomon, S., Greenberg, J., Cohen, F., Pyszczynski, T., Arndt, J., Miller, C.H., Ogilvie, D.M., & Cook, A. (2004). Deliver us from evil: The effects of mortality salience and reminders of 9/11 on support for President George Bush. *Personality and Social Psychology Bulletin, 30*, 1–14.

Luthans, F., & Avolio, B.J. (2003). Authentic leadership: A positive developmental approach. In: K.S. Cameron, J.E. Dutton, & R.E. Quinn (Eds), *Positive organizational scholarship* (pp. 241–258). San Francisco: Berrett-Koehler.

Maddi, S. R. (2002). The story of hardiness: Twenty years of theorizing, research, and practice. *Consulting Psychology Journal, 54*, 173–185.

Maddi, S.R., & Khoshaba, D.M. (2001). *HardiSurvey III-R.* Newport Beach, CA: Hardiness Institute.

Toner, R. (2004, February 15). Ideas & trends – battle stations; still the question: What did you do in the war? *New York Times Week in Review Editorial*, 12.

Rhen, B. (2005, January 7). General pulls guard duty as holiday gift for soldiers. *Pointer View, 62*(1), 1.

Rosenblatt, A., Greenberg, J., Solomon, S., Pyszczynski, T., & Lyon, D., (1989). Evidence for terror management theory I: The effects of mortality salience on reactions of those who violate or uphold cultural values. *Journal of Personality and Social Psychology, 57*, 681–690.

Seligman, M. (2002). *Authentic happiness.* New York: Free Press.

Stouffer, S.A., Suchman, E.A., DeVinney, L.C., Star, S.A., & Williams, R.M. (1949). *The American soldier: Adjustment during army life* (Vol. 1). New York: Wileys.

Wong, L., Kolditz, T.A., Millen, R., & Potter, T. (2003). *Why they fight: Combat motivation in the Iraq war.* Carlisle, PA: Strategic Studies Institute Monograph.

AUTHENTIC DEVELOPMENT: LEADERSHIP DEVELOPMENT LEVEL AND EXECUTIVE EFFECTIVENESS

Keith M. Eigel and Karl W. Kuhnert

ABSTRACT

Based on research with 21 top executives, we have identified a measurable characteristic that highly effective leaders have in common: Leadership Development Level (or LDL). LDLs are developmental levels of maturity that shape the mental and moral capacities of the leader. While the highest LDLs are associated with authentic leadership, the theory behind LDL focuses on the leader's developmental understanding of his or her world, and how that understanding differs at each LDL. In this way, LDL describes the process by which leaders become authentic leaders. In this chapter, we explain what LDL is, how it works, and it's utility for understanding leadership development and leader effectiveness.

Over the past century we have struggled with how to accurately identify and develop future leaders. The truth is we often know effective leadership when we see it and most of us know from experience the impact of poor leadership

Authentic Leadership Theory and Practice: Origins, Effects and Development
Monographs in Leadership and Management, Volume 3, 357–385
Copyright © 2005 by Elsevier Ltd.
All rights of reproduction in any form reserved

on our organizations based on our personal experience with those leaders. The problem is not so much knowing who our effective leaders are; the problem is we are not good at predicting who will and will not be an effective leader, nor how to help them develop to a place of greater effectiveness. Much of what we know about leadership effectiveness comes from a long history of finding successful leaders and identifying the traits, behaviors, or situations that made them successful (Bass & Stogdill, 1990; Burns, 1978; Sternberg, 2003).

Identifying known leaders and describing their success has a long tradition in management research practice. The thick descriptions of successful leaders in many cases are accurate and often a source of inspiration to others. However, these descriptions often focus more on the characteristics of leader's behaviors once they are successful, but do not necessarily inform us as to how they became successful (Collins & Porras, 1994; Collins, 2001; Covey, 1989; Zaccaro, Rittman, & Marks, 2001). Not withstanding the ample research findings that show relationships between leadership traits, attitudes, and performance, we are left with a formula for selecting and developing leaders that is unreliable and frustrating to utilize (Nadler & Nadler, 1998).

Recently, the concept of authentic leadership has been put forth by several authors (Avolio, Gardner, Walumbwa, Luthans, & May, 2004; Gardner, Avolio, Luthans, May, & Walumbwa, 2005; Luthans & Avolio, 2003), and others from this book. It is proposed by these authors that authentic leadership is related to many different characteristics such as self-awareness, self-esteem, trustworthiness, integrity, respect for others, high emotional intelligence, transformational leadership, and other noble characteristics. This emphasis, we believe, is an encouraging shift in thinking as these characteristics are the destination of a developmental journey. What we hope to accomplish in the following pages is to describe this developmental journey, and to create an understanding of the process by which leaders achieve authentic leadership. The underlying rationale for the developmental theory we will posit is that leaders grow through an increasingly better understanding of who they are and how others see them. Our aim is to advance a *theory of the whole person* that helps lead to more authentic leadership. Thus, our goal is to help identify and develop leaders based on their capacities along a developmental continuum. In other words, we are emphasizing the *development* in leadership development.

Our hope is that this chapter offers a challenge to the existing way we think about leadership and leadership development. We believe leaders, as individuals, develop over the life course and do so in predictable ways

(Drath, 2001; Kegan, 1994; Loevenger, 1976; Slater, 2003). As such, we believe there are measurable differences between individuals and these differences account for differences in effective and ineffective leadership. By placing emphasis on development, we are looking not just at what leaders say and do (either as authentic or inauthentic), but where they say it from in their developmental journey.

A CLOSER LOOK AT DEVELOPMENT

Within the disciplines of developmental psychology, there have been many decades of research investigating individuals' capacities to respond to and make sense of the situations or demands that are placed upon them (Kegan, 1994; Kohlberg, 1981; Loevenger, 1976; Selman, 1980). Research on the capacity of people to respond effectively to complex circumstances has fallen under the general umbrella of *constructive developmental* theory or ego development (Kuhnert & Lewis, 1987; Manners, Durkin, & Nesdale, 2004; Rooke & Torbert, 1998). In applying constructive developmental theory to leadership in this chapter, we will refer to constructive developmental capacity as Leadership Development Level (or LDL). LDL is defined as the measurable capacity to understand ourselves, others, and our situations. Each LDL is the total of who we are; how we think about leading others, the way we see and solve problems, and what we know to be important and true. Our capacity to understand is more than the sum of *what* we know – it is *how* we know what we know that defines LDL. *What* we know is what we learn from our experiences. *How* we know, or the frame for our understanding, is how we understand or make sense of our experiences. LDL is the lens through which we filter our experiences (Kuhnert & Lewis, 1987). The way we differentiate levels of how we know is what determines our LDL.

LDL is an invariant, hierarchical, developmental progression that begins at least at birth and continues to evolve throughout the course of one's life. Fig. 1 shows the developmental progression of LDL and how it is characterized by alternating periods of stability and growth. The progression of this developmental capacity is more predictable in childhood than in adulthood for the reason that development is catalyzed by our experiences and the responses we have to those experiences, and those experiences are more predictable in early years. More specifically, when new experiences contradict our current ways of understanding ourselves, others and our situations, then those contradictory experiences become the fuel for development.

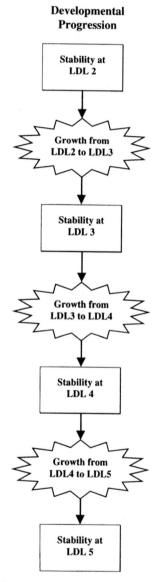

Fig. 1. The Developmental Progression.

Thus, responses to these contradictions help us to develop increasingly more effective ways of knowing, processing, deciding, and relating over the course of our lifetime.

As exposure to experiences that potentially contradict current ways of understanding varies more and more with age, a greater variety of LDLs are found in the 30–60-year age bracket than are seen in younger ages. In other words, the developmental trajectory of childhood and adolescence is generally more predictable than that of adulthood. This developmental phenomenon applied to leadership helps explain why not all leaders of the same chronological age and similar intelligence, personality, and educational background respond similarly to identical (or nearly identical) circumstances – *some, in fact, respond more effectively than others.*

To better understand the differences between the lower (or less developed) LDLs and the higher (more developed) LDLs, we will group the characteristics of the developmental progression around three general areas of experience: *intrapersonal, interpersonal,* and *cognitive* (Kegan, 1982, 1994). We will refer to these three areas from this point forward as knowing ourselves, others, and our worlds respectively, and these ways of knowing differ significantly at each LDL.

As leaders move from lower to higher LDLs, there is a transition in the knowing self realm (intrapersonal) from an externally defined understanding of self to an internally defined understanding of self, in the knowing others realm (interpersonal) from self-focus to other-focus, and in the knowing our world realm (cognitive) from simplicity to complexity. Thus, the lowest LDLs in adulthood can be described as cognitively simple or concrete, interpersonally self-centered, and intrapersonally defined by the immediacy of the moment. In contrast, the highest LDLs exhibit an ability to determine what is important in a situation and do so with an understanding that is complex, principled, inclusive, and stable. It is a more authentic way to lead because high LDL leaders better know who they are and how to make a significant contribution. Table 1 shows examples of this progression in the simplest of terms as it relates to each of these areas of experience.

Due to this aforementioned capacity to respond to the complex demands of the current environment, those individuals at higher LDLs tend to respond to life's dilemmas more adequately than those individuals at lower LDLs (Eigel, 1998; Kegan 1994). All other things being equal (traits, knowledge, skill, and ability), individuals who know, process, decide, and relate at the highest LDLs not only respond to life's dilemmas more effectively, but, as will be suggested by our model, have an increased capacity to lead more effectively as well. Therefore, the research and model presented

Table 1.   Leadership Levels, Sources of Understanding, and the Areas of Experience.

Sources of understanding	LDL 2	LDL 3	LDL 4	LDL 5
	(Understanding from without)		(Understanding from within)	
Knowing what to do (cognitive)	Know and follow the rules	Look for help/ seek support	Figure it out	Explore options
Defining success (intrapersonal)	Did I win or did I lose?	Are we OK?	Did I achieve my goals?	Did I achieve a valued outcome?
Responding to conflict (interpersonal)	Win at all costs	Mend the relationship	Follow a process	Value and learn from the conflict

here posit that only the capacity to know the self, others, and the environment at the highest LDLs will produce sustainable and effective solutions in a complex environment.

WHAT ARE LEADERSHIP DEVELOPMENT LEVELS?

In order to evaluate the veracity of this assertion, it is important to understand more fully the defining characteristics of the different LDLs. In adulthood, LDL is a four-level developmental progression as shown in Fig. 1. We begin at LDL 2 rather than LDL 1 because there is a developmental level that actually precedes LDL 2 that is not relevant to adulthood, but only to childhood development. For more information on this developmental level see Piaget (1970) or Kegan (1982). Each LDL actually has definable and measurable sublevels and in its truest form, is a continuum of development with an infinite number of points along the developmental trajectory.

As the model implies, development is unidirectional and invariant, that is, one does not regress developmentally and levels cannot be skipped. What does vary from person to person, however, is the rate of development and where on the trajectory development stalls and for how long. Individuals at any given level have full access to the levels below it – or as Fowler states: "each new [level] builds on and integrates the operations of the previous [levels]" (Fowler, 1981, pp. 49–50). Nevertheless, they do not have access to the levels above their current developmental level. A metaphor we use for understanding the additive nature of the levels is the artist's palate. The number of colors on our palate defines our developmental level. Our ability to paint a more complete picture of our circumstances is limited by the number of colors we have at our disposal.

Leadership Development Level 2

In our model, the first, and least sophisticated adult LDL is Level 2. LDL 2 leaders understand themselves, others, and the world in essentially the same way as most adolescents. They have failed to develop at the minimum expected pace, and are essentially adults painting with the same two colors as an adolescent. Their picture is more sophisticated than a child's, but disturbingly unsophisticated for an adult leader.

LDL 2 leaders are characterized by an overly simplistic and concrete view of the world. The way that they make sense of their circumstances is very black-and-white, zero sum, win-lose. They are not yet able to consider possibilities or take the perspective of another person. Others' perspectives, if different from their own, are not understood or integrated into LDL 2 thinking – they are just out there and seen as opposing (and usually wrong) points of view. The reason these other points of view cannot be integrated into LDL 2 thinking is because these leaders have not developed an ability to weigh the importance of other opinions against their own – it is not a color on their palate with which they have to work. Consider the following excerpt taken from an interview with an LDL 2 leader:

> You have to understand, I hate to lose. So to me it's a personal loss when I don't convince them that my way was better. Until then I assumed my way was right, or one of the right ways, you know, and we didn't choose it, someone else's way worked, so that's fine too. And that's self-preservation, you know, that way I'm never wrong.

It is easy to see why others experience LDL 2 leaders as self-centered, simplistic, and unbending. The world for them is a set of rules that you play by, and if you do not operate by that set of rules, there are negative consequences. If development to LDL 3 does not take place, and if the egocentric behaviors do not change, then there is a strong likelihood that sociopathic types of behaviors will characterize the LDL 2 leader. LDL 2 leaders, whose focus is exclusively on their own needs, and who are singularly committed to winning at the expense of others, are not usually trusted by others because they lack the capacity to forge and maintain relationships to get work done. They usually fail as leaders because others have difficulty working with them. The good news is that there are few LDL 2 leaders managing in today's organizations – probably less than 10% (Eigel, 1998; Kegan, 1994; Torbert, 1991). Most people have grown beyond this way of understanding the world, at least in its most elementary form, by the time they are promoted to management positions.

Leadership Development Level 3

At LDL 3, a new color is added to the palate that is characterized by the ability to consider the perspectives and influence of others. Individuals at LDL 3 understand the weaknesses and limitations of LDL 2 sense making because they can take a perspective on their old LDL 2 understanding; they are more than their own agenda. It becomes clearer that not every situation is black and white, that not every rule is viable 100% of the time, and that you cannot and should not win at all cost. Others' opinions, or other ways of seeing a situation, are not just "out there" and left unconsidered as they are at LDL 2. Rather, these perspectives can be internalized, empathized with, and even adopted, as one's own if the source is trusted. In this way, LDL 3 leadership is much more effective than LDL 2 for leading in a complex environment; an environment with many factors and points of view that need to be acknowledged, synthesized, and represented fairly.

However, while LDL 3 leaders can be effective, often they are not. As stated in the previous paragraph, and represented in Table 1, the color that is added to their sense-making palate is one that still depends on input from outside sources. The reason these sources are defined as "outside" is because whatever that source is (whether a supervisor, friend, self-help book, or even a political ideology) it does not derive from within. Therefore, other people's opinions matter disproportionately. This is healthy and productive when individuals first develop into it – normally during their teenage years. The expression of this level in its purest form is epitomized by the adolescents who begin defining their world based on the input of peers, teachers, clubs, athletic teams, and hopefully even their parents.

We can all look back at our own lives and recognize these influences as we were growing up. Outside influences were necessary because as teenage and young adult "sense makers," we were unable to understand new complexities without the help of others. However, the dependence on outside sources becomes a liability when one is exposed to a novel situation beyond the scope of previous outside influence. The same holds true for leaders: there are critical times when leaders cannot rely on the counsel of others, the "company line," or "political winds" for that matter, but must turn inward for answers. When LDL 3 leaders are pressed in any given situation, their limits are exposed; they cannot formulate a course of action independent of others' influence. Thus, they show the limited number of colors available on their sense-making palates.

As shown in Table 1, the way that the LDL 3 leader responds to conflict is by getting out of it as soon as possible. Kegan (1982) says that LDL 3 individuals do not have relationships; rather they are their relationships. What he is saying is that an LDL 3 leader has to have relationships in order to know who they are – in order to know they are OK. Notice how in the following LDL 3 interview excerpt, this leader explains her perspective on conflict situations:

> Conflicted situations or having a conflict with anybody is just very uncomfortable and it just gets in the way of everything that you need to get done. In some ways it's almost like I'm conflict avoidant, but I don't avoid it. I just want it to be solved right away. Whatever it takes, I want to clean it up quickly so the next time I see them in the hall, its okay.

LDL 3 leaders can make effective decisions when pressed, but those decisions will not be self-authored or owned in the same way as an LDL 4 or LDL 5 leader. If the picture being painted is a reproduction, they will be able to paint it well. But when the scene demands their own authentic expression, or creativity, LDL 3 palates are shown to be inadequate. For example, an LDL 3 leader who has to make the tough choice of promoting just one of several people will have difficulty because to select one person could potentially harm the interpersonal relationships the LDL 3 leader has fostered with others.

Is the picture that the LDL 3 leader paints more adequate than the picture that the LDL 2 leader paints? Of course, LDL 3 leaders have a new color to paint with and are much more proficient at knowing when and how to use the main color of the LDL 2 artist – concrete rules and ways of acting. They have a perspective on when concrete rules and ways of acting are appropriate, when they are weak, and when their experiences show them to be negotiable or "gray" as opposed to black and white. It was, in fact, seeing the limitations of the LDL 2 palate (the lack of grayness and the virtue of trusting relationships) that promoted development to LDL 3.

What should become clear now is that, as each new color is added to the palate, the colors of the previous levels are still available to the leader. The colors that have been there the longest (from the earlier stages) are the ones that can be used most effectively. The newest color is used in the least sophisticated way and therefore somewhat less effectively (there is not yet enough experience to know fully how to use the new color). This means that when concrete, dogmatic, LDL 2 leadership style is required, those at levels higher than LDL 2 can still use them because the previous ways of knowing oneself, others, and world do not go away, but rather are integrated into a more comprehensive understanding. One reviewer of this chapter asked, "might not a concrete, dogmatic, egocentric person be more effective in some settings, with some types of people?" The answer is, possibly yes. But when that style of leadership defines a leader's capacity rather than a choice he or she makes to address a certain situation, it is easier to see why leaders become increasingly more effective at each LDL. That said, the newest or most current LDL is not only the one that defines current capacity, it is the one that is used the most. It is the newest color on the palate and the one that cannot yet be taken in perspective, but rather the one from which the leader uses the other colors. As stated earlier, the characteristics of the current level are the lens through which leaders understand the world they are painting – a lens to which they are too close to take in perspective.

Leadership Development Level 4

As development moves to LDL 4, a fourth color is added to the palate, and for the first time enough colors are available to paint a picture without imitating the style of others. As Table 1 shows, the source of understanding now originates from within rather from without as well. The LDL 4 leader can, with this more expansive palate, paint a much more realistic, accurate and multidimensional picture than can be painted at either LDL 2 or LDL 3. The newest color added to the leader's sense-making palette is characterized by independence.

By independence we mean that there is no longer a dependence on outside sources to help the leader make sense of self, others and situations. At LDL 4, input from outside sources can be evaluated objectively because the sources *can* be taken into perspective – they become sources that are factored effectively into the sense-making equation. Outside opinions do matter; however, they do not define or determine the leader's decisions. Therefore, LDL 4 leaders have to use all of the past colors in forming their independent views. Consider the following excerpt from an LDL 4 leader as he addresses his understanding of conflict situations:

> First of all, all of us like to get along with one another, but we can have conflict and still go out that evening and have dinner together. That's the best way I can describe it. The real key is making sure that you are totally objective when resolving conflict. Understand

the other, but look at the facts and make decisions based on the facts. They might not always agree with my decision, but they know that I will get rid of the biases that I might have, and that I won't take it personally.

The "we can have conflict and still go out that evening and have dinner together" statement in this excerpt illustrates this independent and self-authored (as opposed to outside-source authored) LDL 4 development well. There is now, for the first time at LDL 4, a separation between business "facts" and personal "feelings." Having the use of all of these former ways of understanding means that traditional rules and laws, winning and losing, the perspectives of others, the input from outside sources, etc. can all be taken into account in the formation of this more complex ability to understand the world. In fact, these past experiences are what allow LDL 4 leaders to author their own point of view. Moreover, this confident independence ("doing the right thing") is also the reason that LDL 4 leaders inspire confidence and are easier to follow.

It is at LDL 4 that we see the first possibility of leading from an authentic place, a place that is of one's own making. Understanding the self, others, and world solely under the influence of outside sources (i. e., LDLs 2 and 3) is not as authentic. Full self-awareness does not emerge until LDL 4. Likewise, Gardner et al. (2005), propose that levels of internalization and integration (Deci & Ryan, 1995) are related to authentic leadership. *External* and *introjected* regulation mechanisms are descriptive of less authentic leadership styles. These types of feedback mechanisms are also characteristic of LDLs 2 and 3, respectively. *Identified* and *integrated* regulation mechanisms are proposed to be related to more authentic leadership, and are similarly characteristic of LDLs 4 and 5.

LDL 3 leadership is more adequate than LDL 2, but truly effective leadership does not begin until LDL 4. LDL 4 leaders are more successful in generating followers because followers recognize that the LDL 4 picture of the world is a much more complete picture than those painted by leaders at the lower levels. In short, at LDL 4, leading is more authentic than at earlier levels. LDL 4 leaders have use of the colors of the previous levels as well as the ability to use those colors more effectively.

LDL 4 leaders know that the world does not revolve around them and are therefore not beholden to their circumstances for their well being. They know they have needs and an agenda, but that alone will not create an effective team or create value for the company. LDL 4 leaders also know that they can effectively and appropriately use the color of relationships and input from outside sources, which adds drama, life and emotion to the painting, but they also know the limits of an outside authored "paint by the numbers" way of understanding. Finally, LDL 4 leaders add their own technique, their "sense-making palate" to make their art distinguishable, identifiable, unique and potentially more valuable. In the end, like all great works of art, the painting reflects the artist at LDL 4. This aspect, more than anything else, separates LDL 4 art from the creations of those at previous LDLs.

Leadership Development Level 5

LDL 4 is not, however, the be all and end all of leadership effectiveness. If LDL 4 leaders can be characterized as effective, authentic artists, LDL 5 leaders are the master painters capable of using many colors simultaneously. In terms of making sense of their environments, LDL 5 leaders have more colors at their disposal to utilize in effectively understanding and responding to whatever scene they are painting – i.e., leadership situations in which they find themselves. They have all of the colors of the previous levels plus a new color that we will explain in the next few paragraphs. However, we should note that LDL 5 leaders are as interesting as they are rare. In the general population only about 5–8% of adults between the ages of 40 and 60 would be considered LDL 5 (Eigel, 1998; Kegan, 1994; Torbert, 1991; Van Velsor & Drath, 2004).

We believe that it is easier to understand the characteristics of LDL 5 when we juxtapose it to the concept of a *paradigm*. Oxford English Dictionary defines paradigm as "a case or instance to be regarded as representative or typical" (Burchfield, 1987). A paradigm, then, is one's understanding of something that is stereotypical of its nature. By extension, a leader's paradigm is his/her stereotypical way of seeing things. Thus, the popular phrase "paradigm shift" has addressed the idea of changing the stereotypical way that one sees things – a new and different way of understanding the world.

LDL 4 leaders are the authors of their own paradigms. This is another way of talking about the independence that we detailed in the LDL 4 section above – having a way, or paradigm, that identifies the self, both to the self as well as to others. This way, or paradigm, is something that LDL 4 leaders cannot take a perspective on, or, in other words, evaluate objectively. The paradigm is the newest color that dominates the way the LDL 4 leader sees the world. Just as LDL 2 leaders cannot step away from, get a perspective on, and evaluate objectively the rules and order that define who they are, and LDL 3 leaders cannot step away from, get a perspective on, and evaluate objectively the influence of relationships and other external factors that define who they are, LDL 4 leaders have their limitations as well. They cannot step away from the paradigms that shape their understanding of the world – this same understanding that helps them decide how to respond, and even how to lead.

The defining characteristic of LDL 5 leaders, on the other hand, is their ability to step away from, take perspective on, and evaluate objectively the paradigms that defined them at the previous stage of development (LDL 4). LDL 5 leaders are open to the influence of others' paradigms. They are able to be their own critics in assessing the value of the paradigm that they may choose to employ in a given situation. They have the rare capacity to see into a situation *and* themselves at the same time. As such, LDL 5 leaders are open and responsive to internal reports on their performance, their likes and dislikes, their impact on others, and their changing needs. One LDL 5 leader describes his understanding of conflict this way:

> I think conflict is a very positive, very desirable, component of a corporate culture. When you're focused on the things that will result in achieving success, opinions will vary, and the functions that different leaders represent will inherently be in conflict with one another – which is a very healthy thing. I try to create an environment where people are comfortable and don't feel there is any risk in conflict or in disagreeing, but are all committed to the success of the enterprise.

This excerpt is an excellent example of a leader who is grounded in his values while still being open to the experience and opinions that others represent. The LDL 5 leader has the "capacity to meet others of any station in their life in their full height and depth" (Torbert, 1994, p. 186). It is this openness and vulnerability to others and the constant self-transformation that makes LDL 5 leaders so effective at leading others.

LDL 5 leadership is suited for turbulent times because of its ability to reflect, the welcoming of contradictions and paradoxes, and acceptance of incompleteness. LDL 5 leaders have the capacity to weigh differing paradigms against a higher-order core set of values or principles that they hold to be true. In this way, they essentially have a system of paradigms which allows a much more complete understanding of themselves, others, and their situations. The higher-order values and principles that hold this system together are the defining essence of the newest color on their palate (and also the thing from which they cannot step away and take in perspective). It is the tension between others' higher-order values and the possibility of their own transformation that makes the LDL 5 leader so effective. For the very first time, they can fully walk in someone else's shoes.

If we go back to our metaphor of the artist's palate, we would classify the LDL 5 artists as the great masters. This new color that we call "the ability to manage multiple paradigms" allows them to employ the appropriate means to create a picture that makes their followers understand the values that they hold true. This capacity for creating a complete and often brilliant picture evokes something in the admirer, follower if you will, that moves them to action. In the area of art, it may move them to see the world differently, but in the area of leadership, it often moves them to action, growth, or effectiveness.

Our understanding of authentic leadership, as presented by Avolio and his colleagues (e.g., Avolio et al., 2004; Gardner et al., 2005), and others is very closely associated with the characteristics we see in LDL 5 leaders. This higher order of development, higher order of knowing oneself, others, and the world is consistent with the descriptions of authenticity presented by these authors. Authentic characteristics like self-awareness, self-esteem, relational integrity, etc., are the byproduct of development. They come about through the hard work of remaking meaning making systems over the course of one's life. One cannot go from inauthentic to authentic without wrestling with the tough questions about who we are, who we want to be, and how to contribute uniquely to the world. We believe it is possible that individuals can engage in authentic behavior at LDL 3 and 4, but living authentically is actually achieved at LDL5.

DEVELOPMENT VS. DEVELOPING

Understanding the measurable differences between the levels of development is different than understanding what causes development. How one gets to the next level is a different topic than what it means to be at a given level. Over the course of one's life, levels of intelligence and certain attributes remain relatively constant (e.g., Bono & Judge, 2004; Jenkins & Oatley, 1996). That is, for the most part our personalities and intelligence are known and do not dramatically change in adulthood. However, even as these factors stabilize, development does not cease. Instead, there are periods of equilibrium or balance when one functions at a given LDL rather easily for a period of time (Piaget, 1970).

The catalyst for development on the trajectory usually comes from a shake up or challenge to the existing developmental position. Then, depending on the response to the challenge, a new, more effective level can emerge – one that accounts for and incorporates the new experiences. It is in this way that development occurs: experiences contradict the existing or current LDL, which destabilizes the equilibrium of that level. The challenged individual can then choose to reconstruct a new understanding, one that incorporates the new information about the world that is learned from the challenge, or they can choose to shut down and allow the current understanding to account for the experience in an oversimplified way. The former promotes development while the latter tends to arrest it.

Because it takes time to accumulate the kinds of significant experiences that challenge the current level of development, as well as to develop coherent responses to those experiences, it is rare to find individuals at the highest *LDLs* prior to their mid-30s. This is not to say that there are not mechanisms for accelerating development toward a more authentic level, however methods for promoting development are outside the scope of this presentation.

As we have stated throughout the course of this chapter, we believe, and our research shows, that LDL determines leader effectiveness. The propositions by those currently defining authentic leaders add further support to our assertions. In the following paragraphs we will detail some of the research that supports this idea. Thus, we will turn our attention to the relationship between LDLs and leader effectiveness.

LEADERSHIP DEVELOPMENT LEVELS AND EFFECTIVENESS

We believe there is a strong and important relationship between LDLs and leadership effectiveness. We also believe, and there is empirical evidence, that leaders are not even able to be effective in novel leadership situations until they are at LDL 4 or higher in the developmental progression (Rooke & Torbert, 1998). In order to test the hypothesis that LDL is one of the key determinants of a leader's effectiveness, we compared two measures of effectiveness to LDL – one related to position in the organization and the other to a traditional rating scale completed by subject matter experts. The first measure of effectiveness is positional. Twenty-one board-elected executive officers (CEOs, CFOs, COOs, and presidents) of public companies were compared to midlevel managers who were seen as effective but not expected to move into executive level positions in the immediate future.

Because executive effectiveness can be difficult to quantify, and since we were relying on the efficacy of relating leader effectiveness to those performing well in executive leadership positions, we made two assumptions that we felt would control and put some bounds on the artistic nature of determining effectiveness. The first was that a group of individuals with something at stake – the board of directors of publicly held companies – would have a vested and accountable interest in selecting the most effective executive available to them at that time. We believe this to be true in spite of the well-documented exceptions recently revealed in public and corporate America. Additionally, in order to control for other obvious explanations, we eliminated second-generation family businesses that had gone public with the family still in control, short tenure (less than 2 years) executives, and founding entrepreneurs who may have been successful because they were in the right place at the right time more than they were good leaders.

In order to control for industry effects, the 21 CEOs were from industries as diverse as manufacturing, technology, software, banking, distribution, textiles, insurance, and finance. In addition, the organizations that the CEOs were leading were all performing at the top of their industries, if not leading them, and the average gross annual revenue was $5.6 billion. Indeed, when one examines the caliber of the executives and the companies they lead, it is difficult to argue that this is not a group of individuals that are highly effective by most people's standards.

The measurement of LDL is a cognitively demanding and a labor intensive process. Each participant engages in a 60–90 min semistructured clinical interview with an interviewer certified at training workshop in Boston, Massachusetts. The object of the interview was to probe and understand, using hypothesis testing, the participant's experience in a way that identified how or why the participant constructed meaning about a particular experience. This meant that probing for information about the content of the person's experience (e.g., conflict) was not part of the process – the goal was probing for an epistemological construction of the given event (e.g., what does conflict mean). The interviewer wanted to know *how* the person thinks not *what* she thinks (Lahey, Souvaine, Kegan, Goodman, & Felix, 1988).

All of the leaders, in our sample, were assessed using the interview. The interviews were transcribed and scored to 20 distinct scores (five distinctions for each of the four LDLs we have referred to in this chapter). Interrater reliabilities of the interview range from 67 to 89% for exact agreement, and from 82 to 100% for agreement within a one-fifth distinction. In other words, we scored each individual to one of the 20 distinctions mentioned above and interrater reliability was based on that scoring, rather than on the four LDLs (of which each LDL includes 5 distinctions) that we have used to describe LDL throughout this chapter. Construct validity for this interview technique has been established over decades of research (Colby & Kohlberg, 1987; Lahey, 1988).

The second measure of effectiveness was instituted in order to mitigate the explanation that it is really position and not leader effectiveness that is related to higher LDLs. Positional references were removed from 150 excerpts taken from over 2000 pages of LDL interviews. These 150 excerpts were of varying LDLs and were rated by subject matter experts (SMEs) as to their effectiveness in a given area (such as conflict management, visioning, success, participation, etc.). The SMEs had an average tenure of 14 years of doctoral-level work in academia and/or business in the area of leader effectiveness. The SMEs were asked to "rate the effectiveness of the responses on a six-point scale – 1) atrocious, 2) ineffective, 3) somewhat effective, 4) effective, 5) very effective, and 6) exceptional." In blind review, two different, independent SMEs, scored each of the excerpts for the LDL the excerpts would represent if the entire interview were consistent with the excerpt. These two measures were then used as effectiveness measures in comparison to LDL.

The hypotheses that LDLs were positively related to leader effectiveness was confirmed on both the positional (or board-elected executive) measure of effectiveness as well as on the effectiveness ratings measure. That is, as LDL increases, leader effectiveness increases.

The first analysis correlates LDL with the position of board-elected executive. As explained in the previous section, we contend that being a board-elected executive (henceforth referred to as the executive group) is an indicator of effectiveness as determined by the more holistic approach of board selection. If individuals who are viewed as effective by a group of stakeholders are, in fact, effective, and if LDL is positively correlated with (or related to) effectiveness, then we should see significantly higher scores in the board-elected executive population than we would in a comparable population of individuals not necessarily seen as effective leaders.

In order to illustrate the data, we have included in Fig. 2 the distribution of LDL scores from 764 highly educated professionals in the same age demographic as the executive group. We have labeled this group "The General Leadership Population." The normative sample was created by combining three data sources: Kegan (1994), Torbert (1991), and our own LDL scores of the comparison group of the 20 upper-level managers from the same organization as our executive group. As Fig. 2 illustrates, the distribution of scores generally fits the normal distribution.

It follows that if LDL was not related to leader effectiveness, we would expect to see a similar distribution of scores with the executive group – one

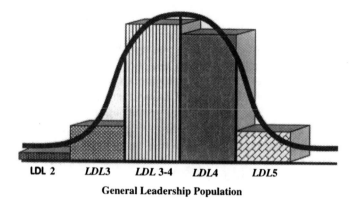

General Leadership Population

Fig. 2.   The Distribution of *LDL* Scores for the General Leadership Population.

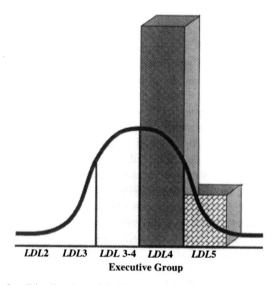

Executive Group

Fig. 3.   Distribution of *LDL* Scores for the Executive Group.

that approximates the normal distribution, just as the General Leadership Population and the comparison group did. However, as can be seen from the dramatic results presented in Fig. 3, the distribution of scores from the executive group far from approximates the normal distribution. It is re-markable, and in fact exceeded what we expected to find, that none of the scores from the executive group were even below LDL 4. Needless to say the results are statistically significant: the χ^2 analysis of the differences between the executive group and the highly educated professional group yielded an asymptotic significance of $p < 0.000$, while the Mann–Whitney U and Moses (SPSS, 1996) yielded significance values of the comparison between the executive and comparison groups of $p < 0.001$ and $p < 0.000$, respectively. This relationship between LDL and effectiveness emphasizes what we have said from the beginning of this chapter – it is not necessarily what you do, but rather, from where you do it that determines your effectiveness.

Whereas we have just illustrated the relationship between position and LDL, we now want to look at the relationship between effectiveness ratings and LDL. We hypothesized that LDL would also be related to measures of effectiveness independent of position – Fig. 4 shows the results of the relationship between LDL scores on 150 excerpts and leader effectiveness scores for the same excerpts. As seen, when the LDL score of an excerpt increases, the corresponding effectiveness rating for that score increases as well. Interestingly, and similar to the previous finding, it is not until the LDL scores approach LDL 4 that the leaders are really seen as effective at all. As in the previous hypothesis, the test of significance for this comparison of effectiveness scores and LDL scores yielded a significant difference on the Spearman Rank-Order correlation of $p < 0.000$.

Just as Fig. 3 shows that leader effectiveness really begins at LDL 4, Fig. 4 shows that response effectiveness begins at LDL 4 as well. We find that examples of responses at various LDLs can help illustrate this relationship. The following excerpt was taken from an interview and rated for its

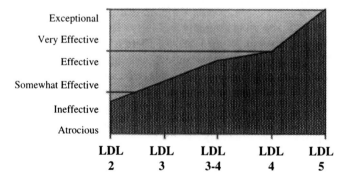

Fig. 4. The Relationship between *LDL* Scores and Leadership Effectiveness Ratings.

effectiveness as a response to the question, "how do you know the right thing to do?" It was rated as an ineffective response. It was also rated LDL 2 as can be seen by the inability to hold opposing view points simultaneously, and because of the black and white, concrete nature of the understanding that is displayed.

> I like to preach that there is always more than one right answer and they are both equally good, it's the question of which one you choose.
>
> INTERVIEWER: Do you practice that actively, the idea of seeking multiple right answers?
>
> Multiple right answers come from having multiple opinions. I suppose all of us sometimes think I don't know if I should do A or B. I can usually wrestle that one to the ground or close my eyes and guess. It will tend to be if I feel strongly about something and a peer feels strongly about something else, then somebody has got to make the call and that's why there is another level.
>
> INTERVIEWER: How do you know when you're wrong?
>
> Well, if you are working with the right people, you are never wrong because they just picked another right way and your way was right, you just didn't get chosen. You're wrong when you get to the end of the game and it didn't work. And I'm wrong every day. There are a lot of things we try that don't work, but that's not a reason not to try, you know, to me, that's losing again if my way didn't work. But you don't know until you try it. Until then I assumed my way was right or one of the right ways, you know, and we didn't chose it, someone else's way worked, so that's fine too. And that's self-preservation, you know, that way I'm never wrong.

Fortunately, there are not many LDL 2 responses coming from leaders in most organizations. Nonetheless, it is easy to imagine the frustration one must feel when attempting to follow this type of leader. The unreconciled contradiction between simple points of view, the win–lose perspective on who was right and wrong, and the utter simplicity of this LDL 2 response make it easy to see why it was rated as ineffective.

In Fig. 5, we have extended the Developmental Progression illustrated in Fig. 1 to include the environments and ways that those at each LDL are effective. As can be seen, we do believe there are few if any environments where LDL 2 leaders are effective. In fact, we would contend that most LDL 2 leaders are ultimately destructive to any environment in which they lead. While strategies that are concrete and rule driven may be appropriate in some extraordinary environments, we do not believe that LDL 2 strategies performed at LDL 2 understanding lead to effective outcomes in most organizations.

As leaders stabilize at LDL 3, there are some limited environments in which they can be moderately effective. These environments are routine, known, and stable. In such environments, learned strategies in a specific content area can be employed with some degree of effectiveness. Whereas

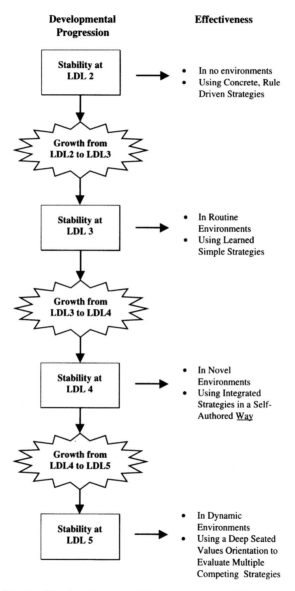

Fig. 5. The Developmental Progression and Effectiveness.

there are few LDL 2 leaders in most organizations, there are many more LDL 3 leaders. However, as the following excerpt illustrates, while an LDL 3 response may be less offensive, and even more likeable, it is nonetheless often ineffective. This LDL 3 response to the "how do you know the right thing to do?" question is characterized by uncertainty and a need to get outside input on how well things are going. The interdependent nature of LDL 3 is also evident.

> I think it's important to get input from others because one person can't have all the ideas. I like to think that there is this broad objective that we are all trying to get to. And I have a little slice of it that kind of comes down and if I do my little piece and everybody else does theirs, it all works. I can't be successful unless I'm going in the same direction as the others. And I can't know if I'm going in the same direction unless somebody over here is telling me, "you're off track;" "don't do that;" or "that's a good idea, but don't do it because we are trying to go that way."

As Fig. 4 illustrates, LDL 3 responses to leadership situations are at best rated only as somewhat effective by our SMEs. In the preceding excerpt, it is understood that interdependence and common goals are needed. However, there is no ownership of the situation outside of what is immediately known without the input of outside sources. In fact, there is little ability, if any, shown that would indicate that this leader is even able to rate his own performance in pursuit of a known outcome. However, when leaders develop to LDL 4, they are able to own or take responsibility for the outcome of a situation. Responsibility, or ownership, is not to be confused with worrying about the outcome, behavior characteristic of LDL 3. Both LDL 3 and LDL 4 leaders would feel that they are taking responsibility, but what responsibility means to them would be very different at the different levels. It is worth noting that LDL 3 leaders can and often do make excellent employees but because so much of their self-esteem is derived from and through others they do not make effective leaders.

At LDL 4 we see, for the first time, consistently effective responses to leadership situations. LDL 4 leaders can respond effectively in novel environments where self-authored, integrated strategies are required. In the following LDL 4 excerpt, you can hear that there is a way that is owned; a way that integrates various perspectives, exuding a confidence others will more readily follow.

> Well, I think you often get better ideas for heading in the right direction from a structured brainstorming, thinking out loud, pushing against each other session than any one individual could come up with standing alone. Very quickly then, once we've gotten our alternatives laid out, we begin to identify what are the potential weaknesses in each one of the models…and so then we narrow it down. So, one, you get a better idea, but just as

importantly, you've gotten a consensus built with some of the key opinion shapers in the organization; you've created a group of disciples that are going to go out and help you then implement and sell and create understanding around what it is that you are going to do.

In this excerpt, it is easy to see the integration of perspectives and ideas, the confidence in the way the leader responds, and how he could transfer this way to many novel leadership situations. While LDL 3 leaders are looking for outside input to *de-fine* themselves, LDL 4 leaders look for input to *re-fine* themselves. It is from this LDL 4 position that leaders can begin to lead others effectively. That said, where we really begin to see highly effective responses that are able to meet the challenges of today's dynamic environments is at LDL 5. It is from LDL 5 that leaders are most authentic in who they are and what they have to offer. In the following LDL 5 excerpt, the response to the question "how do you know the right thing to do?" is given an effectiveness rating of exceptional by both SMEs. Note the openness to, and synthesis of, contradictory options as well as the strong values orientation.

If we had an unlimited amount of time, I could probably find pieces from many different places and times, but one of the things that still stays with me today is from my sociology class and one of the philosophers, maybe Socrates, who said "the unexamined life is not worth living," so that it's important to continue to reevaluate what you believe. It doesn't necessarily mean that you change your beliefs, but you leave them open. You sort of leave them exposed...and I think too many people don't do that. You know, they form their beliefs and their opinions, but they're not open to evaluating them. But if you think about them, there's less to think about when you need to use them...And so decisions [about the right thing to do], I think, become easier as opposed to harder.

As we relate this LDL 5 way of understanding the world and how this LDL 5 response addresses decision making, it is easier to see the relationship between LDL and effectiveness. As Fig. 5 shows, LDL 5 leaders have the ability to go beyond LDL 4 leaders to evaluate multiple LDL 4 ways or strategies and, simultaneously be open to change, whereas the LDL 4 leaders are limited to the effective use of their own way or strategy.

MOVING FORWARD

It is our hope that the research and thinking presented here has put some structure to your ability to know why you know effective leadership when you see it and what leadership development looks like from a theory of the person. Our primary goal in this chapter was to present a descriptive analysis of our findings that all of the high-performing leaders in our sample are LDL 4 or 5, and to provide a theoretical basis (grounded in four decades of research in human development) for why this might be. This is a first step in the process of understanding the ramifications of LDL on leader effectiveness, not the last. There remain many implications for future research that emerge from our discussion.

First, we did not investigate many of the possible relations between LDL and authenticity as is recently presented by Gardner et al. (2005). There seem to be a great number of factors they propose to be related to authenticity that we believe are specifically characteristic of LDL 5. If, as proposed by other authors in this book, there is a connection between authenticity and effectiveness, and we can establish a direct connection between LDL 5 and authenticity, both constructs would be strengthened through further research.

Another application that we have explored with our clients, but not researched fully, is the viability of LDL assessment for selection purposes. Knowing a leader's LDL, given relevant knowledge, skills and abilities for a particular role, would give us potential insight into his or her ability to function effectively in leadership roles. Similarly, assessment of LDL could be a useful tool for mapping developmental strategies for individual leaders as well as helping to determine meaningful training interventions.

A potential weakness of the research presented here is that we did not directly deal with the leadership context. Gardner et al. (2005) propose that organizational context will influence the organization's readiness for and likelihood for the emergence and efficacy of authentic leadership. We agree. In our research, we made every effort to not be context specific in terms of type of industry, but made no measurement of the cultural aspects of context within a given organization. We believe context does matter but what matters more is the LDL at which the environment is experienced; we see the world not as it is, but rather from where we are. For researchers, this means that the person and environment are mutually defined and should not be considered independent of one another. Future leadership research would focus on leader-in-environment rather than examining the independent effects of the leader *and* environment. If we are correct, critical aspects of the leadership context will matter more or less depending on the leader's LDL.

Furthermore, we do not really understand what the "triggers" are for development. There is significant research on the life experiences of leaders (Douglas, 2003; McCall, Lombardo, & Morrison, 1988; Moxley & Pulley, 2004), but we also know experience alone does not facilitate development (Velsor & Drath, 2004). We also know that formal leadership interventions (e.g., 360-degree feedback, job assignments) fuel development, but developmental results are "frustratingly individual" (Barrett & Beeson, 2002; Hollenbeck & McCall, 1999). From the standpoint of LDL, we believe that triggers for development will be those that have meaning for the individual at their LDL and that the transition from one level to the next will be dependent on the leader's readiness and willingness for development. In Fig. 6, we highlight what we believe are the fundamental growth challenges for leaders at each LDL. At each LDL, leaders use this challenge to fuel their own development. Going forward it would be beneficial for practitioners and researcher to find ways to utilize methods and techniques that would "trigger" these growth challenges in leaders.

Additionally, we did not investigate or propose anything about the developmental implications on followers as it relates to LDL. Our practice in working with high LDL leaders suggests anecdotally that higher LDL leaders (i.e., more authentic leaders) are more intentional in the development of their direct reports – they raise other's aspirations of who they are. LDL 5 leaders know that to grow the organization they have to grow the people around them. This is consistent with the propositions advanced by Gardner et al. (2005). Likewise, we do not really know the impact of lower-level leaders on higher-level subordinates even though there is some evidence that developmental level can be promoted in adults (Hurt, 1990; MacPhail, 1989; White, 1985). Exploring LDL dyads and team LDL member composition is a rich area for future research and consistent with Schriesheim, Castro, and Cogliser's (1999) call for improved theorizing about leader–member exchanges.

Finally, the viability of analyzing the relationship between LDL and self-esteem, self-awareness, self-acceptance, unbiased processing, relational openness, or other measures of authenticity is important for establishing what behaviors and characteristics may facilitate development and which may tend to arrest it. While there is preliminary research linking levels of development with moral and ethical development (Avolio & Locke, 2002; Kegan & Lahey, 1984; Lucius & Kuhnert, 1999), clearly more research is needed. Correlating developmental level with behavioral measures of performance (e.g., multisource ratings) is necessary to validate our theory of leadership development. As we have discussed earlier, defining leader effectiveness is difficult and highly idiosyncratic to researcher interest and what data are available to the researcher at the time. Understanding better the relationship between measures of effectiveness like follower behavior, follower satisfaction and how they interface with LDL should be pursued.

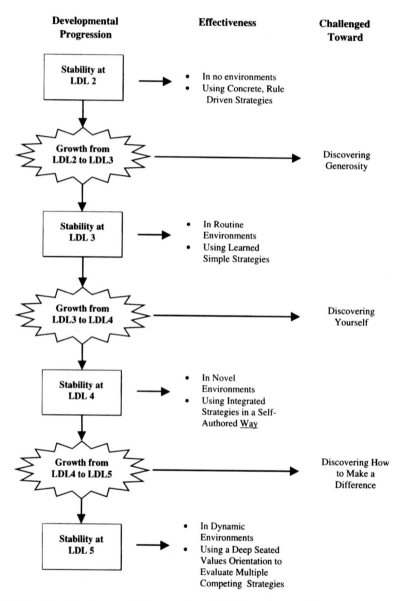

Fig. 6. The Developmental Progression, Effectiveness, and Growth Challenges.

It seems clear that there is an endless list of techniques, strategies, styles, methods, and "irrefutable laws" that leaders can employ in their quest for effectiveness. However, we believe that without understanding the underlying framework of how people develop to a place of greater effectiveness, the selection and development of leaders will continue in the piecemeal ways of the past. Leaders will do their best to respond to and make sense of the experiences, perhaps gaining confidence from the exercise, but not strength toward an intentional developmental challenge related to LDL.

We believe until we target the goals of a leadership development program to the leader's developmental capacity to lead, we will not equip companies to meet the demands of this new century. The intellectual giant of the 20th century, Albert Einstein, stated the problem succinctly: *Today's problems cannot be solved by thinking the way we thought when we created them.* We conclude that leadership effectiveness is not gained simply by piling more skills onto the same level, or by increasing the capacity to recite company leadership competencies. It is gained by fundamentally changing the way we address leadership development – it is not just what you know, but where you know it from that matters. The future of our organizations depends on successfully identifying and developing all leaders to higher LDLs – to a place of greater authenticity – so that they can respond effectively to the increasingly complex demands of our times.

REFERENCES

Avolio, B. J., Gardner, W. L., Walumbwa, F. O., Luthans, F., & May, D. R. (2004). Unlocking the mask: A look at the process by which authentic leaders impact follower attitudes and behaviors. *The Leadership Quarterly, 15,* 801–823.

Avolio, B. J., & Locke, E. A. (2002). Contrasting different philosophies of leader motivation: Altruism versus egoism. *The Leadership Quarterly, 13,* 169–191.

Barrett, A., & Beeson, J. (2002). *Developing business leaders for 2010.* New York: Conference Board.

Bass, B. M., & Stogdill, R. M. (1990). *Bass & Stogdill's handbook of leadership: Theory, research, and managerial implications* (3rd ed.). New York: The Free Press.

Bono, J. E., & Judge, T. A. (2004). Personality and transformational leadership: A meta-analysis. *Journal of Applied Psychology, 89,* 901–910.

Burchfield, R. W. (Ed.). (1987). The compact edition of the Oxford English dictionary (Volume III). USA: Oxford University Press.

Burns, J. M. (1978). WICS: A model of leadership in organizations. *Academy of Management Learning and Education, 2,* 386–401.

Colby, A., & Kohlberg, L. (1987). *The measure of moral judgment* (Vol. 1). Cambridge, MA: Cambridge University Press.

Collins, J. C. (2001). *Good to great: Why some companies make the leap...and others don't.* New York: Harper Collins.

Collins, J. C., & Porras, J. I. (1994). *Built to last: Successful habits of visionary companies.* New York: Harper Business.

Covey, S. R. (1989). *The seven habits of highly effective people: Restoring the character ethic.* New York: Fireside.

Deci, E. L., & Ryan, R. M. (1995). Human autonomy: The basis for true self-esteem. In: M. H. Kernis (Ed.), *Efficacy, agency, and self-esteem* (pp.31–49). New York: Plenum Press.

Douglas, C. A., (2003). *Key events and lessons for managers in a diverse workforce: A report on research and findings,* Greensboro, NC: CCL Press.

Drath, W. H. (2001). *The deep blue sea: Rethinking the source of leadership.* San Francisco: Jossey-Bass.

Eigel, K. M. (1998). *Leadership effectiveness: A constructive developmental view and investigation.* Unpublished doctoral dissertation, University of Georgia, Athens.

Fowler, J. W. (1981). *Stages of faith: The psychology of human development and the quest for meaning.* New York: Harper Collins.

Gardner, W. L., Avolio, B. J., Luthans, F., May, D. R., & Walumbwa, F. O. (2005). "Can you see the real me?" A self-based model of authentic leader and follower development. *The Leadership Quarterly, 16,* 373–394.

Hollenbeck, G. P., & McCall Jr., M. W. (1999). Leadership development: Contemporary practices. In: A. Kraut, & A. Korman (Eds), *Evolving practices in human resource management.* San Francisco: Jossey-Bass.

Hurt, B. L. (1990). Psychological education for teacher-education students: A cognitive-developmental curriculum. In: V. L. Erickson & J. M. Whitely (Eds), *Developmental counseling and teaching* (pp. 339–347). Monterey, CA: Brooks/Cole.

Jenkins, J. M., & Oatley, K. (1996). Emotional episodes and emotionality through the life span. In: C. Magai & S. H. McFadden (Eds), *Handbook of emotion, adult development, and aging* (pp. 421–442). London: Academic Press.

Kegan, R. (1982). *The evolving self: Problem and process in human development.* Cambridge, MA: Harvard University Press.

Kegan, R. (1994). *In over our heads: The mental demands of modern life.* Cambridge, MA: Harvard University Press.

Kegan, R., & Lahey, L. L. (1984). Adult leadership and adult development: A constructivist view. In: B. Kellerman (Ed.), *Leadership: Multidisciplinary perspectives.* Englewood Cliffs, NJ: Prentice Hall.

Kohlberg, L. (1981). *The philosophy of moral development: Moral stages and the idea of justice.* New York: Harper & Row.

Kuhnert, K. W., & Lewis, P. (1987). Transactional and transformational leadership: A constructive/developmental analysis. *Academy of Management Review, 12,* 648–657.

Lahey, L. L., Souvaine, E., Kegan, R., Goodman, R., & Felix, S. (1988). *A guide to the subject-object interview: Its administration and interpretation.* Cambridge, MA: The Subject-Object Research Group.

Loevenger, J. (1976). *Ego development: Conceptions and theories.* San Francisco: Jossey-Bass.

Lucius, R. H., & Kuhnert, K. W. (1999). Adult development and the transformational leader. *The Journal of Leadership Studies, 6*(1), 73–85.

MacPhail, D. D. (1989). The moral education approach in treating adult inmates. *Criminal Justice and Behavior, 16,* 81–97.

McCall, Jr., M. W., Lombardo, M.M., & Morrison, A. M. (1988). *The lessons of experience: How successful executives develop on the job.* San Francisco: New Lexington Press.

Manners, J., Durkin, K., & Nesdale, A. (2004). Promoting advanced ego development among adults. *Journal of Adult Development, 11,* 19–27.

Moxley, R. S., & Pulley, M. L. (2004). Hardships. In: C. D. McCauley & E. Van Velsor (Eds), *Handbook of leadership development* (pp. 183–203). Center for Creative Leadership, San Francisco: Jossey-Bass

Nadler, D. A., & Nadler, M. B. (1998). *Champions of change: How CEOs and their companies are mastering the skills of radical change.* San Francisco: Jossey-Bass.

Piaget, J. (1970). *The principles of genetic epistemology.* London, UK: Routledge & Kegan Paul.

Rooke, D., & Torbert, W. R. (1998). Organizational transformation as a function of CEO's developmental stage. *Organization Development Journal, 16,* 11–28.

Schriesheim, C. A., Castro, S. L., & Cogliser, C. C. (1999). Leader-member exchange (LMX) research: A comprehensive review of theory, measurement, and data-analytic practices. *The Leadership Quarterly, 10,* 63–113.

Selman, R. L. (1980). *The growth of interpersonal understanding: Developmental and clinical analyses.* New York: Academic Press.

Slater, C. L. (2003). Generativity versus stagnation: An elaboration of Erickson's adult stage of human development. *Journal of Adult Development, 10,* 53–65.

SPSS (1996). *Base 7.0 for windows user's guide.* Chicago: SPSS Inc.

Sternberg, R. J. (2003). WICS: A model of leadership in organizations. *Academy of Management Learning and Education, 2,* 386–401.

Torbert, W. R. (1991). *The power of balance: Transforming self, society, and scientific inquiry.* Newbury Park: Sage.

Torbert, W. R. (1994). Cultivating post-formal development: Higher stages and contrasting interventions. In: M. Miller & S. Cook-Greuter (Eds), *Transcendence and mature thought in adulthood* (pp. 186–201). Lanham, MD: Rowman & Littlefield.

Van Velsor, E., & Drath, W. H. (2004). A lifelong developmental perspective on leader development. In: C. D. McCauley & E. Van Velsor (Eds), *Handbook of leadership development* (pp. 183–203), San Francisco: Jossey-Bass.

White, M.S. (1985). Ego development in adult women. *Journal of Personality, 53,* 561–574.

Zaccaro S. J., Rittman, A. L., & Marks, M. A. (2001). Team leadership. *The Leadership Quarterly, 12,* 451–483.

AUTHENTIC LEADERSHIP DEVELOPMENT: EMERGENT THEMES AND FUTURE DIRECTIONS

William L. Gardner, Bruce J. Avolio and Fred O. Walumbwa

ABSTRACT

Reflecting on the confluence of forces that lead to the Gallup Leadership's (GLI) founding and the inaugural GLI Summit on authentic leadership development, we identify several themes (both convergent and divergent) that have emerged in its wake. We discuss and present our views on these themes, and provide theoretical and philosophical arguments in support of our opinion that any effort to develop authentic leaders, or any leader, must consider the leader's moral development, for genuine development to occur. We conclude with recommendations for future theory building and research on authentic leadership and its development.

A variety of forces have coalesced to fuel the emergence and growth of theory and research on authentic leadership development reflected in the chapters of this book. First, in the wake of highly visible ethical scandals involving organizational leaders, there is a growing recognition among leadership scholars

Authentic Leadership Theory and Practice: Origins, Effects and Development
Monographs in Leadership and Management, Volume 3, 387–406

(Bass & Steidlmeier, 1999) and practitioners (George, 2003) alike of the importance of integrity, character, and genuine and trustworthy leader–member relationships to effective leadership. Second, the emergence of positive psychology (Seligman & Csikentmihalyi, 2000; Snyder & Lopez, 2002), positive organizational scholarship (Cameron, Dutton, & Quinn, 2003), and positive organizational behavior (POB) (Luthans, 2002a, b) as fields of study that emphasize positive facets of human functioning has generated interest in positive approaches to leadership, and authentic leadership in particular (Luthans & Avolio, 2003). Third, the strengths-based approach to individual and organizational development (Buckingham & Coffman, 1999; Clifton & Harter, 2003; Harter, Schmidt, & Hayes, 2002; Harter, Schmidt, & Keyes, 2003) pioneered and championed by Don Clifton and associates at the Gallup Corporation has stimulated the application of positive approaches to leadership and leader development within corporate circles.

The confluence of these forces, along with the support of the Gallup Corporation and the University of Nebraska-Lincoln, led to the creation of the Gallup Leadership Institute (GLI), and the inaugural GLI Summit in June 2004.[1] The objective of the GLI Summit was to draw from diverse disciplines and theoretical perspectives to generate new thinking about the development of authentic leadership, authentic followership, and authentic relationships in organizational settings. Given the diverse perspectives of the chapters included in this volume, as well as those published in the recent special issue on authentic leadership development of *The Leadership Quarterly* that emerged from the GLI Summit, we believe the Summit's success has been in generating serious dialogue on what constitutes authentic leadership and more importantly its development. Other chapters arose from work conducted within GLI and reflect the current thinking of its associates regarding the nature, measurement, and development of authentic leadership.

The purpose of this concluding chapter is twofold. First, we highlight some themes related to authentic leadership development that we see as emerging from the prior chapters and earlier work. Second, we recommend some directions for future theory and research on authentic leadership development that we believe are especially interesting and promising.

EMERGENT THEMES AND FOCAL RESEARCH AREAS

In our search for divergent perspectives on authentic leadership, we secured excellent insights from contributors to this volume on the implications of such disparate topics and areas as humor and transparency (Hughes, 2005), re-siliency (Youssef & Luthans, 2005), moral development (Hannah, Lester, & Vogelgesang, 2005), personalized and socialized charismatic leadership and group social capital (Varella, Javidan, & Waldman, 2005), followers' emo-tional reactions (Dasborough & Ashkanasy, 2005), spiritual leadership (Fry & Whittington, 2005), political skill (Douglas, Ferris, & Perrewé, 2005), au-thenticity markers for African-American political leaders (Pittinsky, 2005), leadership development and perspective-taking capacity (Eigel & Kuhnert, 2005) and what we have learned from 100 years of leadership interventions (Reichard & Avolio, 2005). Despite the diversity of these topics, some com-mon themes regarding the nature and development of authentic leadership and related constructs are emerging. Below, we examine these areas of con-vergence, as well as areas of divergent thinking, and future directions for defining and expanding authentic leadership theory's nomological net.

Components of Authentic Leadership: Areas of Convergence

As illustrated numerous times in this volume and elsewhere (Erickson, 1995; Harter, 2002), authenticity is often described using the injunction from the Ancient Greeks, "To thine on self be true." Erickson (1995) points out that this adage implies that one has a true, self that exists independent from other persons. Of course, the self is shaped by prior developmental interactions with other persons and the environment. Nonetheless, at any given point in time, the self can be viewed as a distinct entity to which a person can strive to remain true, despite external pressures to do otherwise. Yet, we have also learned in compiling this volume and the special issue, that there may also be multiple selves comprising the true, let us call it the "composite self," which shows the self is more dynamic and complex than philosophers, prior leadership researchers, and practitioners have conceived.

When the construct of authenticity is applied to leadership, however, it is no longer purely self-referential, since leadership by definition involves interpersonal influence processes between a leader and followers. Hence, current conceptions of authentic leadership focus on the formation of au-thentic relationships between the leader and followers that are characterized by trust and integrity (Avolio, Gardner, Walumbwa, Luthans, & May, 2004; Chan, Hannah, & Gardner, 2005; Gardner, Avolio, Luthans, May, & Walumbwa, 2005; Ilies, Morgeson, & Nahrgang, 2005). What this means is that one's authenticity when associated with leadership versus describing say an "authentic person," is fundamentally attached to the relationship between leaders and followers. Similarly, there is growing consensus that the authenticity of leaders is best viewed as existing on a continuum, ranging from less to more authentic leadership (Avolio & Gardner, 2005; Chan, 2005; Chan et al., 2005; Gardner et al., 2005), as opposed to starting with it being either present or not present. The importance of self-awareness and authentic self-regulation as basic components of authentic leadership and its development is likewise widely recognized and accepted (Avolio & Gardner, 2005; Avolio et al., 2004; Chan et al., 2005; Gardner et al., 2005; Hannah et al., 2005; Ilies et al., 2005; Klenke, 2005; Luthans & Avolio, 2003; May, Chan, Hodges, & Avolio, 2003; Shamir & Eilam, 2005; Sparrowe, 2005). Thus, one can say it is not sufficient to simply be self-aware of what constitutes the moral and ethical "right thing to do," it requires that the leader and follower are able to focus their choices, actions and behaviors via self-regulation to take what they know to turn it into moral and ethical behavior. Indeed, we discover in these chapters that acting authentically effects what constitutes self-awareness and vice versa.

The areas of convergence described above reflect basic components of authentic leadership development theory that have been part of the theory since its inception. In addition, to these components, contributors to this volume have extended authentic leadership development theory through the consideration of additional potential components, or through further elaboration of existing elements of the theory. Below, we discuss conceptual developments and refinements that were introduced in six promising areas.

Authentic Emotions

While several authors have previously considered the importance of emotions to authentic leader–follower relationships (Avolio et al., 2004; Gardner et al., 2005; Michie & Gooty, 2005), the role of emotions and emotional processes within authentic leadership receives additional attention and elaboration in this volume. For example, Hannah et al. (2005) examine leader affect, arguing that more as opposed to less morally developed authentic leaders possess a greater capacity for regulating their emotions during moral decision making, which in turn contributes to more effective moral solutions. Similarly, Hughes (2005) argues that while authentic leaders will be predisposed to express transparently their true emotions to followers, they will also regulate such expressions to ensure that they are appropriate for the context and audience. Finally, Klenke (2005) includes emotional intelligence, hope/optimism, and passion/compassion as part of an affective compassion of authentic leadership.

Shifting attention to follower affect, Dasborough and Ashkanasy (2005) advanced a model of authentic leadership that explicates the relationships between follower attributions of leader authenticity and their emotional reactions. Specifically, they argue that when a leader's moral behavior and intentions are perceived as genuine and trustworthy, attributions of authenticity and positive emotional reactions will follow. In contrast, if follower's attribute manipulative and self-serving intentions to the leader, negative emotional reactions will arise. Consistent with Dasborough and Ashkanasy's model, Hughes (2005) likewise identifies positive follower affect as a potential consequence of the transparency that characterizes authentic leadership. Because authenticity, by definition, involves remaining true to both one's thoughts *and* one's feelings, we believe that efforts to further explicate the role of affect in leader–member relations such as these are particularly promising, especially as they apply to authentic leadership and followership development.

Relational Transparency
The importance of transparency to authentic leader–follower relationships has been recognized by Luthans, Avolio, and their colleagues from the outset (Avolio et al., 2004; Gardner et al., 2005; Luthans & Avolio, 2003). However, several contributors to this volume provide additional insights into the importance of transparency to authentic leadership, including Hughes (2005) and Hannah et al. (2005). Building directly on the work of Gardner et al. (2005), Hughes introduces the GIVE acronym to highlight four key elements of relational transparency: *G*oals/motives, *I*dentity, *V*alues and *E*motions. In addition, he explains how humor can be used to great effect by authentic leaders to achieve relational transparency and elicit positive affective reactions and trust from followers. Hannah et al. (2005) describe how continual activation of an authentic moral leader's values and ethical standards as part of his or her working self-concept will promote relational transparency, and likewise contribute to elevated levels of follower trust. Given the central role that transparency plays in current conceptions of authenticity (Kernis, 2003), as well as growing recognition of the importance of transparency to effective leadership and organizational processes (George, 2003; Pagano & Pagano, 2004), we consider such efforts to further explicate the nature and effects of relational transparency to be especially timely.

Developmental Focus
From the outset, Luthans and Avolio (2003) have made a distinction between authentic leadership and authentic leadership development, where the

latter construct refers to both: (a) the processes whereby leaders become self-aware of their values, beliefs, identity, motives and goals, and grow to achieve self-concordance in their actions and relationships, and (b) authentic (open, transparent, veritable) processes for developing leaders (Avolio & Gardner, 2005; Gardner et al., 2005; Luthans & Avolio, 2003). The contributors to this volume have extended this work by considering the implications of their ideas and research for the development of authentic leaders.

For example, Eigel and Kuhnert (2005) draw upon research with 21 board-elected executives of publicly traded Fortune 100 and 500 firms to identify leader development level (LDL) as an explanatory construct. LDLs refer to levels of developmental maturity based on the work of Kegan (1982) that determine leaders' mental and moral capacities. Eigel and Kuhnert apply the LDL construct to explain the process whereby individuals become authentic leaders. Specifically, they argue that to achieve at a level of self-awareness and moral capacity that supports authentic leadership requires a certain level of cognitive capacity, which Kegan refers to as perspective-taking. In other words, to be an authentic leader one must be the author of one's own self-concept and have the ability to change it over time. Most importantly, as Eigel and Kuhnert (2005) and Hannah et al. (2005) point out, that level of cognitive capacity and perspective-taking can be developed.

LDLs are also seen as providing a broader and more dynamic framework for studying and explaining leadership effectiveness. We agree that higher levels of moral development are characteristic of authentic leaders, as we have argued elsewhere (Gardner et al., 2005; May et al., 2003), along with other contributors to this volume (Chan et al., 2005; Hannah et al., 2005). Eigel and Kuhnert's research offers support for this assertion, and their LDL framework provides a promising platform for future research.

Also noteworthy is Reichard and Avolio's (2005) discussion of the implications of a 100-year meta-analysis of leadership intervention studies conducted by GLI associates for the study and development of authentic leaders. What they report is that after examining over 100 years of leadership research, they were able to quantify the results of 200 empirical studies that spanned all major theories, field and lab research, organizational types, cultures, and various dependent measures. Their main question was whether in fact leadership interventions mattered. Their answer is an emphatic yes, but the impact varied depending on a number of moderators including the type of theory, sample, and dependent variables. Their recommendations include choosing an intervention strategy that will be in line with the nature of the theory and constructs being tested. For example, if you are going to truly test how leaders transform followers into leaders, likely you will need more than a few hours of interactions between the leader and follower to test this hypothesis. They also call for leveraging top management support to implement high-quality research designs/interventions. They specifically suggest that practitioners demand from leadership providers what is the return on development (ROD) attributable to the investments they are being asked to make in leadership interventions/development. Evaluation of the leadership development interventions will no doubt serve to advance what we know and do not know about leadership development.

We strongly encourage basic and applied researchers interested in studying and developing authentic leaders to follow these recommendations. At present, dramatic claims are frequently made by leadership scholars, consultants and "gurus" about the efficacy of assorted developmental programs that are largely unsubstantiated. When those who make grandiose claims fail to produce meaningful results, as is often the case, cynical assessments by intervention targets and other consumers of leadership research inevitably follow. Equally dangerous are cases where leadership training programs are deemed to be successful based on satisfaction surveys of participants, without collecting any evidence of long-term changes in criterion outcomes. In fact, it is very possible that participants can initially be less satisfied with the leadership intervention, but yet have more positive impact on their development over time. This is analogous to those individuals who go through some dissatisfying life difficulties and "discover who they are," which helps them become a better person. Of course, we would like to have both highly satisfying and highly effective leadership development interventions, which may occur over time depending on what aspect of leadership is being developed.

Finally, erroneous claims of intervention effectiveness may be made when changes in criterion outcomes are observed that are confounded by uncontrolled variables. To avoid these problems and truly advance our knowledge regarding the developmental utility of leadership interventions, more rigorous research designs, measures, and longitudinal assessments are required, which will help serve to not only determine if the intervention was successful, but also to enhance the theory that guided those interventions (Avolio, 2003, 2005).

Contextual Factors
Although existing conceptions of authentic leadership (e.g., Avolio & Gardner, 2005; Avolio et al., 2004; Gardner et al., 2005; Luthans & Avolio, 2003) recognize the role that contextual factors (e.g., a positive, strengths-based and inclusive ethical climate) play in the development of authentic

leadership, some new contextual factors were examined in this volume. For example, Kolditz and Brazil (2005) consider the unique challenges that confront leaders who attempt to achieve authenticity in *in extremis* settings, or "at the point of death," along with the posited benefits that accrue to leaders who succeed in doing so.

In extremis settings include life-threatening situations (e.g., war, fire-fighting, sky diving, and mountain climbing) that enhance participants awareness of their own mortality. Kolditz and Brazil (2005) posit that in such situations, the high levels of optimism, hope, resiliency, confidence, and moral capacity that are posited to be characteristic of authentic leadership (Luthans & Avolio, 2003; May et al., 2003), "provide the key to understanding why leaders who are authentic are also effective at commanding follower loyalty, obedience, admiration, and respect" (p. 346). Preliminary results reported from three on-going field research projects of leaders in *in extremis* settings (e.g., mountain climbing guides, New York and San Francisco FBI SWAT team chiefs, a national parachute event leader, an outward bound leader, a jungle video team chief, military officers in combat situations, etc.) provide tentative support for these assertions.

Another chapter in this volume that sheds light on the impact of contextual factors on authentic leadership is Pittinsky's (2005) report on the authenticity markers associated with African-American political leaders. The results highlight the difficulties that such leaders, and perhaps leaders of other ethnic minority groups, face in convincing potential followers of their authenticity. In particular, African-American political leaders who appear to be too assimilated into the majority white culture, as well as those who appear to advertise stereotypical attributes associated with their minority group, run the risk of having inauthentic markers attributed to them. Indeed, this and Hogg's (2001) work on group prototypicality suggest that we may need to change the prototypes associated with a minority group's leadership, in order to achieve a more universal profile of what constitutes authentic leadership. The change in prototypes may occur not only with the minority group, but also with the majority. Perhaps a recent example of that change is the shift toward both male and female leaders being viewed more positively if they are more individually considerate, which traditionally would have been associated with feminine and not masculine leadership.

Together, Kolditz and Brazil's (2005) and Pittinsky's (2005) studies demonstrate well the importance of contextual factors (e.g., in extremis settings, African-American politics) as determinants of perceived leader authenticity, while suggesting the potential positive effects of authentic leadership in such settings. We applaud these scholars for exploring the effects of context on authentic leadership and its development. We encourage others to follow their example by specifying the context for their research, and extending the study of authentic leadership to novel settings. We see the definition of authentic leadership and its development as being inseparable from the context in which it is embedded.

Components of Authentic Leadership: Areas of Divergence

In addition to the areas of theoretical convergence described above, there are also some areas where current conceptions of authentic leadership theory diverge. We compare these areas of divergence and their implications for future research in this and the following sections.

Moral Component of Authentic Leadership

As originally conceptualized by Luthans and Avolio (2003) and elaborated by May et al. (2003), authentic leadership is posited to include an inherent moral component. Specifically, authentic leaders are described as transparent decision makers who develop and utilize their reserves of moral capacity, courage, efficacy, and resilience to address ethical issues and arrive at authentic and sustainable moral solutions (May et al., 2003). Moreover, several contributors to this volume (e.g., Chan et al., 2005; Hannah et al., 2005; Kolditz & Brazil, 2005) have argued that an advanced level of moral development is a requirement for the achievement of leader authenticity.

This assumption has been challenged, however, by Shamir and Eilam (2005) who omit consideration of the content of the leader's convictions and values from their conception of authentic leadership, arguing that a leader can be authentic and "true to the self" without reaching a high level of moral development or adhering to high ethical standards. We disagree with this position. Why? We have definitional, theoretical/empirical, and philosophical reasons.

With respect to our definitional reasons, we believe the construct of "authenticity" as involving self-awareness and self-ownership is inconsistent with a low level of moral development. Of course, people can be true to themselves, at a moderately low level of moral development, although we still maintain they will not have the capacity to fully understand themselves nor others for that matter. To be clear, we have specifically taken the stand that authentic leaders by our definition and in terms of development are of high moral character (see discussion below), which is a prerequisite for such leadership, in the same way that Burns (1978) defined transforming leaders as being of high moral character. Recall that Bass (1985) originally labeled leaders such as Adolph Hitler as transformational, but corrected that mistake when he agreed that transformational leaders had to be "morally uplifting" and Hitler was *clearly not* such a leader.

Sparrowe (2005) echoes Shamir and Eilam's (2005) concerns about the moral component of authenticity, arguing that "because 'to thine own self be true' looks inward before recognizing others, its basic orientation is narcissism" (p. 5). In our view, this is a very limited perspective on what we now have defined as authentic leadership and does not fully capture our definition. However, again using Burns' description of transforming leaders as leading based on their "end values" of justice and liberty, disqualifies all of the narcissistic leaders throughout history as satisfying our definition of authentic leadership. Thus, we strongly disagree with such limited definitions of authentic leadership. We consider the inclusion of a positive moral perspective as a basic component of authentic leadership to be crucial to advancing a theory of authentic leadership development.

We also believe there is solid theoretical and empirical justification for including a moral component. Here it is useful to revisit Kernis' (2003) conception of authenticity, which serves as a theoretical foundation for recent extensions of authentic leadership theory (Gardner et al., 2005; Ilies et al., 2005), including some of the contributions to this volume (e.g., Hannah et al., 2005; Hughes, 2005). Based on extensive research within the field of social psychology, Kernis (2003) identifies four basic dimensions of authenticity: self-awareness, unbiased (or balanced) processing, relational transparency, and authentic behavior. Furthermore, he reviews empirical evidence (Deci & Ryan, 1995, 2000; Kernis, Greenier, Herlocker, Whisenhunt, & Abend, 1997; Sheldon & Kasser, 1995; Ungerer, Waters, Barnett, & Dolby, 1997; Vaillant, 1992) that suggests authentic persons: (1) possess awareness of, and trust in their thoughts, feelings, and motives; (2) are capable of perspective-taking in processing information about themselves and others in a relatively unbiased fashion; (3) are open and comfortable engaging in self-disclosure to form genuine relationships with close others; (4) accept themselves for who they are, and are nondefensive with respect to personal shortcomings; (5) follow internal self-regulation processes in sticking to their believes and values to exhibit authentic behavior; and (6) possess optimal levels of high and secure self-esteem.

As described by Kernis (2003), authentic persons have much in common with individuals who have progressed to the advanced stages of moral development. Hence, we see his conception of authenticity as being consistent with May et al.'s (2003) assertion that more versus less authentic leaders will possess higher levels of positive moral capacity. Indeed, we expect authentic leaders to have reached an advanced level of moral development, such as Stage 6 (universal ethical principles) in Kohlberg's (1969) model or Stage 4 in Kegan's (1982) model.

We are also in agreement with the assertion advanced in the chapters by Chan et al. (2005) and Hannah et al. (2005) that authentic leaders possess well-developed meta-cognitive abilities (Metcalfe & Shimamura, 1994) that enable them to not only think about moral issues, but reflect on how they think about and evaluate such issues. Hence, they are capable of looking at moral issues using a wide variety of lenses and perspectives (see Eigel & Kuhnert, 2005; Kuhnert & Lewis, 1987, in this volume), providing them with a more balanced and sophisticated understanding of the intricacies and tradeoffs involved in complex ethical issues, as well as potential biases and blind spots that may impact and distort their assessments. Therefore, we believe there is a sufficient theoretical basis and empirical evidence to support our assertion that authentic leaders are particularly attuned to ethical issues, and pursue high-quality moral solutions as they consider the interests of diverse stakeholders. This clearly disqualifies the notorious and narcissistic leaders throughout history who were anything but "balanced processors."

Our philosophical reason for including a moral component to authentic leadership theory is that we believe any effort to develop leaders should devote attention to their moral development (Avolio, 2005; Avolio & Gardner, 2005; Kanungo & Mendonca, 1996). As Cuilla (2004) persuasively argues, ethics lies at the heart of leadership and we add to that "development." Hence, we believe leader development will be incomplete and miss the mark if it does not result in increased awareness of, and attention to, the ethical responsibilities that accompany the leader role. In this respect, we are consistent with Burns (1978) in advancing his theory of transforming leadership, which clearly incorporated a positive moral perspective for such leaders. And, as noted above, Bass (1990) added a moral component to his transformational leadership theory after omitting it from his original model (Bass, 1985), in recognition of its importance to leader and follower development.

Positive Psychological Capital
When Luthans and Avolio (2003) introduced their model of authentic leadership development, they defined authentic leadership as including the positive psychological states of optimism, confidence, hope, and resiliency as fundamental components. Moreover, the chapter by Youssef and Luthans

(2005) included in this volume further explicates the implications of employee, leader, and organizational resiliency for authentic leadership and its development.

As was the case for the positive moral perspective component discussed above, however, some authors (e.g., Cooper, Scandura, & Schriesheim, 2005) have expressed concerns about including positive psychological states in the definition of authentic leadership for fear that the meaning of the construct will be diluted. Subsequent models of authentic leadership (Gardner et al., 2005; Ilies et al., 2005), including those introduced by Chan et al. (2005) and Hannah et al. (2005) in this volume, have chosen to focus exclusively on the self-awareness and self-regulatory processes posited to be fundamental to authentic leadership. Thus, additional theory building and empirical research is needed to determine if positive psychological capital is best conceived as an antecedent, core component and/or consequence of authentic leadership. Again, from the very start we have viewed these positive components as being core elements until proven otherwise.

Levels of Analysis and Dimensionality
In their critique of emerging theoretical perspectives on authentic leadership and authentic leadership development, Cooper et al. (2005) expressed concerns about current conceptions of authentic leadership, which define it as a multi-level and multi-dimensional phenomenon. Their concerns centered upon the difficulties involved in operationalizing and measuring the construct. We share these concerns and recognize that many challenges lie ahead for scholars interested in advancing our knowledge of authentic leadership and its development (Avolio & Gardner, 2005).

One of Luthans and Avolio's (2003) initial intents in introducing their model of authentic leadership was to make the construct multi-level and multi-dimensional for one simple reason: leadership is a multi-dimensional and multi-level phenomenon. Hence, we believe it is important that our definitions and models capture this complexity if we are to fully advance our understanding of authentic leadership development (Avolio & Gardner, 2005). Indeed, it is impossible to conceive of leadership development without taking a multi-level view. We recognize that this approach poses measurement challenges, many of which are articulated by Chan (2005) in his chapter of this volume, along with suggestions for addressing them. Nonetheless, we believe it makes sense to begin with a broad and inclusive definition given criticism of prior leadership theories that have not sufficiently recognized the complexity of leadership processes, or have overlooked the importance of context (Bass, 1990; Rost, 1991; Yukl, 2002). Moreover, since there does not exist a general theory of leadership development, putting forth a multi-level theory of authentic leadership development seemed to be a more inclusive starting point for efforts to understand "how good leaders develop."

MOVING FORWARD

Throughout this book, the contributors have highlighted directions for future theory development and research. For example, the authors proposing conceptual models (Chan et al., 2005; Dasborough & Ashkanasy, 2005; Douglas et al., 2005; Eigel & Kuhnert, 2005; Fry & Whittington, 2005; Hannah et al., 2005; Klenke, 2005; Youssef & Luthans, 2005) have either provided propositions for testing their models and/or recommendations for further theory building and research. Others have presented preliminary findings and considered their implications for this emerging area of research (Dasborough & Ashkanasy, 2005; Eigel & Kuhnert, 2005; Kolditz & Brazil, 2005; Pittinsky, 2005; Reichard & Avolio, 2005). Still others have focused primarily on authentic leader development and advanced recommendations for making intervention strategies effective (Eigel & Kuhnert, 2005; Reichard & Avolio, 2005; Youssef & Luthans, 2005). Finally, Chan (2005) has described the measurement challenges confronting researchers interested in studying authentic leadership and provides recommendations for addressing these challenges.

We do not wish to repeat the recommendations of these authors here. Instead, we will highlight a few broad directions for future research that we consider to be essential to the advancement of theory and research on authentic leadership and authentic leadership development.

Assessments and Interventions

When considering directions for future research, it is important to reiterate that authentic leadership and authentic leadership development are related but separate phenomena. Authentic leadership involves the processes whereby leaders form genuine, transparent, and trusting relationships of influence with followers. In contrast, authentic leadership development involves the planned and unplanned processes whereby individuals come to identify the leader role as part of their core self-concept (Chan et al., 2005; Gardner, 1993; Hannah & Chan, 2004), and achieve self-awareness, balanced processing, relational transparency, and authentic behavior when enacting that role with followers (Gardner et al., 2005; Ilies et al., 2005). It may also involve genuine, transparent, and veritable planned efforts to develop authentic leaders (Avolio & Gardner, 2005).

Given these differences, it is important for researchers to clearly identify which of these phenomena are of interest and design their studies accordingly. For instance, if the research objective is to clarify the processes involved in authentic leadership, nonexperimental and preferably longitudinal designs using existing and newly constructed measures of leader authenticity and tests of their impacts on key follower outcomes such as trust, well-being, engagement, commitment, and performance (Avolio et al., 2004) would be appropriate. If, instead, the objective is to assess authentic leadership development, designs that include interventions for the purpose of accelerating leader development may be required (Reichard & Avolio, 2005).

Regardless of the methodology, however, we believe it is essential that the predictions advanced by authentic leadership development theory, as is the case for any model of leadership development, be empirically tested and validated. Unfortunately, as the 100-year meta-analysis described by Reichard and Avolio (2005) in this volume indicates, to date, very few studies of leadership development have employed interventions that extend beyond an hour or two. Therefore, to avoid the problems and limitations that have thus far slowed the generation of knowledge about how leaders develop, studies of authentic leadership development should employ more rigorous and longitudinal designs that include more extensive and impactful interventions. Although this may sound like standard "boiler plate" recommendations in a future research section, it is quite essential for the phenomena that we are venturing to understand, especially when it is authentic leadership development. Indeed, in order to determine what "genuinely" develops good leaders, it is impossible to conceive of a study where the manipulation of leadership and the observance of leaders and followers could occur at one point in time. Leadership development as a research area will clearly be a "tougher game" to play than most previous work on leadership theories.

Nontraditional Evaluation Criteria and Measurement at Multiple Levels

We encourage researchers to use a wider array of dependent variables to assess the effects of authentic leadership and efforts to develop it. Examples of human capital measures that are popular among HR practitioners but underutilized by leadership researchers include human capital Return on Investment (ROI) [revenue-operating expenses−(compensation + benefit costs)/(compensation + benefit costs)], revenue per employee (revenue/full time equivalent no. of employees), profit per employee (profit/full time equivalent no. of employees), and labor cost as % of revenue [(compensation + benefits costs)/full time equivalent of no. of employees]. Other underutilized criterion variables that we would expect to be impacted by authentic leadership include employee safety and safety climate (Zohar, 2002; Zohar & Luria, 2004). Here we posit that leaders who are more transparent and ethical are going to promote a safety climate as they said they would, so one can look at consistency between espoused beliefs and actions.

Perhaps one of the most important areas to now measure are those constructs and corresponding variables that gauge changes that one intends to create via some "genuine" and/or authentic leadership development intervention. The range of constructs and variables that need to be included can involve variables that assess intrapersonal change, interpersonal change, group-level change, and ultimately organizational-level change.

Starting at the individual level, we need to explore how the moral self-concept of leaders and followers is configured when we associate them with high moral character. We then need to research what stimuli impact the moral working self-concept of a leader and follower, perhaps examining most to least impact and under what time frame. Are there some interventions that would be more of an accelerant to authentic leadership development, and if so what are they? Emphasized throughout the various models of authentic leadership development is the core idea that individuals will come to see themselves and situations from a different moral perspective, and we need to understand how to shift that moral perspective through planned interventions. Of course, all of what we said above applies to all aspects of the self, and not just moral self concept, although that is of critical importance.

On an interpersonal level, we must examine how the leader shapes the followers' self concept and the way they choose to think and act across the full range of moral dilemmas. Quite simply, what are authentic leadership behaviors, and how do they differ from charismatic, transformational and/or servant? What is the nature of the relationship formed between the leader and follower where the leader is seen as transparent, consistent, and of high moral character? How does the follower's level of development filter what the leader exhibits and how does what the leader exhibit impact the follower's perceptions, thinking, emotions, behavior, and development? To what extent can we capture authentic leadership in the exchange between leaders and followers, and at what point does it actually emerge as "shared" authentic leadership?

At the group and organizational level, we would advocate further research on how authentic leaders and followers impact subsequent exchanges within groups in terms of positivity, trust, respect, self-sacrifice, citizenship, extra effort, willingness to tell the truth, and the social networks that form as a consequence of this type of leadership. It would be interesting to track the development of social networks in groups and organizations who work with authentic versus inauthentic leaders across a broad spectrum of organizational types and cultures. We suspect that the patterns associated with the social networks will differ dramatically and this will affect the organization's ability to adapt, change, transform, focus, share relevant knowledge, be responsive to clients, and to sustain performance over time.

As we move to more macro levels, we clearly need to explore how our operational definitions at all levels, measures, and interventions apply across different individuals, groups and especially cultural contexts. We have no doubt that a majority of what we learn about authentic leadership development in one culture will apply equally well across different cultures. We are also confident that there will be differences and that culture will become an important moderator to be routinely included in tests of authentic leadership and its development.

FINAL THOUGHTS

In December 2003, we distributed the call for papers for the inaugural Gallup Leadership Institute Summit on authentic leadership development. The stated objective of the Summit was to "produce original views on authentic leadership development and ground-breaking insights for future theory, research, and practice." Together, we believe the chapters of this volume and the articles included in the recent 2005 special issue of *The Leadership Quarterly*, *16*(3), focusing on authentic leadership development go a long way toward fulfilling this objective. We recognize, however, that this is only the beginning of a long journey we and others have embarked upon with the goal of advancing theory, research, and practice regarding this root leadership construct. We are hopeful that the eventual destination of this journey will be the development of a larger cadre of leaders and followers who know themselves, know what they value and believe in, and are true to those values and beliefs as they exercise the highest standards of ethical conduct in pursuit of sustained and veritable performance. Yet, if over time authentic leadership is shown to simply enhance our application of more traditional forms of leadership, such as ethical and transformational leadership, through the establishment of authentic leader–follower relationships, the journey will have been worthwhile.

NOTES

1. Other sponsors of the inaugural GLI Summit include Howard and Rhonda Hawks, Connectivity Solutions, Peter Kiewit Sons, Inc., and *The Leadership Quarterly*. We are grateful for the generous support of this event.

REFERENCES

Avolio, B. J. (2003). Examining the full range model of leadership: Looking back to transform forward. In: D. Day & S. Zaccarro (Eds), *Leadership development for transforming organizations: Grow leaders for tomorrow* (pp. 71–98). Mahwah, NJ: Erlbaum.

Avolio, B. J. (2005). *Leadership development in balance: Made/Born*. Mahwah, NJ: Erlbaum.

Avolio, B. J., & Gardner, W. L. (2005). Authentic leadership development: Getting to the root of positive forms of leadership. *The Leadership Quarterly, 16*, 315–338.

Avolio, B. J., Gardner, W. L., Walumbwa, F. O., Luthans, F., & May, D. R. (2004). Unlocking the mask: A look at the process by which authentic leaders impact follower attitudes and behaviors. *The Leadership Quarterly, 15*, 801–823.

Bass, B. M. (1985). *Leadership and performance beyond expectations*. New York: Free Press.

Bass, B. M. (1990). *Bass & Stogdill's handbook of leadership: Theory, research, & managerial applications*. New York: Free Press.

Bass, B. M., & Steidlmeier, P. (1999). Ethics, character and authentic transformational leadership. *The Leadership Quarterly, 10*, 181–217.

Buckingham, M., & Coffman, C. (1999). *First, break all the rules*. New York: Simon Schuster.

Burns, J. M. (1978). *Leadership*. New York: Harper & Row.

Cameron, K. S., Dutton, J. E., & Quinn, R. E. (Eds) (2003). *Positive organizational scholarship*. San Francisco: Barrett-Koehler.

Chan, A. Y. L. (2005). Authentic leadership development: Measurement challenges and suggestions. In: W. L. Gardner, B. J. Avolio & F. O. Walumbwa (Eds), *Authentic leadership theory and practice: Origins, effects and development*. Oxford, UK: Elsevier Science.

Chan, A. Y. L., Hannah, S. T., & Gardner, W. L. (2005). Veritable authentic leadership: Emergence, functioning, and impacts. In: W. L. Gardner, B. J. Avolio & F. O. Walumbwa (Eds), *Authentic leadership theory and practice: Origins, effects and development*. Oxford, UK: Elsevier Science.

Clifton, D. O., & Harter, J. K. (2003). Investing in strengths. In: K. S. Cameron, J. E. Dutton & R. E. Quinn (Eds), *Positive organizational scholarship* (pp. 111–121). San Francisco: Barret-Koehler.

Cooper, C., Scandura, T. A., & Schriesheim, C. A. (2005). Looking forward but learning from our past: Potential challenges to developing authentic leadership theory and authentic leaders. *Leadership Quarterly, 16*, 474–493.

Cuilla, J. B. (2004). Leadership ethics: Mapping the territory. In: J. B. Cuilla (Ed.), *Ethics: The heart of leadership* (pp. 3–26). Westport, CT: Praeger.

Dasborough, M. T., & Ashkanasy, N. M. (2005). Follower emotional reactions to authentic and inauthentic leadership influence. In: W. L. Gardner, B. J. Avolio & F. O. Walumbwa (Eds), *Authentic leadership theory and practice: Orgins, effects and development*. Oxford, UK: Elsevier Science.

Deci, E. L., & Ryan, R. M. (1995). Human autonomy: The basis for true self-esteem. In: M. H. Kernis (Ed.), *Efficacy, agency, and self-esteem* (pp. 31–49). New York: Plenum Press.

Deci, E. L., & Ryan, R. M. (2000). "What" and "why" of goal pursuits: Human needs and the self-determination of behavior. *Psychological Inquiry, 11*, 227–268.

Douglas, C., Ferris, G. R., & Perrewé, P. L. (2005). Leader political skill and authentic leadership. In: W. L. Gardner, B. J. Avolio & F. O. Walumbwa (Eds), *Authentic leadership theory and practice: Origins, effects and development*. Oxford, UK: Elsevier Science.

Eigel, K. M., & Kuhnert, K. W. (2005). Authentic development: Leadership development level and executive effectiveness. In: W. L. Gardner, B. J. Avolio & F. O. Walumbwa (Eds), *Authentic leadership theory and practice: Origins, effects and development*. Oxford, UK: Elsevier Science.

Erickson, R. J. (1995). The importance of authenticity for self and society. *Symbolic Interaction, 18*(2), 121–144.

Fry, L. W., & Whittington, J. L. (2005). In search of authenticity: Spiritual leadership theory as a source for future theory, research, and practice on authentic leadership. In: W. L. Gardner, B. J. Avolio & F. O. Walumbwa (Eds), *Authentic leadership theory and practice: Orgins, effects and development*. Oxford, UK: Elsevier Science.

Gardner, J. W. (1993). *On leadership*. New York: The Free Press.

Gardner, W. L., Avolio, B. J., Luthans, F., May, D. R., & Walumbwa, F. O. (2005). Can you see the real me? A self-based model of authentic leader and follower development. *The Leadership Quarterly, 16*, 343–372.

George, W. (2003). *Authentic leadership: Rediscovering the secrets to creating lasting value*. San Francisco: Jossey-Bass.

Hannah, S. T., & Chan, A. (2004). *Veritable authentic leadership: Emergence, functioning, and impacts*. Paper presented at the Gallup leadership institute summit, Omaha, Nebraska.

Hannah, S. T., Lester, P. B., & Vogelgesang, G. R. (2005). Moral leadership: Explicating the moral component of authentic leadership. In: W. L. Gardner, B. J. Avolio & F. O. Walumbwa (Eds), *Authentic leadership theory and practice: Origins, effects, and development*. Oxford, UK: Elsevier Science.

Harter, J. K., Schmidt, F. L., & Hayes, T. L. (2002). Business-unit level relationship between employee satisfaction, employee engagement and business outcomes: A meta-analysis. *Journal of Applied Psychology, 87*, 268–279.

Harter, J. K., Schmidt, F. L., & Keyes, C. L. M. (2003). Well-being in the workplace and its relationship to business outcomes: A review of the Gallup studies. In: C. L. M. Keyes & J. Haidt (Eds), *Flourishing: Positive psychology and the life well-lived* (pp. 205–224). Washington, DC: American Psychological Association.

Harter, S. (2002). Authenticity. In: C. R. Snyder & S. Lopez (Eds), *Handbook of positive psychology* (pp. 382–394). Oxford, UK: Oxford University Press.

Hogg, M. A. (2001). A soical identity theory of leadership. *Personality and Social Psychology Review*, *5*(3), 184–200.

Hughes, L. (2005). Developing transparent relationships through humor in the authentic leader–follower relationship. In: W. L. Gardner, B. J. Avolio & F. O. Walumbwa (Eds), *Authentic leadership theory and practice: Origins, effects and development*. Oxford, UK: Elsevier Science.

Ilies, R., Morgeson, F. P., & Nahrgang, J. D. (2005). Authentic leadership and eudaemonic well-being: Understanding leader–follower outcomes. *Leadership Quarterly*, *16*, 373–394.

Kanungo, R. A., & Mendonca, M. (1996). *Ethical dimensions of leadership*. Thousand Oaks, CA: Sage.

Kegan, R. (1982). *The evolving self: Problem and process in human development*. Cambridge, MA: Harvard University Press.

Kernis, M. H. (2003). Toward a conceptualization of optimal self-esteem. *Psychological Inquiry*, *14*, 1–26.

Kernis, M. H., Greenier, K. C., Herlocker, C. E., Whisenhunt, C. W., & Abend, T. (1997). Self-perceptions of reactions to doing well or poorly: The roles of stability and level of self-esteem. *Personality and Individual Differences*, *22*, 846–854.

Klenke, K. (2005). The internal theatre of the authentic leader: Integrating cognitive, affective, conative and spiritual facets of authentic leadership. In: W. L. Gardner, B. J. Avolio & F. O. Walumbwa (Eds), *Authentic leadership theory and practice: Origins, effects and development*. Oxford, UK: Elsevier Science.

Kohlberg, L. (1969). Stage and sequence: The cognitive-developmental approach to socialization. In: D. A. Goslin (Ed.), *Handbook of socialization theory and research* (pp. 347–480). Chicago: Rand McNally.

Kolditz, T. A., & Brazil, D. M. (2005). Authentic leadership in *in extremis* settings: A concept for extraordinary leaders in exceptional situations. In: W. L. Gardner, B. J. Avolio & F. O. Walumbwa (Eds), *Authentic leadership theory and practice: Origins, effects and development*. Oxford, UK: Elsevier Science.

Kuhnert, K. W., & Lewis, P. (1987). Transactional and transformational leadership: A constructive/developmental analysis. *Academy of Management Review*, *12*, 648–657.

Luthans, F. (2002a). The need for and meaning of positive organizational behavior. *Journal of Organizational Behavior*, *23*, 695–706.

Luthans, F. (2002b). Positive organizational behavior: Developing and managing psychological strengths. *Academy of Management Executive*, *16*(1), 57–72.

Luthans, F., & Avolio, B. J. (2003). Authentic leadership: A positive developmental approach. In: K. S. Cameron, J. E. Dutton & R. E. Quinn (Eds), *Positive organizational scholarship* (pp. 241–261). San Francisco: Barrett-Koehler.

May, D. R., Chan, A. Y. L., Hodges, T. D., & Avolio, B. J. (2003). Developing the moral component of authentic leadership. *Organizational Dynamics*, *32*, 247–260.

Metcalfe, J., & Shimamura, A. P. (1994). *Metacognition: Knowing about knowing*. Cambridge, MA: MIT Press.

Michie, S., & Gooty, J. (2005). Values, emotions, and authenticity: Will the real leader please stand up? *The Leadership Quarterly*, *16*, 441–458.

Pagano, B., & Pagano, E. (2004). *The transparency edge: How credibility can make or break you in business*. New York: McGraw-Hill.

Pittinsky, T. L. (2005). Leader authenticity markers: Findings from a study of African-American political leaders. In: W. L. Gardner, B. J. Avolio & F. O. Walumbwa (Eds), *Au-*

thentic leadership theory and practice: Origins, effects and development. Oxford, UK: Elsevier Science.

Reichard, R. J., & Avolio, B. J. (2005). Where are we? The status of leadership intervention research: A meta-analytic summary. In: W. L. Gardner, B. J. Avolio & F. O. Walumbwa (Eds), Authentic leadership theory and practice: Orgins, effects and development. Oxford, UK: Elsevier Science.

Rost, J. C. (1991). Leadership for the twenty-first century. New York: Praeger.

Seligman, M. E. P., & Csikentmihalyi, M. (2000). Positive psychology. American Psychologist, 55, 5–14.

Shamir, B., & Eilam, G. (2005). "What's your story?": A life-stories approach to authentic leadership development. The Leadership Quarterly, 16, 395–418.

Sheldon, K. M., & Kasser, T. (1995). Coherence and congruence: Two aspects of personality integration. Journal of Personality and Social Psychology, 68, 531–543.

Snyder, C. R., & Lopez, S. J. (Eds) (2002). Handbook of positive psychology. Oxford, UK: Oxford University Press.

Sparrowe, R. T. (2005). Authentic leadership and the narrative self. The Leadership Quarterly, 16, 419–440.

Ungerer, J. A., Waters, B., Barnett, B., & Dolby, R. (1997). Defense style and adjustment in interpersonal relationships. Journal of Research in Personality, 31, 375–384.

Vaillant, G. (1992). Ego mechanisms of defense: A guide for clinicians and researchers. Washington, DC: American Psychiatric Press.

Varella, P., Javidan, M., & Waldman, D. A. (2005). The differential effects of socialized and personalized leadership on group social capital. In: W. L. Gardner, B. J. Avolio & F. O. Walumbwa (Eds), Authentic leadership theory and pratice: Origins, effects and development. Oxford, UK: Elsevier Science.

Youssef, C. M., & Luthans, F. (2005). Resiliency development of organizations, leaders and employees: Multi-level theory building for sustained performance. In: W. L. Gardner, B. J. Avolio & F. O. Walumbwa (Eds), Authentic leadership theory and practice: Origins, effects and development. Oxford, UK: Elsevier Science.

Yukl, G. (2002). Leadership in organizations (5th ed.). Upper Saddle Creek, NJ: Prentice-Hall.

Zohar, D. (2002). Modifying supervisory practices to improve subunit safety: A leadership-based intervention model. Journal of Applied Psychology, 87, 156–163.

Zohar, D., & Luria, G. (2004). Climate as a social-cognitive construction of supervisory safety practices: Scripts as proxy of behavior patterns. Journal of Applied Psychology, 89, 322–333.

SUBJECT INDEX

AUTHOR INDEX

CPSIA information can be obtained at www.ICGtesting.com
Printed in the USA
239367LV00001B/56/P